HUMAN DIGNITY IN BIOETHICS AND BIOLAW

HUMAN DIGNITY IN BIOETHICS AND BIOLAW

DERYCK BEYLEVELD
ROGER BROWNSWORD

OXFORD
UNIVERSITY PRESS

OXFORD
UNIVERSITY PRESS

Great Clarendon Street, Oxford OX2 6DP

Oxford University Press is a department of the University of Oxford.
It furthers the University's objective of excellence in research, scholarship,
and education by publishing worldwide in

Oxford New York

Athens Auckland Bangkok Bogotá Buenos Aires
Cape Town Chennai Dar es Salaam Delhi Florence Hong Kong Istanbul
Karachi Kolkata Kuala Lumpur Madrid Melbourne Mexico City Mumbai
Nairobi Paris São Paulo Shanghai Singapore Taipei Tokyo Toronto Warsaw
with associated companies in Berlin Ibadan

Oxford is a registered trade mark of Oxford University Press
in the UK and in certain other countries

Published in the United States
by Oxford University Press Inc., New York

© D. Beyleveld and R. Brownsword 2001

The moral rights of the author have been asserted
Database right Oxford University Press (maker)

First published 2001

British Library Cataloguing in Publication Data
Data available

Library of Congress Cataloging in Publication Data
Beyleveld, Deryck.
Human dignity in bioethics and biolaw/Deryck Beyleveld, Roger Brownsword.
p. cm.
Includes bibliographical references.
1. Medical ethics. 2. Bioethics. 3. Dignity. I. Brownsword, Roger. II. Title.
R725.5.B485 2001
174'.2—dc21   2001052071
ISBN 0–19–826826–2

1 3 5 7 9 10 8 6 4 2

Typeset in Times by
Cambrian Typesetters, Frimley, Surrey

Printed in Great Britain
on acid-free paper by
T.J. International Ltd. Padstow, Cornwall

Acknowledgements

This book is the culmination of reflections on the concept of dignity that first began to concern us as participants in the EU Concerted Action on Basic Ethical Principles in Bioethics and Biolaw, coordinated by the Centre for Ethics and Law, Copenhagen. During the course of this action we published a number of working papers (Beyleveld and Brownsword 1998*a*; 2000*a,b*) that we have not otherwise found occasion to reference in the body of the text. In 1998 we participated in a conference run by the *Modern Law Review* on 'Human Genetics and the Law' at the University of Cambridge, leading to the publication of Beyleveld and Brownsword (1998*b*), which was an important staging post in our thinking, but which we have also not referred to in the text.

Participation in these projects was invaluable to us, and we benefited enormously from the discussions and arguments we had with fellow partners and participants in these projects. We wish to thank them all.

Some of the ideas in this book stem from work undertaken by Deryck Beyleveld with Shaun Pattinson. Although this is acknowledged in the text, Shaun's general input was considerable over a period of time.

We also wish to thank Mark Taylor for helping us check for any serious errors in the final manuscript.

Alan Gewirth's thought is, of course, absolutely core to our thinking, and it is his work that we interpret, extend, and apply. He may not agree with everything that we say, and we are, on occasion, critical of his own position on applications of his theory. Nevertheless, this book would not have been possible without him. With the deepest regard and affection, we dedicate this book to him.

D.B.
R.B.

Sheffield
15 May 2001

Contents

List of Abbreviations

ASA	Argument from the Sufficiency of Agency
ECHR	European Convention on Human Rights
EPC	European Patent Convention
IBC	International Bioethics Committee (of UNESCO)
ICCPR	International Covenant on Civil and Political Rights 1966
ICESCR	International Covenant on Economic, Social and Cultural Rights 1966
IVF	in vitro fertilization
PGC	Principle of Generic Consistency
PVS	persistent (or permanent) vegetative state
UDHR	Universal Declaration of Human Rights 1948
UNESCO	United Nations Educational, Scientific, and Cultural Organization

Introduction

To say that modern bioscience should respect human rights is almost a statement of the obvious. If one adds that modern bioscience should also respect human dignity (a requirement that is now increasingly voiced, not least in the context of international conventions and declarations), the meaning of this further demand is less clear. Is such an appeal, as some sceptics believe, no more than empty rhetoric? Or does an appeal to human dignity meaningfully precede or qualify reliance on human rights—could it be that human dignity is in some sense a more profound value than that of human rights?

In Part I of this book (Chapters 1 to 6) we seek to bring human dignity more clearly into focus. Initially, we survey the way in which human dignity features in a number of international legal instruments, some (such as the UN Universal Declaration of Human Rights) declaring human rights, others (such as the Council of Europe's Convention on Human Rights and Biomedicine) prescribing the limits of modern science and medicine. This generates (in Chapters 1 to 3) a sketch of two opposed conceptions of human dignity. However, although opposed, each conception attaches fundamental importance to the idea of respect for human dignity. One conception, 'human dignity as empowerment', treats human rights as founded on the intrinsic dignity of humans and, characteristically, this issues in a reinforced plea that individual autonomy should be respected. The other conception, 'human dignity as constraint', is more concerned with human duties than with human rights. Treating this conception (much of which is captured in what we call the 'new bioethics' in Europe) as an umbrella for a number of duty-driven approaches, we can find not only a duty to respect the dignity of others but also a duty not to compromise our own dignity as well as to act in a way that is compatible with respect for the vision of human dignity that gives a particular community its distinctive cultural identity.

The tension between these two conceptions of human dignity is vividly brought out by the famous French dwarf-throwing case.[1] There, the Conseil d'État upheld local bans on dwarf-throwing in clubs despite the fact that all parties who participated were consenting adults. While the dwarfs argued that the bans evinced a lack of respect for their dignity (interfering with their free choice and undermining the sense of self-respect that they gained by virtue of being employed), the Conseil ruled that such 'entertainment' compromised human dignity and, as such, was rightly prohibited as contrary to *ordre public*.

Each of these conceptions of human dignity is problematic. In the case of the former conception, notwithstanding the widespread commitment to human rights backed by human dignity, it is unclear in what sense humans have *dignity*,

---

[1] Conseil d'État (October 27, 1995) req. nos. 136–727 (Commune de Morsang-sur-Orge) and 143–578 (Ville d'Aix-en-Provence).

whether it is distinctively *humans* that have dignity, and how the having of dignity justifies the having of (human) rights (especially the right to autonomy). In the case of the latter conception, the idea of a duty owed to oneself (as in a duty not to compromise one's own dignity) is controversial; and it is unclear why the fact that a particular vision of human dignity is the ruling view in a particular place at a particular time grounds matching duties for those who happen to be located within the jurisdiction (irrespective of whether they have freely accepted this view and irrespective of whether such a view must necessarily be accepted by rational beings). Thus, while there are competing conceptions of human dignity available for those who are committed to signing up to a dignitarian agenda, a rationally defensible view remains to be articulated.

In the opening chapters of the book, we also meet the idea that dignity is a virtue. To the extent that this idea implies disapproval of those who conduct themselves in an undignified fashion, we might think that this is a matter of no great importance. For, while we might not welcome undignified behaviour and, indeed, might think that there is far too much of it about, it is surely not something that touches and concerns the intrinsic and inalienable dignity of humans—as liberal human rights theorists and Kantians alike might say, the intrinsic dignity of humanity holds good, instances of undignified conduct (failing to act with dignity) notwithstanding. Nevertheless, we suggest that the idea of responsible behaviour that underlies the notion of dignity as a virtue should be taken seriously. However, what merits serious consideration is not responsibility relative to local custom and etiquette, nor the semblance of composure or the like. Rather, it is responsibility that goes to questions of character as much as to appearance, and that is relative to the human condition itself. Specifically, it is the idea of dignity as a particular practical attitude to be cultivated in the face of human finitude and vulnerability (and, concomitantly, the natural and social adversity that characterizes the human condition). In the course of this discussion, we find an important thread that links dignity as a virtue to the theory of practical legal authority that we first published in *Law as a Moral Judgment* (Beyleveld and Brownsword 1986), namely that citizens have a responsibility to respect the good faith attempts made by legal officials to reason their way to morally defensible decisions. To be disposed to accept decisions so produced, even though one judges them to be mistaken, is to have a character shaped by this virtue. These thoughts also foreshadow one of the key moments of the book (in Chapter 6). This is the idea that dignity as a virtue indicates the aspirational path of responsible (and rational) agency in the context of the existential anxiety that is part and parcel of the human condition—that is to say, an anxiety arising from the limits of reason when focused on questions of human mortality and vulnerability (see below).

The elaboration of a defensible understanding of respect for human dignity is a challenge within practical (and particularly moral) reason. In Chapters 4 to 6 we proceed on the basis that the moral theory articulated by Alan Gewirth (which we take to be the most powerful theory yet developed to establish the rational necessity of the moral point of view and, within that, of a particular moral principle, the Principle of Generic Consistency, PGC) is where we must root our thinking about human dignity. While we recognize that this is far from being an uncontroversial vantage point, it is not the principal purpose of this book to engage in a further defence of the Gewirthian approach (or, indeed, of any similar approach—famously, Kant's transcendental argument—that shares such justificatory ambitions for its moral project). Nevertheless, there are three segments of our discussion that are intended to support our taking this line. First (in Chapter 4), we present a rendition of Gewirth's dialectically necessary argument, this being designed to demonstrate that, from any standpoint in practical reason, no agent can coherently deny being bound by the PGC. In addition to addressing the needs of readers who are not familiar with the Gewirthian argument, this section addresses those critics of the argument who have failed to understand its essential basis in agency. The dialectically necessary argument, as we have said, is designed to run from any starting point in practical reason. However, less comprehensive (dialectically contingent) arguments to the PGC can be made out. Thus, in a second segment, we show how the PGC is presupposed by an agent committed to the idea of human rights (which, of course, is precisely the context for much of the current debate about human dignity); and, in a third segment, via a comparison of Kant and Gewirth (in Chapter 5), we consider how commitments to the idea of categorically binding impartial standards or categorically binding standards *simpliciter* also entail a commitment to the PGC.

In Chapter 6 our reflections on dignity lead us to contextualize the Gewirthian argument from agency in a way that makes explicit the implicit vulnerability of agents. As Gewirth rightly says, the context for moral and practical reason is that of agency and action. However, the context for agency and action (at any rate, as human beings experience it) is one of human finitude and vulnerability. When we say this, we do not mean merely that even the strongest of agents (of the human species) must eat and sleep, and are capable of being harmed in all sorts of ways. The vulnerability that we have in mind goes deeper than this, stemming from the fact not only that reason has its limits but that agents, as rational beings, are aware of these limits (and, in this respect, are self-consciously vulnerable). In Chapter 6 we focus on two enduring puzzles about the human condition, each of which takes reason to its limits, and in relation to each of which responsible agents will be guided by dignity as a virtue. First, there is the great metaphysical question that all agents confront as to their own mortality. Reason dictates a radical agnosticism in response to this question; however, it is an agnosticism that underlines the necessity of serious engagement with morality. Second, there is the question of other minds, specifically with regard to the agency-status of other life forms. Again, reason dictates a degree of agnosticism. However, because of the importance of avoiding (even innocent) harm to the generic conditions of other agents, we argue for a precautionary approach that (for practical purposes) issues in an ontology that allows for the possibility of agency in others (backed by a scheme of protective responsibilities). In both cases, dignity as a virtue is a beacon guiding the path of responsible agency when we are operating at the frontiers of our capacities; in both cases, agents act in line with this virtue when they strive to take forward the moral project as far as reason permits but, at the same time, have the humility and integrity to recognize that they are not omniscient.

From such a vantage point of (self-consciously) vulnerable agency, an analysis of dignity must be developed in terms of agents' rights and responsibilities. So far as agents' rights are concerned, the conception of human dignity as empowerment seems to be well inspired. However, dignity is to be understood as relating to the distinctive capacities of agents (not *humans* as such) and, in this way, as grounding the regime of rights and duties within, and flowing from, the PGC. Because these capacities particularly relate to an agent's power to make informed choices—about the selection and pursuit of particular ends but also about the waiving of the benefits of PGC-derived rights—the clearest way in which we affront the dignity of agents is by acting towards them as if they lacked these capacities. We also compromise the dignity of agents where we deny them the conditions in which they can flourish as operators of informed choice including denying them conditions in which they lose their own sense of value or self-respect. To be sure, in a broad sense, we can say that each and every violation of the PGC (that is, each and every violation of an agent's generic rights) involves a lack of respect for the dignity of that agent. However, if violation of an agent's dignity is to occupy its own conceptual space, it needs to be focused in the way that we have just indicated.

If respect for dignity, tied to the distinctive capacities of agents, is to be taken seriously, and if the idea of dignity as a virtue (underlining the responsibilities of agents) is accepted, we have the ingredients for a framework of dignity-driven rights and responsibilities. What precisely does this imply though? What are the key guidelines for a regulatory framework that enables agents to live and die with dignity? In Part II (Chapters 7 to 11) we address a range of issues, running from birth with dignity to death with dignity, that invite a response to such questions.

In almost all cases, the dignity-agenda is opened by proponents of human dignity as constraint, the contention being that various choices or practices should be treated as off limits (legally and morally). For example, in the name of respect for dignity, it is contended that parents should be denied the opportunity to sex-select their children or engage in more sophisticated genetic specification of their offspring ('designer children'); that agents should be prohibited from engaging in commerce in the human body or body parts (this militating directly against prostitution, surrogacy, organ-selling, baby-selling, dwarf-throwing, and the like, and indirectly against patenting inventive work on the human genome); that agents should be denied the opportunity to clone human cells (whether reproductively or non-reproductively); and that agents who wish to bring their lives to a 'premature' end should not be permitted to do so (with or without assistance), and so on.

Such dignity-based denials of entitlement, running from 'eugenics' to 'euthanasia', are reinforced in various ways. For instance, the dignitarian argument against commerce in human body parts is backed by the thesis that agents cannot have property in their own bodies or body parts; elsewhere, slippery slopes and speculative adverse consequences abound, and so on.

In general, our response is to stick pretty strictly to the limited question of the bearing of respect for dignity (under our Gewirthian-guided analysis) upon these various issues. To this general approach, however, there is one major exception. In Chapter 8, we advance what we call the 'rule-preclusionary' conception of property. Taking on the orthodoxy that agents cannot have proprietary rights in their own bodies or body parts, the rule-preclusionary conception has it that the idea of property in our own bodies, far from requiring an unacceptable extension of property thinking, is precisely where proprietary rights should begin. This one major detour apart, the persistent theme of our discussion is that, if (as we hold) the essence of the dignity of agents resides in their capacity to choose, to set their own ends, then we respect that dignity by creating the conditions and opportunities for choice and recognizing agents as sources of informed choice. In short, to respect the dignity of agents is to recognize that they have the right to choose and to act upon that recognition accordingly.

Having said this, there are three important qualifications to enter against the right to choose. First, choice (including consent or refusal) is to be respected only so long as it is free and informed. Unpacking what this qualifier involves would take a book in its own right. Occasionally, we remind readers that this qualifier is in play. However, it is important to understand that it is implicit in all our discussions. Second, one agent's right to choose is limited by the rights of other agents. The right to choose is not a blank cheque. Like any other right, it is to be exercised only in ways that are compatible with respect for the rights of fellow agents (and, under the precautionary thesis that we elaborate in Chapter 6, in ways that respect the possibility of agency in those who are not ostensible agents). It follows that, while dignity might not be an argument against particular choices (at least, not for the reasons relied on by those who draw on ideas that we find under a 'dignity as constraint' approach), this does not amount to treating the particular action as permissible relative to the PGC. To this extent, our commentary is incomplete. Even if the dignitarian objections are off the mark and point, rather, to a prima facie right to choose, the particular choice made by an agent is legitimate only so long as it is compatible with the PGC-protected rights of other agents. Third, we must not forget the significance of dignity as a virtue. For much of our commentary, we underline the role of dignity in driving forward an agenda of agents' rights. This, however, is not an agenda of rights without responsibilities. Of course, Gewirthian rights translate into duties, both negative and positive, to others. Beyond this, though, dignity as a virtue points to the necessity of serious engagement with moral reason and to our responsibilities in the face of good faith attempts to bring moral order to individual and collective social life.

To return to modern bioscience, it is trite that rapid developments in modern genetics and the like carry both a promise (of benefit to humans) but also various risks. On this negative side, concerns focus on radical (and perceived-to-be-detrimental) changes to the terms of human existence, to the currency of human relationships, to the boundaries of inclusion and exclusion, and to our cultural understanding of birth, life, and death. Faced with this unfolding picture, it is understandable that a degree of caution and conservatism should enter into our calculations. In what we have called the new bioethics, this reaction has expressed itself in (*inter alia*) appeals to human dignity (and human vulnerability). While we have no doubt that there should be an ongoing ethical scrutiny of the revolution in bioscience and that respect for dignity (like vulnerability) is an important element of that scrutiny, we believe that the bearing of dignity is dynamic rather than static—for what gives agents dignity is that they have the capacity to choose that things might be otherwise than they are. In a rapidly changing scientific environment, it is tempting to try to apply the brakes. However, we cannot give agents their dignity-based due unless we recognize their distinctive decision-making capacities. This is not to say that there are no limits to agency, nor that agents have no responsibilities—far from it. However, if we are to respect the dignity of agents in a morally problematic and technologically developing world, we must anchor ourselves to the idea that it is a serious wrong to deny to agents their distinctive capacity to choose and the concomitant right to shape their own destinies.

PART I
Making Sense of 'Human Dignity'

1

Human Dignity as Empowerment

Introduction

It is not surprising that the revolution in the biosciences, particularly in the new human genetics, has raised concerns that human rights should be respected. In a culture committed to human rights, scientific 'progress' requires more than new discoveries, the formulation of illuminating new theories, the development of new biotechniques, or the invention of new biotechnological products and processes. In all its phases, from research and development through to application and use, bioscience must be compatible with respect for fundamental rights—such as the right to refuse to participate in research, the right to decide whether or not to undergo a proposed intervention or course of treatment, the right not to be discriminated against unfairly on genetic grounds, the right to control access to or circulation of confidential information about oneself, and so on.

What is surprising, perhaps, is that the bioscientific revolution has provoked a parallel demand for human dignity to be respected. As Philippe Séguin, president of the National Assembly of the French Republic, remarked in the mid-1990s, not only is there a trend towards the enactment of bioethics laws (such as the three French Acts on bioethics of July 1994), but this 'trend illustrates a growing awareness around the world that legislators must, despite the difficulties, act to ensure that *science develops with respect for human dignity and fundamental human rights*, and in line with national democratic traditions' (Séguin 1995: 120; our emphasis). This trend is further illustrated by, for example, the Preamble to the Council of Europe's Convention on Human Rights and Biomedicine,[1] which requires its signatories to resolve 'to take such measures as are necessary to safeguard human dignity and the fundamental rights and freedoms of the individual with regard to the application of biology and medicine'. Similarly, the Preamble to UNESCO's Universal Declaration on the Human Genome and Human Rights[2] states that while 'research on the human genome and the resulting applications open up vast prospects for progress in improving the health of individuals and of

---

[1] This Convention is sometimes referred to as 'the Bioethics Convention'. Its full title is Convention for the Protection of Human Rights and Dignity of the Human Being with Regard to the Application of Biology and Medicine: Convention on Human Rights and Biomedicine, 1996.

[2] This Declaration, adopted unanimously at the 29th Session of the General Conference on 11 Nov. 1997, was the result of more than four years' work carried out by the International Bioethics Committee of UNESCO. On 9 Dec. 1998 the United Nations General Assembly adopted Resolution A/RES/53/152 endorsing the Declaration.

humankind as a whole . . . [it is imperative] . . . that such research should fully respect human dignity, freedom and human rights'.

Even in the Directive on the Legal Protection of Biotechnological Inventions[3] (which deals *inter alia* with the vexed question of the patentability of biological material, including copies of human gene sequences), the need for patent law to respect dignity is emphasized—Recital 16, for example, proclaiming that 'patent law must be applied so as to respect the fundamental principles safeguarding the dignity and integrity of the person'.[4]

Yet is it so surprising that modern bioscience should provoke renewed appeals to respect human dignity? After all, the idea of human dignity is fundamental to religious traditions that hold human beings to be created in God's image, from which perspective it stands for a 'culture of life' opposed to those elements of modern bioscience that represent a 'culture of death' (see Bristow 1997)—which renders it is easy to agree with Pope John Paul II that the rediscovery of 'the inviolable dignity of every human person is an essential task'.[5] However, the new legal frameworks within which the importance of human dignity is being emphasized once more are secularized codes. Furthermore, even if 'the bioethics movement [itself] was born in a predominantly religious cradle' (Rae and Cox 1999: 1), bioethics today is largely an exercise in applied moral philosophy in which, it has been argued, 'religious voices no longer carry much weight' (Rae and Cox 1999: 2).

Our puzzle, then, is to understand why the idea of human dignity—which tends to lie in the background of (secularized) humans rights instruments *in general*—is now being thrust into the foreground of instruments dealing *specifically with biomedicine*. Is this just a coincidence? Is it simply an opportunistic rhetorical flourish to which we should pay no particular attention? Or does it signify substantive concerns about the impact of new biomedical techniques and technologies—particularly about the impact of the new genetics? If the latter, then is the function of human dignity to reinforce or complement the claims to fundamental freedoms historically advanced in the name of human rights? Or does respect for human dignity have its own distinctive script for the twenty-first century, limiting, qualifying, and possibly competing with our twentieth-century understanding of respect for human rights? If there is a tension between human rights and human dignity, how is it to be resolved? These are the kinds of questions to which we need answers if we are to determine whether there is a defensible conception of human dignity; and, if so, what respect for human dignity implies.

---

[3] Council Directive 44/98, [1998] OJ L213/13.

[4] See, too, Recital 38, which provides: 'Whereas the operative part of this Directive should also include an illustrative list of inventions excluded from patentability so as to provide national courts and patent offices with a general guide to interpreting the reference to *ordre public* and morality; whereas this list obviously cannot presume to be exhaustive; whereas processes, the uses of which offend against human dignity, such as processes to produce chimeras from germ cells or totipotent cells of humans and animals, are obviously also excluded from patentability.'

[5] *Christifideles laici*, 37 (cited in Bristow 1997: 10).

First Steps

Our first task is to elucidate and distinguish two conceptions of human dignity—'human dignity as empowerment' and 'human dignity as constraint'. This distinction correlates broadly with the contrast between the background role typically assigned to human dignity in the founding international instruments of human rights as against the foreground role assigned to it in the recent instruments that set the framework for modern bioscience. Where human dignity plays a background role, the governing conception is human dignity as empowerment; where it plays a foreground role, the distinctive conception is human dignity as constraint.

We start (in this chapter) with the post-Second World War international instruments that laid the foundations for the culture of human rights that was to develop throughout the second half of the twentieth century. Here, intrinsic human dignity is a seminal idea that acts as the background justification for the recognition of human rights and as the source of the fundamental freedoms to which all humans (*qua* human) are entitled. In this context, human dignity as empowerment (specifically, the empowerment that comes with the right to respect for one's dignity as a human, and the right to the conditions in which human dignity can flourish) is the ruling conception.

In Chapter 2, having elaborated the conception of human dignity as empowerment, we compare it with the conception of human dignity as constraint that is to be found in the Convention on Human Rights and Biomedicine and the Universal Declaration on the Human Genome and Human Rights. Here we find human dignity acting as a constraint on free choice. However, this constraint is open to interpretation. On one reading, human dignity constrains by virtue of being a collective good that represents each society's vision of the kind of society it wants to be. On another reading, the constraint springs from the view that it is as wrong to compromise one's own dignity as it is to compromise the dignity of others.

In these opening two chapters we will find that the tension between the two conceptions of human dignity mirrors a familiar tension between the claims of autonomy (human dignity as empowerment) and the claims of other social values (human dignity as constraint). Where the tension is most acute, individual choice is either given free rein (the preferences of others notwithstanding), or it is restricted (paternalistically, in the interests of the individual, or defensively for the sake of collective values). So far as bioethics is concerned, these tensions translate in a striking fashion. Where human dignity as empowerment holds court, and autonomy is prioritized, bioethics is organized largely around the notion of informed consent. On the other hand, where human dignity as constraint rules, and either paternalism or social defence prevails, consent (no matter how free or informed) is no longer decisive. Indeed, a fairly dramatic way of expressing the emergence of human dignity as constraint is to say that, in bioethics, it threatens to overtake the ruling paradigm of informed consent.[6]

Human Dignity and International Human Rights Instruments

In the leading post-Second World War human rights instruments the idea of human dignity, as we have said, tends to take its place in the general normative context and background. Indeed, in the case of the European Convention on Human Rights (ECHR), so muted is the role of human dignity that the drafters make no explicit reference to the idea, leaving it to others to tease out the principle of respect for human dignity as immanent in the Convention.[7] In this respect, the Convention is not alone: for in the case of the US Bill of Rights, too, the founding fathers left it to later generations to find the deep principle of respect for human dignity implicit in the Constitution (see Meyer and Parent 1992).[8]

When we turn to the three constituent instruments comprising the so-called 'International Bill of Rights'—the Universal Declaration of Human Rights 1948 (UDHR), the International Covenant on Economic, Social and Cultural Rights 1966 (ICESCR), and the International Covenant on Civil and Political Rights 1966 (ICCPR)—we find a little more guidance. For, in each case, human dignity is explicitly declared as one of the foundational ideas. Thus, the Preamble to each instrument provides that 'recognition of the inherent dignity and of the equal and inalienable rights of all members of the human family is the foundation of freedom, justice and peace in the world'.[9]

In the ICESCR and ICCPR it is recognized that 'these rights derive from the inherent dignity of the human person'; and Article 1 of the UDHR proclaims that 'All human beings are born free and equal in dignity and rights'. However, only twice thereafter do the drafters of the UDHR draw explicitly on the concept of dignity—first, in Article 22 (concerning the right to social security and the economic, social, and cultural rights indispensable for dignity and the free development of personality) and then in Article 23(3) (concerning the right to just and

---

[6] We interpret this ruling paradigm as a kind of bioethical pluralism in which autonomy and informed consent are the most strongly weighted values. However, there is a more radical interpretation, amounting to an ethics of process, where the principle of autonomy is read as a principle of permission (see Engelhardt 2000: 35–46).

[7] However, as David Feldman (1999: 689) has pointed out: (i) the preambular reference in the ECHR to the UN Universal Declaration of Human Rights does indirectly connect the Convention to human dignity; and (ii) in practice, 'the Strasbourg organs have frequently referred to human dignity as one of the values underpinning the rights'. For example, Article 3 of the ECHR (concerning torture, inhuman or degrading treatment, or punishment) invites an analysis in terms of human dignity.

[8] The same applies to the French Declaration of 1789: the rights of man explicitly identified are equality, liberty, and fraternity, while human dignity is the unexpressed basis for the Declaration.

[9] This preambular principle is also the basis of Article 1 of the recently agreed Charter of Fundamental Rights of the European Union, according to which 'The dignity of the person must be respected and protected'.

favourable remuneration such as to ensure an existence worthy of human dignity). Similarly, there are just two further references to human dignity in the ICESCR and ICCPR: in Article 13 of the former (where it is agreed that 'education shall be directed to the full development of the human personality and the sense of its dignity'), and in Article 10 of the latter (to the effect that 'All persons deprived of their liberty shall be treated with humanity and with respect for the inherent dignity of the human person').

These provisions are firmly tied to an important cluster of preambular ideas: namely, that each and every human being has inherent *dignity*; that it is this *inherent* dignity that grounds (or accounts for) the possession of human rights (it is from such inherent dignity that such rights are *derived*); that these are *inalienable* rights; and that, because all humans have dignity, they hold these rights *equally*. So understood, human dignity is the rock on which the superstructure of human rights is built. The logic of this conception of human dignity as the ground of human rights, however, is that the primary *practical* and *political* discourse is that of human rights rather than that of human dignity. In other words, while philosophers might recur to the idea of human dignity as the deeper justification for human rights, the practical business of pressing one's interests against others (particularly against powerful States) will be conducted in terms of claimed human rights. On this analysis, it is perfectly clear why human dignity, having done its work in grounding human rights, then slips into the background (see e.g. Kolnai 1976: 257–9; Goodin 1981: 91–100).[10]

However, human dignity does not always remain in the background. For example, section 10 of the Constitution of the Republic of South Africa provides that 'Everyone has inherent dignity [implying a background idea] and the right to have their dignity respected and protected [implying a foreground claim]'. Furthermore, section 35 requires that the conditions of detention (of arrested, detained, and accused persons) must be 'consistent with human dignity, including at least exercise and the provision, at state expense, of adequate accommodation, nutrition, reading material and medical treatment'. And, as we have seen, even in the International Bill of Rights, references to human dignity are occasionally made in the Articles. Yet if human dignity is the foundation on which human rights are constructed, what are we to make of human dignity when it is incorporated into general rights claims (such as the right to have one's dignity

---

[10] According to Goodin, 'it is wholly appropriate that arguments for respecting "inalienable human rights" have long been couched in terms of dignity. . . . However, such rights guarantees are not in themselves enough. Protecting people's dignity requires more than just prohibiting degrading political outcomes, as rights traditionally do. People show each other respect or disrespect through their attitudes and motives whether or not they culminate in action. . . . Respecting people's dignity thus requires not only filtering the outcomes of social decision procedures . . but also filtering the inputs into the social decision machinery, censoring the sorts of demands of which society will even take cognisance . . .' (1981: 98–9). Nevertheless, in principle, we see no reason why human rights should not focus on inputs as much as outcomes; and thus no reason why human dignity should not remain in the background.

respected and protected) or specific claims? The frequent appeal to the principle of respect for human dignity in the context of the deprivation of liberty (an appeal found, as we have seen, in both Article 10 ICCPR as well as section 35 of the South African Constitution) is a good test case.[11]

For guidance on the meaning of respect for human dignity in the context of deprivation of liberty, we can turn to the German *Life Imprisonment* case.[12] There the Federal Constitutional Court said,

Respect for and protection of human dignity form part of the constituent principles of the Basic Law. The free human personality and its dignity constitute the highest legal values within the constitutional order. . . . This means that . . . the individual must be recognised as a member with equal rights and an intrinsic value. It is therefore contrary to human dignity to make persons the mere object of the state. . . . The phrase 'the human being must always remain an end in himself' is of unlimited validity in all areas of law; for the dignity of the human being as a person which cannot be lost consists exactly of the maintenance of his recognition as an autonomous personality.[13]

These general remarks suggest two spheres (or focal points) for applications of the principle of respect for human dignity. First, there is the idea that those who have the relevant dignity-related *capacity* (for instance, the capacity for autonomous action) have the right to be recognized as such (that is to say, if the capacity for autonomous action is the relevant capacity, then respect for dignity demands that those who have such a capacity are treated as beings with autonomous personalities). Even where offenders are deprived of their liberty following the commission of a crime, they do not lose their inherent dignity and, by implication, their membership of a community of rights; thus, they retain the right to be recognized as autonomous (or, at any rate, as having the capacity for autonomous action). In the same vein, persons must not be made 'the mere object of the state'. Notwithstanding their commission of an offence, offenders are not to be treated as mere means, objects, or things; they remain ends in their own right by virtue of their capacity to control and take responsibility for their actions. As the Court elaborates this idea, because the dignity of the human person is inviolable, punishments must be proportional to the severity of the offence and the guilt of the offender; which is to say, those offenders who are deprived of their liberty should not be made 'the mere object of crime prevention'.[14] Second, there

---

[11] Similarly, the consultation process concerning the New Democratic Constitution of Zimbabwe poses the following questions under section 7.7.3 ('The Right to Human Dignity'): whether the Constitution should protect prisoners from sexual abuse, overcrowding, transmission of diseases, and any other 'infringements to dignity'; whether people should be protected from torture, and cruel and degrading treatment; whether corporal punishment of children under 18 should be permitted; whether a deceased person's body should be treated with dignity and respect; whether the death penalty should be executed within a prescribed time; how such a penalty should be executed; whether such a penalty should be carried out in private or public; and whether persons on death row should have access to their next of kin.

[12] BVerfGE 45 (1977) 187.   [13] Ibid. 227–8
[14] Ibid. 228.

is the idea that humans have a right to the *conditions* or circumstances in which they can exercise their dignity-related capacities fully—in which, for example, their autonomous personalities can flourish. According to the Court, it follows that cruel, inhuman, and degrading punishments are strictly prohibited by the 'commandment of human dignity';[15] and, in the more recent *Honecker* Decision,[16] the Court suggested that human dignity is violated where an individual is 'degraded to a mere object of state action' by being kept in custody when he is seriously ill and close to death.[17] Although this latter suggestion was controversial, the deeper idea that human dignity is violated where persons are subjected to conditions that are demeaning or degrading is commonly relied on—not merely in the context of deprivation of liberty, but also in relation to housing and employment conditions.

In these reflections we can discern both a formal and a substantive scheme of thinking about human dignity. The *formal* scheme starts with the preambular ideas that we have already noted as the foundation of the International Bill of Rights: human dignity signifies that each human has inherent value; each human is worthy of respect; and each human has inalienable rights to the protection of his or her value. Formally, this foundational idea is articulated as the general right, held by each human, to respect (for one's dignity) by other humans. This right (to be treated as one who has worth) may then be cashed more specifically as:

(*a*) a right to be respected as one who belongs to the class of human beings, that is, as one who has the distinctive capacities of being human;

(*b*) a (negative) right against unwilled interventions by others that are damaging to the circumstances or conditions that are essential if one is to flourish as a human; and

(*c*) a (positive) right to support and assistance to secure circumstances or conditions that are essential if one is to flourish as a human.

So stated, this formal scheme invites *substantive* completion. What is it about humans that gives them value? What distinctive human property is it that dignity picks up in purporting to ground human rights? Is it simply that humans are capable of thinking the (ascriptive) thought 'We are the ones with value; we have dignity';[18] or is it that they can translate this thought into a prescription demanding respect from others; or is it that they can act on such a prescription? In the *Life Imprisonment* case, as in much other thinking about the distinctiveness of humans, it is the capacity for autonomous action that is singled out as special. As Joseph Raz has expressed this point, 'Respecting human dignity entails treating humans as persons capable of planning and plotting their future. Thus, respecting

---

[15] Ibid.   [16] BerlVerfGH NJW 1993, 515.
[17] Ibid. 517.
[18] See e.g. Parent (1992: 64) for the contention that the language of moral dignity should be interpreted as 'essentially ascriptive'.

people's dignity includes respecting their autonomy, their right to control their future' (1979: 221). Raz goes on to suggest that offences to a person's dignity, so understood, can be divided into three classes—insults, enslavement, and manipulation.

An insult offends a person's dignity if it consists of or implies a denial that he is an autonomous person or that he deserves to be treated as one. An action enslaves another if it practically denies him all options through the manipulation of the environment. . . . One manipulates a person by intentionally changing his tastes, his beliefs or his ability to act or decide. Manipulation—in other words—is manipulation of the person, of those factors relevant to his autonomy which are internal to him. Enslavement is the elimination of control by changing factors external to the person. (p. 221)

It follows that, if the capacity to control one's actions by reference to the choices one has made is the distinctive source of human worth, then to deny a human the opportunity to choose and control, whether by insult, enslavement, or manipulation, is to offend against his or her dignity—it is, in fact, a double offence, a denial of rights as well as a denial of responsibility.

We can take this discussion forward by considering how one might elaborate the two sets of rights that capture the thrust of this approach to human dignity: a right to respect for one's dignity as a human; and a right to the conditions in which human dignity can flourish.[19]

A Right to Respect for One's Dignity as a Human

There are several ways in which a person's right to respect for their dignity as a human might be said to be violated—for example, if one were treated as having no worth (or less than equal worth *as a human* relative to other humans); if one were treated incorrectly as though one lacked the distinctive human capacities, or as lacking the capacities in a sufficiently developed form (as with children);[20] or if one were treated as a mere thing or object. These all seem to be egregious violations: in each case, a human being is treated as though he or she is not a human

---

[19] For a fairly similar approach, see Clapham (1993: 148–9), where protection of human dignity is suggested to involve (i) respect for everyone's humanity, and (ii) the creation and protection of 'the conditions for everyone's self-fulfilment (or autonomy or self-realization)'. While the former is said to relate to *direct* attacks on dignity (such as 'killing, torture, slavery, traffic in persons, coercion, verbal abuse, discrimination, maltreatment—these could be categorized as *indignities*'), the latter can be understood as relating to *indirect* attacks (such as 'denying the right to associate, to make love, to take part in social life, to express one's intellectual, artistic, or cultural ideas, to enjoy a decent standard of living and health care'). This latter approach, Clapham points out, is picked up in Article 22 of the UDHR—and the same point could be made in respect of Article 23(3).

[20] See e.g. Fortin (1999). Here, while discussing the majority's approach in *Nielson* v. *Denmark*, (1989) 11 EHRR 175, Fortin remarks that the 'Court's assumption that a twelve year old with no mental impairment had no right to object to his mother's wishes [that he be placed and retained in a psychiatric ward] seems completely contrary to the spirit of the Convention [ECHR], with its respect for human dignity, as expressed in its preamble' (1999: 358).

(or not fully human); in each case, there is a serious affront (or insult) to human dignity. The sense of such an affront is clearly conveyed by Victor Frankl's recollections of his treatment in a Nazi concentration camp. In one incident, Frankl recalls, when he rested for a moment from his repair work on a railroad track, a guard threw a stone at him. As Frankl saw it, 'That, to me, seemed the way to attract the attention of a beast, to call a domestic animal back to its job, a creature with which you have so little in common that you do not even punish it' (1984: 43).[21] Such treatment represents a particularly profound violation of human dignity. It is not simply a matter of treating someone badly (which might be the case if, in Frankl's account, the guard had told Frankl to get back to work at once); it is treating a human being as though he or she were not human at all.

If one were to specify this right (to respect for one's dignity as a human) more precisely, it would be important to address questions of *intent* (of the alleged wrongdoer) and *effect* (upon the alleged victim). For example, it might be argued that the sufficient conditions for such an affront to human dignity are: either (*a*) that the wrongdoer, knowing (or suspecting) that the victim is a human being (or has the relevant human capacity), intentionally (or recklessly) fails to acknowledge the latter as being such; or (*b*) that the wrongdoer, without realizing (or suspecting) that the victim is a human being (or has the relevant human capacity), nevertheless fails to acknowledge the latter as human.

If adverse effect is not part of the specification, we might agree with Stephen Munzer (writing with regard to the question of whether it would be incompatible with respect for human dignity if property in body parts were to be recognized) that 'If I have an unconditioned and incomparable worth, and if you insult that worth by treating me as a repository of body parts, you have offended my dignity even if I have the strength to resist your impositions' (1994: 274). On the other hand, we might hold that, irrespective of the question of intent or knowledge, the necessary and sufficient condition for such an affront to human dignity is that non-recognition actually causes the victim to experience a reduction in self-esteem. In other words, the critical question is not whether A intends to treat B as a mere object, but whether B experiences being treated in this way. Or, again, we might combine the variables relating to intent and effect in some other way to produce the relevant conditions for this particular violation of human dignity.

One (quite commonly employed) way of expressing the idea that persons have a right to respect for their dignity as humans is to say that they have a right against being 'instrumentalized'. For this is an evocative way of articulating the complaint that one has been treated as a mere thing, as an object, as having no intrinsic value, or as lacking the distinctive human capacities. However, the language of instrumentalization is pretty elastic and, at its broadest, it simply conveys the complaint that one feels that one has been 'used' or exploited. The fact that the language of instrumentalization is employed fairly freely when it is

---

[21] Cited by Parent (1992: 60).

alleged that a violation of human rights and/or human dignity has taken place puts us on notice in two ways. On the one hand, where it is alleged that some action or practice involves a violation of human dignity because victims are being instrumentalized, we need to look carefully to see precisely what violation is alleged. On the other hand, where it is alleged that some action or practice involves a violation of human dignity *even though the victims are not being instrumentalized*, then we need to inspect the claim even more carefully, because it suggests that a quite different conception of human dignity is in play (a conception of the kind that we will consider in the next chapter).[22]

A Right to the Conditions in which Human Dignity can Flourish

If the foundational human rights idea is that each human being, having dignity, has a general right to respect (for his or her dignity) by other humans, then we have suggested that, *formally*, this might be translated into (i) a (negative) right against unwilled interventions by others that are damaging to the circumstances or conditions that are essential if one is to flourish as a human being; and (ii) a (positive) right to support and assistance in securing circumstances or conditions that are essential if one is to flourish as a human being. To give this form some *substance*, we have further suggested that those capacities that are distinctively human need to be brought into the account. For the sake of argument, let us suppose that the capacity for autonomous action (in the morally neutral sense of the capacity to control one's future, or to be author of one's own life, or to exercise choice free from the unwilled coercion or manipulation of others)[23] is the distinctive capacity. If so, then rights relating to the circumstances and conditions in which one can flourish as a human relate to the context in which the capacity for autonomy can flower and be realized.

Consider two notorious contexts, those of slavery and apartheid, in which it would be widely agreed that respect for human dignity is compromised. How would these contexts be argued to be incompatible with the right of the victims to conditions in which human dignity can flourish?

Enslavement, as Raz says, is one form of offence to human dignity, and the institution of slavery is enslavement writ large. Now, no matter how 'enlightened' the treatment of particular slaves by particular slave-owners, there is an inescapable sense in which the very institution of slavery necessarily represents

---

[22] See e.g. Hilary Putnam, who says, 'Of course, some proposed uses of cloning do violate the great Kantian maxim against treating another person solely as a means—for example, cloning a human being solely so that the clone would be a kidney donor or bone-marrow donor. . . . [However,] I will argue that cloning humans (if and when that happens) may, indeed, violate human dignity even when the purpose is not as blatantly instrumental as producing an organ donor' (1999: 1).

[23] For the several senses in which the idea of 'autonomy' might be used, see e.g. Engelhardt (2000: 37).

a denial of the slaves' dignity.[24] Granted, some slave-owners might show genuine concern for the well-being of their slaves and would not dream of treating them as though they were mere things, but the fact remains that, according to the rules of the institution, slaves are to be regarded as the 'property' of the slave-owner. Whatever the actual practice, therefore, the institution of slavery stands for a relationship that necessarily is incompatible with human dignity. Nevertheless, the details of the practice are important, for there may well be some variation in the extent to which slaves experience conditions in which their institutionally limited opportunity for autonomous action is supported and can be exercised. In other words, even though there is no way in which even the most benign practice of slavery can be redeemed (relative to human dignity), the more benign cases of this dignity-violating practice will at least respond positively to the slaves' right to have some degree of autonomy.

When we say that some slaves may do rather better than others in experiencing conditions in which they can exercise a degree of autonomy, it is not simply a matter of having the material wherewithal (adequate food, clothing, and shelter and the like), nor of having some space in which one makes one's own decisions. Over and above such matters, the right to the conditions in which human dignity can flourish presupposes a certain level of self-respect or self-esteem. The deep problem with the institution of slavery, however, is that it invites precisely the opposite perception of oneself—far from cultivating self-respect, this is an institution that brands a section of humans as mere property; and, even those slaves who experience the most benign treatment must ponder in their more reflective moments whether they have any intrinsic value as humans. Underlining this point, we find in nineteenth-century America the proponents of the 'free labour' ideology in the Northern States contrasting 'the dignity and vitality of the free white workers' with 'the laboring man's poverty, degradation, and lack of opportunity for advancement in the South' (McCurdy 1998: 168). Of course, emancipation was not everything. For, free workers in the industrial North as in the rural South came to experience deplorable living conditions that were wholly unconducive to the flourishing of autonomous individuals. Nevertheless, emancipation was the first demand of human dignity; and, with the removal of the chains of enslavement, a deep impediment to the recovery of a sense of dignity (to the recovery of self-esteem) dropped away.

Apartheid, like slavery, is an institution that represents a deep violation of human dignity. By treating a section of human beings within the community as inferior *qua* human, apartheid represents a standing violation of the right to respect for one's dignity as a human. It is also a case where the conditions of social organization militate against humans flourishing with a sense of their dignity. As with slavery, we can say of apartheid that: (*a*) so long as the institution persists, there is a standing threat to the universal sense of dignity; (*b*) there

---

[24] In similar vein, see Boxill (1992).

is no guarantee, when the institution is brought to an end, that the material conditions of life will be any more conducive to the promotion of autonomy (although the spiritual conditions will now be more favourable); and (c) it is nevertheless possible, within the (dignity-violating) practice, to identify further independent violations of human dignity. Picking up this third feature, the old South African case of *Purshotam Dagee* v. *Durban Corporation*[25] is an interesting example. There, the plaintiff Indian was a fare-paying passenger in the defendant's tramcar. The local bye-laws provided for separate buses for 'coloureds' and the plaintiff was travelling in compliance with this provision. Nevertheless, the conductor ordered the plaintiff to sit at the back of the tram. The plaintiff having refused to do so, the conductor told him to leave the tram. Applying the local law of delict (in which there is a somewhat ill-defined remedy for impairment of human dignity) (see Burchell 1988), the court held that the plaintiff was entitled to damages for injury to his dignity. If we assume that the local bye-laws already represented a standing violation of the plaintiff's human dignity, nevertheless the conductor's conduct involved a further violation—whether by openly treating the plaintiff as having no worth or by restricting even further the plaintiff's autonomy in relation to his mode of transport (not even allowing him to choose his own seat).

It should also be said that, in post-apartheid societies (like post-slave-owning societies), the possibility of there being crude violations of human dignity remains. Anton Fagan, discussing a trio of recent decisions handed down by the South African Constitutional Court, cautions against the invocation of dignity as a mere 'rhetorical flourish' (1998: 221)—which is not at all to say that the protection of human dignity has no place in the new constitutional settlement (where it is specifically protected by section 10), but that we should have a clear sense of how this particular protection fits in with the regime of rights (against unfair discrimination, in favour of equality, and so on).[26] But how precisely are we to disentangle dignity from these other ideas? Fagan suggests the example of access to a scarce health resource, such as the situation where the State can offer renal dialysis to only 10 per cent of those who (equally) need it. How is the State to decide who is to have access and who is not? A lottery of some kind is one possibility; or perhaps race, gender, or class might serve as the criterion. According to Fagan, criteria of the latter kind (unlike a lottery, or date of birth, or some such method) clearly breach the principle of respect for human dignity. Thus, 'to provide renal dialysis only to whites or middle-class men, in my view, violates the dignity of blacks, of women, and of the working class. For it suggests that members of the latter groups (blacks, women, the working class) lead less valuable lives and thus deserve less concern than do members of the former groups

---

[25] NLR (1908) 391.

[26] Fagan's remarks about dignity being invoked as a rhetorical flourish are directed against the reasoning of Goldstone J in *President of the RSA* v. *Hugo* 1997 (4) SA 1 (CC).

(whites, men, the middle class)' (1998: 223). Similarly, if the State were to decree that 'whites should collect unemployment benefits on Mondays, blacks on Tuesdays through to Fridays' (p. 223), this, too, at any rate in the South African context, would involve an impairment of the dignity of blacks.[27] This, surely, is correct: if blacks, like whites, have value as humans, then they have that worth equally.

Fagan's qualifying remark—concerning the specificity of the South African context—prompts the thought that the requirements of human dignity as empowerment might involve some elements of contingency. Although contingency in the sense that Fagan has in mind is not something that need detain us long, the possibility of contingency undercutting a supposedly 'universal' scheme of human rights is a more troublesome thought, and it is a recurrent issue for us. Accordingly, we need to pause in order to understand the particular sense in which contingency could be a serious problem for the conception of human dignity as empowerment.

Contingency

It is axiomatic within the conception of human dignity as empowerment (in which human dignity operates as the ground for human rights) that human dignity is inherent and non-contingent: human beings have dignity universally; and, no matter how badly particular individuals might behave, they retain their human dignity (although they might forfeit some of their ordinary rights). However, once we take a harder look at these foundational claims, the supposed universality of this conception can soon be brought into question.

At the very heart of the conception of human dignity as empowerment is the contention that human dignity *grounds* human rights. Whatever human dignity means, this conception only hangs together if human rights are justified by reference to human dignity. How might the justifying linkage between human dignity and human rights be presented?[28]

---

[27] Even if the arrangement is not unfair (see Fagan 1998: 233).

[28] The taken-for-granted nature of this linkage is highlighted by Louis Henkin: 'Links between individual rights and human dignity are now commonly assumed. Such links are declared explicitly in the preamble to the Universal Declaration of Human Rights, and in the preamble to the two international human rights covenants that derive from that declaration. . . . The framers of the international instruments did not define human dignity; perhaps they thought it needed no definition, in any language. Nor were they precise about the relationship between human rights and human dignity. It was apparently assumed that it went without saying that respect for a person's human rights is necessary to maintain his (her) human dignity. . . . Having linked human rights to human dignity, the framers of the Universal Declaration proceeded to declare a catalogue of rights. Whether the concept of human dignity determined the specific content of that catalogue is not clear. There has been no studied attempt to invoke human dignity to justify the inclusion of any particular right (or the exclusion of others), either in the declaration or in the many human rights covenants and conventions that derive from it' (1992: 211).

In a bold version of this conception, the premiss would be that human dignity signifies, quite simply, that humans have intrinsic worth and, thus, humans represent a value to be nurtured, respected, and protected. From this premiss, it is easy to argue that human rights are required; for even a passing familiarity with human experience puts us on notice that, although humans are quite good at recognizing value in their own persons, they do not always recognize the corresponding value in others. Hence, human beings are vulnerable and a regime of human rights goes some way towards shielding them against one another (particularly against overbearing State-organized governance). Human dignity, thus, justifies a protective regime of human rights in a very straightforward way. Without doubt, this bold version of human dignity as empowerment suggests a clear link between the ground of human rights (humans having intrinsic worth) and the need for human rights. Admittedly, the linking premiss (that humans do not always recognize intrinsic worth in one another) introduces a contingency; but this is not a contingency that in any sense damages the conception—at worst, human rights become redundant in some idealized future state. However, the foundational premiss itself (that humans have intrinsic worth) is put forward without any supporting reasons. We (humans) may well be disposed to accept that human beings have intrinsic value, but is there any reason why we should accept this proposition? If we have no reason, there is a serious (epistemological) contingency at the base of this conception. As Joel Feinberg has said,

In attributing human worth to everyone, we may be ascribing no property or set of properties, but rather expressing an attitude—the attitude of respect—toward the humanity in each man's person. That attitude follows naturally from regarding everyone from 'the human point of view', but it is not grounded in anything more ultimate than itself, and it is not ultimately justifiable. (1973: 94)

The problem with this version of human dignity as empowerment, therefore, is that its universal attribution of protective rights to humans rests entirely on contingent acceptance—it depends on humans having the right attitude, namely a human rights attitude.

It is also the case, of course, that such a conveniently contingent pro-human account invites the charge of question-begging speciesism. As Helga Kuhse makes the point:

What reasons might one have for holding that all human beings and only human beings have dignity? On the face of it, the principle seems to merely presuppose what needs to be shown—namely that the property of dignity is a property uniquely possessed by human beings. Here it would not do to respond by saying that human life has dignity because it is *human* life, or relates to the lives of members of the species *homo sapiens*. These sorts of claims would be near-tautological. Something more would need to be said—and it would not be enough to say that human life has dignity because it takes the form of a featherless biped or because humans have opposing thumbs. Such justifications would fall foul of the charge of 'speciesism'. (2000: 69–70)

The question, then, is whether we can find something else to say about the properties of humans (or, at any rate, some humans) to justify the premiss that they (or, at least, some of them) have dignity and, concomitantly, moral status as bearers of human rights.

A less brazen version of human dignity as empowerment holds that humans have worth because some persons at least are capable of valuing their own existence[29] or possess some distinctive capacity (such as the capacity for autonomous action). In this version the dignity of humans relates directly to this particular capacity or property. Assuming, for the sake of argument, that autonomy is the relevant property, the linkage to human rights would then run along something like the following lines.[30]

1. The dignity of humans (the reason for their value or worth) resides in their capacity for autonomous action.
2. Humans express their value (dignity) when they act autonomously.
3. It follows that a setting in which humans are able to act autonomously is to be preferred to one in which they are not able to do so.
4. Thus, an autonomy-supporting regime of human rights not only signals respect for human dignity but assists in creating a context in which such dignity can be realized in practice.

The identification of human dignity with the capacity for autonomy does not, however, eliminate the contingency that we have identified already in the bold version of human dignity as empowerment. Quite possibly, many will think it self-evident that the capacity for autonomous action is to be valued (and respected). Nevertheless, unless there are reasons for thinking that autonomy is a thing of value, this conception of human dignity rests on a contingent willingness to accept such a founding claim. Moreover, the identification of human dignity with the capacity for autonomy introduces a further significant contingency. Precisely because human dignity is identified, not with being human as such, but with having the capacity for autonomy, it is only those humans who have a developed capacity for autonomy who have dignity and to whom the regime of human rights applies directly. It follows that this version of human dignity as empowerment is not universal in applying to *all* human beings; strictly speaking, it applies contingently only to those humans who have the capacity for autonomy. To be sure, by fixing on a capacity such as autonomy, there is no arbitrary discrimination of the kind contemplated by human rights instruments (where rights are enjoyed by humans irrespective of sex, race, colour, language, religion, and so on). Even so, strictly speaking, human dignity and, concomitantly, human rights are not enjoyed universally by all members of the human species.[31]

---

[29] As argued, for example, by John Harris (1985; 1995*a*, esp. at 9).

[30] Compare Henkin (1992: 211).

[31] The same contingency applies to 'persons', understood as those humans who have the capacity to value their own existence.

These comments point to two troubling features of human dignity as empowerment. One problem relates to the way in which human dignity operates as a justifying ground for the set of human rights it supposedly supports. The other problem arises from the identification of human dignity with a particular capacity or property that is not possessed necessarily by all human beings. In our view, any adequate theory of human dignity (and moral rights) must have defensible responses to the question marks that we have now pencilled in the margin against the conception of human dignity as empowerment. We will have occasion to return to these issues during the course of the next two chapters, but it is in Chapters 4 to 6 that we give our own view on these matters.

Beyond these difficulties, there are two other forms of contingency that we must mention. However, these are not contingencies that occasion any real concern.

First, as we have remarked, there is a background sense in which all violations of human rights necessarily offend against human dignity and, in principle, any such violation might be seen as an assault on our dignity (or our *sense* of dignity). Whether, then, we elect to express our moral claims in terms of human rights or human dignity or both seems to be a contingent matter, probably depending on a mixture of variable factors concerning custom, culture, and perceived political advantage.[32] For example, William Parent says that 'a distinctively moral conception of human dignity should be available to condemn' those practices or actions involving 'arbitrary, unfair devaluation', such as 'the practice of placing less value or worth on groups of human beings for no other reason than they happen to be black, Jewish, old, female, and so forth' (1992: 61). The perceived advantage of employing such a conception is not altogether clear. However, having observed that we have a wide choice of terminology to describe (and implicitly condemn) actions that arbitrarily put a person down, Parent seems to think that a community that relates such wrongdoing to a lack of respect for human dignity will fare better (morally speaking) than if it lacks this organizing idea.

> ... any culture with a shared understanding of the concepts that belong to the dignity family—for example, moral respect, just or fair treatment, arbitrariness, debasement, contempt, moral character—will also have a concept of dignity. Of course, this concept may not have received anything like a precise philosophical formulation. And responsible citizens of the culture may differ over the proper interpretation of 'unjust debasement' in resolving particular hard cases. Furthermore, the concept of dignity may enjoy little legal protection. But the root idea, that people suffer a grievous personal wrong when they are devalued for irrelevant reasons and that we have a valid moral claim, therefore, not to be so disparaged, will occupy a place in that culture's moral ideology. (1992: 63)

Put in these terms, we might remain to be convinced; we might think that the culture will do just as well provided that it is understood that every citizen has a

---

[32] For a good example of this thesis, see Scheingold (1974).

general right to equal concern and respect and specific rights against being treated as inferior, being unjustly debased, or treated with contempt, and so on. However, this is not a matter worth contesting in the abstract: each context will have its own particular features, in the light of which a judgement can be made about the relative effectiveness of a discourse of human dignity versus a discourse of human rights.[33]

Second, in so far as dignity is aligned with the bases of self-respect, and to the extent that self-respect hinges upon the respect of others, then Robert E. Goodin is surely right to say that the 'entitlements arising out of [respect for human dignity] may vary somewhat with time and place. . . . [For] what [others] *mean* by their actions is crucial, and performance intended to humiliate in one culture might be intended to honour in another' (Goodin 1981: 99). Similarly, the background context may affect the interpretation of particular practices. For example, in some contexts, 'separate but equal' practices may imply no lack of respect and might be compatible with full regard for human dignity; in other contexts, the message is very different.

In sum, proponents of human dignity as empowerment need lose no sleep over contextual contingency. However, epistemological contingency is a cause for concern. If the modern human rights movement rests on axioms about intrinsic and equal human dignity that, in turn, rest only on commitment and acceptance, then what is widely recognized to be a progressive and civilizing culture is vulnerable to those who simply dissent. This is not to say that the development and acceptance of human rights is of no importance. On the contrary, for practical purposes, whether or not human rights are recognized may be, quite literally, a matter of life and death to many. For philosophical purposes, too, acceptance of human rights is important, for, as we will argue in Chapter 4, a commitment to human rights (whether to particular human rights, or simply to the idea of human rights) has an immanent logic implicating commitment to a very particular moral theory. However, the bottom-line logic of epistemological contingency is less reassuring: it is that we are right to think of human dignity as empowerment only so long as we think it right to so think.

Human Dignity as a Two-Edged Sword: The Case of the French Dwarfs

Before we draw this chapter to a close, we should recall and underscore the point that there is potentially a tension between human dignity in support of autonomy and human dignity as a constraint on autonomy. In this sense, human dignity is a

---

[33] The paradigms in Parent's discussion are racism and the Holocaust. However, one might take another case, torture perhaps, as paradigmatic. For example, Raylene Keightley (1995: 379) says 'Torture and related activities represent the most basic denial of human dignity which lies at the very heart of the concept of human rights.' Again, however, whether torture is more effectively resisted in the name of human rights or human dignity seems to us to be a contingent matter.

two-edged sword. As David Feldman, in a rare discussion of human dignity as a
legal value, makes the point:

we must not assume that the idea of dignity is inextricably linked to a liberal-individualist
view of human beings as people whose life-choices deserve respect. If the state takes a
particular view on what is required for people to live dignified lives, it may introduce regulations to restrict the freedom which people have to make choices which, in the state's
view, interfere with the dignity of the individual, a social group or the human race as a
whole. . . . The quest for human dignity may subvert rather than enhance choice. . . . Once
it becomes a tool in the hands of lawmakers and judges, the concept of human dignity is a
two-edged sword. (1999: 685)

The potential cut of the illiberal edge of the sword is vividly illustrated by the
famous French dwarf-throwing (*lancer de nain*) case.[34]

In this case, the Conseil d'État, having affirmed that respect for human dignity
was one of the constituents of *ordre public*, confirmed a municipal police power
to prohibit any spectacle that represented a threat to such respect. Accordingly, it
was held that, where police powers had been exercised in Morsang-sur-Orge and
Aix-en-Provence to ban the attraction of dwarf-throwing in local clubs, such
steps were lawfully taken in order to secure respect for human dignity and *ordre
public*. However, the legality of the bans was challenged by, among others, one
of the dwarfs (one Manuel Wackenheim), who argued that he freely participated
in the activity, that the work brought him a monthly wage (as well as allowing
him to move in professional circles), and that, if dwarf-throwing was banned, he
would find himself unemployed again. To this, the Conseil d'État responded that
the dwarf compromised his own dignity by allowing himself to be used as a
projectile, as a mere thing, and that no such concession could be allowed.[35]

What are we to make of this? On the one side, the dwarfs were relying on the
conception of human dignity as empowerment. For the dwarfs, the central issue
was whether others were acting against their (the dwarfs') dignity. Their argument
was that they were *not* being treated as mere things; others were not disregarding
their capacity to control the situation. It was only to the extent that the dwarfs freely
chose to participate that the activities took place. Moreover, from the dwarfs' viewpoint, to be deprived of their status as employed persons was to undermine the
conditions in which they experienced a sense of their own dignity. So interpreted,
it was the well-meaning paternalism of the Conseil, rather than the actions of the
dwarf-throwers, that represented a threat to the dignity of the dwarfs.[36]

---

[34] Conseil d'État (October 27, 1995) req. nos. 136–727 (Commune de Morsang-sur-Orge) and
143–578 (Ville d'Aix-en-Provence). We are grateful to Professor Irma Arnoux, who first drew our
attention to these two decisions.
[35] See Marie-Christine Rouault's note on the two decisions (Rouault 1996: 32). And, for reflections on the case, with dignity being interpreted as the essence of humanity, see Edelman (1997:
187–8).
[36] For a rather different concern with the conditions in which human dignity may be realized (in
the context of housing provision), see the decision of the Conseil Constitutionnel no. 94–359 (19
January 1995), *Journal Officiel de la République Française* (21 January 1995) 1166.

On the other side, the Conseil d'État was operating with a rather different conception of human dignity (one that we will develop in the next chapter). Central to this conception is the idea that the dwarfs might compromise *their own* dignity and/or, with that, the dignity of fellow humans as understood in contemporary France. This is the idea of human dignity as an overriding value (whether grounded in individual humans or in groups of humans), a value to be respected by all members of human society. On this view, the fact that the dwarf-throwers did not intend to demean or degrade the dwarfs, or that the dwarfs freely consented to their participation, is immaterial: *ordre public* (including respect for human dignity) sets limits to autonomy—certain expressions of free choice are, quite simply, out of bounds. As for undermining the conditions in which the dwarfs recovered a sense of self-esteem, presumably the Conseil judged that this must be a case of false consciousness; for, surely, no genuine sense of self-esteem could be derived from participation in dwarf-throwing when (as Feldman might put it) such an undignified activity could not stand alongside respect for human dignity.

Conclusion

According to the conception of human dignity as empowerment that we have sketched in this chapter, it is the intrinsic dignity of humans that acts as the foundation for human rights. Such a conception fits the thinking that can be traced through the key international human rights instruments of the post-Second World War period—for example, in the ICESCR and ICCPR the equal and inalienable rights of human beings are said to 'derive from the inherent dignity of the human person'.[37] On this view, it is because human beings have dignity that they are entitled to respect from others—that is, by virtue of their dignity, human beings are entitled (*a*) to be recognized as members of the class of humans (a class of beings having value) and (*b*) to have the conditions in which they can experience their own dignity and exercise the distinctive human capacities that account for their dignity.

So elaborated, this conception of human dignity purports to ground a set of rights claims against others. Whether it succeeds in doing so depends on one's willingness to accept the value attributed to humans (or their distinctive capacities) in the constitutive premises of the conception. However, so long as the culture of human rights prevails, the epistemological contingency of the conception might well be of philosophical rather than practical concern.

If human dignity is equated with the capacity for autonomous action then this

---

[37] Although, by contrast, in the Preamble to the African Charter on Human and Peoples' Rights 1981, fundamental human rights are said to 'stem from the attributes of human beings'; and, similarly, the Preamble to the American Convention on Human Rights 1969, states that 'the essential rights of man . . . are based upon attributes of the human personality'.

will feed through into a regime of human rights organized around a right to one's autonomy. On this reading, the function of human dignity is to reinforce claims to self-determination rather than to limit free choice; it is a conception of individual empowerment rather than of social or collective constraint. So interpreted, human dignity fits squarely within the informed consent paradigm, and even bioethicists, like John Harris, who argue strongly against reliance on human dignity would find this conception of human dignity on their side.[38]

All too plainly, though, this is not the only conception of human dignity or, at any rate, this is not the only way of extending this particular conception. As the French dwarfs found to their cost, appeals to human dignity can serve to confine rather than to support one's freedom. And, as Harris suspects, the emerging role of human dignity in bioethics is precisely to close down rather than to open up the freedom to take advantage of the technology now being developed in the biosciences. It is to such a rival understanding of human dignity—human dignity as constraint—that we next turn.

---

[38] See e.g. John Harris (1999); but note the contrasting position outlined by Putnam (1999: 1).

2

Human Dignity and the New Bioethics: Human Dignity as Constraint

Introduction

Modern bioethics has its origins in the Code of Nuremberg of 1947 and gathers pace with the Declaration of Helsinki in 1964. Central to these developments is the idea that human beings should not be subjected to scientific and medical research without their free and informed consent. To the extent that human dignity has a role to play in such thinking, it is as the foundation for human rights, specifically the right of human beings to decide whether or not they will subject themselves to medical trials or treatments.[1]

At the turn of the twenty-first century the culture of human rights (typically related to the value of autonomy, and expressed through the requirement for informed consent) continues to exert its influence on bioethics. Thus, in the Council of Europe's Convention on Human Rights and Biomedicine and in UNESCO's Universal Declaration on the Human Genome and Human Rights, we find the familiar demand that bioscience and biomedicine should respect human rights. However, as we remarked at the beginning of the previous chapter, we also find in these instruments an explicit demand that human dignity should be respected. If this demand is interpreted in line with the conception of human dignity as empowerment, then the higher profile accorded to human dignity in the emerging bioethics can be treated as a shift merely in style rather than as a shift in substance. This, however, is not our reading of the new bioethics.

Contrary to the view that the bioethical framework now being crafted reflects no substantive change of direction, we suggest that a conception of human dignity as constraint is implicated in much recent thinking about the limits to be placed on biomedicine, reflecting the belief that biomedical practice in the twenty-first century should be driven, not by the vagaries of individual choice, but by a shared vision of human dignity that reaches beyond individuals. In other words, if we think of respect for human dignity as one of the constitutive values of our society (whether as an element of the public interest, or of *ordre public,* or as one of the fundamental values of our community), then those individual preferences and choices that are out of line with respect for human dignity are simply off limits.[2]

---

[1] Article 7 ICCPR, for example, provides that 'no one shall be subjected without his free consent to medical or scientific experimentation'.

[2] Similarly, see Kuhse (2000: 62): 'In bioethical contexts, "human dignity"' is but rarely invoked in attempts to affect [*sic*] liberalizing change; rather it is more often appealed to by those who seek to

The Convention on Human Rights and Biomedicine

In the Council of Europe's Convention on Human Rights and Biomedicine (adopted by the Committee of Ministers in November 1996), it is not immediately obvious that a sea-change might be taking place in the way that human dignity and human rights are understood to relate to one another. For (as in the Universal Declaration of Human Rights), having recited 'the importance of ensuring the dignity of the human being' in the Preamble, and having declared in Article 1 that the parties 'shall protect the dignity and identity of all human beings', the drafters of the Convention do not make any further explicit reference to human dignity. However, the Explanatory Report accompanying the Convention suggests a much less settled picture.

What the Report emphasizes is that 'human dignity . . . constitutes the essential value to be upheld . . . [and] is at the basis of most of the values emphasised in the Convention' (paragraph 9); that all Articles must be interpreted in the light of the aim of the Convention—'which is to protect human rights and dignity' (paragraph 22); and that the principle of respect for human dignity is central to Articles 15 (the general rule with regard to scientific research) (see paragraph 96), 17 (protection of persons not able to consent to research) (see paragraphs 106 and 111), and 21 (which provides that 'The human body and its parts shall not, as such, give rise to financial gain') (paragraph 131). Furthermore, the Preamble to the Protocol to the Convention dealing with the cloning of human beings tells us that the Protocol is guided by the consideration that 'the instrumentalisation of human beings through the deliberate creation of genetically identical human beings is contrary to human dignity and thus constitutes a misuse of biology and medicine'.[3]

While these explanatory comments suggest a greater readiness to identify human dignity with a number of specific offences, this kind of tagging does not of itself indicate that a rival conception is incorporated in the Convention. Nevertheless, there are grounds for thinking that the Convention reflects more than a new fashion for drafting. In particular, there are two developments in the substance of the latest bioethics (as per the Convention) that seem significant precisely because they draw heavily on a new articulation of the idea of human dignity. In both instances, respect for human dignity imposes additional

---

prevent change, particularly in such areas as artificial modes of reproduction and genetic interventions of various kinds.' Kuhse goes on to cite the mid-1980 German and Australian reports on IVF and related technologies as instances of such constraining appeals to human dignity.

[3] Similarly, see the consultation document of the Human Genetics Advisory Commission and Human Fertilisation and Embryology Authority (1998a, section 8), where human reproductive cloning is said to raise 'serious ethical issues, concerned with human responsibility and instrumentalisation of human beings' (p. 16). And, then, it is observed: 'There are moral arguments to support the claim that human dignity forbids the use of human beings only as a "means", holding that they are to be treated as an "end" in their own right' (p. 18).

constraints—in the first case constraining actions that concern human life from the point of conception and, in the second case, constraining actions which, although prima facie merely self-affecting, are judged to compromise human dignity (whether located in the actor's own person or humanity or, so to speak, in the community's collective conscience).[4]

The Protection of All Human Life

According to Article 1 of the Convention, the parties 'shall protect the dignity and identity of all human beings and guarantee everyone, without discrimination, respect for their integrity and other rights and fundamental freedoms with regard to the application of biology and medicine'.

The drafting of this provision is obscure and its underlying thinking is quite complex. Crucially, a distinction is drawn between 'everyone' and 'all human beings'. When the drafters use the term 'everyone', they self-consciously copy the language of the European Convention on Human Rights. In neither Convention, however, is this term defined (see the Explanatory Report to the Convention, paragraph 18). 'Everyone', therefore, refers to the potentially contested concept of a bearer of human rights. This is to be contrasted with 'all human beings', this term apparently signalling 'a generally accepted principle that human dignity and the identity of the human being [must] be respected as soon as life [begins]' (ibid., paragraph 19).

To appreciate the significance of the distinction drawn in Article 1, we must pause briefly to sketch the sense in which the concept of 'everyone-as-a-bearer-of-human-rights' might be contested. If we start with the restrictive view that the possession and protection of human rights extends only to developed humans who have their faculties, then 'everyone' will not include 'every living one'. On this view (commonly associated with 'will' theories of rights), the paradigmatic bearer of human rights will be the person who is able to operate his or her rights (claiming and waiving the benefits to which he or she is entitled). This is not to say that non-qualifying humans, such as the young (whose capacities for practical reasoning have not yet developed) or the elderly (whose capacities no longer function as they should), merit no protection. However, taking a restrictive approach, such protection must be elaborated on an indirect basis (i.e. a basis other than the direct possession of human rights). Such an indirect strategy might employ a number of justifications—for example, protection might be argued for on the ground that mistakes might be made because there are no bright lines dividing qualifiers from non-qualifiers, or that respect for human rights is strengthened by practices that respect life itself, and so on. If we take a less

---

[4] In this chapter we will tend to focus on 'communitarian' interpretations of human dignity as constraint. However, human dignity as constraint is open to non-communitarian interpretations (on which, see Ch. 3), and the instruments that we consider are, in this respect, open to more than one interpretation. See further pp. 38–41 below.

restrictive view, we might hold that 'everyone' covers all independent human life, that is, all humans from the cradle to the grave. Even on this less restrictive view, though, there are non-qualifying members of the human species, such as embryos, foetuses, and the like. Once again, this is not to say that potential qualifying human beings merit no protection, simply that, in the absence of a functioning capacity for practical reasoning or independent existence, the case for protection of such life forms cannot be made out as if they were bearers of human rights. We might, however, eschew both of these (restrictive) views and, instead, hold that 'everyone' includes 'every instance of human life, biologically defined'. On this relaxed view, the possession and protection of human rights applies from conception onwards.

Now, the difficulty facing the drafters of Article 1 of the Convention was that, while some of the signatories adhered to a restrictive conception of 'everyone-as-a-bearer-of-human-rights', the general view was that human life should be protected from the point of conception onwards. How was this difficulty to be resolved? One response would have been to have adhered to a restrictive conception of 'everyone-as-a-bearer-of-human-rights', alongside which a protective approach might then have been developed on the basis of indirect support for human rights. This, however, was not the response adopted. Instead, we find the category of 'all human beings' being introduced in order to signal that the value of human dignity kicks in from the point of conception. Conceding that such a conception of dignity is 'not obvious', Peter Kemp explains:

if one transforms the idea of dignity as a virtue of the other into a universal principle for understanding the worth of human being as such, then dignity can be ascribed not only to men or women as rational beings, but also to the human being who has not yet, or has no longer, an autonomous will, and who is therefore unable to be a master of his or her own life. (2000: 19)

Whatever the plausibility of this conception and concomitant justification of human dignity, Article 1 brokers a clear compromise: while those signatories who cannot agree that the *conceptus* is a bearer of human *rights* are to be allowed to persist with this belief, all signatories are required to accept that, in the name of human *dignity*, the *conceptus* is a protected entity.[5]

The idea that respect for human dignity is the key to protection of the *conceptus* might be thought to be relatively unobjectionable, simply supplementing the ruling scheme of human rights by protecting early human life at a stage when the capacities to which autonomy is generally thought to relate are not yet developed. This, however, is not without implications for the centrality of autonomy; it is not as though dignity simply functions to protect life where autonomy runs out. Rather, if embryonic and foetal life is protected under the cover of respect for human dignity (in its new extended sense), then the autonomous choices of

---

[5] This strategy also allows sleeping dogs to lie in the sense that it does not open up awkward questions about the bearing of the ECHR on the domestic abortion laws of Contracting States.

researchers (for example, to create, test, manipulate, and store embryos) and of women (to terminate pregnancies) must be measured for their legitimacy against, not only the general regime of human rights, but also against the special dignity-based regime protecting such early human life. Having said this, we should not overstate the impact of recognizing that, *by reference to respect for human dignity*, embryonic and potential human life forms have a protected moral status. In the light of our earlier remarks concerning *indirect* protective justifications, it will be appreciated that the significance of human dignity is not in retrieving a protected status for potential life; what human dignity does is to offer a *direct* justification for protection (human life having dignity) rather than the *indirect* justification that must be constructed alongside a restrictive human rights theory. Whether this radically alters the calculation depends on the relative strength of the respective protective arguments. However, other things being equal, we would expect a direct (dignity-based) justification to be more protective of life than an indirect (human rights-based) justification. In other words, the emergence of human dignity as constraint does not here place a limitation on autonomy where previously there was none; rather, it puts in place a limitation with a direct justification where previously the limitation only had an indirect justification. Nevertheless, the acceptance of human dignity as a direct covering protection for early human life represents, at the very least, a significant change to the terms of debate;[6] and it almost certainly signals a much more restrictive approach to early-stage biomedical interventions.

Constraining Apparently Merely Self-Affecting Conduct

While many of the provisions in the Convention are directed at protecting persons against unauthorized interferences by *others*, Article 21 relies on respect for human dignity in order to prohibit financial gain from commerce in the human body or body parts—much in the way that the Warnock Committee noted that some opposition to surrogacy was based on the ground that 'it is inconsistent with human dignity that a woman should use her uterus for financial profit and treat it as an incubator for someone else's child' (Warnock Committee 1984, paragraph 8.10). It is obvious that such a conception of human dignity (as a constraint on what is apparently merely self-affecting conduct) is on a collision course with human dignity as autonomous empowerment.

In the last chapter we encountered an example of such a collision in the case of the French dwarfs.[7] There, it will be recalled, the Conseil d'État held that dwarf-throwing is incompatible with respect for human dignity. Furthermore, the fact that the dwarfs who freely engaged in dwarf-throwing considered such

---

[6] Compare Ronald Dworkin's (1993) attempt to change the terms of the debate about abortion and euthanasia.

[7] Conseil d'État (October 27, 1995) req. nos. 136–727 (Commune de Morsang-sur-Orge) and 143–578 (Ville d'Aix-en-Provence).

employment to be the basis of their dignity, and themselves led the challenge to the legality of the banning orders, counted for nothing: as the Conseil d'État ruled, if a form of conduct compromises human dignity, it is simply not a legitimate option.

Not surprisingly, this same tension between (dignity-based) autonomy and human dignity as constraint has also been problematic in the German case law. For example, in the well-known *Peep-Show* Decision,[8] the Federal Administrative Tribunal (anticipating the thinking of the Conseil d'État in the dwarf-throwing case) denied a licence for a mechanical peep-show on the ground that the performance would violate Article 1(1) of the Basic Law. Having affirmed that 'respect for and protection of human dignity are constituent principles of the Basic Law', and, having said that in the peep-show 'the woman is placed in a degrading position' and 'treated like an object', the Tribunal continued:

The consent of the women concerned can only exclude a violation of human dignity if such a violation is based only on the lack of consent to the relevant actions or omissions of the women concerned. However, this is not the situation here because in the case at issue . . . the human dignity of the women concerned is violated by the exposition typical of these performances. Here, human dignity, because its significance reaches beyond the individual, must be protected even against the wishes of the woman concerned whose own subjective ideas deviate from the objective value of human dignity.[9]

In other words, human dignity represents an 'objective value' or good (reaching beyond the individual) such that, if an act violates this value, human dignity is compromised irrespective of whether the party so acting freely agrees to perform the act in question. As we have been at pains to emphasize, where human dignity so conceived is at stake, free choice is irrelevant.

Unlike the law in France and Germany, English law (both public and private) is less explicitly committed to the value of human dignity (as constraint).[10] Nevertheless, the tension found in the French and German cases is readily found both in English jurisprudence and in the case law. To take an obvious instance, the classic mid-century exchange between Patrick Devlin (1959, 1965) and H. L. A. Hart (1963), concerning the enforcement of 'private morality', can be understood precisely in terms of this tension. Traditionally, the essence of the exchange is put in terms of the following kind. On the one side, Devlin contended that even merely self-affecting conduct is legitimately regulated where it offends against the constitutive values of a particular social order; and, since each society

---

[8] BVerwGE 64 (1981) 274.

[9] Ibid. 277–9. See Kadidal (1996) for commentary. We are grateful to Sabine Michalowski for drawing our attention to the *Peep-Show* case.

[10] In a well-known paper Dawn Oliver (1997) has contended that dignity, together with autonomy, respect, status, and security, is a key value underlying both public and private law. In this analysis, however, dignity relates quite closely to autonomy and respect, and it is in line with empowerment rather than constraint.

will define itself in its own distinctive way, there is no private sphere (for autonomous action) that holds good against regulation at all times and in all places. On the other side, Hart (1967) argued that modern societies are constituted by economy rather than culture, by common markets rather than by shared values; that any society that takes individual freedom seriously must recognize that a price is to be paid; and that, in modern freedom-respecting societies, that price is regulatory restraint. However, if we recast the terms of this debate, we can say that Devlin's position is that, even in secular societies, there will be a collective understanding of human dignity; and that, where particular forms of conduct seriously compromise human dignity as understood in a particular society, then that society legitimately takes steps to regulate the offending conduct. By contrast, Hart's position is that human dignity is expressed through autonomous action and that regulation in the name of dignity as social constraint must not be allowed to subvert dignity as individual empowerment.

More recently the much-debated sado-masochist case *R* v. *Brown*[11] provides an equally compelling illustration of the tension. There, the question was whether the consent of the participants provided a defence to what would otherwise be criminal acts of assault and wounding (inflicted during sado-masochistic encounters). In a split three to two decision, the majority of the House of Lords held that the consent of the participants (who were all adults) was no defence. Although each of the opinions given in *Brown* adopts its own distinctive approach, the underlying question of principle is most clearly an issue for Lords Templeman (majority) and Mustill (minority). Put shortly, Lord Templeman's view (echoing that of Devlin) is that the criminal law is for the protection of society, including the protection of society's basic values. So regarded, sado-masochism, even fully consensual sado-masochism, might be an appropriate case for regulation. As Lord Templeman evocatively put it:

Society is entitled and bound to protect itself against a cult of violence. Pleasure derived from the infliction of pain is an evil thing. Cruelty is uncivilised.[12]

For Lord Mustill (echoing Hart), however, a key consideration is

that the state should interfere with the rights of an individual to live his or her life as he or she may choose no more than is necessary to ensure a proper balance between the special interests of the individual and the general interests of the individuals who together comprise the populace at large.[13]

If not quite a whole-hearted endorsement of autonomy, Lord Mustill's dissenting opinion at least gave encouragement to the defendants to appeal to the European Court of Human Rights—which they duly did, arguing principally that the decision of the House of Lords violated Article 8(1) of the ECHR (the right

---

[11] [1993] 2 All ER 75.   [12] Ibid. 84.   [13] Ibid. 116.

to respect for private and family life).[14] At Strasbourg, as at Westminster, the Court was divided; but the majority again ruled against the appellants. For present purposes, the most striking opinion was given by Judge Pettiti, who took the view that Article 8 was not applicable, saying that the concept of 'private life' was not to be stretched indefinitely. According to the Judge:

Not every aspect of private life automatically qualifies for protection under the Convention. The fact that the behaviour concerned takes place on private premises does not suffice to ensure complete immunity and impunity. . . . The protection of private life means the protection of a person's intimacy and dignity, not the protection of his baseness or the promotion of criminal immoralism.[15]

In one sense, this is uncontroversial. Each human right has a recognized scope and application. The right to one's private life (understood as the right to respect for one's intimacy and dignity) is no different. It follows that, unless the conduct or interest in question falls within the scope of the right, it does not apply. Reading between the lines of Judge Pettiti's opinion, however, we might sense that human dignity here represents a preferred version of the good life, in opposition to a life of baseness and immoralism, which version is then used to constrain individual autonomy. In other words, within what we assume to be a human rights perspective, we find human dignity functioning (controversially) as a source both of empowerment and of side-constraint.

Before we move on to the UNESCO Universal Declaration on the Human Genome and Human Rights, it is as well to put down a marker as to the different ways in which human dignity as a constraint on apparently merely self-affecting action might be theorized. In principle, politico-moral theories of human rights (as theories of individual entitlement and responsibility) might be rights-driven (typically, on the side of the citizen) or duty-driven (typically, on the side of the State). Whether rights-driven or duty-driven, such theories are deontological in the sense that respect for human rights is understood to have an intrinsic value that is morally necessary and sufficient. Such theories stand opposed to goal-based theories, in which not only may individual rights and duties relating to respect for humans be subordinated to some governing goal (whatever that goal might happen to be), but, in so far as respect for human rights is understood as having value, it is purely for the instrumental reason that such respect promotes the particular governing goal. For present purposes, we can put goal-based theories to one side. For, the contest between human dignity as empowerment and human dignity as constraint is located within deontological ethics.

In a rights-driven theory of human rights, why might human dignity be thought to require regulation of apparently merely self-affecting actions? To be sure, such a theory will require that each person should respect the (dignity-underpinned) rights of *other humans*. But in what way might human dignity

[14] *Laskey, Jaggard and Brown* v. *United Kingdom*, (1997) 24 EHRR 39.
[15] Ibid. 61.

justify constraining merely self-affecting exercises of the right of autonomy? Individuals might express their autonomy by entering into compacts that impose limits on otherwise merely self-affecting actions and, at community level, acceptance of certain self-denying ordinances might be the price of membership of a particular society. If this were the context in which we met Judge Pettiti's opinion (which seems pretty implausible), then we could make sense of human dignity operating as an *internally* generated constraint on merely self-affecting conduct arising within a rights-driven theory. Such exceptional cases apart, it is difficult to see how a rights-driven theory can appeal to human dignity to restrict the right to self-determination—as we have said, the conception of human dignity that fits with this approach is one of emancipation and empowerment.[16]

In a duty-driven theory of human rights, human dignity can ground constraints on an individual's otherwise legitimate exercise of freedom in three different ways; namely, by reference to duties to others, duties to oneself, and duties to the community.

First, there are the duties that we (including officials of the State) owe to others (and, correlatively, the human rights that others have against us and that we have against others). Such duties are designed to articulate respect for the dignity-related interests of others; and, if a duty-driven theory of human rights stopped here, it would be very close to a rights-driven theory.

Second, in addition to duties to others, a particular theory might recognize duties to oneself, in which case there might be a duty to respect not only the dignity-related interests of others, but also one's own dignity. Here we run into a clutch of questions about the coherence of a concept of duty to oneself, to which we will return in the next chapter. If we can make sense of this idea, though, there is clearly a potential tension between merely self-affecting autonomy and the duty to respect one's own human dignity.

Third, a particular theory might recognize duties to one's community or the like, so that, in addition to the *direct* duty that one has to others to respect their dignity-related interests, one also might have an *indirect* duty to others (as members of one's community) to respect their vision of human dignity. Gilbert Hottois, writing about the commodification of the human body, explicates the sense in which such a duty goes right to the core of social solidarity:

Introducing the body and its parts into the market dominated by money, technique and individual desire (this means: false personal freedoms) amounts to [destroying] all those beautiful symbolic [syntheses]: the body is separated from the person who may dispose of it, the integrity of the body is atomized to an indefinite number of parts, the body becomes a plastic changeable thing, it may be modified and exchanged following irrational, individual desires. . . . These temptations are literally seen as diabolical, i.e. anti-symbolical, destroying not only the dignity of persons but still more solidarity, the ties at the very basis of society. The members of a society who would consider themselves and each other as

---

[16] For discussion of the question of rights against oneself, see further Chs. 3 and 5.

arbitrarily open to such dismembering practices would necessarily destroy their society. (2000: 95)

Whether such a vision of human dignity (and the duty that it entails) is understood locally as constituting a particular society or more imperialistically as constituting any civilized society (or even any society), where that vision decrees that certain apparently merely self-affecting acts are contrary to human dignity, then the conflict between autonomy and respect for human dignity is present.

The Universal Declaration on the Human Genome and Human Rights

When we turn from the Convention to the Universal Declaration on the Human Genome and Human Rights—an instrument already described as 'the first international text to bring the question of human dignity face to face with the problems raised by scientific progress' (Ralaimihoatra 1996: 46)[17]—reliance on human dignity is pervasive. Following a number of preambular references, including the significant recognition that respect for human dignity must take precedence over the progress promised by research on the human genome and its applications, the first four Articles (comprising Part A of the Declaration)[18] are grouped under the heading 'Human Dignity and the Human Genome'.

According to Article 1, 'The human genome underlies the fundamental unity of all members of the human family, as well as the recognition of their inherent dignity and diversity. In a symbolic sense, it is the heritage of humanity.' This provision is in line with Article 1 of UNESCO's Declaration on Race and Racial Prejudice,[19] which, having proclaimed that all human beings belong to a single species, goes on to say that they 'are born equal in dignity and rights and form an integral part of humanity'. In other words, whatever the superficial differences between members of the human species, whatever the diversity of human projects, there is an underlying unity: quite simply, all humans belong to the same family and, as such, have equal dignity and rights.

The key prescription in this Part of the Universal Declaration is in Article 2,[20] according to which,

> (*a*) Everyone has a right to respect for their dignity and for their rights regardless of their genetic characteristics.

---

[17] Reporting the speech by Mrs. Noëlle Lenoir, president of the International Bioethics Committee.

[18] The Declaration comprises twenty-five Articles divided into seven Parts, namely, A. Human Dignity and the Human Genome; B. Rights of the Person Concerned; C. Research on the Human Genome; D. Conditions for the Exercise of Scientific Activity; E. Solidarity and International Co-operation; F. Promotion of the Principles set out in the Declaration; and G. Implementation of the Declaration.

[19] Adopted on 27 Nov. 1978.

[20] Article 4, providing, 'The human genome in its natural state shall not give rise to financial gains', is also an important prescription in this Part of the Universal Declaration.

(*b*) That dignity makes it imperative not to reduce individuals to their genetic characteristics and to respect their uniqueness and diversity.

Commenting on this Article, Hectór Gros Espiell, the chairman of the Legal Commission of UNESCO's International Bioethics Committee (IBC) has said,

Article 2 of the Declaration asserts that the genetic characteristics of the person can in no way justify limits on the recognition of his or her dignity or the exercise of his or her rights. This is a fundamental principle whose corollary is the prohibition of all discrimination based on genetic characteristics [see Article 6]. This article is derived from Article 2 of the Universal Declaration of Human Rights . . . and adds the genetic criterion to it.

Many other instruments adopted by UNESCO also refer to this principle of non-discrimination. . . . In taking the dignity of the human person as its reference, the Declaration seeks above all to condemn any attempt to draw political or social inferences from a purported distinction between 'good' genes and 'bad' genes. (Espiell 1999: 3)

Part A of the Declaration is completed by Article 3, which purports to reject genetic reductionism and genetic determinism, and by Article 4, which, running parallel with Article 21 of the Convention on Human Rights and Biomedicine, provides that 'The human genome in its natural state shall not give rise to financial gains.'

Thereafter, dignity is explicitly referred to in seven Articles.[21] These Articles prohibit 'discrimination based on genetic characteristics' such as would infringe human dignity (Article 6); 'research or research applications concerning the human genome' that fail to respect human dignity (Article 10); and 'practices' that are 'contrary to human dignity, such as reproductive cloning of human beings' (Article 11). They require parties to make available to all 'advances in biology, genetics and medicine' but 'with due regard for the dignity . . . of each individual' (Article 12); to 'take appropriate steps to provide the framework for the free exercise of research on the human genome' but in such a way as to 'safeguard respect for . . . human dignity' (Article 15); and to take steps to raise awareness of 'responsibilities regarding the fundamental issues relating to the defence of human dignity' arising from research in human genetics and the like (Article 21). Finally, the IBC is required, *inter alia*, to 'give advice concerning the follow-up of this Declaration, in particular regarding the identification of practices that could be contrary to human dignity, such as germ-line interventions' (Article 24).

In these provisions, we find that human dignity is relied on in more than one way. Many of the provisions—particularly the central provisions in Part A (coupled with Article 6) designed to protect humans against discrimination on genetic grounds—are perfectly compatible with the first conception of human dignity. Indeed, the vision of a dignity-driven bioethics as a promoter of a culture

---

[21] This was no last-minute conversion to the importance of respect for human dignity. In the Revised Preliminary Draft (of 20 Dec. 1996) leading to the final version of the Universal Declaration, dignity appeared explicitly six times in the first twelve Articles, see Articles 1, 2(c), 4(b), 5, 7, and 12 (as they then were).

of freedom and responsibility fits very nicely with this first conception. However, at a fairly early stage of the discussions leading to the drafting of the Declaration, the principle of respect for human dignity was seen as encompassing a broader project than this. Thus, it was said of the Declaration: 'The aim is not only to protect the individual, in his rights and his freedoms, since dignity concerns the human being as such, in its [*sic*] largest sense.'[22] In line with this larger agenda, the Declaration's dignity-based concerns about human reproductive cloning and germ-line intervention seem to be less concerned with protecting autonomous choice than with preserving the sanctity of life or the integrity of the genome (as the 'heritage of humanity'). Again, to quote, Hectór Gros Espiell:

The technologies derived from genetic engineering and biology could lead to practices, contrary to human dignity, that should not be permitted. . . . [Article 11] mentions the example of cloning for the purpose of reproducing human beings. But other technologies are concerned, and some of them are already in use such as sex-based embryo selection or, in the more distant future, the creation of chimeras by transgenesis. (1999: 5)

The Universal Declaration, it should be said, is far from being alone in citing such practices as contrary to human dignity. As we have seen already, the Convention on Human Rights and Biomedicine takes this same line in relation to sex selection. Moreover, Article 6(2) of the Directive on the Legal Protection of Biotechnological Inventions[23] specifically excludes from patentability (as immoral) (*a*) processes for cloning human beings and (*b*) processes for modifying the germ-line genetic identity of human beings; and Recital 38 of the Directive provides that 'processes, the uses of which offend against human dignity, such as processes to produce chimeras from germ cells or totipotent cells of humans and animals, are obviously also excluded from patentability'.

During the drafting of the Declaration, questions were raised about the coherence of the drafters' understanding of human dignity. At the Fourth Meeting of the Legal Commission of the IBC, for instance, the International Federation of Philosophical Societies commented that 'the declaration that the human genome is [the] common heritage of humanity was not immediately understandable. Moreover the outline seemed to oscillate between protecting the rights of the individual in relation to genetics and protecting the human genome, which was seen as a sort of essence of human being.'[24]

With hindsight, one might say that the Declaration betrays a dualism that runs through much modern thinking in bioethics. On the one hand, because human beings have equal dignity they are entitled to be shielded against bioscientists

[22] *Birth of the Universal Declaration on the Human Genome and Human Rights* (Paris: Division of the Ethics of Science and Technology of UNESCO, 1999) (Report of the Second Meeting of the Legal Commission of the IBC), 39.

[23] Council Directive 98/44, [1998] OJ L213/13.

[24] *Birth of the Universal Declaration on the Human Genome and Human Rights* (Paris: Division of the Ethics of Science and Technology of UNESCO, 1999) (Report of the Fourth Meeting of the Legal Commission of the IBC), 54.

who might otherwise subordinate individual interests, choices, and preferences to the (supposedly) greater good of the advancement of science and medicine; on the other hand, because human dignity itself may be regarded as representing a larger value or good, individual interests, choices, and preferences must be checked where bioscience facilitates their pursuit in a way that threatens this value. In other words, the Declaration betrays a dualism involving, on the one hand, human dignity as empowerment and, on the other hand, human dignity as constraint.

Taking stock, in the Declaration (as in the Convention), we find elements of human dignity as empowerment (as one would expect in traditional human rights instruments), but the particular concern with biomedicine and genetics elicits a number of quite different (unfamiliar) responses—that the key to the protection of embryonic and potential human life might be human dignity rather than human rights; that dignity might be compromised by our own (self-affecting) actions as much as by the unwilled interferences of others (signalled most clearly by the prohibition on commercialization of the human body); and that some practices (for instance, human reproductive cloning, germ-line intervention, sex selection, and the creation of chimeras) are contrary to human dignity. In these restrictive responses, we have the ingredients of human dignity as constraint.

The New Bioethics in Europe

During the last quarter of the twentieth century the emerging discipline of bioethics was dominated by the seminal work of Beauchamp and Childress (1979). As is well known, Beauchamp and Childress proposed that bioethical thinking should be guided by the four values of autonomy, beneficence, non-maleficence, and justice. Since there were notable episodes during the twentieth century when it was not recognized that a precondition for legitimate medical research and treatment is that those who participate in research trials or who are to be treated should do so on the basis of their informed consent, the importance of highlighting the value of personal autonomy should not be understated. Respect for autonomy transforms the relationship between health care professionals and patients, empowering the latter and signalling that, even if doctors purport to know best, it is ultimately patients who choose and control. Moreover, respect for autonomy signals in the clearest way that no individual is to be sacrificed for the greater good of medical progress.

While no one would doubt that biopractice should be sensitive to the value of autonomy, some European bioethicists argue that there has been an over-correction in favour of individual choice.[25] They argue that, where there is a background ethic

---

[25] Generally, on the competing bioethical discourses now evident in the United States and Europe, see Parizeau (2000). Specifically, see Rendtorff and Kemp (1999).

of care and concern for others (and, concomitantly, a sense of solidarity with and responsibility for others), bioethics needs to be guided by a regime of values that reflects not only a degree of control over one's own flourishing but also a measure of commitment to the flourishing of others. Furthermore, ethical biopractice needs guiding values that cover those cases where the capacity for autonomous judgement is impaired or not yet developed. To put this another way, where there is respect for autonomy, autonomous actors can take care of themselves, but non-autonomous human life needs to be protected. In contrast to the scheme elaborated by Beauchamp and Childress, the new European bioethics takes dignity, integrity, and vulnerability to be the guiding (protective) values (alongside autonomy).[26]

In this European scheme, human dignity is recognized as a multi-textured idea comprising six strands (see Rendtorff and Kemp, 1999: 31). First, human dignity is said to emerge 'as a virtue of recognition of the other in an intersubjective relationship', human dignity constituting 'a capacity that the person has because of his or her social position'. Second, dignity is said to indicate 'the intrinsic value and moral responsibility of every human being'. Third, the intersubjective understanding of dignity is said to lead to the view that a person must 'be considered as without a price', from which it follows that 'human beings cannot be objects for trade or commercial transaction'. Fourth, dignity is said to be 'based on self–other relations of shame and proudness, e.g., in degradation and self-esteem'. Fifth, in the process of human civilization, dignity is said to set the limits of civilized behaviour; i.e. dignity indicates 'that there are certain things that a [civilized] society should just not do'. Finally, 'dignity includes the individual's openness to the metaphysical dimensions of life, referring to dignified behaviour at the limit-situations of existence such as birth, sufferance, death of a beloved other, one's own death, etc.' What should we make of this inventory?

Although the precise meaning of these strands is not always clear, there are distinct echoes of the two conceptions of human dignity already sketched. As we have seen, the first conception of human dignity (human dignity as empowerment) builds upon the idea of the intrinsic value of every human being (*qua* human being); respect for the dignity of others certainly entails that we should not regard others as mere 'objects for trade or commercial transaction'; and actions that degrade others, or that are calculated to undermine their self-esteem, are often expressed to be assaults on their human dignity. The second conception (human dignity as constraint), too, is picked up here, perhaps most neatly in the fifth strand, according to which human dignity sets the limits to conduct in a civilized society—thus, for 'human dignity as an objective value', or humanity in its

---

[26] Interestingly, Article 3 of the Charter of Fundamental Rights of the European Union, having provided that 'Everyone has the right to respect for his physical and mental integrity', then lists the following implications in the fields of medicine and biology, namely: respect for free and informed consent, prohibition of eugenic practices, prohibition on making the human body and its parts a source of financial gain, and prohibition on reproductive human cloning.

larger sense, read 'those things that simply should not be done in a civilized soci-ety'. On this view, it is not enough that we should care that others flourish rela-tive to their own particular lights; we must care that collectively we flourish relative to the standards of a civilized society. There is, though, at least one other interpretation of human dignity that stands out in this list. This is the idea of dignity as dignified behaviour (stated in metaphysical terms in the sixth strand). What are we to make of this notion?

On the face of it, the idea of dignified or undignified behaviour is very differ-ent from that of dignity as the intrinsic value of human beings (as per the first conception of human dignity as empowerment). So, for instance, in cases such as that of the French dwarfs or the sado-masochists in *R* v. *Brown*, we might judge that the conduct in question was 'undignified'; and yet we would not think that the intrinsic human dignity of the parties was thereby affected. For, as Alan Gewirth has written,

The sense of 'dignity' in which all humans are said to have equal dignity is not the same as that in which it may be said of some person that he lacks dignity or that he behaves with-out dignity, where what is meant is that he is lacking in decorum, is too raucous or obse-quious or is not 'dignified'. This kind of dignity is one that humans may occurrently exhibit, lack, or lose, whereas the dignity in which all humans are said to be equal is a characteristic that belongs permanently and inherently to every human as such. (1982*a*: 27–8)

By the same token, while we might admire dignified conduct, we would not think that this adds to the intrinsic human dignity of those whose conduct we so admire.

Would we also say that the concept of dignified or undignified behaviour is different and distinguishable from that of human dignity as constraint? To the extent that undignified behaviour is equated with matters of etiquette, while such conduct might cause offence and meet with disapproval, it hardly seems to be in the same league as those forms of evil and corruption that simply cannot be toler-ated in a civilized society. Nevertheless, we are dealing with differences of degree here, which suggests that we should be slow to dismiss this idea as having no bearing on our discussion. Indeed, as will become apparent in due course, we think that it is a mistake to marginalize the notion of dignified behaviour—although, contrary to these initial indications, our later analysis of human dignity as a virtue connects up more closely to the conception of human dignity as empowerment than to that of human dignity as constraint.

Even if we are not yet clear how dignified behaviour fits into the picture, we have said enough already to understand why dignity as intrinsic human value and dignity as the limits of civilized society are potentially at odds with one another. Indeed, as the proponents of the new bioethics openly recognize, 'the principles will always be characterised by fundamental tensions, tragic dilemmas and mutual contradictions' (Rendtorff and Kemp 1999: 12). At its sharpest, the tension lies between those who rely on human dignity to argue for autonomy, choice, and control over one's own life and those who rely on human dignity to assert collective control over the exercise of autonomy. In this light, it becomes perfectly clear that the agenda of the new European bioethics, in correcting for the weight given to autonomy, is not about restoring physicians' power over their patients but about asserting collective control over individual choice—whether it is the choice of couples to destroy or donate an embryo, to terminate a pregnancy, to select the sex of their child, or to manipulate the genome of their child; the choice of dwarfs to earn their living in nightclubs or to trade in their body parts; or the choice of individuals (who, perhaps paradoxically, wish to die with dignity) about how and when their lives are terminated.

The new bioethics, then, reopens a very old question. As Mill (1962: 135) famously put it, is the individual to be respected as sovereign over his own body and mind—in this context, especially his own body—or is the sphere of individual choice always contingent on collective preference? We know that there is no simple answer to this question. And, in the light of the foregoing discussion, we know that the notion of respect for human dignity can be fashioned to lend support to either side of the debate.

Contingency

At the core of the new bioethics there is the question 'In the light of emerging biotechnology, what sort of a culture do we want for our society?' Do we want Europe to be a place where we allow sex selection, human reproductive cloning, genetic manipulation, commerce in human organs, and so on? If these questions are gathered together under the rubric of respect for human dignity, then the question is 'What conception of human dignity shall we operate with in our society?'

Far from being worried about contingency, the new bioethics (so understood) celebrates contingency. Each group, each society, each region is invited to articulate its particular conception of human dignity. For the purposes of external relations, each culture may or may not adopt a tolerant attitude to conceptions of human dignity that it does not share. For the purposes of internal relations, though, the constitutive conception of human dignity governs—hence, even if sado-masochism or dwarf-throwing might be tolerated elsewhere (i.e. externally), they cannot be tolerated within the jurisdiction (i.e. internally) if the local conception of human dignity decrees that such activities evince a lack of respect for human dignity. Recalling Mill's strictures against the tyranny of the majority, though, is such a culturally relative conception of human dignity defensible?

In an idealized version of this conception, every member of the particular society would participate in a debate about human dignity. Such a debate would be informed; everyone's voice would be heard; the views of the economically powerful would not be privileged; no one would be coerced or cajoled; no one would be deceived; no one who would be bound by the outcome would be ignored or discounted; reason and reasonableness would prevail; and so on.[27] At the end of the debate, there would either be complete consensus or, at least, there would be a widely shared view from which no reasonable participating person could dissent. To say that the ensuing conception of human dignity rested merely on accidental consensus or acceptance would be to undersell what such a group had achieved. Moreover, because such an exercise displays at a collective level the best practice of informed consent and autonomous choice, proponents of human dignity as empowerment would find it difficult to deny to individuals who have participated in such a debate the right subsequently to live by their agreed conception of human dignity as constraint.

However, if this is the ideal version of human dignity as constraint, in practice the processes by which collective values are articulated are somewhat less attractive. In practice the worst case is that of intolerant voices (whether of the majority or of an influential minority) expressing negative attitudes about certain practices, which attitudes are then translated into restrictions ostensibly in the interest of respect for human dignity. Any suggestion that a community's morality might be identified with such negative attitudes was famously subjected to a withering critique by Ronald Dworkin (1978, ch. 10) (commenting on Lord Devlin's 'enforcement of morals' thesis). As Dworkin rightly argued, the community's attitudes or opinions could amount to a 'moral position' or 'a moral point of view' only if certain formal conditions (defining a position as a 'moral' position) were satisfied. To be sure, philosophers continue to debate the details of the list of formal conditions (universalizability, categoricality, impartiality, and so on) but it is common ground that there is something distinctive about having a moral position—there is more to it than having a practical attitude (positive or negative) towards some matter or making a practical judgement in relation to some action (for it or against it). In the light of Dworkin's critique, we might think that the case for human dignity as constraint is improved provided that the position staked out meets formal moral requirements—at least, we might then respect such a position as a moral position even though we might disagree with it. However, this only repairs one aspect of the worst case. We might still be left with the tyranny of the (moral) majority or of the influential (moral) minority; and, in the absence of processes such as those contemplated by the idealized version, it is difficult to see how this aspect of human dignity as constraint might be remedied.

The practical problem with the conception of human dignity as constraint is that modern societies are often pluralistic societies. While there may be a consensus condemning slavery, torture, and so on as incompatible with respect for human dignity, there is less agreement (and sometimes deep disagreement) once we get beyond the few paradigm cases. For example, North Americans can coexist with

---

[27] Chiming in with the ideas associated with, for example, Alexy (1989), Habermas (1984) (and even more so Habermas 1988); and Scanlon (1992).

one another despite being deeply divided over the permissibility of abortion, some thinking that respect for human dignity requires a pro-choice position and others thinking that it requires a pro-life position. Similarly, in the United Kingdom some think that respect for human dignity requires a pro-choice position in relation to end of life issues while others believe that human dignity decrees that liberalizing moves should be resisted; some think that consensual sado-masochism is compatible with human dignity, others that it is deeply offensive to human dignity, and so on. Faced with such a mix of points of agreement and disagreement, Dworkin argues that we can tease out the 'critical cultural morality' of a community, and in this spirit we could argue for the best interpretation of the community's conception of human dignity. The limitations of such a strategy, however, are fairly obvious. While a particular (critical) interpretation of the community's conception of human dignity as constraint might be defensible relative to the paradigmatic moral commitments of the particular community, how does one respond to a person who does not accept those commitments?

Next Steps

The human rights instruments that we have considered in this and the previous chapter reveal human dignity in a variety of guises: sometimes as the source of human rights; at other times as itself a species of human right (particularly concerned with the conditions of self-respect); sometimes defining the subjects of human rights; at other times defining the objects to be protected; and, sometimes reinforcing, at other times limiting, rights of individual autonomy and self-determination. We have suggested that these various aspects of human dignity can be gathered together under two rival conceptions, human dignity as empowerment and human dignity as constraint. We have also suggested, however, that neither conception can be defended very far down. The plausibility of human dignity as the ground of human rights, like that of human dignity as the source of a constraining collective good, depends on contingent culture and disposition. Put this way, we have to regard the tensions emerging in modern bioethics as a clash of mere ideologies or cultures; and those who are inclined to dismiss 'Appeals to human dignity . . . [as] comprehensively vague' (Harris 1998: 31), or as a mere 'conversation stopper' (or a slogan seized upon by pressure groups when it suits their interests) (Birnbacher 1998: 325[28]), surely have some ground for their scepticism. What, then, are our next steps?

First, we need a little more philosophical context for our competing conceptions of human dignity. In particular, we need to begin our engagement with Kantian thinking, for it is in Kant's writing that we have not only the seeds of many of our ideas about human dignity but also a serious attempt to ground those

---

[28] See also Beyleveld (1998a: 335).

ideas. If we are to elaborate a conception of human dignity that is rationally defensible and that can then be applied to the bioethical puzzles of today and tomorrow, it is a fair bet that we can learn some important lessons from Kant.

Secondly, and at the same time, we need to locate the idea of dignified conduct in our philosophical sketch. For, as we have already indicated, we believe that dignified conduct as a virtue is an idea worth following up as we attempt to construct a theory of human dignity for the twenty-first century.

3

Dignity, Human Dignity, and Dignified Conduct

Introduction

Writing nearly thirty years ago, Michael Pritchard remarked that 'The notion of human dignity has not fared well in contemporary moral philosophy. It seems to have suffered the fate of notions such as virtue and honor, by simply fading into the past' (1972: 299). Yet, prior to its demise (and very recent revival), the idea of human dignity has a considerable history of some complexity. The notion of a 'right to dignity', as Ronald Dworkin (1993: 233) has remarked, has been used in many senses by moral and political philosophers.[1] To catalogue each of these senses would be a work in its own right; and, more importantly, it would be unlikely to take us any nearer to our objective of determining whether a defensible conception of human dignity can be articulated.

Nevertheless, we can at least sketch the philosophical landscape, picking out, in particular, the landmark Kantian claim that humanity, so far as it is capable of morality, is the only thing having dignity. By reference to Kant, we can sharpen the analysis of our two competing conceptions of human dignity (human dignity as empowerment and human dignity as constraint), as well as highlighting some of the key issues to be discussed in detail in Chapter 5 (in which we explore the principal features of Kant's (1948) moral methodology(ies), leading to the

---

[1] Dworkin tries to isolate a distinctive strand in the pattern of modern thought by focusing specifically on 'a right not to suffer indignity' (meaning a right not to be treated in ways that evince disrespect) as against a general right to dignity (the latter often relating to the 'conditions in which genuine self-respect is possible') (Dworkin 1993: 233). However, such a right is not to be given an experiential interpretation: it is not the experienced distress occasioned by a lack of respect that matters. What matters is that there is a failure to respect a person as having 'critical' interests—that is, a failure to respect one as a being for whom 'it is intrinsically, objectively important how [one's] life goes' (p. 236). Hence, 'Understanding that dignity means recognizing a person's critical interests, as distinct from advancing those interests, provides a useful reading of the Kantian principle that people should be treated as ends and never merely as means. That principle, so understood, does not require that people never be put at a disadvantage for the advantage of others, but rather that people never be treated in a way that denies the distinct importance of their own lives' (p. 236). According to Dworkin, although (at one level) the right not to suffer indignity is subject to local custom and practice, in the sense that what counts as a lack of respect is a matter of convention, (at a deeper level) 'the right that all people have—that their society recognize the importance of their lives, expressed through whatever vocabulary it has—is not itself a matter of convention' (pp. 236–7). Allowing that Dworkin's analysis is open to some interpretation, it seems to be quite close to what we have called the conception of human dignity as empowerment. As we suggested in Ch. 1, this conception can be unpacked to yield a right to be recognized as a being with distinctive *capacities* (e.g. as one who is capable of giving meaning, purpose, and direction to one's own life and, thus, in Dworkin's terms, identifying for oneself one's critical interests, including a critical interest in life itself) as well as rights pertaining to the conditions and circumstances in which a being with such *capacities* can flourish.

Categorical Imperative, alongside the dialectically necessary method found in Alan Gewirth's moral theory (see, principally, Gewirth 1978*a*)).

In the history of ideas, the Kantian conception of intrinsic human dignity is to be contrasted with the more limited notion of dignity as a function of a person's social rank (as found in the so-called tradition of the dignity of the nobles). While this latter idea persists to the present day—being expressed, for example, on those occasions when 'commoners' gather to celebrate the dignity of the monarch—it is not so much the dignity of high rank that interests us as the idea that those who exemplify the virtue of dignified conduct are to be highly regarded (ranked). On the assumption that dignified conduct is the expression of a character imbued with dignity, then in what sense is dignity a virtue? Tentatively, we suggest that the context for the virtue of dignity is one in which humans, confronted with adversity (whether social or natural) and the limitations of human finitude, seek to balance the will to resist (to overcome) with the will to submit (to accept): in such a context, those whose character is attuned to the virtue of human dignity will find an appropriate balance. If we are to rehabilitate human dignity as a virtue, it needs to be clarified, and its relationship with the conceptions of human dignity as empowerment and as constraint needs to be thought through.[2]

Dignity and Human Dignity

Thus far, we have drawn no significant distinction between dignity as such and *human* dignity. However, in a valuable analysis of the idea of human dignity, Herbert Spiegelberg draws attention to the fact that there is a significant difference between our understanding of dignity in general and human dignity in particular. Thus,

Dignity in general . . . is a term of many meanings. It applies to all sorts of carriers, human and non-human, and indicates primarily certain distinctive qualities which give them a rank above others that do not have these qualities. In fact, dignity in the general sense is a matter of degree. It reflects an aristocratic picture of reality in the tradition of the 'Great Chain of Being' with higher and lower dignities. Such dignity is subject to change, to increase and decrease; it can be gained and lost. It finds its expression in such dignities as are conferred on 'dignitaries' through honors or titles, and can be expressed in dignified or undignified comportment.

Human dignity is a very different matter. It implies the very denial of an aristocratic order of dignities. For it refers to the minimum dignity which belongs to every human being qua human. It does not admit of any degrees. It is equal for all humans. It cannot be gained or lost. In this respect human dignity as a species of dignity differs fundamentally from the genus. (Spiegelberg 1970: 55–6)

---

[2] In Ch. 6, we suggest that the existential anxiety that is characteristic of the human condition is a case of adversity writ large; and, in that context, the virtue of dignity implies holding in balance the optimism that goes with belief in immortality with the pessimism that goes with belief in the possibility of extinction.

According to Spiegelberg, although usage of the *term* 'dignity' has an ancient pedigree, it is not until the Enlightenment that we find the phrase 'dignity of man' (or 'human dignity') gaining currency. Not only this, the very *idea* of 'human dignity' is also a relatively recent arrival, the notion that human beings are worthy of respect *qua* human coming to be formulated (possibly for the first time with Locke) alongside the idea of subjective rights inherent in individuals (see Spiegelberg 1970: 42–3). Alas, having arrived on the scene, human dignity has rarely been exposed to careful philosophical analysis. Indeed, apart from Kant's well-known treatment of the intrinsic dignity of man (which we will deal with shortly), Spiegelberg is able to find only a few scattered or suggestive remarks in the philosophical literature starting with Pico della Mirandola (at the beginning of the Renaissance) and running through to Sartre's existentialism. On this account, philosophers are little wiser than anyone else. Spiegelberg concludes (with considerable prescience as events have proved) that the challenge to philosophers is to 'present and exchange their interpretations of human dignity and their justifications for it . . . [otherwise] a vital idea of our time . . . [may] degenerate into a mere slogan, soon to be discarded as outmoded and old-fashioned' (1970: 62).

Introducing a collection of papers teasing out the idea of human dignity that is implicit in the US Constitution, Michael J. Meyer sees the history of the idea in much the same terms as Spiegelberg. Thus, according to Meyer,

In political thought at the time of the Enlightenment revolutions two quite distinct concepts of dignity were in use, not only in politics proper but also in philosophical thought. The divide can, at the outset, be understood quite simply. On the one hand, some political thinkers used the idea of dignity to refer to a rank within a recognized and established social hierarchy—for example, the dignity of a king, of a noble, or of a bishop. For these thinkers a person's dignity was simply a function, or a sign, of an individual's elevated social rank. In contradistinction other thinkers understood the notion of dignity to have a much wider application—for example, the dignity of man or the dignity of humanity. (1992: 4)

If Burke (1973) can be taken as representative of the former mode of thought (which, Meyer is prepared to grant, was in line with standard usage of the pre-revolutionary period), then Paine's (1973) promotion of the natural dignity of man was representative of the latter. Clearly, the trajectory of radical Enlightenment thought was away from hierarchy and towards the 'equal recognition of individual human dignity' based on 'a belief in the citizenry's capacity for self-government and a commitment to their equal right to the same' (Meyer 1992: 7).

It has been often said that, in matters of philosophy, one has to be either with Kant or against him. In relation to the idea of human dignity, this commonplace offers a helpful starting point. For, while we cannot assume that the framers of the revolutionary declarations of rights in the late eighteenth century, or the proponents of human rights two centuries later, were or are self-consciously followers of Kant, Kantian thinking signifies the clearest break with hierarchical notions of dignity, it is the best-known articulation of the idea of intrinsic human dignity, and it suggests a natural anchoring point for theories of human rights and duties.

Kant and Intrinsic Human Dignity

As is well known, it is the Categorical Imperative that is the organizing concept of Kant's moral philosophy. However, as is also well known, Kant presents several versions (or formulas) of the Categorical Imperative and no one can claim to be a Kant scholar without having a particular theory about how we should read each of these versions and the way that they relate to one another. In Chapter 5, with a view to reconstructing Kant's moral theory, we will focus on two versions of the Categorical Imperative—the Formula of Universal Law ('Act only on that maxim through which you can at the same time will that it should become a universal law'; Kant 1948: 83–4) and the Formula of the End in Itself ('Act in such a way that you always treat humanity, whether in your own person or in the person of any other, never simply as a means, but always at the same time as an end'; pp. 90–1). In the present chapter, however, our concern is not so much with entering into debates about the best interpretation of Kant as with noting the way in which much modern thinking can claim to be guided by his suggestive remarks on the subject of human dignity. For, whatever one makes of Kant's writing, there is no denying that, in what is largely uncharted territory, it shines out as a beacon.

The classical locus of the seminal features of Kant's moral thinking is the *Groundwork of the Metaphysic of Morals*. There Kant maintains that, in the Kingdom of Ends, everything has either a price (in which case something else can be put in its place as an equivalent) or a dignity (in which case it has intrinsic value and is, so to speak, beyond price) (Kant 1948: 96). Given, as Kant puts it, that 'morality is the only condition under which a rational being can be an end in himself'—because only in this way is it possible to be a law-making member in a Kingdom of Ends—then it follows that 'morality, and humanity so far as it is capable of morality, is the only thing which has dignity' (pp. 96–7). In other words, 'the dignity of man consists precisely in his capacity to make universal [moral] law, although only on condition of being himself also subject to the law he makes' (p. 101). A dozen years later, in *The Metaphysics of Morals*, Kant gathers together his thoughts as follows:

Every human being has a legitimate claim to respect from his fellow human beings and is *in turn* bound to respect every other. Humanity itself is a dignity; for a human being cannot be used merely as a means by any human being . . . but must always be used at the same time as an end. It is just in this that his dignity (personality) consists, by which he raises himself above all other beings in the world that are not human beings and yet can be used, and so over all *things*. But just as he cannot give himself away for any price (this would conflict with his duty of self-esteem), so neither can he act contrary to the equally necessary self-esteem of others, as human beings, that is, he is under obligation to acknowledge, in a practical way, the dignity of humanity in every other human being. Hence there rests on him a duty regarding the respect that must be shown to every other human being. (1991: 209)

In these much quoted remarks, modern writers can (and do purport to) find support for a variety of supposed applications of Kantian morality, not just in practical matters generally, but specifically within the field covered by bioethics (see e.g. Wolbert 1998). For example, Kant's remarks, if taken literally, are an open invitation to claim that commercialization of the human body is an affront to dignity (by putting a price on something that is beyond price). More generally, though, we can see how Kantian thinking can be invoked to give support not only to one of the foundational axioms of human dignity as empowerment[3] but also to one of the more problematic aspects of human dignity as constraint.

First, it will be recalled that, in the conception of human dignity as empowerment, it is the assumed dignity of humans that grounds human rights. The unresolved question here is 'What precisely is it about humans that gives them special value (dignity)?', to which Kant's answer is that it is by virtue of their having dignity that humans raise themselves 'above all other beings in the world that are not human beings and yet can be used, and so over all *things*'. It is the possession of dignity, in other words, that is the special property of humankind, marking out humans from other living things. According to Werner Wolbert, this Kantian response is not to be mistaken for 'speciesism', for an arbitrary privileging of the human species per se:

This accusation [speciesism] would be justified if dignity were granted to the human being simply as a member of the biological species. The relevant feature, however, is not membership [of] the species *homo sapiens*, but . . . the moral capacity of the person. This idea may become clearer, if one keeps in mind that for Kant *two* things have dignity: first, the moral attitude (moralische Gesinnung) or moral goodness, and second, the human person insofar as he or she is capable of morality. Morality in this sense is the willingness to act according to the Categorical Imperative. (Wolbert 1998: 19)

So, for Kant, we find dignity in the capacity of rational beings to reason their way towards, and then to abide by, the moral law. In the case of humanity (unlike, say, the angels), compliance with the moral law cannot be taken for granted; it is constantly subject to weakness of the will, prey to temptation, inclination,

---

[3] See, too, Bedau (1992, esp. 153–5). According to Bedau, the key strands in Kant's thinking about human dignity are: (1) a person's dignity refers to a person's worth; (2) dignity is a value that all humans have equally and essentially; (3) human dignity is intimately related to human autonomy; (4) human dignity is inseparably connected to self-conscious rationality; and (5) human dignity provides the basis for equal human rights. Thus, 'the (Kantian) idea of human dignity involves and consists of a certain cluster of interrelated attributes, which together confer on persons a certain *status*. This status is constituted by equal worth and capacity for autonomy and rationality of all persons, a status not shared with other things or even other creatures. It is reflected above all in the equal human rights that all persons enjoy' (p. 155).

convenience, insouciance, and the like. Nevertheless, humans have the capacity to participate fully in a moral community and, for the purposes of according dignity to humans, it is the capacity that counts.

If dignity is to be equated with the capacity for moral thought and action, and if it is only for this reason that humans have value, then dignity-based human rights (as in the conception of human dignity as empowerment) do not rest merely on the stipulation that humans have value. What has value is the capacity for moral thought and action, and it is only those beings (humans, so Kant assumes) who have this capacity who have dignity. From this it follows that the bearers of dignity-based human rights must be restricted to those beings with the relevant moral capacity. As we saw in Chapter 2, it does not follow from such a restrictive approach that those humans who lack the relevant capacity (who, thus, lack dignity in this sense) are accorded no protected status or standing. However, any moral theory that takes such a restrictive approach needs, as a matter of urgency, to articulate its position on the standing of those who do not qualify directly as rights-bearers; and, in Chapter 6, we will set out in detail our own precautionary approach in response to just this question.

Although Kant's identification of human dignity with the capacity for moral reason and morally directed action shields the conception of human dignity as empowerment against the charge that it conveniently (but arbitrarily) declares that human beings have value, it remains unclear that human dignity requires acceptance of any kind of moral code let alone a code of human rights. Having seen in Chapter 1 that the identification of human dignity with autonomy (in the sense of a freely operating capacity for practical reason) fails to ground human rights in a non-contingent way, it should be no surprise that the substitution of moral reason proves no more convincing.

For the sake of argument, let us suppose that a human being recognizes in herself the capacity for moral reason and morally directed action and thus accepts that she has dignity. What follows? If this particular person wishes to exercise her moral reason and endeavour to lead a moral life, and if we also assume that it is not in the nature of human beings to lead a moral life without self-conscious reference to moral norms, then she will express her dignity by legislating her understanding of the moral law for herself and others. From within such a human's internal viewpoint, a recognition of one's own dignity (coupled with the commitment to lead a moral life) leads to legislation and acceptance of a moral code. Crucially, though, such an entailment between human dignity and morality holds good only so long as the particular practical viewpoint includes a commitment to the moral life. Given that an amoralist or moral agnostic may, without obvious contradiction, admit to understanding what it is to have a capacity for moral reason and yet deny that there is any compelling reason for leading a moral life, there seems to be a gap between the 'can' and the 'ought' in this line of reasoning. In other words, if Kant's rendition of human dignity claims only that humans can be moral (and, thereby, have value as moral beings), it remains to be shown why humans ought to be (or must be) moral. Famously, Kant attempted to close this gap by way of a transcendental deduction centring on the autonomy of the will. However, in Chapter 5, we will follow many others in holding that this particular attempt fails.

In the light of these comments, we must continue to have reservations about the conception of human dignity as empowerment. Certainly, this conception can incorporate the idea that the dignity of humans resides in their capacity for moral reason and morally directed action; and it can follow Kant in treating this capacity as the necessary and sufficient condition (regardless of race, colour, or creed, or the like) for moral status as a rights-bearer. However, human dignity, even in the Kantian sense, gives no firmer foundation for human rights than the contingent acceptance that we have remarked upon already.

Turning to the rival conception of human dignity as constraint, on the face of it, Kant's writing is pregnant with supportive statements. For example, would Kant not have endorsed the Conseil d'État in the dwarf-throwing case, when the Conseil said that the dwarfs, by allowing themselves to be treated as projectiles, treated themselves as mere things? Similarly, surely Kant would have approved the reasoning in the German *Peep-Show* decision, where the Tribunal held that the women compromised their dignity by allowing themselves to be treated as mere objects. Equally, in both cases, supporters of human dignity as constraint might take their script from Kant by saying that the parties were wrong in that they gave themselves away for a price. Underlying such apparently supportive statements, however, there is a critical general claim, namely that, in principle, we have duties to ourselves (whether expressed as a duty of self-esteem, a duty to treat oneself as an end, a duty not to compromise one's own dignity, and so on). If we follow Kant in accepting that there can be duties to oneself, then one interpretation at least of human dignity as constraint has some plausibility (although the contingency already identified remains in the sense that respect for one's own dignity will only bind those who are minded to lead the moral life).

Three brief preliminary remarks about a duty not to compromise one's own dignity are in order. In each case, the purpose of these comments is simply to put down a marker in relation to the extent of the constraint imposed.

First, if we accept the idea of a duty against compromising one's own dignity, the scope and substance of such a duty remains to be specified and, clearly, this is a matter of considerable importance. For instance, in the case of the French dwarfs, a self-regarding duty cast in terms of attempting to preserve one's sense of self-esteem might be much more favourable to the dwarfs than a duty cast in terms of not allowing oneself to be treated as a mere thing.

Second, if we assume that the duty against compromising one's own dignity operates as a form of exclusionary reason, then it takes normative priority over certain other kinds of practical considerations, in particular, one's simple inclinations and preferences. To this extent, the duty to oneself clearly acts as a constraint on free choice. However, before we have the measure of the full practical weight of this duty, it needs to be set alongside whatever other duties to oneself one might have as well as one's duties to others. For example, can a short-term breach of the duty (say, by prostituting oneself) be justified by reference to a duty to remove oneself (and members of one's family) from demeaning living conditions, or by reference to a duty to assist others in some way?[4] Of course, this point should not be misunderstood: where one compromises one's own dignity for the sake of a higher duty, this is not a case of the freeing of constraint so much as one form of constraint overriding another.

Third, even if we accept the normative idea of a duty against compromising one's own dignity, the *practical* impingement of such a duty upon a person's power of self-determination is likely to be affected by the way in which this duty is enforced. To state the obvious, the distinctive feature of a duty-led moral regime is that moral wrongdoing is identified with breach of duty. Where A's breach of duty involves a violation of B's correlative right, we might expect B (or B's representatives) to hold A to account (at least, in the first instance). However, where A's breach is simply of a duty owed to A himself or herself, how is A to be held to account? Some duty-led communities might take the view that duties (whether to others or to oneself) are to be self-enforced; but, in other such communities, public measures will be taken to prevent and discourage agents from compromising their own dignity, and a range of sanctions will be in place for duty violations. However, because breach of such a duty is a 'victimless' form of offence, even an active policy of public enforcement—at any rate, so long as it relies heavily on 'complaints' being made—will have its limits.

These preliminary remarks about a duty not to compromise one's own dignity are predicated on the hypothesis that we accept the general idea of a duty to oneself. Is this, however, a hypothesis that we should accept? Here, we need to disentangle two ideas, which are easily obscured when we talk about duties to oneself. The first idea is strictly that of a duty to oneself, with oneself being both the obligor and the obligee in relation to the duty. The second idea is that of a duty which, on the face of it, concerns the promotion of one's own interests (one's own dignity, self-esteem, freedom and well-being, and so on).

To focus on the first of these ideas, is the notion of a duty to oneself (with the self standing as both obligor and obligee) coherent? In the paradigmatic case A owes a duty to B to do (or not do) X; correlatively, B has a right against A that X be done (or not done). Moreover, where B's right is understood under a will theory, B has the option of waiving the benefit of the right: in other words, B has the option of releasing A from performance of X. To bring the case of a duty to oneself into line with this paradigm, we must say that A, having a duty not to

---

[4] Stephen Munzer suggests that sellers of body parts might compromise their own dignity 'if the strength of the reason for selling is insufficient in relation to the nature of the part sold' (1994: 271). Munzer's theory of sufficiency turns on biological factors such as the renewability and vitality of particular parts as well as on the necessity for the use of body parts and whether the part retains a close personal link with the seller (pp. 275–7).

compromise A's own dignity, owes this duty to A. (The possibility of A owing the duty to some other party Z will be considered shortly; but this is not, *ex hypothesi*, a case of a duty *to* oneself.) In other words, the rights-holder (obligee) in relation to this duty is A himself (who is also the obligor).

Does it make sense to conceive of A owing the duty to A? On the face of it, it does not. For, if A (*qua* rights-holder) has the option of waiving the benefit of the right and, thus, releasing A (*qua* duty-bearer) from performance of the duty, then A is bound only as far as he chooses—which is hardly a case of being bound at all. There is also something mysterious about casting A in more than one role relative to himself. No doubt, A is capable of acting as both rights-holder (for one transaction) and duty-bearer (for another transaction) in a relationship with B. But there is only one A and it is unclear how A can put distance between himself as rights-holder and himself as duty-bearer for the purposes of a self-regarding duty. In Chapter 5 we will return to these questions to consider them in more detail.

If there are difficulties about A owing the duty to A, does it make more sense to conceive of A owing a self-regarding duty to a third party, Z? Clearly, if A does owe a duty not to compromise A's own dignity to Z, the separation of A (as duty-bearer) and Z (as rights-holder) means that the difficulties that we have just sketched drop away. However, the question that we are now posing is not about the coherence of a duty to oneself (strictly speaking) but about the idea of a duty, apparently concerning only one's own interests, being owed to a third party. The puzzle here is how it might come about that A owes such a duty to Z. One possibility is that such a duty arises by virtue of a special transaction between the parties, as where A promises Z that he, A, will not act in ways that are agreed to compromise A's own dignity. On this account, A's interests assume significance for Z only by virtue of the special commitment made by A. In the absence of such special undertakings, how might such a duty arise? Unless we presuppose a communitarian model of the kind sometimes associated with human dignity as constraint, it is difficult to see how A can be held accountable to anyone other than A for the welfare of A's own interests. Indeed, in the absence of a communitarian model, there is a definite resistance to the common identification of interests: my interests are my business, not yours, and vice versa. However, if we presuppose a communitarian model, the discreteness of individual interest is weakened. Each member of the community owes it to fellow members to respect the values that identify the community as the particular community that it is. If respect for one's own dignity is one such value, then each member of the community has an obligation to fellow members to act in accordance with this duty. In other words, where the communitarian model obtains, what is apparently one's own interest is also a matter in which every other member of the community has an investment—we are, thus, each trustees of our own dignity for the benefit of one another.

The Dignity of the Nobles and Dignified Conduct

In contrast with the idea that *all* humans have dignity, or at any rate (in Kant's case) all those humans with the capacity for moral reason, at the time of the Enlightenment, there was, as we have said, a rather more exclusive interpretation of dignity. This was the idea of dignity as the mark of a rank, such as the dignity of a king or a noble. From this tradition, we can draw a contrast between conduct that is dignified (as befitting those of higher rank) and that which is undignified (as one might expect of those of lower rank). And, with a little imagination, we can derive the idea of dignity as a virtue. In what sense, though, might dignity constitute a virtue?

It is possible that, in some social orders, matters of grace and presentation are valued so highly that the cultivation of a dignified demeanour—even though no guarantor of respect for others[5]—is regarded as a virtue for its own sake. We might thus admire those nobles in revolutionary France who retained their composure (and dignity) even while being barracked on their way to the guillotine. However, such commonly cited exemplars of dignity as Socrates and Nelson Mandela have a depth that goes well beyond matters of personal presentation and bearing. If Socrates and Mandela personify the virtue of dignity, they do so not so much as a matter of how they present themselves (particularly in adverse situations) but of the practical attitude that they have towards certain kinds of social adversity. Or, to put this another way, if dignity is a virtue, it is found in the *character* of humans wrestling with the limitations of human finitude and the problems of social order.[6]

The much debated case of Diane Blood[7] provides a very interesting illustration of the way in which a number of strands of dignity-based thinking can be brought together, including the virtue of dignity. It will be recalled that the case arose when the Human Fertilisation and Embryology Authority refused to allow Diane Blood to have access to the sperm that had been taken from her terminally ill husband, Stephen. The Authority's refusal rested on its view that there was non-compliance with the provisions of the Human Fertilisation and Embryology Act 1990, under which Stephen's written consent was required before the sperm could be lawfully released to Diane for the purpose of her attempted impregnation. Approaching the question from the standpoint of human dignity as empowerment, one would argue in favour of Diane's right to have access to the sperm provided that one was satisfied that the taking and use of the sperm was backed by Stephen's informed consent. The fact that no written consent had been given

---

[5] For example, according to William Parent, 'evil men like Hitler often displayed . . . presentational dignity, at least in their public behaviour. And so, for that matter, do Mafia hit men. So from a moral standpoint, this conception of dignity is wholly bankrupt' (1992: 55).

[6] For the standard emphasis on character in virtue ethics, see e.g. Crisp and Slote (1997).

[7] *R* v. *Human Fertilisation and Embryology Authority, ex p DB* [1997] 2 All ER 687 (CA). On which, see e.g. Feldman (2000: 71–2).

(as required by the legislation) would not of itself be fatal to Diane's claim. On the other hand, if one approached the issue from the standpoint of human dignity as constraint, one might well argue that, regardless of whether there was evidence (written or otherwise) of consent, this was simply not the kind of action that should be tolerated in a civilized society. In fact, the public debate generated by the case suggested that the majority saw this as a question about facilitating individual choice (legal literalism notwithstanding) rather than as a threat to the community's sense of human dignity. Whichever side of the debate one was on, however, all agreed that Diane Blood conducted her campaign with dignity; and, for our immediate purposes, it is this consensus that is worth pausing over.

What was it about Diane Blood's handling of the case that attracted this consensus? Possibly, for some, it was simply a matter of Diane maintaining a dignified demeanour, particularly when dealing with the media and the press. Having failed with her initial application before the High Court, Diane did not rant and rage; despite her obvious disappointment and the emotional stress that she was under, there was no loss of self-control; and, despite disagreeing with thosê who decided against her, she did not attempt to castigate them—instead, she quietly (but determinedly) went about lodging what was to prove her successful appeal. Possibly, for others, it was the sense that here was a young woman who not only was prepared to put her case to the courts, but would get on with her life after the final decision *whatever it proved to be*. Of course, the fact that the appeal succeeded before the Court of Appeal, following which the Authority reconsidered its earlier decision to deny Diane Blood access to the sperm (now with a view to her exporting it to a clinic in Belgium where she would be treated) meant that, unlike Socrates and Mandela, she did not actually have to live (or, for that matter, die) with an adverse decision. For some, though, this is the acid test: when the final decision goes against you, do you accept it? Do you take defeat, like victory, with dignity? Only if you do can you claim to represent the virtue of dignity.

It seems to us that, if dignity as a virtue merits a significant place in the moral scheme of things, it is in connection with one's attitude to adversity, both social and natural. William Parent has come quite close to this idea when talking about an agent's 'empirical understanding of himself and of his natural powers, limitations, and aspirations'—that is, 'a view of dignity that doesn't demean but instead elevates the status of beings who are struggling to cope in the natural world' (1992: 55). David Feldman, too, although not talking explicitly about dignity as a virtue, has said much the same: 'Dignity is . . . not an end in itself, or even a means to an end. It is rather an expression of an attitude to life which we as humans should value when we see it in others as an expression of something which gives particular point and poignancy to the human condition' (1999: 687). Feldman goes on to suggest that, typically, what he calls the 'subjective' aspect of human dignity (which is concerned with one's sense of self-worth) is 'reflected in a readiness to confront the realities of one's circumstances, including talents and physical and mental limitations, and make the best of them without losing hope and a sense that one's life is worthwhile' (p. 687). So conceived, the practical virtue of dignity is centred on the way in which we confront the many forms of adversity that we encounter. If we want an Aristotelian figure for this, the virtue of dignity holds the right balance between, on the one side, our attempts to overcome and, on the other side, our readiness to submit to adversity.

In the examples that we have given so far, it has been the political and legal order that has been the source of the particular adversity encountered. In each case, though, it is not *mere* adversity. Crucially, what makes both Socrates and Nelson Mandela exemplars of human dignity is the fact that we view their cases on the basis that they were unjustly treated; their confinement, even if in accordance with the rules of the positive 'legal' order, was illegitimate. In *Law as a Moral Judgment* (Beyleveld and Brownsword 1986), we set out at some length a legal idealist account of legal obligation, this account being aligned with a twin theory of accountability (on the side of legal officials) and restraint (on the side of citizens). Revisiting this account in the light of the present discussion, we might well regard it as being constructed around a dialectic between two virtues. On the one side, the virtue of accountability holds legal officials responsible relative to a balance between moral idealism and moral indifference; on the other side, the rights and responsibilities of citizens are conditioned by the reciprocal virtue of restraint under which much the same balance is sought after. Provided, then, that the legal system has the right kind of moral orientation, the virtue of restraint is such that the practical authority of the decision-makers and their decisions is recognized even where particular decisions (resulting from what we called a 'good faith attempt') are thought to be incorrect. Tragically, even a legal order with an appropriate moral trajectory will make mistakes, convicting the innocent and perpetrating various injustices. Where one is a victim, it takes a special attitude to accept one's fate, to cope with adversity of this kind. However, this is one manifestation of the practical virtue of human dignity.

If the case of Diane Blood prompts some thoughts about the virtue of dignity in the face of politico-legal adversity, the tragic case of Tony Bland (who, following the Hillsborough disaster, lay for several years in a persistent vegetative state) perhaps tells us something about the virtue of dignity in the face of physical adversity.[8] This is a case to which we will return in Chapter 11, because it has served as a focal point for a great deal of comment about what respect for human dignity dictates (see Feldman 1999: 688; 2000: 70). For present purposes, the only question is what it might hint at in relation to the *virtue* of dignity. So far as Bland himself was concerned, he was in no position to evince any kind of virtue—at most, one might have said that he was the kind of person who, during his conscious life, had understood how to balance the will to overcome with the

---

[8] *Airedale NHS Trust* v. *Bland* [1993] 1 All ER 821. For comment straddling *Blood* and *Bland*, see Morgan and Lee (1997).

will to submit. Thus, those who knew Bland's character might have said that, once he knew that his situation was hopeless, he would not have wanted to prolong matters. One step removed from this, the immediate members of Bland's family might have brought to the hospital bedside not so much their knowledge of Bland's character, but their own understanding of what dignity required of them if they were to handle the situation as this particular virtue requires. Yet what does dignity require in such cases? The British bioethicist Alastair Campbell (2000: 107–8) tells the poignant story of a baby boy born with a genetic defect affecting his capacity to breathe. The defect was so severe that, although the boy could return home with a home ventilation unit, he would never be able to lead a normal life nor be capable of being without a carer available day and night. The boy's mother, thinking that such a life was intolerable for her child, wanted the respiratory support removed so that the boy could die in peace. The father, however, took a different view, insisting that the support should continue. As Campbell says, whereas in Bland's case there was 'nothing but the mockery of human existence' (p. 107), in the case of the neonate the position is altogether less clear. Does the virtue of human dignity indicate that, in these circumstances, the mother was right to submit or the father right to resist? Or does the virtue allow for a range of acceptable responses between resistance and submission? (See Hursthouse 1997.[9]) Perhaps we can make headway with this question if we ask why we should value such a practical attitude? Is it because we simply value an attitude that evinces a middle way between stubborn resistance and supine submission? Or is it because we believe that such an attitude will be instrumental in promoting other values or desired states of affairs? If dignity is a virtue, is it so as an intrinsic or as an instrumental expression of good character?[10]

In principle, just as a society might purport to define itself by declaring its commitment to a particular regime of values, so it might purport to define its people by reference to their character—by their willingness 'to get on with their lives', 'to accept their fate', 'to abandon a course of action when it is seen to be futile', or whatever. In such a society, human dignity (plotted at a particular place on the spectrum between resistance and submission) might be identified and inculcated as a defining virtue. If so, it would not be thought important as serving some higher purpose (such as making people happier or the like) or as having beneficial consequences for others; the virtue of dignity would simply be regarded as one of the defining elements in a person of good character (and, concomitantly, the expression of human flourishing). If, by contrast, the virtue of

---

[9] Having specified that an action is right 'if it is what a virtuous agent would do in the circumstances' Hursthouse says: 'this premiss intentionally allows for the possibility that two virtuous agents, faced with the same choice in the same circumstances, may act differently. For example, one might opt for taking her father off the life-support machine and the other for leaving her father on it. The theory requires that neither agent thinks that what the other does is wrong . . . but it explicitly allows that no action is uniquely right in such a case—both are right' (p. 219 n. 1).

[10] Generally, see e.g. Chapman and Galston (1992).

dignity is valued instrumentally, it is not prized for its own sake but only in so far as it promotes some other value(s). For example, we might believe that those who act in accordance with this virtue will be happier, or add to the collective welfare, or respect the rights of others, and so on. It follows that the particular place on the spectrum between resistance and submission at which a dignified character is located will be sensitive to the instrumental function of this virtue; in other words, the virtue will be elaborated in a way that is designed to optimize promotion of the value(s) served by dignity.

To return to the case of the baby boy, and in the light of the distinction between a non-instrumental and an instrumental conception of dignity as a virtue, can we be any more confident about evaluating the different responses of the parents? Where a society takes a non-instrumental view, the culture will give guidance on what kind of character one will have if one is to internalize the virtue of dignity. Such guidance will involve a mixture of general precepts (giving persons a sense of where this particular society sets out its stall on the dignity spectrum) and specific responses (in situations of relatively common occurrence). Where guidance is simply at the general level, it is possible that even those tutored in the culture will reasonably disagree about particular cases—and one can imagine a society setting out its stall in a broad enough way to allow for each of the opposed views of the parents to qualify as reasonable responses relative to the virtue of dignity. If, however, the particular case falls under a specific directive, then the parents cannot both be right. Of course, this does not tell us which parent is right other than relative to the particular lights of a particular society. For, given the relativistic nature of a society-by-society rendition of the virtue of human dignity, the father might have the right response in some places, the mother in others.[11]

If the virtue of human dignity is understood in an instrumental way, its requirements will be set relative to the values that it is designed to serve. Once again, guidance might be available at both a general and a specific level. In the former case, the operative (to be served) value(s) will be declared and judgements must be made about which particular response to adversity will best promote the value(s) in question. In the latter case particular rules of thumb might have developed to the point where we can say that, relative to those rules of thumb, one of the parents is right. However, unless the operative values themselves (together with their rules of thumb) are necessarily or self-evidently correct, the sense in which the parent is right is relatively weak.

These remarks suggest that the distinction between a non-instrumental and an instrumental account of dignity as a virtue can only take us so far in determining which attitude is right in a particular situation. This is so for two reasons. First, even if a culture has a developed appreciation of dignity as a virtue, and even if we can characterize its appreciation as non-instrumental or instrumental, and even if we can then flesh out the substantive sense that goes with that character-

---

[11] Even, some might contend, in the same place. See Hursthouse (1997).

ization, there might still be some indeterminacy in the application of a culture's scheme of values and virtues. Of course, the less well articulated a community's sense of dignity as a virtue, the greater the indeterminacy. Second, even if there is no question of indeterminacy, so that we can all agree that relative to a particular community's appreciation of dignity as a virtue, a certain attitude is right (or wrong), the judgement is relative to that community's scheme of values and virtues. Hence, if we want to be able to make a stronger judgement about a case such as that outlined by Campbell—in other words, if we want to be able to judge whether the mother or the father was right in a sense that goes beyond British (or some other) culture—then we need a rationally defensible theory of human dignity on which we can ground the idea of dignity as a virtue.[12]

Human Dignity: Four Secular Conceptions and a Virtue

For many bioethicists, the rediscovery of the value (or virtue) of human dignity is a cause for concern. Even if this is not an attempt to reverse the secularization of the discipline, it is a retrograde step. According to Helga Kuhse,

the notion of human dignity plays a very dubious role in contemporary bioethical discourse. It is a slippery and inherently speciesist notion, it has a tendency to stifle argument and debate and encourages the drawing of moral boundaries in the wrong places. Even if the notion could have some use as a short-hand version to express principles such as 'respect for persons', or 'respect for autonomy', it might, given its history and the undoubtedly long-lasting connotations accompanying it, be better if it were for once and for all purged from bioethical discourse. (2000: 74)

Without doubt, Kuhse is right to say that human dignity is a slippery idea. However, it is also an extremely powerful idea, and the thought that we might do better if we purged it from bioethical discourse is whistling in the wind; and, by bringing the key strands of dignity discourse more sharply into focus, we can at least eliminate some of the slipperiness and open, rather than close, argument and debate.

It is time, therefore, to draw together the threads of these opening chapters. Thus far, the salient features of our account include: (*a*) the identification of a deep tension between what we have called human dignity as empowerment and human dignity as constraint; (*b*) a number of reservations about the claim that human dignity serves as the justifying ground for human rights (and duties); (*c*) the observation that we might arrive at human dignity as constraint (as in the new European bioethics) either by a Kantian approach (emphasizing the duty not to compromise one's own dignity) or by a communitarian approach (under which

---

[12] In so far as the tradition of so-called 'virtue ethics' sets itself against rational grounding (see Crisp and Slote 1997), then this project might require a view of dignity as a virtue which takes us away from this tradition.

autonomous choice, as understood in the prevailing human rights culture, is constrained by reference to the value of human dignity); and (*d*) the seeds of an idea of human dignity as a virtue that applies in circumstances of social and/or natural adversity. Quite how we are to locate human dignity as a virtue in this field remains moot. However, ideal-typically at least, we might order the field by fixing upon two very different starting points in relation to human dignity. The first starting point is the idea that human dignity speaks to what is special about human beings—that is to say, what is intrinsically and universally distinctive about humans—such that the human community can justifiably be regarded as a moral community. The second ('communitarian') starting point is the idea that human dignity speaks to what is distinctively valued concerning human social existence in a particular community—so much so that the particular community is defined by and identified with its own distinctive valuation and vision of human dignity. Whichever starting point we take, we can generate a conception of human dignity as empowerment as well as of human dignity as constraint. Hence, ideal-typically, there are two conceptions of human dignity, each with two variants, as well as the conception of human dignity as a virtue.

Human Dignity as the Distinctive Feature of Humanity (and as the Justifying Ground for Human Rights and Duties)

Where human dignity is understood as the essence of humanity and as the ground on which a regime of human rights and duties is to be constructed, proponents are looking for some distinctive (and relevant) human capacity or characteristic that explains and justifies the favoured scheme of rights and duties. According to the two leading claims of this kind, each of which is concerned to avoid the charge of 'speciesism', humans are special by virtue of having the capacity (*a*) to make unforced choices, to act in a way that is both purposive and voluntary or (*b*) to engage in moral reason, to act as a moral legislator and to act in a way that is morally directed. In the language that we have employed, these ideas can be taken forward in more than one way, to yield conceptions of human dignity as either empowerment or constraint.

As Empowerment

What we have called 'human dignity as empowerment' equates human dignity with the capacity to make unforced choices and, from here, constructs a regime of human rights centred on the promotion of individual autonomy. Accordingly, working with this liberal conception of human dignity, the principal human rights are designed to ensure that persons are recognized not only as having the capacity to make their own choices, but also as being entitled to enjoy the conditions in which they can flourish as self-determining authors of their own destinies. With human dignity as empowerment, life is not free of tragic choices; but it is for each person to make his or her own informed choice, tragic or otherwise.

As Constraint

Starting with the idea that human dignity relates to the human capacity for moral reason, Kant constructs a scheme of moral duties (rather than moral rights) designed to promote individual autonomy. However, for Kant, the will operates autonomously only where it directs action in such a way as is compatible with respect for the human dignity of both others *and oneself*. In this version of what we have called 'human dignity as constraint', and in line with the Kantian scheme, we find 'free' action (as it would be characterized under human dignity as empowerment) distinctively limited by reference to the duty not to compromise one's own dignity.

Human Dignity as a Value that Gives a Community its Particular Identity

Where a communitarian approach is taken, human dignity speaks less to what is special about human beings *qua* human and more to what is special about a particular community's idea of civilized life and the concomitant commitments of its members. In this light, we can see the new bioethics in Europe as aspiring to do much more than put human dignity back on the map. It aspires to represent Europe as a community that stands for a certain vision of human dignity; and, what is more, it is this particular vision of human dignity that identifies Europe as the particular community that it is. In principle, a particular community might conceive of human dignity in terms that give priority to the exercise of free choice, such that individual autonomy is seen as the highest expression of human dignity. However, the European project takes a different turn by conceiving of human dignity as setting limits to individual autonomy.

As Empowerment

The particular conception of human dignity as empowerment that we have focused on thus far locates human dignity at the base of an autonomy-centred scheme of human rights—it is *because* humans have dignity that they have rights *qua* humans. If, however, we had tried to develop a communitarian version of human dignity as empowerment, these ideas would be arranged in a slightly different way. Rather than picking out a distinctive human capacity, human dignity itself would be treated as a fundamental value towards which conduct should be orientated; and, in the case of a communitarian version of human dignity as empowerment, that value would be identified with the primacy of autonomous individual action. To put this another way, in such a community the reason why individuals would be treated as having a right to autonomy would not be because they, as human beings, have dignity but because in this particular community the value and vision of human dignity is understood in terms of an obligation to facilitate autonomous action.

As Constraint

Like the Kantian version of human dignity as constraint, the modern European bioethical version prescribes duties that set limits to the free choices of individuals. However, unlike the Kantian version, the new bioethics does not appeal to human dignity in order to emphasize the intrinsic value of each individual. Rather, each community has its own vision of human dignity and it is the particular vision within one's own community that specifies the values that represent the constraints on free action. Of course, such a constraining vision does not have to be static. As we have seen with the new bioethics, there is an ongoing monitoring of bioscience with a view to proscribing new practices or possibilities where they are regarded as contrary to human dignity.

Human Dignity as a Virtue

If human dignity is a virtue, we have suggested that it pertains to a practical attitude that enables humans, when confronted by adversity, to strike the right balance between the will to submit and the will to overcome or resist. Whether such an idea can be related to any of the conceptions of human dignity that we have outlined remains to be seen. To put the matter more pointedly, whether any of the conceptions of human dignity that we have outlined is rationally defensible, and, if so, whether dignity as a virtue can be tied in to that conception, remains to be seen.[13] This being so, what can we say about the rational defensibility of the conceptions identified?

Rational Defensibility

The conception of human dignity as empowerment upon which we have focused incorporates the move from recognizing the capacity to make unforced choices to acceptance of the right to choose. Whether this is in the particular context of transferring decision-making power from paternalistic physicians to their patients or in the general context of human rights, the fact that persons can choose is presented as entailing that they have the right to choose. However, is this necessarily so? While no one would suggest that there is any contradiction involved in accepting (*a*) that human beings have such a capacity and (*b*) that human beings, *qua* human, have rights, what is unclear is whether, having accepted (*a*), one

---

[13] Compare William A. Galston (1992: 2): 'Within any type of moral theory, it is always possible to find a subordinate place for virtue understood as the enduring and effective disposition to do whatever that theory requires. So, for example, there are subsidiary conceptions of virtue associated with following deontological rules or utilitarian precepts. To give virtue pride of place, however, is to reverse this relation: within a particular situation, the right thing to do is defined relative, not to a rule, but rather to what a person with a virtuous disposition would do if he or she were in possession of the pertinent facts.'

would then be involved in a contradiction if one denied (*b*). Does this not look like a violation of the fact–value distinction? What kind of logic can lead from the mere fact of human purposiveness to universal moral entitlements of the kind represented by human rights? It follows that, if human dignity as empowerment is to be rationally defensible, some considerable foundational work remains to be done.

Turning to human dignity as constraint (as in the Kantian version), the fact that such a conception comes into tension with human dignity as empowerment, or seems counter-intuitive to those who prioritize individual choice, or employs a dubious idea of duty to the self, does not give us decisive reasons for its rejection—at least, not if there are good reasons for its acceptance. We have suggested, however, that there are obvious difficulties with an account of human dignity that builds on the human capacity for moral reason. Notoriously, from an amoralist perspective, even if the capacity for moral reason is recognized in the landscape of practical reason, there is no reason why it should be privileged in any way and nor is there any reason why humans should not keep morality at arm's length. It also should be said that, even if a moral standpoint (formally speaking) is conceded, it is by no means clear that a duty-led morality is entailed.[14] Once again then, if this version of human dignity as constraint is to be shown to be rationally defensible, some considerable foundational work remains to be done.

In the communitarian versions of human dignity there is no concern with epistemological questions that look for answers beyond the fact of community self-definition and acceptance. Granted, we must assume that ideas or representations of human dignity are sufficiently significant to distinguish one community from another. From this point on, however, the only issue is whether one accepts the vision of human dignity as per community A, B, C, or D, and so on. If one purports to be a member of community A (or if one falls under its jurisdiction), one has a duty to respect its view of human dignity. In this light, relative to the aspiration of rational defensibility, the European bioethical project could be said to be both ambitious and modest. Its ambitiousness resides in its attempt to articulate a vision of human dignity that commands acceptance across a region as pluralistic as Europe; its modest nature, by contrast, resides in its lack of concern with defensibility beyond acceptance—if X is accepted, then X requires no further justification. Or, to put this another way, the project is more interested in breadth (of acceptance) than in depth (of justification).

Finally, there is the virtue of human dignity. If such an idea, akin to the communitarian version of human dignity as constraint, rests only on acceptance within a particular community, this is as far as our quest for rational defensibility can take us. However, if human dignity as a virtue can be locked into a scheme of thinking that makes foundationalist claims, then we might yet be able to press

---

[14] See e.g. Hare (1981) for the argument that, within moral reason (i.e. from the standpoint of moral reason) a split-level utilitarianism is entailed.

the rational defensibility of this idea rather harder. Whether or not this is possible, as we have just said, remains to be seen.

Next Steps

However we conceive of human dignity, it is worth emphasizing that it is a matter of *moral* concern. If human dignity is the foundation of human rights and duties, it is the foundation of moral rights and responsibilities. If human dignity is a value to be respected over and above respect for human rights, it sets a moral requirement. Even if human dignity is a virtue, it prescribes, morally, a particular practical attitude and response.[15] In one way or another, then, human dignity presupposes participation in moral reason. It follows that each conception of human dignity represents a particular exercise in moral reason.

Now, in a milieu of moral scepticism, we will find many disputing that there can be any 'right answers' within moral reason and others denying that any kind of moral viewpoint is required by participation in practical reason. To overcome such scepticism, we need to be able to locate human dignity within a moral theory that is not only good against all comers within moral reason but that is presupposed by practical reason itself. This is a tall order. Kant famously tried to place human dignity within such a secured moral theory. However, the Kantian project is commonly judged not only to have failed but to be impossible. Nevertheless, if we want rational defensibility in anything resembling a strong sense (as we do), then a secured theory of human dignity is what we must seek out. Our next step, therefore, is to see whether we can take this project forward.

---

[15] Although it bears repetition that the relationship between traditional morality and virtue ethics is contested (see Crisp and Slote 1997).

4

The Principle of Generic Consistency and its Justification

Introduction

In this chapter we introduce Alan Gewirth's Principle of Generic Consistency (PGC), and offer two arguments for using it as the governing principle in appeals to human dignity in bioethics and biolaw.

The first argument is Gewirth's own argument that agents contradict that they are agents if they do not accept that the PGC is the supreme principle governing the permissibility of actions. We, hereby, aim to show that the PGC is the supreme principle of bioethics and biolaw (indeed, of all ethics and law), *in so far as* these are concerned with prescription. If this argument is valid then, in so far as the preservation or violation of human dignity is relevant to the permissibility of actions, the PGC must (on pain of contradicting that one is an agent) be taken to govern the making of all such judgements.

The second argument aims to show that anyone who accepts that there are human rights—*on the assumptions that* to be human is necessary and sufficient to possess human rights, and holders of human rights may, in principle, waive the benefits that exercise of these rights confers[1]—must grant the PGC a similar status or contradict acceptance of such rights.

The second argument has less radical implications than the first. It aims to show that any legal system that recognizes human rights (*under the requisite conception of these*) must regard actions that violate human rights as legally invalid. Therefore, the PGC must be considered to govern judgements about the preservation or violation of human dignity by any legal system that recognizes human rights on pain of contradicting recognition of such rights. Thus, the PGC is the yardstick for the analysis of human dignity in biolaw, but only in so far as we are dealing with biolaw within a legal system that recognizes human rights. Similarly, the PGC is only established as the essential governing principle for the analysis of human dignity in bioethics for those who accept that there are human rights. However, although some persons or legal systems might (and do) reject human rights (at least under the requisite conception), acceptance of such rights is common enough to require widespread acceptance of the PGC as the governing principle for analysis of human dignity if our second argument is valid.

Under either argument, with the PGC as the governing principle, we have a

---

[1] The idea that rights are such that rights-holders may, in principle, waive the benefits that exercise of the rights confers is generally known as the 'will conception of rights'.

regime of thinking that attaches fundamental importance to individual choice and responsibility. However, because this regime hinges on the characteristics of agents (and agency) rather than humans as such, it is not quite identical to the scheme of thinking that we have identified with human dignity as empowerment. Nevertheless, the spirit of Gewirthian thinking is in line with human dignity as empowerment rather than with human dignity as constraint.

The Principle of Generic Consistency

The PGC requires agents to act in accord with the generic rights of all agents.

Generic rights are rights to generic needs of agency. Some agency needs are not generic because they depend on the purposes being pursued. Thus, for example, someone who wishes to play contract bridge requires three other players and a pack of cards (or, in this day and age, a computer that can simulate these requirements); but these things are not required in order to cycle from Sheffield to Buxton, for which other things are needed. By contrast, needs of agency are generic if they are prerequisites of an ability to act at all *or* with any *general* chances of success, *regardless of the purposes being pursued.* In other words, generic needs of agency are necessary for action or successful action *as such.*

According to Gewirth (1978*a*: 63), some generic needs are more necessary than others. Consequently, generic needs of agency are ordered hierarchically according to a criterion of degree of needfulness for action.

The criterion of degree of needfulness for action discriminates qualitatively and quantitatively. On the one hand, it applies to the idea that some things impinge on being able to act at all (they are needed in relation to the very possibility of acting), whereas other things, while not needed in this way, are needed for the possibility of *successful* action *in general.* On the other hand, the criterion applies to the idea that deprivation of (or interference with) a generic need may have a lesser (or greater) effect on either the possibility of acting at all or of acting successfully than will deprivation of (or interference with) another generic need.

Things that are needed for the very possibility of acting Gewirth calls 'basic' needs (or 'basic goods'). These include life itself, capacities involved in an ability to make choices, possession of mental equilibrium sufficient to enable one to translate one's preferences into active pursuit of one's purposes, as well as the necessary means to these (meaning those things the absence of—or interference with which—will threaten or interfere with life, etc.). In the case of human agents food, clothing, shelter, and health will be included among these necessary means (see 1978*a*: 54).[2]

---

[2] It is possible that concrete things that instantiate the generic needs will vary between different species. There is no assumption that only human beings can be agents.

Things that are needed for the possibility of successful action, Gewirth divides into two categories: 'non-subtractive' needs and 'additive' needs (see pp. 54–6).

Non-subtractive needs are needed to be able to act *successfully*, without thereby being needed for the very possibility of acting. To interfere with a non-subtractive need is to diminish an agent's chances of achieving his, her, or its ('its')[3] purposes regardless of what these purposes might be, without diminishing the possibility of the agent being able to pursue its purposes. Possession of *accurate* information, therefore, is an example of a non-subtractive need (which implicates a need to be told the truth and for others to keep their promises).

Additive needs consist of things that are needed to be able to improve one's capacities for successful action, regardless of one's purposes. The acquisition of special skills, and of new or additional information, are examples of additive needs.

Qualitatively, basic needs are more necessary for action than non-subtractive needs, which are more necessary than additive needs. On the other hand, needs within these categories are capable of quantitative discrimination in terms of their needfulness. Since the PGC grants rights to the generic needs, it follows that the generic rights are also hierarchically arranged according to the criterion of degree of needfulness. Thus, in case of conflict between the generic rights of different agents, basic rights will trump non-subtractive ones, which will trump additive ones, and finer discriminations within these qualitative categories will be possible quantitatively.

It should be clear from this that application of the PGC requires empirical knowledge concerning what concrete things instantiate generic needs, and also about the quantitative needfulness of various generic needs. For this reason, it is not helpful to attempt to give more than a bare minimum of flesh to the abstract categories in terms of which the PGC is couched: what specific actions constitute what, if any, violations of the generic rights must (to a considerable extent) be assessed during judgement applying the principle.[4]

Before we attempt to justify the PGC, however, four other points need to be noted about the generic rights.

First, the generic rights are 'strong' or 'claim' rights, by which we mean that they impose duties on other agents to respect the generic needs of the rights-holder.

---

[3] We use the genderless pronoun in recognition of the fact that agents are, *as an abstract category*, not necessarily human or even gendered beings.

[4] Gewirth divides the generic needs into two categories '(generic) freedom' or 'voluntariness' and '(generic) well-being' or 'purposiveness'. Well-being refers to 'substantive' needs or aspects of action, 'freedom' to 'procedural' needs or aspects (see 1978*a*: 41). We prefer not to discriminate in this way. As Gewirth, himself says, freedom can be regarded as instrumental to well-being (see p. 52). It is better to present the argument for the PGC simply in terms of the abstract category of generic needs, and to leave specification of the generic needs (both abstract and concrete) to application of the PGC. This enables the essence of the argument for the PGC to be presented most simply and also removes any contingency from it.

Second, the generic rights are positive as well as negative—because the PGC imposes duties on agents to assist other agents to secure their generic needs as well as duties on them not to interfere with the generic needs of other agents (see Gewirth 1978*a*: 217–30; Beyleveld 1991, ch. 10).

Third, the generic rights are rights under the 'will conception' of rights. As such, the duties of agents in relation to the generic rights of other agents are duties not to interfere with the generic needs of agents *against their will*, and to assist other agents who cannot secure the generic needs for themselves to do so *if the other agents so wish.*[5]

Finally, the generic rights are *moral* rights, and the PGC is a *moral* principle, for the differentiating reason that the PGC requires agents to take favourable account of the interests (in the case of the PGC, the generic needs) of others— moral principles being viewed by Gewirth as categorically binding other-regarding (i.e. other-respecting) ones.[6]

Justifying the Principle of Generic Consistency

Gewirth's Argument for the PGC

Gewirth (1978*a*) argues that agents and prospective purposive agents[7] contradict that they are agents if they do not accept and act according to the PGC. The reason why he pursues this strategy is, first, that he is attempting to justify the PGC as a moral principle according to his conception of such a principle. To justify a principle *as* categorically binding requires, as Kant also recognized, that it be shown to be 'connected (entirely *a priori*) with the concept of the will of a rational being as such' (Kant 1948: 89).[8] To show that an agent contradicts that it is an agent by not accepting and acting in accord with a principle will satisfy this requirement. This is because, as Gewirth points out (1978*a*: 22–3), since pure logic is presupposed by the use of any alternative criteria of rationality, what it requires is ineluctable. Second, Gewirth takes it for granted that agents (from their own perspectives) have good reason to pursue their own interests if they have good reason to do anything at all. Thus, the specific problem with showing that a *moral* principle is categorically binding is that agents must be shown why,

---

[5] The reason for this is given in our presentation of the argument. See n. 14 below.

[6] According to Gewirth, 'a morality is a set of categorically obligatory requirements for action that are addressed at least in part to every actual or prospective agent, and that are concerned with furthering the interests, especially the most important interests, of persons or recipients other than or in addition to the agent or the speaker' (1978*a*: 1).

[7] An agent is a being who does something voluntarily for a purpose that it has chosen. A prospective purposive agent is a being with the capacities required for agency with at least some disposition to exercise them. We use 'agent' to cover both agents and prospective purposive agents.

[8] Kant's 'rational being with a will' is equivalent to Gewirth's 'agent'. A rational being with a will is a being who follows maxims that are its reasons for acting.

as agents, they are categorically bound to take favourable account of the interests of others in their own actions.

Gewirth argues from the claim of an agent to be an agent within the first-person perspective of that agent. It is appropriate for any person considering the argument to imagine that he or she is that agent ('I'). The argument may be summarized as follows.[9]

By claiming to be an agent, I claim (by definition)[10]

(1) I do (or intend to do) X voluntarily for a purpose E that I have chosen.

Because E is my freely chosen purpose, I must accept

(2) E is good,

meaning only that *I* attach sufficient value to E to motivate me to pursue E (i.e. that I value E proactively). If I do not accept (2), then I deny that I am an agent—which is to say that it is *dialectically necessary* for me to accept (2).[11]

(3) There are generic needs of agency.

Therefore, I must accept[12]

(4) My having the generic needs is good *for* my achieving E *whatever E might be* ≡ My having the generic needs is categorically instrumentally good for me.[13]

Because I value my purposes proactively, this is equivalent to my having to accept

---

[9] We will not attempt to defend the argument here step by step, though we will comment briefly on a very limited number of recent objections. For the main objections, see Regis (1984). The argument is defended against all of these and many others in Beyleveld (1991).

[10] That Gewirth's method seeks to justify practical precepts to an agent (*as defined*) is not a function of a *value judgement* that only the views of agents matter. It follows from the fact that practical precepts can only be directed *rationally* at beings having the capacities of agents, and that only for such beings *can the question arise* of what practical precepts may legitimately be followed. To have a practical point of view, one must be an agent.

[11] Dialectically necessary procedures contrast with dialectically contingent ones. An argument is *dialectical* if it is propounded relative to some claim made by an interlocutor. Its conclusion is *contingent* where

(i) the claim on which it is based can be coherently rejected by the interlocutor; *or*
(ii) the connection between the premiss (claim) and the conclusion is contingent.

Its conclusion is *necessary* where the interlocutor cannot coherently reject the claim *and* the conclusion follows necessarily from the claim. Dialectical procedures contrast with assertoric ones, where considerations with validity independent of claims made by interlocutors are cited for acceptance of conclusions.

[12] By the principle 'Whoever pursues an end must be prepared to pursue the means necessary to achieve the end'. If I do not accept this principle, I deny that I am an agent (because agents, by definition, do things as perceived means to their chosen ends).

[13] The symbol '≡' signifies 'is equivalent to'/'is exactly equal to'.

(5) I categorically instrumentally ought to pursue my having the generic needs.

Because my having the generic needs is necessary for me to pursue my having the generic needs, I must hold

(6) Other agents categorically ought not to interfere with my having the generic needs *against my will,* and ought to aid me to secure the generic needs when I cannot do so by my own unaided efforts *if I so wish,*[14]

which is to say, I must hold

(7) I have both negative and positive claim rights to have the generic needs ≡ I have the generic rights.

It follows (purely logically) that I must hold, not only (7), but also

(7′) I am an agent → I have the generic rights.[15]

Consequently, it follows (purely logically) that I must hold

(8) All agents have the generic rights.

Since I deny that I am an agent by denying (8), every agent denies that it is an agent by denying (8). Thus, (8) (which is the PGC) is dialectically necessary for every agent.

The inference from 'I must hold (7) or deny that I am an agent', to 'I must hold

---

[14] It is because the agent must value the generic needs only instrumentally (albeit categorically so) that the agent cannot be prohibited categorically from waiving the benefits that exercise of the rights would confer. The rights are claimed for the possibility of action and successful action. There is no premiss in the argument that agents must value their agency as such. Such a premiss is an evaluation that would require independent justification that cannot be secured on the mere claim to be an agent. The prescription here is made on the criterion of my interests (satisfaction of my generic needs), and it is said by Gewirth to be 'prudential' in the sense that the basis upon which I hold (and must hold) it to be justified is that the action required by the prescription is required by my interests. Matthew Kramer and Nigel Simmonds (1996: 307–8, 313) claim that, *within the parameters of the dialectically necessary method,* it is *unintelligible* to prescribe that another do something in one's own interests *unless* the interests of the addressee coincide with one's own interests. This is because, in this context, 'the only available reasons for action are prudential reasons' (p. 308); but, on Gewirth's definition of morality, to prescribe that you do X in my interests is to require you to act morally. On Gewirth's definition of morality, it is, indeed, true that what is a prudential reason when cited in a justification addressed to you is a moral reason from your perspective. Kramer and Simmonds, however, are wrong to think that the dialectically necessary method does not permit me to assume that *you might* understand, respect, or accept moral appeals. The method only prohibits me from relying *on your actual acceptance or respect as a premiss to progress the argument,* until it has been established that agents must (on pain of contradicting that they are agents) take favourable account of the interests of agents other than themselves. If, as Kramer and Simmonds concede, 'In ordinary settings of interaction, where moral reasons can be specifically taken into account . . . "From my perspective you ought to abstain from doing φ, even though your interests are not served at all by such abstinence" is fully intelligible' (p. 313), then their objection evaporates. Were the strategy of Gewirth's argument to show that it is prudent (either individually or collectively) to be moral, then Kramer and Simmonds would be on solid ground. This, however, is not the nature of the argument.

[15] The symbol '→' signifies 'entails'.

(7′) or deny that I am an agent' is secured by what Gewirth calls the 'Argument from the Sufficiency of Agency' (ASA) (see 1978*a*: 109–10). This needs explanation, because it is central to our analysis of the concept of dignity in Chapter 6. The ASA may be presented as follows.

(*a*) If my having to hold (7) *does not entail* that I must hold (7′) then I must be able to deny 'I am an agent → I have the generic rights' without denying that I have the generic rights.

(*b*) To deny 'I am an agent → I have the generic rights' is to assert that my having some property D—a quality not necessarily possessed by all agents—is necessary for me to have the generic rights. To deny 'I am an agent → I have the generic rights' is to assert 'I have the generic rights → I have D'.

(*c*) 'I have the generic rights → I have D' logically requires assent to 'I am an agent without D → I do not have the generic rights'. In other words, to be consistent with 'I have the generic rights → I have D', I must consider, *even though I am an agent*, that I do not have the generic rights *if I do not have D*.

(*d*) However, on the basis of my having to hold (7), I must, *provided only that I am an agent*, consider that I have the generic rights—which is to say that I must, *by virtue of being an agent*, consider that I have the generic rights, *whether or not I have D*.

(*e*) 'I must consider, *even though I am an agent*, that I do not have the generic rights *if I do not have D*' contradicts 'I must, *by virtue of being an agent*, consider that I have the generic rights, *whether or not I have D*'.

(*f*) Since 'I have the generic rights → I have D' contradicts what my having to hold (7) entails, 'I have the generic rights → I have D' contradicts that I must hold (7).

(*g*) Since 'I have the generic rights → I have D' is equivalent to denying 'I am an agent → I have the generic rights' to deny 'I am an agent → I have the generic rights' is to deny that I must hold (7).

(*h*) Thus, in order not to deny (7), I must affirm 'I am an agent → I have the generic rights'.

Therefore, if I must hold (7) then I must hold (7′).[16]

---

[16] A number of commentators—e. g. Richard B. Brandt (1981: 39–40)—claim that because agents cannot be assumed to proactively value each other's purposes, the inference from (7) to (8) cannot be secured purely logically. However, they almost invariably fail to attend to the ASA. A rare exception is Marcus G. Singer (2000: 181–3), who has recently objected to the ASA by targeting a claim made in Beyleveld (1991, e.g. 246, 417–18) that to deny the validity of the ASA is to deny the logical principle that [(p & q) → r] → [p → (q → r)]. In Beyleveld (1991) it was argued that, *as an agent*, I proactively value my purposes (have the property IP) and categorically need the generic conditions of my agency (have the property IC). Because IP and IC are connected necessarily with my agency, *and with*

Implications of Gewirth's Argument for Bioethics and Biolaw

If Gewirth's argument for the dialectical necessity of the PGC is valid, then the PGC is the supreme principle not only of all prescriptions that have, in relation to Gewirth's definition of morality, the quality of being moral prescriptions, but of all norms or rules directed at action. Agents, to whom alone norms or rules can be directed rationally, must (*on pain of contradicting that they are agents*) accept that all actions must conform with the requirements of the PGC. The PGC must, in other words, be accepted by agents as the supreme principle of all practical reasoning, not merely of moral reasoning. Since the PGC is a moral principle, agents are rationally required to make moral reasoning (governed by the PGC) supreme in their practical reasoning. Consequently, because law purports to set normative requirements for action, it is rationally necessary for agents to take the PGC as the supreme principle of *legal* validity. Agents cannot rationally set moral requirements (governed by the PGC) aside in their legal reasoning. Moral criteria are not merely related contingently to legal reasoning; agents must (on pain of contradicting that they are agents) take them to be internal to legal reasoning; from which it follows that they must take defects in moral validity (as governed by the PGC) to be defects in legal validity (see Beyleveld and Brownsword 1985, 1986, 1993a).[17]

'Normative ethics' is sometimes equated with 'morality', and sometimes

each other, and because IC functions in the argument not only as a necessary component of my agency (by virtue of which I deny IC if *I do not consider that I have a right to the generic features* ('MyR')), but also as the dialectically necessary criterion that justifies *that I have a right to the generic features*, the inference drawn by the ASA that (within my dialectically necessary viewpoint) (7) →(7'), may be written as [(IP & IC) → MyR] → [IP → (IC → MyR)], which is an instance of the logical principle [(p & q) → r] → [p → (q → r)]. Singer, however, points out that, while this principle holds for material implication, it does not hold in any calculus of strict implication or entailment, and that Gewirth's argument requires it to hold as entailment. Thus, if the ASA requires this principle to be affirmed as a principle in entailment, the ASA must be denied. We believe that Singer is right about this and concede that an error was made in pressing this point *in the way it was* in Beyleveld (1991). However, this does not invalidate the ASA. There are two reasons for this. First, the formula [(p & q) → r] → [p → (q → r)) *is valid* in entailment *on condition that p and q entail each other*, and IP and IC are necessarily connected as aspects of my agency. In other words, the logical principle actually at stake is {[p ↔ q] & [(p & q) → r]} → [p → (q → r). Second, Singer depicts the claim that he attacks as the ASA's proof of (7) → (7') (see 2000: 182). This is not so. The claim he attacks is a supporting and independent argument. (Thus, if the modified supporting argument we have stated in reply to Singer, designed to show that (7) → (7') may be reduced to an incidence of {[p ↔ q] & [(p & q) → r]} → [p → (q → r)], is invalid, then the ASA itself still remains to be assessed in its own right.)

[17] This also vindicates the claim associated with natural law theory (or legal idealism) as against legal positivism (or legal realism) that immoral rules are not legally valid. This claim is not a descriptive one to the effect that positive rules claimed to be law are necessarily morally good or right. Nor is it the normative claim that positive rules claimed to be law morally ought to be good or right. It is the thesis that the practically rational person must, as such, consider claims to legal validity to be governed by criteria of morality.

A similar thesis (though not, we believe, with fully adequate justification) is presented by John Finnis (1984: 3–18), when he claims that law must be viewed from the standpoint of the practically reasonable person, and that the practically reasonable person thinks morally.

distinguished from it. However, regardless of how it is conceived, since normative ethics purports to make judgements relevant to the permissibility of actions, it must also fall under the governance of the PGC. Thus, the PGC must be taken to be the supreme principle of bioethics and biolaw (as indeed of all ethics and law). It follows that, in so far as judgements concerning human dignity are made in bioethics and biolaw, the validity and scope of those judgements must conform with the PGC and considerations that are essentially connected with it.

Alternative Arguments for the PGC

We believe that Gewirth's argument for the dialectical necessity of the PGC is sound. However, there is no denying that resistance to the very project of Gewirth's argument is strong. According to Martin P. Golding, 'Gewirth employs a strategy of argument that might be called the ideal philosophical procedure' in that it involves 'the derivation of powerful or rich conclusions from weak or minimal premises' (1981: 165). However, the weaker (i.e. the less controversial) the premisses, the more sceptical persons are entitled to be that such powerful conclusions can follow from them.

Kai Nielsen expresses such scepticism succinctly when he states that, although in Gewirth's 'astringent sense of "rational"' . . . it is plain and uncontroversial that we ought to be rational' (1984: 65), by employing such a criterion of rationality, 'Gewirth, like Kant, is trying to get categorically binding moral principles (principles binding on every rational agent)—including categorical right-claims—from the sheer concept of agency. . . . [T]rying to get so much out of a bare concept of agency is like trying to squeeze blood out of a turnip' (p. 79). This reflects the reaction of many who are presented with Gewirth's argument, and although both Golding and Nielsen concede that the level of Gewirth's scholarship requires the argument to be taken seriously, such scepticism hinders conscientious consideration of it. Consequently, unless alternative (dialectically contingent) arguments can be given for employing the PGC as the criterion of moral or legal validity, many will not be interested in what the PGC requires for individual actions and social (including legal) rules and practices.[18]

By claiming to have shown that the PGC is dialectically necessary, Gewirth claims to have shown a number of distinguishable things. Most importantly, he claims to have shown that

(a) there are requirements (duties) that agents must (on pain of contradicting that they are agents) take to be categorically binding on agents;

(b) these categorically binding duties require agents to take account of the interests of agents other than or in addition to themselves (i.e. they are moral duties);

---

[18] On the importance of alternative arguments, see Ockleton (1988: 236–7).

(c) these moral duties are correlative to rights of agents, the benefits of which are waivable by their holders;

(d) these moral rights are rights to the generic needs of agency.

Now, instead of beginning with the bare claim of an agent to be an agent, Gewirth might have begun with the claim made by an agent that there are duties that are categorically binding on agents. Alternatively, he might have begun with the claim made by an agent that there are moral duties (*under his conception of morality*); or with the claim that there are moral rights. It should be easier to show that an agent who claims that there are categorically binding duties must, *in consistency with this claim*, accept the PGC than to show that agents who merely claim to be agents must, in consistency with this latter claim, accept the PGC. The task of showing that an agent who claims that there are moral duties must, in consistency with this claim, accept the PGC should be easier still. And it requires no more than the recognition that there are generic needs of agency to show that agents, who accept that there are moral rights under the will conception of these, must accept the PGC. In line with Golding's observation, as the premises become stronger (closer in content to the PGC itself) the easier it becomes to show that acceptance of the PGC follows from acceptance of them. However, while an agent cannot coherently deny that it is an agent, it cannot be assumed that it is incoherent for an agent to deny that there are categorically binding duties, let alone that there are moral duties, let alone that there are moral rights, etc. These claims must be taken to be dialectically contingent—unless valid dialectically necessary arguments have already shown that agents cannot deny them without denying that they are agents, and the closer to the content of the PGC these claims become, the more elaborate such arguments have to be. Correspondingly, the closer that the content of the starting claims come to acceptance of the PGC, the more controversial they become, and the less likely they are to be accepted as starting points.

Nevertheless, there are many who are happy to accept such dialectically contingent claims. On the basis of such commitments, dialectically contingent arguments for the PGC can be presented that, while they do not establish the PGC as dialectically necessary, nevertheless require persons who have them to accept the PGC as the supreme principle of morality and practical reason. While such arguments (without demonstration that these commitments are themselves dialectically necessary) cannot establish that the PGC *is* categorically binding on agents, they nevertheless have justificatory force relative to acceptance of their premises.

We will, here, only present one dialectically contingent argument for the PGC.[19] This argument begins with the claim that there are human rights (as such

---

[19] See Beyleveld (1996) for dialectically contingent arguments from categorically binding duties and from categorically binding other-regarding duties. Modified versions of these will also be presented in Ch. 5.

rights are conceived in the modern human rights instruments and conventions). This claim is not quite the same as the claim that there are moral rights under the will conception, for it raises issues about the relationship between being human and being an agent, and also about the nature of rights in the human rights instruments.

The Dialectically Contingent Argument from the Acceptance of Human Rights

Suppose I (any agent) claim

(1) I have a right to do X.

I must also claim

(2) I have a right to the necessary means to do X.

Since

(3) There are generic needs of agency,

I must also claim

(4) *Whatever X is*, I have rights to the generic needs of agency.

From this, it follows logically that

(5) Any agent who considers that it has a right to do anything must consider that it has rights to the generic needs of agency.

Hence, it also follows that

(6) Any agent who considers that it has a right of kind R to do anything must consider that it has rights of kind R to the generic needs of agency.

Thus, it follows that

(7) Any agent who considers that it has a human right to do anything must consider that it has human rights to the generic needs of agency.

Now, the concept of a human right contained in modern human rights instruments is of a right held for the sufficient reason that one is 'human'. As Scott Davidson says, the modern human rights instruments have their roots in the American Declaration of Independence of 1776, and in the French Declaration of the Rights of Man and the Citizen of 1789, and it is a central feature of human rights instruments with this pedigree that human rights are conceived of as 'by nature inherent, universal and inalienable: they belong to individuals simply because they are human beings and not because they are the subjects of a state's law' (Davidson 1993: 5). This is apparent, for example, from Article 14 of the European Convention on Human Rights, according to which, 'The enjoyment of the rights and freedoms set forth in this Convention shall be secured without discrimination on any ground such as sex, race, colour, language, religion, political or other opinion, national or social origin, association with a national minority, property, birth or other status.' Thus, from (7) it follows that

> (8) Any agent who considers that any being has a human right to do anything must consider that the being has rights to the generic needs of agency simply because it is human.

From this, it follows that

> (9) Any agent who considers that any being has a human right to do anything must consider that all humans have rights to the generic needs of agency.

(9), however, is not the claim that

> (10) Any agent who considers that any being has a human right to do anything must accept the PGC.

This is because, although it may be inferred from (9) that

> (11) Any agent who considers that any being has a human right *to do* anything must accept that all agents have rights to the generic needs of agency,

the generic rights granted by the PGC are rights the benefits of which may be waived by the rights-holder; i.e. they are rights under the will conception of rights. Thus, unless the human rights instruments operate with the will conception of rights rather than the interest conception (according to which rights-holders may not act against their own interests, which are coextensive with the benefits that accrue from being a rights-holder), it cannot be inferred that anyone who holds that there are human rights logically must accept the PGC.

Furthermore, human rights might not necessarily be rights to do things rather than to have them; and, from the claim that A has a right to *have* X, it does not follow, without more, that A has a right to the generic needs of agency.

Thus, for the argument for the PGC from the acceptance of human rights to succeed, it must be shown that, at least centrally, to be human is to be an agent and that the human rights instruments operate with the will conception of rights.

The claim that being human is conceived by the human rights instruments, at least centrally, as being an agent is plausible. Basically these instruments, at least initially, were based on ideas of liberty, equality, *and fraternity*. They were conceived as civil and political rights, and later as social, economic, and cultural rights, concerned with the rights of *citizens* within a democratic order. Consequently, those who were thought of as having rights were also thought of as having reciprocal duties to rights-bearers. In so far as this is so, rights-bearers must be held to be agents, for only agents can have duties.

Certainly, in so far as very young children, foetuses, the dead, and members of the human biological species who are apparently not agents are granted rights under the human rights instruments, this claim is challenged. However, it is fairly clear that most of the rights in the human rights instruments are inapplicable to any but agents, that the extension of human rights to these special groups is controversial and a fairly recent event,[20] and that the foetus is granted only a 'proportional' status by the human rights instruments if they grant it any status at all.[21] Furthermore, it should be recognized that it may be possible for these 'special' groups to fall under the protection of the human rights instruments without actually being granted rights in the central sense that the instruments employ. If this is so, and in Chapter 6 we will argue that it is so, then we suggest that it is altogether more plausible to regard the status granted to the special groups by the human rights instruments as, in some way, derivative of or secondary to the status of agents to whom the protections of the human rights instruments centrally apply.

The fact that the human rights instruments do not outlaw boxing, mountain-climbing, and other dangerous activities, and do not require persons to vote, etc., shows that the will conception (which is only applicable to agents) is to be applied to at least some of the rights. But against the idea that the will conception is to be applied universally, it is to be pointed out that the European Court of Human Rights has, on occasion, ruled that consent to harm does not necessarily absolve a person from wrongdoing.[22] However, this is by no means conclusive, as there can be good reasons grounded in protection of the rights *of others* why persons should not be permitted, in particular circumstances at least, to waive the benefits of their rights. Furthermore, and from a conceptual point of view, perhaps conclusively, it needs to be borne in mind that the will and interest conceptions of rights are conceptions of rights as such. They cannot be applied to some rights and not to others. Thus, if it is clear that, in the main, human rights are considered to confer waivable benefits, then when agents are denied the right to waive these benefits, or 'rights' are apparently conferred on what seem to be non-agents, then coherence of approach requires that such 'exceptions' not be regarded as cases in which the interest conception applies, but as special cases where rights of other agents under the will conception require the waiver-rights of agents in question to be overridden, or duties to or in relation to[23] apparent non-agents to be recognized.[24]

---

[20] For example, the Convention on Rights of the Child, which grants children some independent rights (which was adopted by the General Assembly of the United Nations on 20 Nov. 1989) and the Convention on Human Rights and Biomedicine of the Council of Europe, which grants protections to human embryos and others unable to give consent.

[21] Otherwise they would have to prohibit abortion.

[22] *Laskey, Jaggard and Brown* v. *United Kingdom* (1997) 24 EHRR 39.

[23] Any duty not to harm or to protect X is a duty *in relation to* X. A duty *to* X is a duty owed solely by virtue of properties possessed by X. Thus, the category of duties in relation to X includes duties that the properties of X are not sufficient to generate. Such duties will characteristically be duties owed as a result of the need to protect the rights of others (or duties to others) than X.

[24] We show how the PGC can grant duties to apparent non-agents in Ch. 6. For a discussion of some kinds of mere duties in relation to non-agents/apparent non-agents, see Beyleveld (2000a: 62–4, 75–7).

Thus, our view is that the human rights instruments do operate centrally with the will conception of rights, which entails that they treat being human, centrally, as being an agent. If this is so, then the argument we have presented shows that acceptance of human rights requires acceptance of the PGC.

If this is not so, then our argument will have to be further qualified, as we will have shown only that acceptance of human rights under the will conception of rights requires acceptance of the PGC.

Implications of the Argument from the Acceptance of Human Rights

It follows from the argument from the acceptance of human rights that legal systems that recognize human rights must treat the PGC as a necessary criterion of legal validity, on pain of denying that they recognize human rights. This does not derive from any explicit substantive provisions of human rights in these systems. It follows simply from the concept of a human right as a right that is possessed by human beings on the sufficient condition that they are human under the will conception of rights. Thus, recognition that the PGC is a necessary criterion of legal validity must be ascribed to *any* legal system that recognizes human rights *if it is to be correctly described as a legal system that recognizes human rights*.

An equally direct implication of the argument from the acceptance of human rights is that *any* convention on human rights—hence, for example, the European Convention on Human Rights (ECHR)—must, on pain of contradicting that it is a convention on human rights, be interpreted in line with the requirements of the PGC.

We do not deny that a convention on human rights might, *as a convention*, grant rights that the PGC does not grant, grant rights that the PGC prohibits, or simply fail to grant rights that the PGC requires. We assert only that if a convention 'on human rights' grants rights contrary to the PGC then this contradicts that it is a convention on *human rights*. In this way, the argument for the PGC from the supposition of human rights places severe constraints upon the interpretation of a convention on human rights.

The general rules of interpretation are as follows.

I. Where a convention grants rights explicitly that the PGC does not require then, *provided that the PGC does not prohibit this*, such a grant will be legitimate under the 'indirect' applications[25] of the PGC (*provided that the convention itself is authorized by the PGC*).

---

[25] To apply the PGC directly is to deduce what it requires in the circumstances of its application. However, it may not always be possible to determine what the PGC requires in this way. This is because (*a*) the circumstances may be so complex that persons can reasonably disagree about what the PGC requires in these cases; or (*b*) the decision that needs to be made is optional in terms of the PGC (e.g. driving on the left-hand side of the road v. driving on the right-hand side), but is one that must be made because persons cannot be permitted to perform either option indiscriminately. The

II. Where a convention merely fails to grant rights explicitly that the PGC requires, it is to be taken to grant these rights implicitly, for the same reason that the convention must be regarded as operating with the PGC itself (even when it does not declare that the PGC is its governing principle)—that to fail to accept that the PGC is the governing principle of a convention is to deny that the convention is a convention *on human rights*.

III. Where a convention grants rights explicitly that the PGC requires not to be granted, then, in principle, this must be considered to be an error made by the drafters of the convention. However, *to an extent*, the matter may be viewed pragmatically. What the PGC requires *in its applications* is dependent on particular circumstances. This is because it grants rights according to the criterion of degree of needfulness for action and successful action. This criterion, it will be remembered, determines which rights are to be given precedence when rights come into conflict. However, whether or not the rights of individuals come into conflict depends on contingent circumstances attending social interaction, and, although the PGC is the absolute principle of human rights, the rights it grants are, with one possible exception,[26] not absolute, but depend upon contingent circumstances attending the interaction of individuals. Nevertheless, there are rights that are only capable of being overridden by other rights in extreme situations.[27] Because these rights will obtain in most circumstances, they may be articulated explicitly in a convention even though there are circumstances in which the PGC would overrule them. Consequently, human rights conventions are not to be rejected merely because they enshrine rules that do not have absolute validity under the PGC. Provided that such rules are valid under the PGC in most circumstances, they may be treated as 'rules of thumb' for rights. It is only where rights are granted that the PGC generally would not grant that it becomes necessary to declare the grants to be invalid or, in extreme cases, to reject the convention.

PGC handles these cases by prescribing (in its direct application) legitimate dispute-resolution procedures. Decisions made according to these procedures are indirect applications of the PGC. The conditions of legitimacy and the bindingness of these applications are discussed in detail in Beyleveld and Brownsword (1986: 178–86) and Chs. 7–9.

[26] This is the right of innocent persons not to be killed against their will. See Gewirth (1981). See also the criticism by Jerrold Levinson (1982) and the reply by Alan Gewirth (1982*b*).

[27] The idea that human rights are inalienable does not imply that there are no circumstances in which they may be derogated from. An inalienable right is not necessarily an absolute right. An inalienable right is one that cannot be waived by the right-holder (though benefit of the right can be waived by the right-holder's choice not to exercise it). This implies that if human rights are inalienable, then only other human rights can (in cases of conflict) override them. It is true that the rights of certain groups of persons are restricted in various Articles of the ECHR—e.g. minors, infectious disease carriers, persons of unsound mind, alcoholics, drug addicts, vagrants (all in Article 5), and aliens who are engaged in political activity (in Article 16)—but there is nothing in such provisions per se to challenge the view that the ECHR is about *human* rights. The primary effect of conceiving of the ECHR as a convention on human rights is to place very tight interpretative restrictions upon various derogatory clauses within the ECHR.

A comprehensive examination of the status of the human rights instruments under these rules of interpretation is an enormous task. However, for present purposes, which are merely to illustrate the working of these rules, a broad-brush preliminary perusal of just one instrument, the European Convention on Human Rights (ECHR), will suffice.

In general, the rights granted by the ECHR fall into two groups. The first group consists of a number of rights stated in relatively unqualified terms: the right to life protected by law (Article 2); the right not to be subjected to torture or inhuman or degrading treatment or punishment (Article 3); the right not to be held in slavery or servitude (Article 4); the right to liberty and security of person (Article 5); the right to due process and trial in accordance with the Rule of Law (Articles 6); the right not to be subject to retroactive punishment (Article 7); and the right to marry and to family life (Article 12). These rights, in turn fall into two sub-groups. The rights under Articles 5, 6, and 12 are subject to fairly limited specific qualifications, and to Article 15(1), which authorizes a Contracting Party to derogate from its obligations in 'time of war or other public emergency threatening the life of the nation'. On the other hand, the rights under Articles 2 ('except in respect of deaths resulting from lawful acts of war'), 3, 4, and 7 are (by Article 15(2)) exempted altogether from derogation.

The second group consists of a number of rights that are subject to restriction on specified general grounds. These are the right to privacy (Article 8), the right to freedom of thought, conscience, and religion (Article 9), the right to freedom of expression (Article 10), and the right to freedom of peaceful assembly and association (Article 11). The precise terms of restriction vary from Article to Article. However, there is a common derogatory core, and this is that the rights may only be restricted as prescribed by law, *and then only to the extent* (as Article 9(2) puts it) as is

necessary in a democratic society in the interests of public safety, for the protection of public order, health or morals, or for the protection of rights and freedoms of others[28]

or (as Article 10(2) provides) as is

necessary in a democratic society, in the interests of national security, territorial integrity or public safety, for the prevention of disorder or crime, for the protection of health or morals, for the protection of the rights of others, for preventing the disclosure of information received in confidence, or in maintaining the authority and impartiality of the judiciary.

Additionally, of course, the general public emergency derogation provisions of Article 15 apply to these rights.

Superficially, there might appear to be some difficulty in squaring the ECHR with the PGC. The difficulties are of three general kinds. The PGC places rights

---

[28] Articles 8(2), 10(2), and 11(2) have very similar wording.

in a hierarchy according to the degree to which they are needful for action per se and for successful action generally, but

(a) there is nothing very specific in the ECHR about which rights outweigh which (although there is some sense that, in general, the rights granted in earlier Articles are more important than those granted in later Articles);

(b) many of the conditions specified in the ECHR permitting restriction do not explicitly make the protection of competing rights the reason for the restriction;

(c) the ECHR makes several rights non-derogable, whereas in the scheme justified by the PGC there is at most one absolute right.[29]

None of these observations generates insuperable difficulties. As regards (a), the absence of a specific criterion for dealing with conflicts between rights *at least* does not contradict the construction required by the PGC that the more important rights are those that are more needful for action per se and for successful action in general (with the rights that are needful for the former being more important than those that are merely needful for the latter). As regards (b), although protection of the rights of others is stated alongside the needs of public order, crime prevention, etc., as a condition justifying the restriction of human rights, it is far from implausible (as, indeed, it is necessary) to see the justification of all of these restrictions as lying in the protection of the conflicting rights of others afforded by the satisfaction of such needs.[30] Indeed, it would be highly *implausible* to make anything much of *the contrast* between protection of the rights of others and the other derogating needs, simply because some of the derogating conditions (e.g. the need to defend the confidentiality of information provided in confidence—mentioned in Article 10(2)) refer quite unambiguously to rights that would be granted under the PGC. Finally, as regards (c), even though the rights under Articles 3, 4, and 7 are not absolute under the PGC, they are extremely fundamental within its structure. It is not unreasonable, and almost certainly wise, where the PGC is being operationalized as a political legal instrument, to present the most important of the PGC's protections as absolute in order to protect against abuse of the discretion (as regards the interpretation of derogatory conditions) that Member States will seek every opportunity to exercise.

Of course, if interpretation in line with the PGC becomes very strained, it might be preferable to reject specific provisions as mistakes. On this cursory inspection, however, our impression is that the ECHR is readily enough viewable as a rough guide to rights required by the recognition of human rights (namely, the rights required by the PGC).

---

[29] See n. 27 above.

[30] In this connection, it should be noted that the emerging jurisprudence of the European Court of Human Rights stresses that derogation on various grounds of social necessity requires the existence of a pressing social need, and that the restrictions themselves should be no more than is proportionate to the legitimate aim pursued. The idea of proportionality, here, certainly requires that derogatory provisions themselves be justified in terms of human rights.

However, in the present context, the most important implication of the argument for the PGC from acceptance of human rights is that any views about the nature of human dignity that the PGC requires must govern the interpretation of human dignity in the human rights instruments.

5

Kant and Gewirth

Introduction

The moral theories of Kant and Gewirth share a number of features. Most importantly, Kant and Gewirth agree that

(*a*) morality *purports* to impose categorically binding standards for action;
(*b*) there is a supreme principle of morality, which *actually is* categorically binding;
(*c*) a principle can be justified *as* categorically binding only by demonstrating that it is an absolutely unconditional requirement of reason.

In line with this, Gewirth argues that agents contradict that they are agents if they do not accept and abide by the PGC, and Kant seeks to show that his supreme principle, the Categorical Imperative, is 'connected (entirely *a priori*) with the concept of the will of a rational being as such' (1948: 89). As a result, each considers what he holds to be the supreme principle of morality to be also the supreme principle of practical reason (i.e. of rational action).

How the Categorical Imperative is related to the PGC is important because, as we noted earlier, much contemporary thinking on human dignity (some in line with dignity as empowerment, other with dignity as constraint) draws its inspiration from Kant. For reasons we will give in this chapter, we do not consider Kant's justification of the Categorical Imperative to be successful. Nevertheless, if the PGC and the Categorical Imperative are so related that Gewirth's argument for the PGC also justifies the Categorical Imperative, then we will need to attend carefully to Kant's applied moral philosophy when we apply the PGC, because applications of both principles must then yield mutually consistent results. On the other hand, if the PGC and the Categorical Imperative are incompatible principles, then we need to be clear about how they differ in order not to conflate their implications.

While Kant attempted to *justify* the Categorical Imperative by arguing that there is a necessary conceptual connection between action in accordance with it and the concept of agency (see 1948, ch. 3), he *elucidated* the Categorical Imperative by deriving acceptance of it as a logical implication of acceptance of morality (see 1948, chs. 1 and 2). Gewirth does not provide a corresponding dialectically *contingent* argument for the PGC. However, in the last chapter we derived commitment to the PGC from acceptance of human rights; and other dialectically contingent arguments for the PGC are available that are easier to relate to Kant's project. In particular, it is useful to try to argue that anyone who accepts that there are categorically binding requirements on action, whether other-regarding or not, must accept the PGC.[1] By attending to specific features of these arguments, we will derive a principle that closely resembles Kant's first formula for the Categorical Imperative, the Formula of Universal Law. This derivation will not only provide a Gewirthian version of the Formula of Universal Law, it will show that a common objection to Kant's elucidation of the Categorical Imperative (namely, that pure reason cannot require agents who accept categorically binding requirements on action that are not necessarily other-regarding to accept an other-regarding Categorical Imperative) can be successfully answered. In addition, we will derive a Gewirthian version of Kant's second formula for the Categorical Imperative, the Formula of the End in Itself, by relating one of Kant's arguments for this formula to Gewirth's dialectically *necessary* argument for the PGC.

However, Kant's normative moral philosophy has characteristics that cannot be reconciled with Gewirthian theory. While it is possible that Kant misconstrued his own theory, a comparison between Gewirth's dialectically necessary argument for the PGC and Kant's transcendental deduction[2] of the Categorical Imperative in chapter 3 of *Groundwork of the Metaphysics of Morals* suggests that there are fundamental differences between Gewirthian and Kantian theory, which are rooted in the difference between Gewirthian and Kantian conceptions of 'pure practical reason'.

We will link this difference to the main way in which Gewirthian and Kantian theories differ in their conceptions of human dignity, which centres around the different status within these theories of duties to oneself.

Reconstructing Kant's Categorical Imperative

Kant provides a number of different formulas for the Categorical Imperative. We will attend only to the Formula of Universal Law, 'Act only on that maxim through which you can at the same time will that it should become a universal law' (1948: 84), and the Formula of the End in Itself, 'Act in such a way that you always treat humanity, whether in your own person or in the person of any other, never simply as a means, but always at the same time as an end' (p. 91).

---

[1] These arguments draw on and modify arguments presented in Beyleveld (1996, 1999*a*). Some passages in this chapter are taken directly from the latter article.

[2] Kant does not use this terminology in *Groundwork of the Metaphysics of Morals* (1948). However, it is a standard description and, since he holds his supreme principle to be synthetic a priori (see p. 105), is justified by linkage between synthetic a priori propositions and transcendental deductions in Kant's writings generally, and by its use in his *Critique of Practical Reason* (1956).

Kant's Elucidation of the Formula of Universal Law

The Formula of Universal Law is a universalizability test, which specifies that it is permissible for a 'being with a will' to act on a 'maxim' only if that being can at the same time will that the maxim should become a 'universal law'.

A being with a will is endowed with practical reason, which means that it is able to guide its actions by maxims (which specify standards according to which the being is prepared to act) that it treats as its reasons for acting (see Kant 1948: 76–7). If the Kantian concept of a being with a will is not identical to Gewirth's concept of an agent then it is nonetheless the case that any Kantian being with a will is a Gewirthian agent, and that Gewirthian agents are Kantian beings with a will.[3] Thus, because 'being with a will' is a rather clumsy expression, we will generally refer to 'beings with a will' as 'agents'.

What the Formula of Universal Law's universalizability test amounts to depends on what is meant by 'a universal law' and the 'can will' condition.

As regards 'universal law', Kant distinguishes 'subjective principles' from 'objective principles' (or 'practical laws'). Subjective principles depend on contingent purposes. Objective principles or laws are valid for every agent because what they prescribe is binding on agents simply because they are agents, no matter what contingent properties (including the having of purposes or the holding of maxims) they might possess (see 1948: 84). Therefore, the predicate 'universal' in the expression 'universal law' is redundant unless it signifies more than merely that a practical law is necessarily binding on every agent. What Kant means when he says that a maxim holds as a universal law is not merely that the maxim has prescriptive force for each and every agent simply because each and every agent is an agent, but also that it has the same prescriptive force for every other agent as it has for any particular agent. Accordingly, if it is held that 'Agents ought to pursue their self-interest' is a practical law, then this is consistent with holding only that each agent ought to pursue *its own* self-interest. To hold this principle to be a universal law, however, is to hold that Agent$_1$ must not only endorse action in Agent$_1$'s self-interest, and any other agent must endorse action in that other agent's self-interest, but that Agent$_1$ must also endorse action in every other agent's self-interest, and every other agent must endorse action in Agent$_1$'s and any other agent's self-interest. In other words, to hold a principle as a universal law, Agent$_1$ must value action according to it by any other agent as though it were Agent$_1$'s own action.

Thus, the Formula of Universal Law's universalizability test, which may also be formulated as

> For it to be permissible for an agent to act on a maxim, the agent must be able to will that any other agent at the same time act on the same maxim,

---

[3] This is because maxims specify ends (purposes), and the idea that a being guides its actions by maxims implies that it chooses these maxims and, hence, the purposes they specify.

is a moral test under Gewirth's definition of 'morality', because it requires agents to take favourable (indeed, equal) account of the interests of other (indeed, all) agents.

As regards the 'can will' condition, according to Kant, there are two distinct conditions that the conjunction of $Agent_1$ acting on a maxim with other agents acting on it must satisfy in order for $Agent_1$ to be able to will it (see 1948: 86–7).

(*a*) The conjunction must fall under a conceivable law of nature.

(*b*) The conjunction must not involve $Agent_1$ in a contradiction in its will.[4]

Kant's general reasoning in his elucidation of the Formula of Universal Law in *Groundwork of the Metaphysics of Morals* may be presented as follows.

(1) According to the 'common' idea of morality there are ends that are intrinsically good, to be pursued for their own sakes.
(2) If this idea is true, then there must be categorically binding maxims prescribing these ends.
(3) If there are categorically binding maxims, then pure reason must be capable of being practical (determining ends for the will): i.e. there must be at least one maxim or principle for determining maxims that is connected entirely a priori with the concept of an agent as such.[5]
(4) If pure reason can be practical then its principle must be the Formula of Universal Law.

Kant's argument for (4) is, unfortunately, not clear.

. . . if I conceive a *categorical* imperative, I know at once what it contains. For since besides the law this imperative contains only the necessity that our maxim should conform to this law, while the law, as we have seen, contains no condition to limit it, there remains nothing over to which the maxim has to conform except the universality of a law as such; and it is this conformity alone that the imperative properly asserts to be necessary.

There is therefore only a single categorical imperative and it is this: '*Act only on that maxim through which you can at the same time will that it should become a universal law*'. (Kant 1948: 84)

Certainly, *if* there is a categorical imperative then all maxims that a rational agent may espouse must be consistent with it. And, as the idea of a categorical imperative requires that it be connected entirely a priori with the concept of an agent, any maxim espoused by an agent must conform with the proposition that the categorical imperative is universally valid (i.e. binding on all agents). But, as

---

[4] The 'can will' condition has been much debated. See e.g. the excellent discussion, particularly of the conceivability test, by Christine Korsgaard (1985).

[5] This reading is also supported by Kant's explicit statement in *The Metaphysics of Morals* that there must be ends that 'by their concept' are also duties. 'For were there no such ends, then all ends would hold for practical reason only as means to other ends; and since there can be no action without an end, a *categorical* imperative would be impossible. This would do away with any doctrine of morals' (Kant 1991: 190).

we have already pointed out, there is a gap between the universality of an imperative viewed as a practical law and its universality viewed as a universal law, and numerous commentators have objected that they do not see how Kant can close this gap on the basis of pure reason alone (see e.g. Allison 1990: 205–6).

The source of the problem is that, while respect for others is not part of Kant's *definition* of morality, his Formula of Universal Law is an other-regarding principle; indeed, it is an *impartial* principle that requires agents to take *equal* account of the interests of all agents. Hence, it is claimed, for Kant to show that agents must regard a categorical imperative not merely as a practical law but as a universal (impartial) law, he must assume that agents have an impartial attitude towards the interests of others (for which no warrant has been provided), or else his idea of rationality itself imputes such an impartial attitude (which renders it not 'pure') (see e.g. Gauthier 1986: 6).

Although Gewirth does not provide a parallel dialectically contingent argument to the effect that those who accept morality must accept the PGC, such an argument can be constructed. Of course, Gewirth defines morality not as a set of categorically binding requirements on action *simpliciter*, but as a set of categorically binding *other-regarding* requirements on action. However, in Gewirth's definition, this signifies only that *some* favourable account must be taken of the interests of at least *some* relevant others (agents in Gewirthian theory). For a requirement to be moral (as against non-moral rather than against immoral), it is not necessary that *equal* account be taken of the interests of *all* relevant others. Thus, beginning with the claim that there are moral requirements on action according to *Gewirth's* definition of morality will not automatically solve the problem.

However, many moral theorists do define morality as impartial (e.g. Baier 1958: 200–1; Benn and Peters 1959: 56; Toulmin 1950: 145). Indeed, David Gauthier considers that morality 'is traditionally understood to involve an impartial constraint on the pursuit of individual interest' (1986: 7).

As we shall now see, Gewirthians can show that acceptance of impartial categorically binding requirements on action logically requires acceptance of the PGC. But, more than that, they can show that acceptance of categorically binding requirements on action *simpliciter* logically requires acceptance of the PGC.

Deriving Acceptance of the PGC from the Acceptance of Morality[6]

Suppose that I (an agent, 'Agent$_I$') accept that there are morally binding requirements on action, conceived of as categorically binding *impartial* ones. I, thereby, claim

---

[6] The argument for the PGC from other-regarding categorically binding requirements on action given in Beyleveld (1996) only succeeds if other-regarding requirements are impartial ones, which is not made clear there.

(*a*) There are categorically binding requirements on action, which are impartial.

By virtue of claiming that there are categorically binding requirements on action, I must accept

(*b*) There are requirements that are binding on my actions simply because I am an agent $\equiv$ There are ends that I ought to pursue or contradict that I am an agent.

It follows, logically, that

(*b'*) Any other agent ('$Agent_o$') must accept that there are ends that $Agent_o$ ought to pursue or contradict that $Agent_o$ is an agent.

Given

(*c*) There are generic needs,

it follows from (*b*) that I must accept

(*d*) Regardless of what ends are categorically binding on me, I ought to possess the generic needs as means to my pursuit of whatever I claim to be ends categorically binding on me,

and from (*b'*) that $Agent_o$ must accept

(*d'*) Regardless of what ends are categorically binding on $Agent_o$, $Agent_o$ ought to possess the generic needs as means to $Agent_o$'s pursuit of whatever $Agent_o$ claims to be ends categorically binding on $Agent_o$.

By virtue of claiming that these requirements are impartial (i.e. that equal account of the interests of all other agents must be taken), *I* must accept

(*e*) $Agent_o$ ought to have the generic needs as means to $Agent_o$'s pursuit of whatever $Agent_o$ claims to be ends categorically binding on $Agent_o$,

and $Agent_o$ must accept

(*e'*) $Agent_I$ ought to have the generic needs as means to $Agent_I$'s pursuit of whatever $Agent_I$ claims to be ends categorically binding on $Agent_I$.

Thus, I (and $Agent_o$, hence all agents) must accept

(*f*) All agents ought to have the generic needs as means to their pursuit of whatever they might claim to be ends categorically binding on their actions $\equiv$ All agents have (will claim)[7] rights to the generic needs $\equiv$ the PGC.

---

[7] See Chapter 4, pp. 71–2 for explanation.

Suppose, instead, that I claim *only* that there are, *according to Kant's definition*, morally binding requirements on action. I, thereby, merely claim

(A) There are categorically binding requirements on my action.

From this it follows that I must accept

(B) There are requirements that are binding on my actions simply because I am an agent ≡ There are ends that I ought to pursue or contradict that I am an agent.

Given,

(C) There are generic needs,

it follows that I must accept

(D) Regardless of what ends are categorically binding on me, I ought to possess the generic needs as means to my pursuit of whatever I claim to be ends that are categorically binding on me,

and $Agent_o$ must accept

(D′) Regardless of what ends are categorically binding on $Agent_o$, $Agent_o$ ought to possess the generic needs as means to $Agent_o$'s pursuit of whatever $Agent_o$ claims to be ends that are categorically binding on $Agent_o$.

Thus far, the argument runs parallel to the argument from categorically binding other-regarding requirements on action. However, since these requirements are not now thought of as impartial, it is not permissible to assume that I take equal account of the interests of $Agent_o$, nor that if I treat X as my reason for acting, then $Agent_o$ must accept that it has reason both to help me to do X and not to interfere with my doing X. To demonstrate that I must accept the PGC, it must be shown that I must take equal account of the possession of the generic needs by $Agent_o$, and this must be shown by purely logical means.

That acceptance of (A) requires me to accept (D) means that if I consider that there are categorically binding requirements on action then I must, on pain of *contradicting this claim*, hold that I ought to pursue my having the generic needs as means to whatever I claim to be ends categorically binding on me, whatever these might be, or *contradict that I am an agent*. This is because the idea that an agent is categorically bound to do X is the idea that it is simply by virtue of being an agent that the agent is bound to do X. This, however, implies that there is a contradiction between the proposition 'A is an agent' and the proposition 'A is not bound to do X'. Thus, if I claim that there are categorically binding requirements on action, I must hold

(E) I am an agent → I categorically ought to possess the generic needs as means to my pursuit of whatever ends I claim to be categorically binding on me.

However, we saw from Gewirth's 'Argument from the Sufficiency of Agency' (ASA) in Chapter 4 that it follows *purely logically* from ['I am an agent' → 'I have the generic rights'] that *I* must hold ['I am an agent' → 'I am an agent → I have the generic rights']. Since this inference is purely logical, it must follow *purely logically* from ['I am an agent' → 'I have Q'] that *I* must hold ['I am an agent' → 'I am an agent → I have Q']. Thus, if I must hold (E), then I must hold

(F) I am an agent → I am an agent → I categorically ought to possess the generic needs as means to my pursuit of whatever ends I claim to be categorically binding on me.

And, now, logic alone requires me to accept

(G) $Agent_0$ is an agent → $Agent_0$ categorically ought to possess the generic needs as means to $Agent_0$'s pursuit of whatever ends $Agent_0$ claims to be categorically binding on $Agent_0$,

from which it follows that I must accept

(H) $Agent_0$ has a (will claim) right to have the generic needs.

Just as my having to hold (G) → my having to hold (H), my having to hold (F) → my having to hold

(I) I have a right to have the generic needs.

'(H) & (I)' is the PGC. Since all agents who accept that there are categorically binding requirements on action must reason in the same way, all such agents must accept the PGC or contradict that there are categorically binding requirements on action.

Deriving a Gewirthian Version of the Formula of Universal Law

Our task, here, is not to derive acceptance of the PGC itself from acceptance of morality (as defined by Kant) but to adapt such reasoning to derive acceptance of the Formula of Universal Law. We have stated that Kant holds that if there are categorically binding maxims then pure reason must be capable of being practical. This, Gewirthians will understand as

(Gv1) If there are categorically binding principles then there must be at least one principle prescribing ends that any agent must accept on pain of contradicting that it is an agent.

Starting from this Gewirthians will reason

(Gv2) If there is a principle that an agent must accept on pain of contradicting that it is an agent, then all agents must accept this principle on pain of contradicting that they are agents, which, in Kantian terms, implies that there must be a principle that is a practical law for all agents.

However, implicit in the validity of the ASA (see above) is the proposition

(Gv3) If I must prescribe X on pain of contradicting that I am an agent then I must consider what X prescribes to be justified by the fact that I am an agent or contradict that I am an agent.

From this it follows, purely logically,

(Gv4) If there is a principle that is a practical law for all agents then it is (in Kantian terms) a universal law, meaning that each agent must endorse the action of every other agent acting on this principle as though it itself were acting on, or proposing to act on, this principle.

If there is a practical law for an agent then that agent may not act on a principle that runs contrary to that practical law (without contradicting that it is an agent). But if there is a universal law for agents then, in considering what it may do, an agent must not only consider whether a principle it proposes to act on runs contrary to what is a practical law for itself. It must consider whether the principle it proposes to act on runs contrary to that law considered as a practical law for any other agent ($Agent_0$). It must, in effect, treat a practical law for $Agent_0$ as though it were a practical law for itself. For if there is a universal law for agents, then $Agent_1$ contradicts that it is an agent by acting according to ends that conflict with the ends that $Agent_0$ must follow on pain of contradicting that $Agent_0$ is an agent. Thus, the following criterion of permissible principles follows from Gv4, given the assumption that there is a practical law for agents:

(Gv5) An agent may only act on a principle if action according to this principle is consistent with what is required by practical laws being considered as universal laws,

which may be restated as

(Gv6) An agent ($Agent_1$) may only act on a principle if action according to it does not run contrary to what it must will (or contradict that it is an agent), when what $Agent_0$ must will (or contradict that it is an agent) is at the same time considered as what $Agent_1$ must will or contradict that it is an agent.

This principle we will call 'the Gewirthian Formula of Universal Law'.[8]

From this formula we can derive, not the PGC itself, but the statement that an agent may only act on a principle consistent with the PGC, simply by specifying

---

[8] Gewirth's rejection of universal ethical egoism (see Gewirth 1978a: 82–9), in effect, deploys this principle.

that what an agent must will is governed by the generic needs.[9] Viewed in this way, this formula is equivalent to the statement that agents must obey the Golden Rule 'rationalised' (see Gewirth 1978a: 169–70; 1978b). The Golden Rule requires agents to treat others as they *would wish* to be treated themselves. The Golden Rule rationalized requires agents to treat others as they *rationally must wish* others to treat them; and the PGC is derived from the Golden Rule rationalized by specifying that what an agent rationally must wish others to do is not to interfere with its generic needs/assist it to secure its generic needs as instrumental to its purposes.

Kant's Arguments for the Formula of the End in Itself

Kant presents two arguments for the Formula of the End in Itself. The first is dialectically contingent. It derives the Formula of the End in Itself as part of Kant's elucidation of the concept of morality. Its line (see Kant 1948: 90–1) is as follows.

(1) If there is a categorically binding imperative then something must have absolute value as an end in itself.

(2) If rational nature (agency as such) does not have absolute value as an end in itself, then nothing can have such value.

(3) Therefore, if there is to be any categorically binding imperative, rational nature must be an end in itself.

(4) Therefore the Categorical Imperative (if there is a categorical imperative) must be the Formula of the End in Itself.

The second argument, although (confusingly) presented in chapter 2 of *Groundwork of the Metaphysics of Morals* (and, indeed, overlapping the first argument) actually builds on the transcendental deduction of chapter 3 of the same work. It runs (see p. 91) like this.

(*a*) Every person (read 'agent') necessarily conceives of his/her own existence as an end in itself.[10]

(*b*) The ground upon which every other person conceives of his/her own existence as an end in itself is the same ground that is valid also for me.[11]

---

[9] See the regressions involved in treating Gewirth's dialectically necessary argument as a *reductio ad absurdum* of principles opposed to the PGC provided in Beyleveld (1991: 47–56) to see how the generic needs are to be deployed.

[10] This requires the transcendental deduction.

[11] What Kant writes is ambiguous. He can be read as saying that I must consider that others are ends in themselves, either because they have the same reason for considering that they are ends in themselves as I have (namely, they would contradict that they were agents if they did not consider themselves to be ends in themselves), or because they must cite the same reason for being an end in themselves as I must (namely, that they are agents). The former is open to the objection brought by Brandt (1981) (see ch. 4 n. 16 above) against Gewirth. The latter is not open to this objection. Of course, the ASA shows that if agents must hold the former they must hold the latter, but there is no evidence that Kant was aware of the problem and its solution.

(c) Therefore, I must conceive of the existence of every other person, as well as myself, as an end in itself.

(d) Therefore, the Categorical Imperative is the Formula of the End in Itself.[12]

A Gewirthian Reconstruction of Kant's Argument for the Formula of the End in Itself

Kant's second argument for the Formula of the End in Itself can be related to the PGC by trying to derive the Formula of the End in Itself in a Gewirthian manner. This is achieved by a slightly modified statement of Gewirth's dialectically necessary argument for the PGC expressed in Kantian terminology. (In the sequence that follows, Kantian formulations are in italics.)

If I claim

(Gr1) I am an agent = I pursue purposes voluntarily = *I pursue subjective ends voluntarily,*

then I claim

(Gr2) I value my purposes = *I value my subjective ends.*

(Gr3) In order to be able to pursue or achieve any purposes/*subjective ends*, I need to be an agent.

Therefore, I must hold

(Gr4) That I am an agent is a necessary good = *My agency is an end in itself,*[13] (which entails '*Every agent, if rational,*[14] *views its agency as an end in itself*'). Consequently, I must hold

(Gr5) Any other agent (Agent$_0$) ought not to interfere with my agency against my will[15] $\equiv$ I have a right to my agency = *My agency may not be used as a mere means to the subjective ends of others.*

Given the ASA, I must now hold

---

[12] In a footnote Kant tells us that (b) is to be justified in ch. 3 of *Groundwork of the Metaphysics of Morals*. Since ch. 3 merely purports to justify the Categorical Imperative by showing the dialectical necessity of free will (see below), what Kant must have in mind is the insertion of (i) in his dialectically contingent derivation of the Formula of the End in Itself from the concept of morality (which involves the inference that if it is dialectically necessary for a person to hold that he or she is bound by the Categorical Imperative, then it must be dialectically necessary for that person to consider that he or she has absolute value as an end in itself).

[13] Bearing in mind that to value something as a necessary good is to assign categorical *instrumental* value to it in Gewirth's dialectically necessary argument, this must be interpreted as what Gewirth calls a 'subsistent' end in itself. Agents (through their capacities for agency) are subsistent ends in being necessary means to the setting of desiderative ends (see Gewirth 1991: 68).

[14] In the sense of reasoning properly, by not contradicting that it is an agent.

[15] We state only the negative duty here.

(Gr6) I have a right to my agency because I am an agent → *My agency may not be used as a mere means to the subjective ends of others for the sufficient reason that I am an agent.*

To be logically consistent, I must now hold

(Gr7) $Agent_o$ has a right to its agency = *$Agent_o$'s agency may not be used as a mere means to the subjective ends of others.*

Gr6 together with Gr7 means that I must hold

(Gr8) All agents have a right to their agency = *No agent's agency may be used as a mere means to the subjective ends of others* = the Gewirthian Formula of the End in Itself.

Because to have a right to agency is to have a right to the necessary means of agency as such (which are the generic needs), the PGC can be derived from this formula merely by specifying possession of the generic needs as the necessary means of agency.

The Reconstructed Categorical Imperative versus Kant's Categorical Imperative

Because we have derived Kantian-type conclusions in a way acceptable to Gewirthian theory, we have provided a reconstruction of Kant's position, not a pure exegesis of it. This, by the nature of the exercise, highlights similarities between Kantian and Gewirthian thought. There are, however, reasons for thinking that the Gewirthian Formulas of Universal Law and the End in Itself might not be exactly what Kant had in mind. The most important of these derive from Kant's presentation of duties as falling into four categories—perfect duties to oneself; perfect duties to others; imperfect duties to oneself; and imperfect duties to others (see Kant 1948: 84–6)—which does not fit easily into Gewirthian theory. For example,

(*a*) For Kant, imperfect duties are identified when the universalization of contrary maxims produces contradictions in the will, whereas perfect duties are identified when contrary maxims cannot consistently or possibly be universalized. On the other hand, in our Gewirthian reconstruction, the universalizability test in the Formula of Universal Law is restricted to the avoidance of contradictions in the will (and, indeed, it is difficult to provide any rationale for regarding the *impossibility* of universalization as of any moral significance in Gewirthian theory).

(*b*) Although Gewirthian theory can accommodate the notion of imperfect duties, these must always, in some way, derive from the generic rights (thus from one's perfect duties to others).[16]

---

[16] One of Kant's reasons for considering that agents have only imperfect duties to be kind or loving

(*c*) In Gewirthian theory the benefits of all the rights it justifies may, in principle, be waived by the rights-holder. This is a function of the categorical value that agents must attribute to their having the generic needs being categorical *instrumental* value (see Beyleveld 1991: 33). Thus, in Gewirthian theory even suicide is something that an agent may will and, contrary to what Kant claims (see 1948: 85; 1991: 218–19), there can be no perfect duty not to commit it (see Beyleveld 1991: 32; Gewirth 1978*a*: 264–6). Indeed, the notion of perfect duties *to oneself*, though capable of indirect and analogous constructions, is intrinsically problematic in Gewirthian theory (see further below).

(*d*) Whereas in Gewirthian theory agents have positive as well as negative rights to the generic needs (see Gewirth 1978*a*: 223; 1984: 227–33; Beyleveld 1991: 333–59), Kant considers all rights to be negative only (see 1991: 216) (because he holds all positive duties to be imperfect and rights are correlative to perfect duties to others).

Some of these features—especially those referred to in (*b*) and (*c*)—are simply functions of the fact that Gewirth's theory is a rights theory (under the will conception of rights), whereas Kant's theory gives primacy to duty.

This, however, signifies that there is a difference in the way in which Kant and Gewirth conceive of 'an end in itself'. For Kant, to regard a person as an end in itself is to consider that there is a duty not to interfere with the person's agency that cannot be waived by the person. For Gewirth, but not for Kant, to regard an agent as an end in itself is to grant it a will claim right to its agency, with the implication that the correlative duty not to interfere with or to assist its agency is cancellable by the permission or will of the agent.

We suggest that this difference in Kantian and Gewirthian conceptions of 'an end in itself' derives from different conceptions of 'pure practical reason' (in so far as this idea has application within Gewirthian theory). This is, in turn, linked to the fact that the idea that agents must conceive of themselves as having free will in a strong sense plays no part in Gewirth's dialectically necessary argument for the PGC, whereas it is absolutely central to Kant's transcendental deduction of the Categorical Imperative.

Gewirthian versus Kantian Conceptions of Pure Practical Reason

Kantian moral theory has often been criticized for its 'formalism', for lack of specification of necessary ends in the Categorical Imperative, in consequence of which it has been held to give no specific moral guidance. There are at least two reasons, however, why this accusation is not entirely fair to Kant. First, as Lewis White Beck says, the function of a Kantian formula 'is not to supply variables but

is that agents do not have their dispositions and feelings fully at the disposal of their will. However, while this is true, we see no reason why there cannot be a perfect duty *to try* to cultivate such dispositions (which will generally be protective of the rights of others). This is, in any case, the natural analysis for moral theories that are concerned directly with actions rather than the having of feelings.

to provide the procedure toward a solution' (1965: 25) for which it is the necessary but not sufficient condition. Second, the accusation derives from too much
attention to *Groundwork of the Metaphysics of Morals* at the expense of later
works, particularly *The Metaphysics of Morals*. In the latter, Kant quite clearly
specifies *one's own* perfection and the happiness *of others* as necessary ends (see
1991: 191–2; 195–6). Nevertheless, the material content that this provides for the
Categorical Imperative is very thin when compared with the content provided for
the PGC by the generic needs.

Of course, this under-specification might be due to Kant's failure to appreciate the significance of generic needs of action and successful action. At best,
however, this cannot be the whole story, for in Kantian theory the necessary ends
are imperfect duties that are related to virtue rather than to rights (see 1991:
194–8). But, more importantly, it is possible (even likely) that the relative lack of
material content in the Categorical Imperative is integral to Kant's thought. One
clue to this is that Kant finds it quite meaningful to think of the Formula of
Universal Law as a law (albeit not as an imperative) that governs the actions of
disembodied beings like angels who could not violate the moral law (see 1948:
78). As such, Kant must conceive of the moral law in a way that enables it to
apply not only to those who have generic needs of agency, but also to hypothetical beings that do not. This suggests that there is a difference between Kantian
and Gewirthian conceptions of pure practical reason. It seems to us that when
Kant talks of pure practical reason he is talking about requirements that pure
reason sets for the will quite *independent of* all contingent willing. On the other
hand, in so far as Gewirth may be said to have a concept of pure practical reason,
it is one that sets requirements *irrespective of* what an agent might contingently
will. The generic needs of action are means to an agent's pursuit/achievement of
its ends whatever these might be. They are, in a sense, derived from an agent's
ends, and an agent's motivation to pursue the generic needs derives from its
perception that the generic needs are necessary means to its ends.

Central to both Kantian and Gewirthian conceptions of a categorical imperative is the idea that it is binding *regardless of* the contingent ends that an agent
might set itself. If we focus on this idea, then there is no doubt that both the PGC
and the Categorical Imperative purport to be categorical imperatives, and it is
perfectly appropriate to refer to the 'ought' that an agent is rationally required to
direct to itself to pursue and defend its having the generic needs as a categorical
'ought' (albeit an instrumental one). However, there is another aspect of Kant's
idea of a categorical imperative that renders it more specific than this. Kant
defines 'categorical imperatives' in opposition to 'hypothetical imperatives', and
he *defines* a hypothetical imperative as an instrumental one. 'Hypothetical imperatives declare a possible action to be practically necessary as a means to the
attainment of something else that one wills (or that one may will)' (1948: 78). On
the other hand, 'A categorical imperative would be one which represented an
action as objectively necessary in itself apart from its relation to a further end'

(p. 78). Now, while this definition does not render the PGC a hypothetical imperative but a categorical one,[17] its *content* is derived from the relation of the generic needs as necessary means to what one wills or might will. However, in our Gewirthian reconstruction of Kant's elucidation of the Formula of Universal Law, we have assumed that the proposition that an agent instrumentally ought to pursue its generic needs regardless of its purposes implies the proposition that pure reason is practical. Kant, on the other hand, appears (at least at times) to tie the notion of pure practical reason to the idea of a categorical imperative in its contrast with hypothetical imperatives. This, in turn, relates to Kant's contrast between 'heteronomy' and 'autonomy' of the will.

According to Kant,

If the will seeks the law that is to determine it *anywhere else* than in the fitness of its maxims for its own making of universal law—if therefore in going beyond itself it seeks this law in the character of any of its objects—the result is always *heteronomy*. In that case the will does not give itself the law, but the object does so in virtue of its relation to the will. This relation, whether based on inclination or on rational ideas, can only give rise to hypothetical imperatives: 'I ought to do something *because I will something else*'. (1948: 102)

An autonomous will is defined by Kant positively (as a will that makes its own laws from its nature *as will*) as well as negatively (as a non-heteronomous will— i.e. as a will not conditioned by a specific interest) (see 1948: 94–5).

According to Kant, the Categorical Imperative is the law (or principle) of autonomous willing (see 1948: 94–5). That is to say, to conceive of a will guiding its actions (or better, maxims for action) by the Categorical Imperative is to conceive of a 'free' will, and to display a free will is to guide one's actions by the Categorical Imperative (i.e. to act for no other reason than that this is permitted or required by the Categorical Imperative). For Kant, morality (under the Categorical Imperative) and free will are, in this sense, reciprocal concepts. This idea, as we shall now see, plays a central role in Kant's attempted transcendental deduction of the Categorical Imperative in *Groundwork of the Metaphysics of Morals*.

Kant's Transcendental Deduction of the Categorical Imperative in Groundwork of the Metaphysics of Morals

As we have seen, in chapter 2 of *Groundwork of the Metaphysics of Morals* Kant argues that anyone *who considers that there are morally binding requirements on action* must accept the Categorical Imperative as the supreme criterion for the permissibility of maxims for action (and correlatively, must consider that he/she has free will). However, according to Kant, by doing this

---

[17] The reason why the agent must obey the PGC is not that it serves any end but that the agent would contradict that it is an agent if it does not. This does not make the PGC a logical principle. It only makes the reason for obeying it a logical one (see Beyleveld 1991: 102–5).

We have merely shown . . . that autonomy of the will is unavoidably bound up with it [the concept of morality 'currently in vogue'] or rather is its very basis. Any one therefore who takes morality to be something, and not merely a chimerical Idea without truth, must at the same time admit the principle we have put forward. This chapter [chapter 2], consequently, like the first, has been merely analytic. In order to prove that morality is no mere phantom of the brain—a conclusion which follows if the categorical imperative, and with it autonomy of the will, is true and is absolutely necessary as an *a priori* principle—we require a *possible synthetic use of pure practical reason.* (1948: 106)

In chapter 3 of the same work Kant attempts to show that this requirement can be met. His argument (see pp. 107–9) runs as follows.

(Td1)   'Will is a kind of causality belonging to living beings so far as they are rational' (p. 107).[18]

(Td2)   In the negative sense, a will that is free works independently of determination by alien causes (laws of nature).

(Td3)   A will that is free in the negative sense is also free in the positive sense that it is not lawless but a causality conforming to immutable laws of a special non-natural kind.

(Td4)   Free-will is a self-contradictory notion unless in all its actions the will is 'a law to itself' (p. 107) (i.e. unless the will is autonomous).

(Td5)   An autonomous will is bound by the Categorical Imperative (which Kant claims to have established in the course of his analysis of morality in the previous two chapters).

Therefore,

(Td6)   If free will is presupposed then the Categorical Imperative follows by mere analysis of the concept of such freedom.

(Td7)   Free will cannot be demonstrated (from a theoretical point of view) as a property of a being with a will.

(Td8)   However, free will must be presupposed as a property of all beings with a will, because every being with a will must presuppose that its will is free as the only idea 'under which he can act' (p. 109).

Therefore,

(Td9)   Every being with a will must consider that it is bound by the Categorical Imperative as the only idea under which it can act.

---

[18] Linking the will with rationality in this way raises problems, because it suggests that it is otiose to refer to a rational being with a will. Rationality may, of course, refer either to possession of a capacity or to a proper use of it, and deployment of this distinction may resolve the problems. This merits considerable discussion, which we will not attempt here. For simplicity, we will generally drop reference to 'the will of a rational being', referring only to 'a being with a will'. Kant is essentially interested in what a being with a will (a being with the capacity to act for reasons) is required by the proper use of its reason to accept and do.

As we understand this, Kant argues (though he does not use this terminology) that the Categorical Imperative is dialectically necessary, and his view that it is synthetic a priori is that it is dialectically necessary (see Beyleveld 1999a: 103).

Td8 is crucial. As far as we understand Kant, he reasons as follows.

(Td10) A being with a will possesses 'practical freedom' (possesses reason that is practical, reason that exercises causality in regard to its objects: i.e. its actions are voluntary, under the control of its will).

(Td11) Although its actions are under the control of its will, the will itself could, for all that we can know, be determined by causes outside of its control. If so, the will would not be a free will.

(Td12) However, a being exercising practical freedom *must consider* itself to have free will. If it does not, it must attribute the causality of its will to something external to it, which contradicts the idea that its will is practically free (which is equivalent to contradicting that it is a being with a will).

This, surely, is fallacious reasoning. We may grant that a being with a will must regard its actions as under the control of its will. But to suppose that it does not possess free will (by supposing its will to be determined by causes external to it) is not to contradict the idea that it is a being with a will *unless it is supposed* (and what Kant is trying to show is that it *must be supposed*) that a being with a will not merely exercises causality *through* its will but that in so operating it operates as a 'first cause'. However, a will would not cease to be an efficient cause of action just because it itself had an efficient cause; it would merely cease to be a *self-sufficient* efficient cause. Thus, Kant's reasoning supposes that what it is trying to establish must be presupposed.

How does Gewirth's dialectically necessary derivation of the PGC differ from this? Well, Gewirth and Kant essentially begin in the same place, with the claim of an agent (being with a will, being with practical freedom) to be an agent. To demonstrate that a principle is categorically binding (in the sense of binding *regardless of* any contingent willing) it is necessary to show that the principle is binding on an agent simply by virtue of its being an agent. It is customary, following Kant's own usage (see 1948: 108), to say that such a demonstration requires the introduction of a 'third term' that is capable of linking the notion of being an agent to recognition of the categorically binding principle. In relation to Kant's transcendental deduction, this 'third term' is 'free will' (or better, the idea that an agent must conceive of itself as having a free will—a will the laws of which are free of all contingencies of willing). But, in Gewirth's dialectically necessary argument for the PGC, the 'third term' is the introduction of the idea that there are generic needs, the 'laws' of which derive from the fact that the generic needs are related to any of an agent's possible ends as their necessary means.

Bernard Williams (1985: 62–3) objects to both Kantian (in which he includes Rawlsian) and Gewirthian theories on the ground that they abstract from all the contingencies attached to being an agent. Thus, they require agents to accept requirements that are based on the idea that they are rational agents and nothing else, ignoring the fact that rational agents will always be something else as well, and that what is rational for an agent with one set of capacities, characteristics, and purposes will not necessarily be rational for an agent with another set. However, it should be clear that *if* this criticism does apply to Kant,[19] it does not apply to Gewirth. This is precisely because the Gewirthian notion of pure practical reason is of rational requirements that are derived from the contingent purposes of agents (and other contingent properties that might affect these) as necessary conditions for these purposes *whatever they might be, and not independently of them.* The generic needs are immanent within contingent purposivity; thus, no assumption is made that agents can be rational and no more. That agents are rationally bound by what can be derived from the generic conditions does not ignore their contingent properties.[20]

The full import of this difference becomes apparent as soon as it is appreciated that if Gewirth's dialectically necessary derivation of the PGC is sound, and Kant's Categorical Imperative is related to it as it is under our reconstruction, then *if* Kant is correct that action in accordance with the Categorical Imperative and free will are reciprocal concepts, then demonstration of the dialectical necessity of the PGC is also demonstration of the dialectical necessity of free will (see Beyleveld 1999*a*: 109–10).

To be sure, if the dialectically necessary derivation of the PGC is sound, then the PGC is a law of rational agency as such, or (in Kantian terminology) a law given to the will by its nature as will. The PGC is, thus, a law of an autonomous will as Kant defines this positively.

However, this does not imply that the PGC is a law of free-willed action, *unless* an autonomous will is one that operates free of any contingent motivation (as a will that is free in Kant's negative sense). Now, there is a crucial ambiguity in Kant's *negative* notion of an autonomous will as a non-heteronomous will. As we have already noted, Kant defines a non-heteronomous will as one that is not conditioned by a specific interest (see 1948: 94–5). However, even with the use of the word 'specific', this leaves it open for a heteronomous will to be interpreted in two ways—either as a will that is determined by a specific interest, or as a will that is determined by the having of specific interests *as such*. If the latter interpretation is given, then it seems to us that autonomous action (as non-heteronomous action) must be interpreted as free of any contingent motivation at all, which will require free will in the negative sense. However, if the former

[19] And it will not apply if our reconstruction correctly represents Kant's intentions.

[20] See, further, Beyleveld (1991: 308–10): 'By the same token, while Kant's view of pure practical reason renders motivation to do what it requires mysterious, in Gewirthian theory there is no difficulty comprehending why there is necessarily motivation to follow "laws" of pure practical reason.'

interpretation is given, then autonomy could still be compatible with lack of free will, because autonomous action would not be independent of the pursuit of *any* contingent interests.

In brief, in Kant, the idea that pure reason can be practical is, in part, the idea that agents can be *caused* to act independently of any determination by factors belonging to their nature as physically embodied beings. For Gewirth, on the other hand, the idea that pure reason can be practical is compatible with causality driven by contingent desires and purposes, because the motivation to pursue and defend one's generic needs (as instrumental to one's purposes) remains regardless of one's purposes.

Since this aspect of the Kantian notion of pure practical reason is not involved in our reconstruction of the Categorical Imperative, the dialectical necessity of the PGC (or the reconstructed Categorical Imperative) does not entail the dialectical necessity of free will (at least in the sense that Kant would appear to intend).[21]

Import for the Kantian and Gewirthian Conceptions of Dignity

According to Kant 'killing oneself is a crime (murder)' (1991: 218) quite independently of one's duty to other human beings (e.g. one's family).

Man cannot renounce his personality as long as he is a subject of duty, hence as long as he lives; and it is a contradiction that he should be authorized to withdraw from all obligation, that is, freely to act as if no authorization were needed for this action. To annihilate the subject of morality in one's own person is to root out the existence of morality itself from the world, as far as one can, even though morality is an end in itself. Consequently, disposing of oneself as a mere means to some discretionary end is debasing humanity in one's own person (*homo noumenon*), to which man (*homo phaenomenon*) was nevertheless entrusted for preservation. (p. 219)

Kant, in short, considers self-murder to involve treating oneself as a mere means, which is contrary to human dignity (see p. 255).

This is not the case in Gewirthian theory.[22] The reason, as we have already noted, is that the generic rights are will claim rights, the benefits of which the agent may always waive (unless this would involve violation of the agent's duties *to others*), and this is because the agent's necessary attachment to its generic

---

[21] Our present view, therefore, is that the possibility that it might be, which is mooted in Beyleveld (1991), is to be rejected.

[22] Gewirth himself holds (quite rightly, we believe) that, in the first instance, agents are justified in trying to prevent another agent from taking its own life, on the presumption that the agent is acting under stress that undermines its capacity for free choice. However, if, in the final analysis, it appears that suicide is what the would-be suicide freely wills, then (subject to overriding considerations of the would-be suicide's duties to others) this intention may not be interfered with. (See Gewirth 1978*a*: 324.)

needs is a categorically instrumental one, not an intrinsic one. This, in turn, is co-implicated with the Gewirthian notion of pure practical reason as something that is satisfied by reasons that apply *regardless of* an agent's purposes without having to apply *independently of* an agent's purposes.

We will conclude this chapter by attending to some complexities of this contrast, because it is clearly central to the difference between Gewirthian and Kantian conceptions of human dignity. It also merits attention, because it may not be obvious how Kant avoids the Gewirthian position within his own theory and Gewirth (despite his view on suicide) accepts that there are duties to oneself that are not functions of one's duties to others.

According to Gewirth, the 'very idea of there being duties to oneself incurs important objections', including

if a person has duties to himself, then, because of the correlativity of duties and rights, he also has rights against himself. But any right-holder can always give up his right and thereby release the respondent of the right from his duty. On the other hand, no person can release himself from a duty. Hence, the notion of duties to oneself is contradictory, since it implies that a person both can and cannot release himself from his duties to himself. (Gewirth 1978a: 334)

Nevertheless, Gewirth goes on to say that there can be duties to oneself.

First, the duty that agents have to obey the PGC itself is a duty to oneself as well as to others, because the agent's adherence to the PGC is not given by the contingent purposes the agent has but by being a rational agent as such. Thus, this duty is not correlative to a right against oneself.

Second, if we are to make sense of expressions such as 'being unfair to oneself', 'not doing oneself justice', 'demeaning oneself', or 'degrading oneself' (pp. 335–6), then we need to find room for duties to oneself. However, if we are to make such judgements coherently, we need to remove the contradiction involved in the objection quoted above. According to Gewirth, this can be done by distinguishing, *within* oneself, between the agent that imposes the obligation and the agent upon whom the obligation is imposed. Gewirth suggests three different models for such a separation (see 1978a: 337).

The first model distinguishes between my present self and my future selves. This makes it possible to say that the present me has duties to the future me, because, by analogy, my future selves stand to my present self as other agents stand to me.

The second model differentiates between aspects of the psyche, either on an equilibrium model—where each aspect (such as one's intellectual powers, or sociability) is to be regarded as a person to be treated equally with the other aspects; or on a hierarchical model—in which one's lower self is to be subordinated to one's higher self.

The third model treats various aspects of one's agency (such as one's freedom, or one's physical well-being) as agents that have rights against the other aspects not to be overpowered by them.

Gewirth's first consideration is valid, but open to misinterpretation. Agents, clearly, have an absolute requirement to obey the PGC and cannot waive it. This is because it is by virtue of being an agent that agents are bound by the PGC. We might, therefore, say that an agent, *as an agent per se*, imposes the PGC on itself *as any particular agent*. Thus, we might say that I, as any particular agent, have a 'duty' *to myself as an agent per se* to obey the PGC. However, this cannot be used to argue that I have duties to myself *in relation to the generic rights*. That would mean that agents cannot waive the benefits conferred on them *by* the PGC. It cannot mean this, because the PGC protects generic will claim rights of agents. Furthermore, it is important to appreciate that the absolute requirement to obey the PGC is not a duty *under* the PGC, and thus not a *moral* duty (the PGC being the supreme principle determining what is morally right, wrong, or acceptable), but a *rational* (i.e. logical) requirement (the reason why agents must obey the PGC is that they would contradict that they are agents if they do not), and it is for this reason that the requirement is not correlative to any will claim right.

As regards the second consideration, it is odd for Gewirth to make this suggestion, because he would be the first to insist that moral theory must be driven by dialectically necessary considerations. This means that it cannot be assumed that the expressions need to be accounted for just because they have currency. This must be demonstrated. Furthermore, even if they are proper, it does not follow that they have to be taken at face value, for they could be regarded as duties *in relation to oneself* deriving from one's duties *to others*. In any event, the models Gewirth suggests are fraught with difficulties.

As regards the idea that 'my future selves' may be thought of as other agents in relation to 'my present self', this is not merely subject to the objection that Gewirth himself raises (see 1978*a*: 336–7), that my 'future selves' may be as debauched as my 'present self'. The basic problem is that 'my future selves' develop from, and are extensions of, 'my present self', and this fact distinguishes relations between my 'present' and 'future selves' from my relations to others. This has a number of implications, one of which is that 'my future selves' cannot call 'my present self' to account for harming them. I might well, in the future, wish I had acted differently in the past if my past actions have left me in a state that another agent—had I so acted in relation to it—could claim was a violation of its generic rights. But, whereas another agent can claim rights against me, I can merely regret my past actions. If I could hold my 'past selves' to account, this would imply that I could never be held responsible in the future for my actions in the present. Therefore, in relation to a crucial aspect of rights claims, I cannot properly be said to have past, present, and future selves. All there is is me at different times.

As regards both the equilibrium version of the second model and the third model, the idea that particular aspects of the psyche or agency may be regarded as agents with generic rights against other aspects is untenable. These aspects are only components of agency or personality. As such, to regard the aspects as agents is to regard what is only part of agency or personality as what is sufficient for agency or personality. Furthermore, if the fact that agency requires an integration of aspects is to be used to argue that agents have duties to themselves to preserve this integration, then this can only be done by maintaining that agents have intrinsic duties to be agents. There is, however, nothing in Gewirth's argument that provides justification for this idea.[23]

Finally, as regards the hierarchical version of the second model, this is acceptable if it means no more than that one has a duty to do what is right rather than what is wrong. However, as soon as it is seen as a case of the lower self having a duty to the higher self then the problem recurs that the higher self can waive the benefits of its rights (which means that nothing is gained in the cause of unwaivable duties to oneself). If the higher self cannot release the lower self from its duties, then this can only be because generic rights are not rights under the will conception (which is contrary to the argument to the PGC) or else the duties derive from duties to others.

All in all, therefore, our view is that while agents may properly be said to have duties to develop (or try to develop) integrated psyches and not to act in ways that might be described as self-demeaning, etc., *all* such duties derive from the rights of others.

Interestingly, in *The Metaphysics of Morals* Kant raises an objection to the idea that there might be duties to oneself that is similar to the one we have quoted from Gewirth.

If the I *that imposes obligation* is taken in the same sense as the I *that is put under obligation*, a duty to oneself is a self-contradictory concept. For the concept of a duty contains the concept of being passively constrained (I am *bound*). But if the duty is a duty to myself, I think of myself as binding and so actively constraining (I, the same subject, am imposing obligation). And the proposition that asserts a duty to myself (I *ought* to bind myself) would involve being bound to bind myself (a passive obligation that was still, in the same sense of the relation, also an active obligation), and hence a contradiction. One can also bring this contradiction to light by pointing out that the one imposing obligation (*auctor obligationis*) could always release the one put under obligation (*subiectum obligationis*) from the obligation (*terminus obligationis*), so that (if both are one and the same subject) he would not be bound at all to a duty he lays upon himself. This involves a contradiction. (1991: 214)

Even more interestingly, Kant's strategy of reply is very similar to Gewirth's. First, according to Kant,

Since the law by virtue of which I regard myself as being under obligation proceeds in every case from my practical reason; in being constrained by my own reason, I am also the one constraining myself. (1991: 214)

This is well-nigh identical to the first point made by Gewirth. There is an absolute

---

[23] See, further, the reply to Franklin I. Gamwell (1984: 65) in Beyleveld (1991: 138–40).

duty to obey the Categorical Imperative, which I cannot waive. I am bound by the Categorical Imperative as something I must recognize on pain of contradicting that I am an agent, and this means that I can be said, as an agent, to impose the Categorical Imperative on myself.

Second, like Gewirth, Kant contends that the apparent contradiction incurred by the idea of duties to oneself disappears once it is appreciated that the 'I' that imposes an obligation is not the same 'I' as the 'I' upon which the obligation is imposed. However, he appeals only to the relationship between me as an agent and me as any particular agent (which is involved in both Kant's and Gewirth's first points). According to Kant, the 'I' imposing the obligation ('I' as an agent per se) is an *'intelligible being' (homo noumenon)*, in which the 'incomprehensible property of *freedom* is revealed by the influence of reason on the inner lawgiving will', whereas the 'I' upon which the obligation is imposed ('I' as any particular agent) is 'a *sensible being*' ('a *natural* being') *(homo phaenomenon)*. 'So man (taken in these two different senses) can acknowledge a duty to himself without falling into contradiction (because the concept of man is not thought in one and the same sense)' (Kant 1991: 214). In short, Kant holds that *homo noumenon* claims a right against *homo phaenomenon*, who is placed under a duty that *homo phaenomenon* cannot waive. However, while in Gewirthian theory I, *as an agent per se*, can waive the duties I place on myself *as a particular agent*, Kant appears to hold that *homo noumenon* cannot do so, for *homo noumenon* 'is regarded as a being that can be put under obligation and, indeed, under obligation to himself (to the humanity in his own person)' (p. 214). But, why must this be the case? After all, the whole problem of the contradiction arises from thinking of agents as legislating the duties they impose by their will (which implies that they can waive the duties) and so cannot impose these duties on themselves (as the duty-bearer cannot waive a duty).

It might be responded that this misportrays Kant's position. Kant is not referring to duties to oneself in general, but only to a duty to oneself to obey the Categorical Imperative. However, if this is so, then it must be pointed out that that duty is a rational one (of pure reason), not a moral one. But, just because this is the case, it is unnecessary for Kant to appeal to the distinction between agents as *homo noumenon* and *homo phaenomenon* to rescue his position from contradiction, because the contradiction only threatens when duties are seen as correlative to will claim rights (and the duty to obey the Categorical Imperative, as rational, is not correlative to a will claim right).

Reminding ourselves of the difference between the Gewirthian and Kantian visions of agency per se, might, however, help us to see why Kant might think that *homo noumenon* does not have a will claim right when it legislates duties *under* the Categorical Imperative to *homo phaenomenon*. For both Kant and Gewirth, the essence of agency is autonomy in some sense. However, for Kant, autonomy (in which human dignity as the ground of human rights resides) consists of free will. *Homo noumenon* has free will. As such, the Categorical

Imperative *and its demands in application* do not confront it as imperatives but as laws of nature. The sense in which *homo noumenon* may be said to legislate to *homo phaenomenon* does not involve the notion of choices made. And this is because Kant has the idea that free will involves determination independent of any contingent choices, values, or motivations. Such contingent properties belong only to *homo phaenomenon.* Only in relation to *homo phaenomenon* is the Categorical Imperative an imperative.[24]

On the other hand, Gewirthian theory does not conceive of the distinction between me as an agent per se and me as a particular agent in this way. My agency per se consists of those things I have *as a natural being* that are necessary for me to pursue purposes regardless of their content. My autonomy (hence my dignity), therefore, consists of my ability as a particular *natural* agent to make choices (which Kant would hold belong to *homo phaenomenon), and the auton-omy that I exercise rationally (which Kant views as belonging to *homo noumenon*) remains grounded in this ability.

To sum up. It should be clear that, in both Kantian and Gewirthian theory, to deny that one is bound by the supreme principle of morality is to deny one's dignity. For to deny that one is bound by the supreme principle of morality is not only to deny that one has moral duties, but also that one has moral rights, and dignity is primarily the property by virtue of which one has moral rights. Kant, as well as Gewirth, considers moral rights (i.e. rights under the supreme principle of morality) to be will claim rights. However, while it might be possible in Kantian theory to square this with the idea of duties to oneself under the supreme moral principle, there should be no doubt (despite some of Gewirth's comments to the contrary) that moral duties to oneself *under* the PGC have no place in Gewirthian theory.

---

[24] This is implied by Kant's view (see 1948: 78) that only to those capable of imperfection does the Categorical Imperative appear as an imperative.

6

Dignity, Rights, and Virtue under the Principle of Generic Consistency

Introduction

In this chapter, on the presumption that the PGC is the supreme principle of morality, we develop a conception of human dignity by examining the connection between having dignity and having rights, and having dignity and acting virtuously.

We will address three questions.

1. What constitutes dignity, where this is viewed as the property by virtue of which creatures have generic rights?
2. What creatures have dignity?
3. What are we to make of dignified conduct, where this is viewed as a virtue?

It might be thought that we have already answered the first question. Gewirth's argument that the PGC is dialectically necessary involves the Argument from the Sufficiency of Agency, which establishes that if 'I' (any agent) would contradict that I am an agent by not accepting that I have the generic rights, then I must accept that I have the generic rights because I am an agent. From this, it follows that I must accept that all other agents have the generic rights. Hence the property by virtue of which agents are to be granted the generic rights is their agency, and dignity as the basis of rights is constituted by the property of being an agent.

Consequently, to violate an agent's dignity is to 'act contrary to' the agent's agency. What constitutes such action is open to interpretation; but the following are clear examples of ways in which an agent's (X's) dignity can be violated:

(*a*) by denying that X is an agent (which occurs whenever X's generic rights are violated);[1]
(*b*) by denying that X is a generic-rights-bearer;
(*c*) by denying that X, as a generic-rights-bearer, has generic rights equal to those of all other agents;

---

[1] Indeed, since the PGC is dialectically necessary, the violator of X's generic rights denies its own agency (hence, violates its own dignity) by so doing. It is often said that in order to love others one must love oneself. This dictum is given a specific interpretation as well as being justified by the necessary link between denial of the perpetrator's agency and denial of the victim's agency by the perpetrator of a generic rights violation. Under the PGC all immorality is, as a denial of agency, contrary to human dignity. However, once this is appreciated, it is not illuminating to analyse all ways in which the PGC might be violated as violations of human dignity, and our discussion of violation of human dignity in Part II will be restricted to more specific ways in which it might be violated.

(d) by depriving X of the opportunity to exercise the responsibilities and duties to other agents that are correlative to being a generic-rights-bearer;[2]

(e) by interfering with X's autonomous purposivity *as such*, which characterizes X as an agent.

However, this is not the whole story, and we will argue that it is actually by virtue of *vulnerable* agency that the generic rights are to be granted. An appreciation by agents that they are vulnerable, that their ability to pursue and achieve their chosen purposes is not secure but can be threatened, is implicit in the dialectically necessary argument for the PGC. Essentially, the subjects of this argument have rational capacities that enable them to reflect upon the implications of their bodily and psychological frailties. When, which is the case with human agents, these subjects are embodied, such reflection leads them to suffer existential anxiety, the fear that bodily death leads to personal extinction. We contend that it is the capacity for such anxiety that most profoundly constitutes the dignity that grounds the generic rights.[3]

In relation to the second question, Kant claims that 'morality, and humanity, so far as it is capable of morality, is the only thing which has dignity' (1948: 96–7). Because only agents are capable of morality, Kant hereby claims that only agents have dignity. But, in addition, he implies that only some human beings are agents, thus that only some human beings have dignity.

Is this also the case in Gewirthian theory? Certainly, Gewirth's argument for the PGC establishes that being an agent[4] is sufficient to have the generic rights,[5] and thus that agency is sufficient for dignity. But is being an agent also necessary to have dignity? According to Gewirth, not only agents possess generic rights. While the PGC grants the generic rights in full to agents only, the 'Principle of Proportionality' shows that non-agents with only some of the capacities individually necessary and jointly sufficient to be agents (which we will call 'partial agents') have the generic rights in proportion to the degree to which they approach being agents (Gewirth 1978a: 121–2, and 141).

We will argue that this cannot be so, because only agents can have rights of the kind derived in Gewirth's argument for the PGC. Furthermore, the Principle of Proportionality cannot, by itself, show that agents have duties to partial agents (by virtue of which partial agents might be said to have 'quasi-generic rights') in proportion to their approach to being agents either.

Nevertheless, we will argue that agents must accept that they have *duties to* all living creatures (human or non-human) on a proportional basis.

---

[2] It is this sense that best fits, we think, the idea of a quality of life worthy of human dignity that appears in, for example, Article 4(1) of the European Social Charter in connection with the right to a minimum wage.

[3] A version of this argument was presented in Beyleveld (1999b).

[4] The vulnerability of agents is to be taken as read.

[5] Though, strictly speaking, given the dialectical nature of Gewirth's argument, one should say 'to be regarded as possessing the generic rights'. We will use the assertoric formulation as a shorthand, however.

Our argument involves approaching the matter from the perspective of *applying* the PGC to creatures in the world, rather than attempting to extend the objects of the PGC's protection from agents to partial agents. From the perspective of application, the first question to be answered concerns how creatures in the world (human beings, non-human animals, plants, and so on) are to be identified as agents or not agents.

An agent cannot know with certainty that any being other than itself is an agent. Since this is so, it might be thought that agents are not categorically required to grant the generic rights to any creatures in the world other than themselves, and that, while the PGC is categorically binding in relation to agents *in theory*, it is not categorically binding *in its practical application*. However, we will argue that this is not so. The categorically binding nature of the PGC requires agents to employ precautionary reasoning, which obliges them to presume that all creatures that behave as though they are agents are agents.

This argument, which constitutes nothing less than a moral argument for other minds, is important in its own right. However, the precautionary reasoning it involves can be applied to the case of creatures that are ostensibly only partial agents as well.

It cannot be known with certainty that apparent partial agents (those that do not display all the characteristics, structural or behavioural, expected of agents) are not agents. Thus, precaution requires agents to accept duties to apparent partial agents in proportion to the degree of evidence that they might be agents, appearances to the contrary notwithstanding.

The problem with Gewirth's position is not that he cannot show that various marginal groups (such as the unborn, very young children, the severely mentally incapacitated, non-human animals, etc.) whose status as agents is questionable (even highly unlikely in some cases) are to be accorded intrinsic moral status (though not rights), but with the reasons he has for believing this to be so. Agency-in-full is necessary for rights under the PGC, and intrinsic moral status is to be accorded to apparent non-agents, not as partial agents, but as possible agents (thus as *possible* possessors of dignity) on account of the precaution that the categorically binding nature of the PGC requires to be exercised.[6]

The moral status of children, the severely 'mentally deficient', and mentally damaged raises some special issues, which we will discuss separately, as it requires distinctions to be drawn—in particular, between partial agents, 'intermittent' agents, and 'specific-task-incompetent' agents.

In relation to the third question, we will suggest that there is a link between dignity as the ground of rights and dignity as a virtue in Gewirthian theory, which is to be found in the rational response of agents to the existential anxiety that grounds the attribution of rights.

---

[6] This argument was first developed, and is in its fullest form in Beyleveld and Pattinson (1998). The argument is also used in Beyleveld and Pattinson (2000) and Beyleveld (1999*b*; 2000*a*).

Various strategies are open to agents to alleviate their existential anxiety. One approach involves denying that the self is mortal. An opposed approach involves resignation to, or even embrace of, personal mortality. However, not only does reason not permit either metaphysical proposition to be affirmed, but (or so we will argue) existential anxiety underpins the moral project. Consequently, in imposing a categorical imperative on human agents, reason requires them not to try to overcome their fear of personal mortality yet to hope that they have immortal selves.

Our argument for this will proceed in two stages. In the first stage we will reconstruct Kant's moral argument for the existence of God and immortality to show that the premiss that there is a categorical imperative does not permit the existence of God and immortality to be denied. In the second stage, we will deconstruct Leibniz's claim that if God exists then this must be the best of all possible worlds to show that the premiss that there is a categorical imperative does not permit belief in the existence of God and immortality.

We will suggest that to have a dignified character is to possess a personality in which fear of personal extinction and hope of immortality are in equilibrium, and that dignified conduct is conduct that exhibits such a personality. This suggests a degree of rapprochement between dignity as the basis of human rights (central to Gewirthian theory) and dignity as a property of virtuous conduct (which is associated, more centrally, with both virtue ethics and the elitist 'tradition of the nobles'). This is because being able to display fortitude in the face of adversity (which is a paradigmatic example of dignified conduct in these traditions) is, on the basis of our analysis of having a dignified character, also to be considered virtuous under the PGC.[7]

Dignity and Vulnerable Agency

An intelligible discourse of practical reason needs more than a population of agents considered as beings with the capacity to direct their actions voluntarily towards purposes they have chosen. It supposes that these agents are vulnerable in a number of ways. Most obviously it rests on

1. a capacity of agents to act against the dictates of the moral law. Kant was surely right to assert that to angels, who have no temptation to act against the dictates of the Categorical Imperative, this principle does not appear as an imperative but as a law of nature (see 1948: 78);
2. insecurity of agents, their ability to perceive at least the possibility of their being harmed (i.e. being deprived of the means to pursue or achieve their chosen purposes), or of lacking the means to pursue or achieve their chosen purposes.

---

[7] A less developed version of this argument was presented in Beyleveld (1999*b*).

As we have presented Gewirth's argument, 'I' (the agent who is the subject of the argument) am required to claim that the sufficient reason why I have the generic rights is that I am an agent. It is important, however, to appreciate that it is implicit that agents are vulnerable. While it is true that 'I' (as such a vulnerable agent) must claim that my being an agent is the sufficient reason why I have the generic rights, the argument cannot be applied to non-vulnerable agents (if such can exist). Having the powers of agency is necessary, but it is not sufficient, to generate a need for the objects of rights. Agents have purposes they choose to pursue (by virtue of which they value these purposes), and this value is proactive (i.e. it motivates them to pursue the ends valued). That their capacity to value purposes leads to their having to claim rights, however, requires that they perceive their means to achieve their purposes, and specifically their generic capacities to achieve their purposes, to be insecure. In short, the generic *capacities* must be perceived to be generic *needs*. The most fundamental of these generic needs are the very capacity to reason and make choices, life itself, and mental equilibrium sufficient to translate a wish for something into activity designed to obtain what is wished for.

There are, essentially, two properties that *human* agents have as subjects and objects of intelligible practical precepts. The first property is consciousness of a kind that is capable of reflecting upon itself and its conditions (which, essentially, grounds the capacities for reasoning, practical and theoretical, of human agents *as* agents). The second property is physical embodiment in space and time. In consequence of this second property, a human agent reflecting upon its consciousness can also reflect upon the relationship between its consciousness and symbolic inner identity (its self), and its physical body. The consequence is existential anxiety or dread, fear of extinction of one's self. This is a central theme in theology and existentialism, and also in humanist analytic psychology. Ernest Becker, summarizing his understanding of Kierkegaard's work (see e.g. Kierkegaard 1954, 1980), while also presenting his own view, puts it like this.

[According to Kierkegaard,] man is a union of opposites, of self-consciousness and physical body. Man emerged from the instinctive thoughtless action of the lower animals and came to reflect on his condition. He was given a consciousness of his individuality and his part divinity in creation, the beauty and uniqueness of his face and name. At the same time he was given the consciousness of the terror of the world and of his own death and decay. This paradox is the really constant thing about man in all periods of history and society; it is thus the true 'essence' of man . . . The fall into self-consciousness, the emergence from comfortable ignorance in nature, had one great penalty for man: it gave him *dread*, or anxiety. . . . Man's anxiety is a function of his sheer ambiguity and of his complete powerlessness to overcome that ambiguity, to be straightforwardly an animal or an angel. . . . But the real focus of dread is not the ambiguity itself . . . the final terror of self-consciousness is the knowledge of one's own death. (Becker 1973: 69–70)

Compare Erich Fromm.

Man is the only animal who not only knows objects but who knows that he knows. Man is the only animal who has not only instrumental intelligence, but reason . . . . Gifted with self-awareness and reason, man is aware of himself as being separate from nature and from others; he is aware of his powerlessness, of his ignorance; he is aware of his end: death. . . . He is part of nature, subject to her physical laws and unable to change them, yet he transcends nature. . . . He is never free from the dichotomy of his existence: he cannot rid himself of his mind, even if he would want to; he cannot rid himself of his body as long as he is alive—and his body makes him want to be alive. . . . I propose that man's nature . . . [can only be defined] in terms of fundamental contradictions that characterise human existence and have their root in the biological dichotomy between missing instincts and self-awareness. Man's existential conflict produces certain psychic needs common to all men. He is forced to overcome the horror of separateness, of powerlessness, and of lostness, and find new forms of relating himself to the world to enable him to feel at home. (1974: 225–6)

Whereas, for Fromm, the source of anxiety is fundamentally the ambiguity, for Becker it is the fear of death *simpliciter.* Consequently, Becker develops the thesis that it is only through psychological repression of their mortality, or through various myths of immortality, that human beings can make life bearable. Fromm, on the other hand, maintains that various strategies that involve a flight from freedom (and the responsibility this entails), or from reason itself (as the source of the existential conflict), can also be successful (see, in particular, Fromm 1942).

We draw attention to this tradition, because, provided that its concern is focused properly, it provides considerable insight into the concept of dignity as the basis of human rights in theories that locate the essence of dignity in agency.

To focus it properly, we must consider the existential ambiguity not just as an empirically observed fact about the behaviour of human beings, but as something inherent in the nature of human agents *as* subjects and objects of practical precepts. As such, we must modify some of the statements Fromm and Becker make.

First (for reasons we will give later on), we should not assume as readily as they (and, indeed, Kant) do that human beings alone are agents.

Second, we should be more hesitant than they are to affirm that human agents have mortal *selves.* If we reflect soundly on the limits of our reason in relation to metaphysical matters concerning the relationship between the body and the self, then we must admit that we cannot *know* that bodily extinction does (or does not) lead to extinction of the self. No amount of observation of what happens to physical bodies other than our own at bodily death can tell us anything about what happens to the psyches presumed to exist with those bodies, unless we identify the having of a self with observable behaviour. Certainly, we cannot know what happens to our own psyches until this happens (and maybe not even then). All the scientific knowledge we have about the relation between mind and body is really only knowledge of the correlation between body and observable behaviour presumed to be mental (in others) and between body and subjective experience (in ourselves). To interpret this as knowledge of the real relationship between mind and body is to presume metaphysical propositions about the relationship between mind and body (and 'mental' behaviour) that cannot be validated in any way and which are not self-justifying.[8] Thus, we should side with Fromm against Becker that what is central to the existential condition of human agents is not that they *know* that *they* are fated to die,[9] but anxiety about this outcome. However, this anxiety should be attributed to human agents *as* intelligible subjects and objects of practical precepts, not as a general contingent fact about them. This is because it is difficult to see how beings who lack *any* concern about threats to their agency could be motivated to care about their physical lives and other generic conditions of agency in a way that would make them agents.

However, this line of reasoning implies that what makes being a vulnerable agent at least the sufficient condition of having generic rights is that vulnerable agents are subject to existential anxiety concerning the possibility of extinction of their selves. The capacity for existential anxiety is, thus, the facet of their vulnerable agency that constitutes the dignity of human agents as the ground of their generic rights.

Gewirth's Argument for the Rights of Partial Agents

According to Gewirth, although being an agent is sufficient to possess generic rights, it is not necessary. Being an agent is necessary as well as sufficient only for having the generic rights *in full*. Application of the 'Principle of Proportionality' shows that partial agents, who possess only some of the properties necessary to be an agent, have generic rights in proportion to how closely they approach being agents. Hence, various marginal groups that do not display the properties sufficient for them to be regarded as agents (such as the newly born, very young children, the severely mentally deficient, and non-human animals) nevertheless have at least some of the generic rights.

Gewirth's Principle of Proportionality is as follows.

> When some quality Q justifies having certain rights R, and the possession of Q varies in degree in the respect that is relevant to Q's justifying the having of R, the degree to which R is had is proportional to or varies with the degree to which Q is had. Thus, if x units of Q justify that one have x units of R, then y units of Q justify that one have y units of R. (Gewirth 1978*a*: 121)

According to Gewirth, this principle is necessarily true. It is dialectically

---

[8] These are very sweeping assertions. We will not attempt to justify them here. Were we to attempt to do so, we would, in general approach at least, follow the analysis presented of such matters by Immanuel Kant in his *Critique of Pure Reason* (Kant 1934).

[9] Though they have overwhelming reason to believe that their physical bodies are so doomed. This is not merely because of inductive evidence concerning the fate of known humans. We suggest that physical decay is part of the concept of being a physical object existing in space and time.

necessary for agents to regard being an agent as sufficient justification for having the generic rights in full. Therefore, that it is dialectically necessary for agents to grant the generic rights in part to partial agents in proportion to how close they are to being agents is demonstrated simply by substituting 'being an agent' for Q and 'the generic rights' for R in this principle.

However, this principle (as stated) is not necessarily true. It is necessarily true that, when having Q justifies having R, and the possession of Q varies in degree in the respect that is relevant to having Q's justifying the having of R, the degree to which R is had is *a function* of the degree to which Q is had. However, it does not follow (without further conditions being imposed) that having R is *such a* function of having Q that, if having x units of Q justifies that one has x units of R, then having y units of Q justifies that one has y units of R for *all* values of x and y.

It is also better to make explicit the conditions that must be satisfied for possession of Q to vary in degree in the respect that is relevant to having Q justifying having R. Thus, with it being understood that R can be any property at all, the Principle of Proportionality should be stated as

When having some quality Q justifies having some property R, and the extent of having Q *sufficient* to justify having R in full is *not necessary* to justify having R to any extent at all, the degree to which R is had is a function of the degree to which Q is had.

As we saw in Chapter 4, the Argument from the Sufficiency of Agency (ASA) (Gewirth 1978a: 109–10) shows that being an agent (defined as having purposes that one acts for) is necessary and sufficient for having the generic rights *in full*. While having purposes that one acts for is an *invariant* relational property, to have this property it is necessary to have the generic capacities of agency and possession of these can vary in degree. Agents have all the generic capacities of agency to the degree needed to have this relational property, but partial agents possess the generic capacities of agency to a lesser extent. Gewirth claims that the Principle of Proportionality shows that the degree to which partial agents have the generic rights depends upon the degree to which they possess the generic capacities of agency.

This may sound plausible, but it is false. Having the generic capacities of agency to the degree needed to be an agent is not only necessary (and sufficient) to have the generic rights *in full* (so that agents with the generic capacities of agency to degrees greater than that needed to be an agent cannot, thereby, acquire the generic rights to a *greater* extent), *it is necessary to have any generic rights at all*. This is because, as derived, the generic rights are rights under the will conception of rights; i.e. those who have them can always, by their free choice, waive the benefits that exercise of the generic rights entitles them to—provided only that they do not, thereby, neglect or violate their duties to other agents. This is not a function of an arbitrary espousal of the will conception of rights. It derives from the fact that, in the dialectically necessary argument to the PGC, agents are required to claim the generic rights for themselves, not because they are required to value the generic needs for their own sakes, but because they are instrumental to their pursuit or achievement of their purposes whatever these might be. But, in order to be able to freely waive the benefits of a right, one must have the capacities needed to be an agent. Thus, partial agents cannot have any generic rights.

This objection cannot be evaded by acknowledging that partial agents cannot have any generic rights *strictly speaking*, and claiming, instead, that the Principle of Proportionality nonetheless shows that partial agents have 'quasi-generic rights' (unwaivable protections correlative to duties of agents not to harm partial agents, or to assist them in need) in proportion to their approach to being agents. The Principle of Proportionality can only license inferences about the *quantity* of possession of a property; it cannot (by itself) license inferences that *alter the quality* of what is predicated. To claim that the Principle of Proportionality licenses inferring that, because agents have the generic rights in full, partial agents have quasi-generic rights to some extent, is to commit 'the fallacy of disparateness'.[10] To have a quasi-generic right is not to have a generic right to some extent. It is to have a different quality of protection from that granted by a generic right.

Thus, if it remains possible that it might be dialectically necessary for various 'marginal groups', members of which do not appear to be agents but only partial agents (on the best evidence available) to be granted quasi-generic rights, this cannot be because the Principle of Proportionality, operating on the premiss that agents are to be granted the generic rights, requires partial agents to be accorded quasi-generic rights.

Precautionary Reasoning and Duties to Marginal Groups

If Gewirth's argument for the generic rights of (or at least duties to) partial agents were valid, then the correct statement of the PGC would not be that agents must act in accordance with the generic rights of all agents, but that they must also act in accordance with the generic (or quasi-generic) rights of all partial agents (which are proportional to the degree to which partial agents approach being agents). His argument would affect the ontology of his theory, the abstract categories of being that are the direct objects of the PGC's protection.

We have shown that such modification of the PGC and its ontology cannot be justified. It is possible, however, to approach the matter differently, not by altering or extending the argument *for* the PGC, but by attending to considerations that are involved in applying the PGC's abstract ontology to real objects in the world (that is to say, in judging that a being is or is not an agent).

---

[10] Which Gewirth (1960: 313), himself, has formulated. This fallacy is committed where fields or subject matters are compared on disparate levels or in disparate respects.

The way in which Gewirth defines agency is not a generalization from the empirically observable characteristics of human beings (or any other creatures) assumed to be agents, but is a function of the characteristics that beings must be presumed to have if they are to be thought of intelligibly as subjects and objects of practical precepts. Gewirth defines agents as he does because it is only for beings with the capacity to direct their actions voluntarily towards purposes they have chosen that questions arise about what practical precepts may or should be followed, and it is only to such beings that practical precepts can be directed rationally. Consequently, Gewirth's operative concept of an agent is immune from objections derived from empirical psychology. However, this raises a serious question about how any agent can know that there are any other agents in the world. This is because the capacities of agency are in part mental attributes that 'I' (any agent) cannot observe directly in other beings. Although I know that I am an agent directly, and this is not something I can be mistaken about, the best I can do, when trying to determine whether or not some other being X is an agent, is to construct a model of the behaviour to be expected of an agent, and test X's behaviour against it. But, even if X exhibits all the behaviour and characteristics expected of an agent (as most adult members of the human species do) and is *ostensibly* an agent, this does not *prove* that X *is* an agent. It is *possible* that X is a programmed automaton without a mind, and no amount of empirical observation of X's behaviour and characteristics will be able to prove otherwise. The relevance of empirical evidence cited for X's mental status depends on metaphysical assumptions. In short, the problem of knowing whether or not another being is an agent is a special case of the age-old philosophical problem of other minds.

Gewirth's great achievement is to have demonstrated that the PGC is the supreme moral imperative categorically binding upon agents, and thus that all agents categorically must grant the generic rights to all other agents. However, unless agents can identify other beings as agents *categorically*, it is open to a sceptic to concede Gewirth's achievement but then contend that the achievement has no *practical* application, because I can deny that there are any other agents at all in the world without contradicting that I am an agent.

If the sceptic is seeking to deny that there are any agents in the world, then there are a number of good responses available. First, such a position is virtually impossible to sustain in practice. To sustain it, I must refrain from prescribing anything to any other being. I cannot impose duties on others, or think that there are any beings against whom I can claim the generic rights that I must claim for myself. Indeed, I cannot engage in any discourse of reasons with any being other than myself.

Second, while it might not be dialectically necessary for me to consider that there are any agents other than myself, it would certainly be irrational for me to deny that there are any agents other than myself on the criteria that govern everyday life. Recourse to solipsism is a high price to pay to be able to deny that the PGC has *any* force in its practical application.

Third, the lack of a dialectically necessary application of the PGC would not place the PGC at any disadvantage compared with any other practical principle or moral theory, simply because the denial that there are any other agents will affect any scheme of practical prescriptions equally.

However, our sceptic need not be taken as denying that there are other agents, but can be taken merely as asserting that Gewirth's achievement in demonstrating that I am categorically required to grant the generic rights to all other agents does not show that I am categorically required to grant the generic rights to any creatures other than myself. This more modest assertion is, however, also mistaken.

A Moral Argument for Other Minds

Everything that our sceptic wishes to assert may be conceded to the point of agreeing (*even where* X, on the basis of its behaviour and other characteristics, appears to be an agent) that the propositions 'X is an agent' and 'X is not an agent' are on a par with respect to an ability to demonstrate categorically *the truth* of either. However, these propositions are not on a par *morally*. If I mistakenly presume X to be an agent, then, although this will lead me (mistakenly) to have to restrict my behaviour towards X to some extent, I do not thereby deny my (or any other agent's) status as a generic-rights-holder. But, if I mistakenly presume X not to be an agent, then I deny that X (an agent) is a generic-rights-holder.

Gewirth's argument for the PGC, however, shows that agents are categorically required to treat all agents as generic-rights-holders. Thus, to presume that X is an agent runs no risk of violating the PGC, whereas to presume that X is not an agent runs this risk. But, under the assumption that the PGC is categorically binding, there can be no justification under any circumstances whatsoever for violating it. Thus, to risk the possibility of violating the PGC, *when this can be avoided*, is itself to violate the PGC. Therefore, it is categorically necessary to do whatever one can to avoid this consequence (provided, of course, that the actions taken do not conflict with more important requirements to be derived from the PGC).

Where X displays the behaviour expected of an agent, we might say that X is 'ostensibly an agent' or an 'ostensible agent'. When X is an ostensible agent, by the very nature of the case, it is possible to treat X as an agent. In this case at least, it is possible to avoid the risk *altogether* of mistakenly denying that X is an agent, by presuming X to be an agent and acting accordingly. Hence, it follows that it is categorically necessary to accept

> Where X is an ostensible agent, the metaphysical possibility that X might not be an agent is to be wholly discounted and X's ostensible agency is to be taken as sufficient evidence that X has the capacities needed to be an agent.

Thus, agents do contradict that they are agents if they do not grant the generic

rights to all ostensible agents, and the PGC is categorical in its practical application. By the same token, the dialectical necessity of the PGC entails that it is
dialectically necessary for agents to consider that creatures that display the capacities of agents have minds. Thus, this argument provides a moral argument for the
existence of other minds.

Implicit in the reasoning to this conclusion, which is nothing other than a
version of Pascal's Wager[11] applied under the constraints imposed by the assumption that the PGC is categorically binding, is the following Precautionary
Principle.

> If there is no way of knowing whether or not X has property P, then, in so
> far as it is possible to do so, X must be assumed *to have* property P if the
> consequences of erring in presuming that X *does not have* P are worse than
> those of erring in presuming that X *has* P (and X must be assumed *not to
> have* P if the consequences of erring in presuming that X *has* P are worse
> than those of assuming that X *does not have* P).[12]

Proportionality under Precaution and Duties to Apparent Partial Agents

Suppose, however, that X exhibits (and, as far as I am able to ascertain, only
exhibits in its behaviour or associated characteristics) capacities of agency to a
degree *less than* those of an ostensible agent, by virtue of which X is apparently
only a partial agent. Although X is apparently only a partial agent, *because the
proposition that another creature is an agent is a metaphysical one and human
reason is limited in such matters*, I cannot infer that X *is not* an agent. Just as I
cannot *know with certainty* that X *is* an agent when X is an ostensible agent, so I
cannot *know with certainty* that X *is not* an agent when X is apparently only a
partial agent. So, even though X is apparently only a partial agent, there remains
a risk that if I suppose that X is not an agent, and act accordingly, X is an agent,
and I will have deprived X of the protection of the PGC to which X is categorically entitled. Thus, it is categorically necessary, *all things being equal*, to do
whatever one can do to avoid this consequence, and this will require me to recognize duties not to harm and to protect X.

---

[11] According to Pascal, reason cannot demonstrate either that God exists or that God does not exist.
Even so, there is a choice between believing in or not believing in God (or, at least, of acting in accordance with belief or non-belief). 'Let us weigh up the gain and the loss involved in calling heads that
God exists. . . . if you win you win everything, if you lose you lose nothing' (Pascal 1966: 151). One
must, therefore, wager that God exists. While the underlying principle is sound—that, when there is
a choice between two equally likely outcomes, one only of which is infinitely disastrous, one must
choose the course that avoids that disaster—this is unsuccessful as an argument for believing in God
(or for acting as though one believes in God). First, belief is not something that can be commanded.
Second, the idea that God (at least when conceived of as perfectly good *and* omnipotent) could require
belief in It, or action as though one believes in It (by which Pascal has in mind going to church, etc.),
on pain of infinite penalty, is ridiculous.

[12] Because of its link to the *categorically binding* moral law, this principle is categorically binding
itself.

Suppose, then, that it is categorically necessary (under precautionary reasoning) for me to recognize duties of protection to X and Z (both of whom are apparently only partial agents). What am I required to do if these duties come into conflict?

All other things being equal, such conflicts are to be handled by a criterion of avoidance of more probable harm, according to which

> If my doing y to Z is more likely to cause harm h to Z than my doing y to X (and I cannot avoid doing y to one of Z or X) then I ought to do y to X rather than to Z.

Where y is failing to observe a particular duty of protection, and h is mistakenly denying a being the status of an agent, we can infer by this criterion that

> If my failing to observe a particular duty of protection to Z is more likely to mistakenly deny Z the status of an agent than is my failing to observe this duty of protection to X (and I cannot avoid failing to observe this duty to one of Z or X) then I ought to fail to observe my duty to X rather than to Z.

Since I am more likely to mistakenly deny that a creature is an agent the more probable it is that the creature is an agent, it follows that my duties of protection to those who are more probably agents take precedence over my duties of protection to those who are less probably agents.

The moral status of a creature may be measured by the weight to be given to the duties of protection owed to it by an agent. It follows that the moral status of creatures who are more probably agents is greater than that of creatures who are less probably agents. In other words, the moral status of creatures is *proportional* to the probability that they are agents.

Given that X's display of all the capacities of agency must (under precautionary reasoning guided by a categorical imperative) be viewed as sufficient evidence that X is an agent, it follows that if X displays some, but not all, of the capacities of agency, then this must be viewed as less than sufficient evidence (but evidence nonetheless) that X is an agent. In other words, where X is an ostensible agent, the probability that X is an agent must be taken to be 1; but, where X is apparently only a partial agent, the probability that X is an agent must be taken to be greater than 0 but less than 1 in proportion to the capacities of agency that X displays.

Thus, we establish the following conclusion.

> Apparent partial agents are owed duties of protection by agents in proportion to the degree to which they approach being ostensible agents—not *qua* partial agents—but *qua* possible agents.

The behaviour that living beings are capable of exhibiting can be classified in a number of ways. The following sort of classification is particularly relevant to bioethics and biolaw.

    (I) Patterned behaviour of the kind produced by all living organisms.

   (II) Behaviour that evinces purposivity (motivation by feeling or desire).

  (III) Behaviour that displays intelligence (capacity to learn by experience).

  (IV) Behaviour that exhibits rationality (value-guided behaviour, which is characteristic of agency).

If the argument we have presented is sound, then I must consider creatures capable of exhibiting Category IV behaviour to be agents with a moral status equal to my own, on the grounds that (under precaution) such behaviour is sufficient evidence to justify the attribution of agent status.[13] Those whose behaviour is restricted to Category I are to be accorded less moral status, on the grounds that this behaviour is insufficient evidence that they are agents. As beings acquire Category II and III behaviour, however, they are to be accorded progressively greater moral status, on the grounds that such a progression provides increasingly better evidence for status as an agent.[14]

Do Categories I–III have any absolute moral significance? That is to say, might it be the case that, until a creature reaches a certain stage (perhaps II or III), the status secured for it by proportionality reasoning under precaution may be discounted for all practical purposes?

It seems to us that proportionality under precaution *alone* does not enable us to draw any such conclusion. What it provides is an entirely relative ordering. Because denial of an agent's status as a generic-rights-holder is the ultimate prohibition under the PGC, and is to be avoided if at all possible, it follows that, *unless* the morally protected needs of a being of higher moral status require it, even the creature of least moral status must not be interfered with. Indeed, if it is at all coherently conceivable that a creature could be an agent, then it must be protected unless there are countervailing considerations.[15]

---

   [13] In Beyleveld (1998*b*: 250–1) uncertainty about whether beings like chimpanzees or dolphins might be agents is held to confer moral status on them by means of precautionary reasoning. In that suggestion, precautionary reasoning is applied to uncertainty about whether the behavioural evidence is sufficient to establish that the subject is an ostensible agent or only an apparent partial agent. In the present application, that the behavioural evidence is sufficient to establish that a being is an apparent partial agent (or an ostensible agent, as the case might be) is not in doubt. The relevant uncertainty is over whether, despite what the evidence indicates, the being might (or might not, as the case might be) be an agent.

   [14] Such proportionality reasoning may be extended to within at least some of these categories. For example, those exhibiting Category III behaviour (*but who fall short of exhibiting Category IV behaviour*) are to be accorded greater moral status according to the greater intelligence they exhibit.

   [15] In principle, conflicts between the duties owed to apparent partial agents and duties owed to other beings are to be adjudicated by use of a needs calculus that weighs the risk of relevant harm under the categorical imperative to the apparent partial agent of action to protect the relevant needs of the conflicting party (or parties) (taking into account the relevant 'utility' of such action to the conflicting party) against the risk of relevant harm to the conflicting party of action to protect the relevant needs of the apparent partial agent (taking into account the relevant utility of such action to the apparent partial agent). (See Beyleveld 2000*a* for an indication of some of the complexities involved in applying this calculus under the PGC.)

Finally, it is worth noting that precautionary reasoning requires agents to grant some moral status to creatures that appear to be potential agents. This is *because evidence that a being E is a potential ostensible* [16] *agent is evidence relevant to the probability that E is an agent.* Thus, precautionary reasoning also supports the following claims.

(1) Evidence that E is a potential ostensible agent, *by itself*, requires agents to grant E moral status (in proportion to the strength of this evidence); and

(2) Evidence that E is a potential ostensible agent adds to the moral status secured for E by the degree to which E exhibits the characteristics and behaviour expected of an agent. Thus, if F is apparently only a partial agent with f moral status (by virtue of the extent to which F displays the characteristics and behaviour expected of an agent) *but not apparently a potential agent*, and E is apparently a partial agent with e moral status *and also apparently a potential agent*, then agents must take more seriously the possibility that E is an agent than that F is an agent, by virtue of which their duties of protection to E are greater than their duties of protection to F. (And, of course, the degree to which evidence of potential to become an agent adds to E's moral status is proportional to the strength of this evidence.) [17]

It is important to be clear about what the precautionary argument does and does not establish. It does not establish that agents owe duties to partial agents or potential agents (who are still non-agents) in proportion to the degree to which they approach being agents. We do not believe that agents can be shown to owe any duties *to* non-agents *as such* (though they may have duties *in relation to* them, which derive indirectly from their duties to agents when these agents have particular relationships with non-agents). [18] The argument shows, instead, that agents owe duties to all creatures whose agency is uncertain (which really includes all living beings) in proportion to the degree to which they display evidentially the necessary capacities and characteristics of agents. Thus, it is not to a dog *qua* partial agent that an agent owes duties, but to the dog *qua* possible agent. On the assumption that marginal groups are not agents, they are owed no duties. But, the point is that agents cannot know that marginal groups are not

---

[16] Evidence that E is a potential ostensible agent is, under precaution, to be taken as sufficient evidence that E is at least a potential agent, just as the evidence that constitutes E being an ostensible agent is to be taken as sufficient evidence that E is an agent.

[17] The weakest evidence that one can have that E is a potential ostensible agent is that E is a member of a species S (some of) whose members develop into ostensible agents under specified conditions. To this can be added knowledge of correlations between possession of E's specific characteristics and development into ostensible agents by members of S. All factors of this kind being equal, the further E develops in the direction of becoming an ostensible agent, the more confident one can be that E will develop the whole way. Thus, considerations of evidence for potential and considerations of evidence of degree of approach to being an agent are not wholly independent.

[18] See, further, ch. 4 nn. 23 and 24 above.

agents with sufficient certainty to satisfy the demands of a categorical moral imperative to grant rights to agents. Hence agents may never assume categorically that marginal groups are non-agents, even if that is what the available evidence most strongly indicates.

This has important implications: namely,

(a) marginal groups that are apparently no more than partial agents are to be regarded as having intrinsic moral status, because the possibility that they are agents (and thus possess dignity and generic rights) cannot be ruled out entirely;

(b) the intrinsic moral status of marginal groups varies in degree in proportion to how closely they approach being ostensible agents;

(c) the PGC grants intrinsic moral status to all living human beings (biologically defined) (because there is sufficient evidence that all living human beings are at least partial agents). Consequently, if our argument for the PGC from the acceptance of human rights (presented in Chapter 4) is valid, then the human rights conventions and instruments logically should grant protection (though not necessarily will claim rights) not only to human *agents*, but also to all living humans, animals, and even plants to at least some degree.[19]

Does this mean that marginal groups as well as ostensible agents are to be considered as having dignity? If we regard possession of intrinsic moral status as possession of dignity, then marginal groups must be held to have dignity—which, furthermore, will vary in degree. However, if we think of dignity as the property by virtue of which beings have generic rights (and this is the primary way in which we are approaching the matter), then marginal groups (human or not) are not to be thought of as possessing dignity (only as possibly possessing it); and dignity so viewed does not vary in degree. A distinction must, then, be drawn between possessing intrinsic moral status and possessing dignity. There is no problem with such a distinction, because attribution of intrinsic moral status (which correlates with duties *to* a being) can correlate *either* with attribution of the generic rights (attribution of dignity, incapable of varying in degree) *or* with duties to protect possible possession of dignity when generic rights cannot be attributed (capable of varying in degree).

Although the general principles of precautionary reasoning are clear, children, the 'mentally deficient', and the mentally damaged have some special features that need to be attended to if precautionary reasoning is to be applied correctly to them.

---

[19] We see no reason why androids and 'non-living' beings exhibiting 'artificial' intelligence, if they exhibit certain other capacities (such as feelings), should not also qualify.

The Moral Status of Children, the 'Mentally Deficient', and the Mentally Damaged[20]

Our analysis has, thus far, assumed that a being is either an agent or not an agent. At any particular instant this must be so. However, it is possible for a being that has developed the capacities of agency to lose them and then regain them (and, perhaps, lose them again). Such a being will be an intermittent agent. Furthermore, whether or not we are actually dealing with an agent, that being may display the capacities of agency only intermittently, hence be an ostensible intermittent agent.

Intermittent display of agency sometimes characterizes the behaviour of persons recovering from certain kinds of stroke or other severe brain injuries. It also sometimes characterizes the behaviour of persons with severe mental illness. It is also exhibited by young children during their development, who can at times appear to be capable of rational thought, only to appear to lose this capacity temporarily.

As far as the moral status of intermittent agents *as such* is concerned, they have dignity and the generic rights when they are agents and lack these when they are not. However, it does not follow that if a human being X is ostensibly only an intermittent agent then X is to be treated as having the generic rights only some of the time (while X displays agency).

If we are to treat an ostensible intermittent agent X as an intermittent agent (i.e. as having no generic rights at one time, and all the generic rights at another time) we will need to know whether, at any particular time, X is a partial agent or an agent.

Suppose, then, that we attempt to assess X's status vis-à-vis having the generic rights (i.e. vis-à-vis having dignity). We will find ourselves confronted with at least two serious difficulties. Whatever the result of our test, it cannot be used to justify treating X according to that result for, by the very nature of the case, X might have altered status in the meantime. Furthermore, in order to assess X's status, various procedures will have to be gone through, and the moral permissibility of such procedures will rest, to some extent, on X's status. For these reasons, we will not be able to find out what X's status is in advance of particular interactions.

Of course, while we cannot seek to ascertain X's status at any instant, we might be able to assess, over a moderate period of time, how close X is to having the capacities needed to be an agent in a standing fashion. Thus, it is tempting to say that, if X, over a moderate period of time, more reliably displays the capacities needed to be an agent than does Y, then X is to be accorded more status than Y.

However, while this is not incorrect, it is unclear just how X and Y are to be

---

[20] Most of the analysis in this subsection is taken from Beyleveld and Pattinson (1998).

treated, and it is important that the idea that X and Y are to be treated as having different status not be misunderstood.

If X is an agent, the PGC requires us to grant full dignity to X. The first duty that agents have under the PGC is to grant its protection to agents. *If X is an agent and agents do not grant X the generic rights*, then they have violated the PGC. Since the requirement to obey the PGC is absolutely categorical, it might seem that the PGC requires agents to treat X as an agent to the extent that it is possible to do so, unless it is absolutely certain that X *is not* an agent.

However, matters are not quite so simple. For, *if agents assume that X is an agent*, and try to treat X accordingly *and X is not in fact an agent*, then they will be attempting to impose duties on X that X is unable to discharge (in particular, the duty to abide by the PGC). Furthermore, in cases where the interests of X come into conflict with the generic rights of agents, agents may be required to restrict their exercise of the generic rights for the sake of generic rights that X is presumed to have, but does not have. Thus, it might seem that agents should not treat X as an agent unless it is absolutely certain that X *is* an agent.

However, since we cannot know (at the relevant point in time) whether X is an agent or a partial agent, we must apply precautionary reasoning. This reveals that the apparent antinomy is not real. The negative consequences of an error *in failing to grant* X *the generic rights* are not commensurable with the negative consequences of an error *in granting* X *the generic rights*. The burdens that are placed on agents by restricting their actions in relation to X, on the basis of the presumption that X is an agent when X is not, do not deny the generic rights to agents. What will be restricted is various actions that agents can perform as an exercise of the generic rights, not the generic rights themselves. Furthermore, if it is an error to grant X the generic rights, thereby placing burdens on X that X cannot discharge, then this is not something that affects X's generic rights (for if it is an error, X has no generic rights). It is, therefore, under the PGC, worse to err in assuming that X is not an agent than to err in assuming that X is an agent. Thus, *for practical purposes*, precautionary reasoning requires that X be assumed to be an agent.

That said, partial agents and intermittent agents must not be confused with agents who lack competence to perform specific tasks without unintentionally harming themselves or others ('specific-task-incompetent agents'). All agents lack competence to perform some specific tasks, and their task competence varies. Consequently, although all agents have all the generic rights equally, it does not follow that they all have equal rights to perform specific tasks. For example, the fact that X and Y are agents with all the generic rights equally does not give X and Y an equal right to be airline pilots, or even an equal right to train as airline pilots. This, however, does not impact on their possession of the generic rights. It impacts, rather, on their right to exercise the generic rights for particular purposes, which does not depend on their having the capacities needed to be agents (to be able to act at all), but on their having the capacities beyond this that are necessary for the successful performance of particular actions only.

The tasks that an agent must be able to perform without unintentionally harming itself or others vary from society to society. Thus, specific task competences that an agent must achieve to enable it to lead an independent existence without unintentionally harming itself or others will vary from society to society. We may designate as 'societally competent agents' those agents who have achieved such a level of task competence (the level of competence to be expected of a normal adult) relative to the demands of life in their particular society.

With this in mind, we can be more precise about how ostensible intermittent agents are to be treated. If X is an ostensible intermittent agent then X will sometimes not be able to exercise intentional control over its actions, and sometimes will behave in ways that cause unintended harm to itself or others because of its inherent inability at these times ostensibly to *act*. In relation to specific actions, generally ostensible intermittent agents will behave no differently from the way in which ostensible specific-task-incompetent agents will act. So ostensible intermittent agents are, in practice, to be treated as societally incompetent agents— agents of restricted task competence who (as agents) possess all the generic rights, but lack the capacities of agency to the degree necessary for them to be able to cope independently with some of the 'normal' interaction situations they are likely to encounter in their social environment without causing unintended harm to themselves or others.

With this as background, it is useful to examine what Gewirth himself has to say about the status of children and mentally deficient humans.

According to Gewirth,

Children are potential agents in that, with normal maturation, they will attain the characteristics of control, choice, knowledge, and reflective intention that enter into the generic features of action. A potential agent is not the same as a prospective agent, for the latter already has the proximate abilities of the generic features of action even if he is not occurrently acting. Insofar as children are not such prospective agents, they are not among the recipients whose right to freedom the PGC requires agents to respect fully. But insofar as children are potential agents, they have rights that are preparatory for their taking on the generic rights pertaining to full-fledged agency. In keeping with these preparatory rights, the PGC requires that children be given a kind of upbringing that will enable them to become both agents who can make their behavior conform to the PGC and prospective agents whose generic rights must be respected by agents. The preparatory rights include as much respect for freedom and well-being as is consistent with the goal of agency. Hence, children must increasingly participate actively in decisions affecting themselves as they increase in maturity. Rules providing for education, parental guidance, and other policies and institutions affecting children are justified and indeed required because of their contribution to such fostering of children's having the generic abilities and rights of action. (1978a: 141)

Insofar as mentally deficient persons are not able, even as physical adults, to exercise the kind of control over their behavior that normal prospective agents do, they do not have to the same degree the right to freedom. Since for any prospective agent the point of having and respecting the generic rights derives from their necessary contribution to action in pursuit of purpose-fulfilment, persons who are not capable of such action have the right to freedom only to the extent to which their free conduct would not directly interfere with the conditions of their own freedom and well-being or with the generic rights of other persons. But to the extent to which mentally deficient persons have human potentialities, the PGC requires both that these be protected and that efforts be made to effect whatever improvements may be possible in the direction of normal agency. (pp. 141–2)

Therefore,

In the case of children and mentally deficient persons, the Principle of Proportionality requires only so much diminution of the generic rights, especially freedom, as needed for the protection of their own well-being and their maturation into full-fledged agency. (pp. 142)

Gewirth claims that

(*a*) in so far as children and mentally deficient humans are not agents-in-full, they do not have the generic right to freedom in full, but do have the generic right to freedom to the degree that they are capable of acting freely without causing harm to themselves and others; and

(*b*) in so far as children and mentally deficient human are potential agents, they have
  (i) rights to have this potential 'protected'; and
  (ii) rights that are preparatory for their being able to be granted the generic rights in full. Thus, as children mature into agents-in-full, they should increasingly participate in decisions that affect themselves.

When considering human foetuses, we saw that precautionary reasoning imposes duties on agents to allow the foetus's potential to display agency to develop (and to assist this development, when necessary), and that this duty is subject to proportionality reasoning. This reasoning applies equally to all beings for whom there is evidence that they are potential agents. Thus, we can agree with (*b*)(i), subject to making the usual terminological adjustments required by precautionary reasoning.

(*a*) and (*b*)(ii), however, raise additional issues. Central to (*a*) (and also implicated in (b)(ii)) is the claim that the criterion that determines the extent to which partial agents are to be accorded the generic rights is the extent to which they can be left to pursue their purposes without harming themselves or others (see e.g. Gewirth 1978*a*: 122, 141).

Gewirth's use of this criterion present enormous problems. If this criterion is the reason for the proportionality between having the capacities of agency and having the generic rights (see 1978*a*: 122) then Gewirth must intend it to apply to all recipients of the generic rights in part. Given his identification of those who have the generic rights only in part, this means that he intends it to apply to human foetuses, children, and mentally deficient humans in so far as these are only potential agents, and non-human animals. However, because Gewirth holds that foetuses lack purposivity altogether (see 1978*a*: 142), it cannot be applied to foetuses as he conceives them. To be applied to foetuses, it must be modified, so that the having of purposes or intentions does not come into it—to something like

> Partial agents are to be granted the generic rights to the extent that they can be left alone without harm to themselves or others being caused.

However, precisely because purposes do not come into this statement, the criterion it states cannot be a criterion for the having of any generic rights, for generic rights are rights to act, or rights to possess things that enable one to act, and actions are things done voluntarily for purposes that the agent has chosen.

As Gewirth states it, it may appear that it can be applied to beings that pursue purposes (plausibly children, mentally deficient humans, and some non-human animals). However, if these beings are conceived of as not being agents (thus lacking the degree of the capacities of agency to the extent needed to be agents), then precisely because having this extent of the capacities of agency is needed to have a freely chosen purpose, it cannot be applied to link the degree to which their having the capacities of agency permits them to 'act' without harm to themselves or others to the having of any generic rights.

When replying to James F. Hill's charge that he commits the fallacy of disparateness (see Hill 1984: 180), Gewirth restates the criterion that links the degree to which the capacities of agency are had to the having of the generic rights: 'the varying degrees of having the abilities of agency justify varying degrees of having the rights, because of the way in which the having of the abilities bears on individuals' inherent capacity of exercising the rights without harm to themselves or others' (Gewirth 1984: 226). Such a criterion can, indeed, be applied to the having of rights. However, although the rights that individuals can have are dependent upon whether or not they are able to act in various ways without causing unintended[21] harm to themselves or others, these rights cannot be generic rights. In order to be able to exercise any rights, individuals must be agents and, thereby, be accorded the generic rights in full.

It is interesting, therefore that Gewirth refers to children and mentally deficient humans as having rights to freedom in proportion to the degree to which 'their *free conduct* would not directly interfere with the conditions of their own freedom and well-being or with the generic rights of other persons' (Gewirth 1978*a*: 142; our emphasis), for it should be clear that *if* children and mentally deficient humans have any capacity to act freely then they are agents, and while proportionality is correctly applied to their having of rights, these rights are not generic rights. In other words, Gewirth must here be thinking of children and mentally deficient humans as specific-task-incompetent agents.

In fact, depending on the degree of development of their ability to display the

---

[21] If we are talking about will claim rights, then intentional harm to self could be a legitimate exercise of these rights. What is relevant to limiting rights is inability to control actions in intended ways.

capacities of agency, children and mentally deficient adults are to be regarded as apparent partial agents having no generic rights but to whom we owe proportional duties under precaution, or intermittent agents (in which case they are to be treated as specific-task-incompetent agents—i.e. as having the generic rights in full but non-generic rights in proportion to their task competence), or as agents on a standing basis (in which case they might still have specific task incompetence).

When exactly most human beings become ostensible agents is not something we need to determine here. However, if the findings of developmental psychology are to be believed, then full ostensible agency is usually achieved at about 7–11 years of age, and often much earlier. This raises questions about the justification of having, for example, the voting age only at 18, the age of consent for medical treatment only at 16, and the age of consent to medical research only at 18 (as is currently the case in England).

As regards the voting age, the right to vote (not a generic right in and of itself) is a method of observing the generic right to participate in decisions or decision-making processes affecting oneself. However, the right to vote also empowers agents to make decisions affecting the lives of others. As such, it is permissible to restrict it to those who possess a specific level of task competence. Given that the right to vote is given to all 18-year-olds, this raises two questions. First, since not all 18-year-olds will have this competence, should not those who lack it be deprived of the vote? Second, since many agents younger than 18 will have this competence, should they not be given the right to vote earlier? *In the abstract*, the answer to both questions must be yes. However, *in practice*, attempting to individualize the voting age and deprive some human beings of it altogether not only runs into practical difficulties and the precautionary need to give the benefit of the doubt to unclear cases, it is also open to outright abuse. All three grounds argue for universality. The issue, then, is whether the rule may be a *qualified universal* rule (e.g. one which restricts the franchise to *all* human beings *above a certain age*). In our opinion, this is permissible provided that the restriction is not one that disqualifies any agents as such (as, for example, gender or race, religious belief, or level of education would do) but is something that all agents (barring factors beyond anyone's control) can expect to achieve automatically (such as a particular age).[22]

Similar considerations apply to the age of consent for treatment and research. However, unlike the vote, decisions about one's treatment or participation in research do not empower decisions affecting others. Thus, one reason to restrict on considerations of task competence does not apply. However, other such considerations remain. In general, the generic right to autonomy can only be exercised if there is adequate information and an ability to understand it, and this can justify qualified universal rules in these areas.

---

[22] Whether or not 18 is the right age is another matter, which we cannot go into here.

The legal position in England is unclear as to whether persons under 18 may consent to research on their own (see Mason and McCall Smith 1999: 471–6), but persons need only be 16 to consent to treatment on their own.[23] Indeed, persons under 16 may consent on their own to *treatment* if it is impracticable or against their interests to seek the consent of the parent or legal guardian and they are mature enough to understand what is involved in *that* treatment (i.e. are 'Gillick-competent'),[24] though (in our opinion) it would be unsafe for doctors to rely on this for *research* without applying to a court for permission.[25]

While, for *research*, the objection of under-age persons (under 18) is to be respected (even where the parent or legal guardian consents) (see Mason and McCall Smith 1999: 475), the objection of under-age persons to *treatment* (if deemed to be in their best interests) may be overridden by the parent, legal guardian, or the courts[26] (even if the under-age person is Gillick-competent).[27]

Our analysis supports the principle that greater maturity is required to consent to research than to treatment (because the context of the former poses a greater threat of exploitation of the vulnerability of young persons). It also supports the principle that Gillick-competent children (as assessed on a case-by-case basis) should be allowed to consent on their own to treatment on the conditions specified above.[28]

It is less clear that it supports the view that the consent of a parent or legal guardian is needed for a Gillick-competent child to consent to research. If Gillick competence really is competence in relation to the specific intervention involved, rather than some broad general competence, then the dignity of the child surely requires that the child be granted the right to make decisions affecting himself or

[23] See s. 8(1) of the Family Law Reform Act 1969. 'The consent of a minor who has attained the age of sixteen years to any . . . medical . . . treatment which, in the absence of consent, would constitute a trespass to the person, shall be as effective as it would be if he were of full age; and where a minor has by virtue of this section given effective consent to any treatment it shall not be necessary to obtain any consent for it from his parent or guardian. . .'. The age of consent for both treatment and research is, however, 16 in Scotland. See s. 1(1)(b) of the Age of Legal Capacity (Scotland) Act 1991.

[24] See *Gillick* v. *West Norfolk and Wisbech Area Health Authority* [1985] 3 All ER 402. The concept of Gillick competence is not the concept of ostensible agency but a concept of specific task competence.

[25] However, in Scotland it is possible to interpret s. 2(4) of the Age of Legal Capacity Act 1991 so that it permits Gillick-competent children to consent to both treatment and research on their own. This is because the Act refers to the legal capacity of a 'person under the age of 16 years' who 'is capable of understanding the nature and possible consequences of the procedure or treatment' to consent 'on his own behalf to any surgical, medical or dental procedure or treatment', and 'procedure' might include research.

[26] See e.g. the interpretation of s. 8(3) of the Family Law Reform Act 1969 (according to which 'Nothing in this section shall be construed as making ineffective any consent which would have been effective if this section had not been enacted') in *Re W (a minor/medical treatment)* [1992] 4 All ER 627. See also *Re E (a minor/wardship: medical treatment)* [1993] 1 FLR 386.

[27] See *Re W (a minor/medical treatment)* [1992] 4 All ER 627 and *Re E (a minor/wardship: medical treatment)* [1993] 1 FLR 386.

[28] This relaxation is a specific function of the fact that these decisions are not other-affecting in the way in which the right to vote is.

herself with regard to the child's specific task competence. However, it is arguable that the practical implementation of this, which requires the child to be properly informed, requires an independent oversight in the potentially exploitative context of research.

On the other hand, our analysis surely does not support the overriding of informed refusal of *treatment* made by a Gillick-competent child, as it is difficult to see what considerations are to be set against what the dignity of the Gillick-competent child demands in this context.[29]

Dignity and Virtue

If being subject to existential anxiety is central to what constitutes possessing dignity as the basis for generic rights then what *attitude* should the rational agent have towards this anxiety? Certainly, it does not follow merely from the fact that the rational agent cannot know either that it has a finite mortal self or that its self is immortal that it may not believe that it has an immortal self (or, alternatively, that it is mortal) or act on either assumption. To believe what reason does not require to be believed is not on a par with believing what reason requires not to be believed.

Thus, unless reason positively prohibits belief in both mortality and immortality, rational (i.e. not irrational) solutions to the existential anxiety produced by reason are available to those who are capable of faith in God and immortality; to those who, alternatively, find the idea of extinction positively comforting; as well as to those 'heroic' individuals who are able to cope without commitment to either metaphysical possibility.

It is time to take the bull by the horns! We will now attempt to show that practical reason, by binding agents to a categorical imperative, does not permit 'denial of death' or 'escape from freedom' strategies, but positively requires the heroic stance to be cultivated that most persons (on overwhelming empirical evidence about human psychology) appear to find quite beyond them.

Kant's Moral Argument for God and Immortality Reconstructed

Our starting point is Kant's claim that practical reason, through justifying the Categorical Imperative, requires God and immortality to be posited (see Kant 1956, esp. 126–36). This claim is easy to ridicule if Kant is portrayed as holding that acceptance of the Categorical Imperative necessitates *belief that* God exists and that the self is immortal. After all, one of Kant's greatest achievements in *Critique of Pure Reason* (Kant 1934) was to show that there is no possible proof

---

[29] Again, to assess the appropriateness of the specific age limits involved here would take us too far from pure consideration of issues of the dignity of the child.

of metaphysical theses of the existence of God or of immortality. Hence, practical reason cannot require belief in the existence of God or immortality. If practical reason requires such beliefs then there is an antinomy in pure reason itself—which makes a mockery of the central aim of Kant's moral epistemology, which is to demonstrate the unity of theoretical and practical reason.

What, however (and regardless of what Kant might or might not actually have thought),[30] if the argument for these posits (or postulates) is not portrayed as an argument for *belief* that God exists and that each human agent's self is immortal? As we understand Kant, his reasoning is as follows:

(1) The moral law prescribes duties that have a final end, which Kant calls the '*summum bonum*' ('the highest good'). The *summum bonum* is a state in which happiness and worthiness for it are in complete harmony. This harmony requires not merely that every agent receives its just rewards and punishments, but ultimately that the moral law is observed by all—so that every agent carries out its duty and no agent has its rights violated.

(2) The *summum bonum* is an 'Ideal of Reason'. Agents who guide their actions by the moral law have no duty actually to bring it about (for this is not within their power alone), but must want it brought about, and must try their best to bring it about. In this sense, the *summum bonum* is a necessary object of the will.

(3) However, the *summum bonum* is not an attainable state of affairs—*unless* agents have immortal selves (because in this world what is and what ought to be are not in harmony) and God exists (because only if God exists can what is and what ought to be actually be brought into harmony). Unless there is life after bodily death, wrongs perpetrated can never be righted. However, even life after bodily death is not enough, because such a life may be subject to all the imperfections of this life. For the *summum bonum* to be attainable, there must be guaranteed an endless progress to perfection for all agents, which can only be guaranteed if the God of rational theology (an omnipotent, omniscient, perfectly good Being) exists.

(4) Therefore, the immortality of the self and the existence of God must be posited.

Does this show that anyone who believes that there is a categorically binding moral law must accept that agents are immortal and that God exists; hence, that the dialectical necessity of the PGC renders it dialectically necessary for agents to suppose that they are immortal and that God exists? No! What this reasoning establishes is only that the *summum bonum ought to be* and, therefore, that immortality and God *ought to be as necessary objects of the will*. The categorical imperative requires the *summum bonum* as an Ideal of Reason, the 'ought'

---

[30] This is by no means clear, and we recommend the reader to consult the excellent commentary by Beck (1960: 242–83).

contained in the statement 'The *summum bonum* ought to be' being an 'ought of evaluation' presupposed by the action-guiding 'oughts' that the categorical imperative directs at agents. It cannot be inferred from this that God and immortality exist. Thus, acceptance of the PGC as the categorically binding moral law cannot require *belief in* immortality and the existence of God.

However, though the moral law does not require agents to believe in God and immortality, it does require them *not to believe* that God and immortality *do not* exist. This is because the moral law requires agents to strive their utmost to bring about a situation that cannot exist unless God and immortality exist. Thus, to believe that God and immortality do not exist is to believe that the moral law commands one to bring about what cannot be brought about. Since 'ought' implies 'can', the moral law cannot command this. Therefore, to deny that God and immortality exist is to deny that there is a moral law.

Thus, the rational agent's options are reduced to two: the rational agent may adopt the heroic stance of agnosticism or relieve its existential anxiety by faith in God and immortality.

This, however, is not all that may be inferred from the argument. If the rational agent is not required to believe that God and immortality exist, and may adopt the stance of agnosticism, then the rational agent is nevertheless required to *at least* want God and immortality to exist (for these are necessary objects of the will). Indeed, the rational agent is required to do more than *merely want* this to be the case. This is because it is not irrational to want something to be the case that one knows not to be the case. It is not even irrational to want something to be the case that one knows cannot possibly be the case. Thus, merely wanting God and immortality to exist is compatible with believing that God and immortality do not exist, even that they cannot exist. Since the rational agent may not believe such things, the rational agent is required to *at least hope* that God and immortality exist, for hope is precisely that state of wishing something to be the case that is conditioned by absence of belief that it is not the case.

Leibniz's Theodicy Deconstructed

But is faith in God and immortality really an option open to the rational agent? Belief in immortality and God entails belief that the *summum bonum* will necessarily be realized. Indeed, does it not require, as Leibniz held (see e.g. 1934: 27) and Voltaire satirized in his novel *Candide* (Voltaire 1971), the belief that the world *as it is, with all its apparent imperfections*, is the best of all possible worlds?[31] While it is not necessary to believe that the apparent imperfections (including violations of the PGC) are *in themselves* only apparent, it does seem

---

[31] In *Candide* Voltaire has the court philosopher Dr Pangloss (a follower of Leibniz), who contracts syphilis (from which he is cured at the cost of an eye and an ear) and experiences hanging, dissection, whipping, and being a galley slave, accepting all his 'misfortunes' cheerfully on account of his conviction that all is for the best in this best of all possible worlds.

to require belief that the entire scheme of things, *including all the imperfections*, is the best possible scheme of things. This, in turn, entails that if anything were done other than what has been, is, or will be done, then that would make the world less than the best possible. If this is not so, then there cannot be a Being that is omnipotent, omniscient, *and* perfectly good, and thus there cannot be a God.

But, if this is correct, then there can be no point to a categorical imperative. For the agent who is certain of immortality and God, bodily extinction should hold no terrors of the kind necessary for the Gewirthian line of reasoning to the categorical imperative to succeed. Such an agent may well *prefer* others not to interfere with the generic needs of its embodied agency. But it should be certain that these do not ultimately matter, for its *bodily* extinction is not *its* end, and, *come what may*, it will eventually and finally enjoy a state of blessedness that justifies perfectly everything that has ever happened to it. For bodily death to matter to an agent enough to require it to consider that it has categorically binding rights not to have its bodily integrity and embodied life threatened against its will, it must fear that such threats are final threats to its agency. If God and immortality exist, however, then this is not the case. Belief in God and immortality, therefore, renders any such fears irrational.[32]

Having established that agents may not deny God and immortality, this reasoning implies that agents cannot resolve their existential anxiety rationally. There are no propositions compatible with acceptance of a categorical imperative that imply that there are no grounds for fear of extinction of the self; and, yet, the categorical imperative requires agents to hope that they are immortal. Thus, fully rational agents cannot employ strategies of faith in God and immortality or any other psychological strategies that deny death; but neither can they employ strategies that resolve their anxiety by resignation to final extinction and embrace of the ultimate meaninglessness of all things. They are rationally required to accept a radical agnosticism or questioning stance that compels them to attempt to live with open-eyed fear of extinction and mere hope of immortality.[33]

Something of the nature of this stance, and particularly of the humility it involves, is magnificently captured in Kant's famous peroration in his conclusion to *Critique of Practical Reason*, which shows, if nothing else, that awareness of the existential anxiety of human agents was central to Kant's own moral philosophy.

---

[32] Theodicy (which attempts to explain how evil in the world is compatible with the existence of the God of rational theology) is a huge subject. We are aware that we are nailing our colours very much to the mast of the Irenaean tradition, in which God (*if* It exists) must have created human agents imperfect as a necessary condition of their growth to perfection, rather than to that of the Augustinian tradition, which attempts to get God off the hook by blaming all evils on free-willed actions of beings that God created perfect. An excellent monograph on theodicy is Hick (1977).

[33] We are already deep into the realms of rational theology, so it is worth noting that this line of reasoning has a radical consequence: namely, that *if* there is a God, then God does not require belief in It. Indeed, it implies that God's purpose for human agents is for them to have to learn to stand on their own two feet without any such belief.

Two things fill the mind with ever new and increasing admiration and awe, the oftener and more steadily we reflect upon them: the starry heavens above me and the moral law within me. . . . I see them before me, and I associate them directly with the consciousness of my own existence. The former begins at the place I occupy in the external world of sense . . . The latter begins at my invisible self, my personality. . . . The former . . . annihilates, as it were, my importance as an animal creature, which must give back to the planet (a mere speck in the universe) the matter from which it came, the matter which is for a little time provided with vital force, we know not how. The latter . . . in which the moral law reveals a life independent of all animality . . . at least so far as it may be inferred from the purposive destination assigned to my existence by this law . . . reaches into the infinite. (Kant 1956: 166)

A Dignified Character and Dignified Conduct

Dignified conduct may be said to reflect a dignified character, which may be viewed as the personality to which reason requires human agents to aspire. With this in mind, we might view a dignified character simply as a personality disposed to respect the moral law. Relative to this, dignified conduct is action in accordance with the moral law performed out of commitment to obey the moral law.[34]

Correlative to this, character qualities that are inconsistent with or threaten to undermine respect for the moral law may be said to display an undignified character. For example, some persons attach enormous significance to the possession by agents of qualities that are not necessary for agency (such as skin colour, physical attractiveness, sporting prowess, etc.). If the significance that a person attaches to 'agency-irrelevant' qualities is such that it leads him or her to violate the generic rights of others then this is clearly against dignity as the basis of human rights, and displays an undignified character. But what we may term 'the fetish of irrelevance' also has application to conduct directed at oneself. If agents' pursuit of agency-irrelevant qualities *for themselves* leads them to violate the generic rights of others, then this is equally against human dignity and displays an undignified character. In addition, we suggest, to permit oneself to be rendered unhappy in a way that interferes with one's ability to function properly as an agent may (by extension) also be referred to as undignified conduct (though this will not be immoral, merely tragic, if it does not correlate with dispositions or actions that threaten generic rights violations).

Our reflections in the previous section are fully consistent with such observations. What they do is provide a positive account of the essence of the personality disposed to respect the moral law: they lead us to view a dignified character as formed in equipoise between fear of death and hope of God and immortality, and dignified conduct as conduct that expresses this equipoise.

As we saw in our opening chapters, theories in which dignity is viewed

---

[34] Which is, basically, how Kant viewed virtue in *Groundwork of the Metaphysics of Morals* (Kant 1948).

primarily as the property by virtue of which beings are possessors of generic rights and their correlative duties are not the only ones that use the concept of dignity. For example, there is, on the one hand, 'the tradition of the nobles'—in which dignity is viewed as a property belonging to an elite social class, office, or station, and dignified conduct is viewed as conduct appropriate to that position. On the other hand, there is the tradition of virtue ethics, in which Aristotle is pre-eminent—in which dignity is viewed primarily as the property of a virtuous character or of virtuous conduct.

However, our reflections in the previous section on the attitudes appropriate to the rational agent suggest a connection between our Gewirthian view of dignified conduct and the conceptions employed by the tradition of the nobles and by virtue ethics. We will conclude this chapter by spelling out this connection, which requires us to be able to characterize an ability to display fortitude in the face of adversity as a virtue in Gewirthian theory.

An ability to display fortitude in the face of adversity is almost universally admired conduct, with the degree of 'virtue' displayed being in proportion to the seriousness of the threat involved—as exemplified by the equanimity displayed by Socrates in the face of his unjust death sentence, or the way in which Nelson Mandela behaved during his imprisonment. Such behaviour does not even have to be manifested by those who are thought of as especially good to qualify. The outwardly calm way in which many of the nobles who were executed during the French Revolution went to the guillotine is also widely regarded as admirable in itself. Indeed, such fortitude is not merely regarded as admirable: it is, we think, a paradigmatic instance of what would be regarded as *dignified* conduct.

Of course, particular instances of fortitude in the face of adversity can have causes that might temper judgements of how admirable they are, or indeed, whether they are admirable at all. For example, the ability of nobles facing the guillotine to behave in a 'dignified' manner by displaying a 'stiff upper lip' was due substantially to their conviction that they were intrinsically superior to other classes, and that to display this kind of fortitude was a way of showing this superiority.

There are, however, more acceptable reasons than this for regarding an ability to display fortitude in the face of the threat of terminal adversity as virtuous. For example, since bodily extinction is the fate of all of us, those who are able to reconcile themselves to this eventuality and to anticipate it with equanimity will be happier for it. Those who have this ability, therefore, possess a character that instrumentally rational persons have reason to hope and wish that they will be able to develop, if they do not have it already. Furthermore, by actually displaying such fortitude, they show that the wished for equanimity not merely is something that is desirable, but that it is attainable. As such, their behaviour is able to set an effective example, and those who have this ability are to be commended for that. They display an ability that enables their lives and the lives of others to go well (or, at least, better).

Virtues may, generally (including within Gewirthian theory), be viewed as dispositions of character to act rightly or well. However, in Gewirthian theory, dispositions of character to act rightly or well must be analysed in terms of dispositions that, in some way, protect or support the rights and duties of agents, rather than as desirable dispositions that can be justified independently of any links to rights or duties. Unless displaying fortitude in the face of adversity is to be considered virtuous because it in some way protects or supports the rights and duties of agents, it might be viewed by Gewirthian theory as a prudential and other-regarding good, but not as a moral one.[35]

There are two ways in which it can be argued that the ability to display fortitude in the face of adversity is to be regarded as a moral virtue in Gewirthian theory. The first argument is consequentialist, the second is necessitarian.

The consequentialist argument maintains that fortitude in the face of adversity is something that aspiring to radical agnosticism tends to produce, and that the ability of an agent to display such fortitude makes it less likely that the agent will violate the rights of others. If we were to argue in this way, we might appeal to analyses presented by, for example, Erich Fromm,[36] which provide good reason to believe that various 'denial of death' and 'denial of freedom' strategies directly threaten agents' rights. On this basis, we might argue that, while all denial strategies are not necessarily malignant in actual consequence, avoidance of them (involving radical agnosticism) is to be encouraged generally as a means to protect agents' rights.[37]

However, is it not the case that radical agnosticism, which requires rational agents to attempt to live poised between fear of personal extinction and hope of God and immortality, directs rational agents to aspire to fortitude in the face of adversity? Since the rational agent fears that its bodily extinction signals its end, it will be justified in resisting its bodily death as strenuously as it can. But, when it becomes apparent that resistance is futile, or will threaten the equal right to bodily life of other innocent agents, since it must hope that there is a life beyond, it must resign itself to the inevitable and look forward with hope to a possible beyond. Since it hopes for God and immortality, despair is inappropriate.[38] But, since it does not believe in God or immortality, its acceptance of its fate requires genuine fortitude. Thus, because it is dialectically necessary for agents to aspire to radical agnosticism rather than employ 'denial of death' or 'denial of freedom' strategies, it is dialectically necessary for agents to aspire to fortitude in the face of adversity. If our argument for radical agnosticism is sound, then to employ

---

[35] It should be remembered that we conceive of morality as categorical as well as other regarding.

[36] See esp. Fromm (1974, chs. 10–13).

[37] We might also argue that radical agnosticism disposes against the fetish of irrelevance.

[38] Erich Fromm, referring to hope concerning humanity's ability to create a better future for itself, puts the point elegantly: '*Optimism* [which hope requires] *is an alienated form of faith; pessimism an alienated form of despair. . . .* The basis of rational faith in man is the presence of a real possibility for his salvation; the basis for rational despair would be knowledge that no such possibility can be seen' (1974: 577).

'denial of death' or 'denial of freedom' strategies is to deny that there is a categorical imperative, and thus that there are any moral duties or rights at all as conceived of in Gewirthian theory. Thus, if radical agnosticism requires aspiration to such fortitude then not to aspire to such fortitude is to deny the moral project of the PGC as the categorical imperative.

If this is sound, then it shows that displaying fortitude in the face of adversity is to be considered virtuous in Gewirthian theory. [39] Although such conduct will only be genuinely dignified if it is a product of a dignified character (and thus of radical agnosticism), at least outwardly, a degree of rapprochement is formed between Gewirthian theory and opposed traditions that view dignity primarily in terms of dignified conduct.

---

[39] Neither a personality disposed to respect the moral law, nor a character immune to the fetish of irrelevance, nor an ability to display fortitude in the face of adversity conditioned by radical agnosticism are dispositional states that agents can guarantee to achieve. As such, agents have only imperfect duties to achieve them; though they do have perfect duties *to try* to achieve them. Thus, possession of these dispositional states may be regarded as virtuous rather than mandatory and conduct in accordance with the moral law that is produced by having these dispositions is, *in this aspect*, virtuous, rather than mandatory (which is to say, action in accordance with the moral law is mandatory, but action in accordance with the moral law out of respect for the moral law, or due to immunity from the fetish of irrelevance, etc., is not).

PART II
Applications

7

Being Born with Dignity: Selecting the Genetic Characteristics of Offspring

Introduction

Developments in modern biotechnology and biomedical science enable those wanting children to control the genes of their offspring to a far greater extent than ever before.

For example, it is technically possible for a couple intending to have a child to undergo genetic tests, on the basis of which an estimate can be made of the probability that the child will inherit particular genes. On this basis, the couple can decide whether or not to have a child together. If the woman is already pregnant, she can have the foetus tested in her womb. If the foetus has unwanted genes (or does not have wanted genes), she might be able have the pregnancy terminated. Alternatively, in the context of *in vitro* fertilization, embryos can now be tested for genes before implantation in the womb—enabling only those embryos that have 'acceptable' genes to be implanted—thus avoiding abortion.

When technical problems of delivering genes are overcome (as they will be sooner or later), somatic gene manipulation[1] will enable the genetic make-up of the unborn child to be modified in the womb. Manipulation of the genes of embryos before implantation (or at subsequent sufficiently early stages) can affect the germ-line of the embryo, thus passing on the modifications to future generations. Alternatively, germ-line gene manipulation can be effected by genetic modification of the germ-cells of the parents.

Indeed, it is now possible to choose to have a child with the identical genetic make-up of some existing or dead person (including oneself) by inserting the nuclear genetic material from a cell of that person into an enucleated ovum and having the embryo that develops implanted into a woman who is to bear the child.[2]

While these things are possible (or soon will be), it does not follow that they

---

[1] The term 'somatic gene therapy' is inappropriate if modification is not directed at treatment of a medical condition. Since we will deal with possibilities outside a treatment context, we will use more neutral terminology.

[2] This has not yet been officially recorded as having happened in humans, as against sheep, mice, cows, pigs, and some other animals. But there can be little doubt that it is an imminent possibility. Unlike embryo-splitting, this technique (the so-called 'Dolly the sheep' technique) will not produce an identical 'clone' unless the enucleated ovum is from the mother or sister or any other woman in the maternal line of the person who is being cloned. This is because the mitochondria in the cytoplasm of the ovum also contain genetic material (about 1 per cent of the total in the ovum).

are morally permissible. Indeed, some countries have found some of them so abhorrent that they have prohibited them by law. Although other reasons may be given for outlawing them, the claim that they violate human dignity figures strongly whenever moral fault is found with them, and it is claims of this kind rather than more general claims about immorality that we will, of course, focus on.[3]

On the other hand, and this is only to be expected because human dignity can dress itself up in the clothes of empowerment instead of the clothes of constraint, it might be claimed that *not* using technology to prevent children from being born with genetic disorders violates the dignity of the children, or even that preventing parents from choosing the genes of their offspring is a violation of the dignity of the parents, whether or not the aim is to prevent 'disorders' or to ensure that the child has 'desirable' characteristics.

Selection of the genes of offspring can be evaluated at two levels. First, the end of genetic selection itself—which might be either the selection of phenotypic characteristics[4] (to which the selection of genes is a means), or the selection of genes as such—might be held to violate human dignity. Second, it might be specific means used to select genes that are objected to.

We will, first, consider whether selection of phenotypic or genotypic characteristics *as an end to be achieved* is contrary to human dignity. It might seem logical for us then to consider whether various means to select genes are contrary to human dignity. Were we to do this, we would consider techniques such as somatic gene manipulation, germ-line gene manipulation, cloning, abortion, pre-implantation genetic diagnosis, etc. separately. The advantage of this would be that we would not lose sight of any differences between these various activities. However, this approach would inevitably produce considerable repetition, because specific objections in relation to human dignity will often apply to more than one of these techniques or technologies. Instead, we will assess claims about what constitutes violation of human dignity that might be alleged to apply to one or more of the techniques of selection. Thus, we will focus on general reasons that have been given for why one or more techniques of selection are contrary to human dignity—e.g. that the technique involves killing a human being, or treating a human being as a means to the ends of others, or predetermining the characteristics of a human being.

Therefore, while we will occasionally discuss a particular technique, our focus will be on it not as such, but only as the context of a particular claim about what amounts to a violation of human dignity.

---

[3] As we pointed out in the last chapter, in so far as human dignity is the ground of human rights, then at least within a rights theory like that of Gewirth, any violation of human rights is a violation of human dignity. We will, for the most part, concentrate on claims that are more specific than this.

[4] Phenotypic characteristics are any observable characteristics (e.g. eye colour, height, intelligence, diseases, lifespan, proteins) which genetic theory holds to be produced by genes operating in interaction with environmental factors.

Does Basing Selection of Genes on Judgements of Desirable Phenotypes or Genotypes Violate Human Dignity?

In this chapter our attention is on selection that aims to ensure that a child *will be born* with (or without) specific targeted *genes*.[5]

However, although some would-be parents might be concerned about the genetic characteristics *as such* of their offspring, most would-be parents are probably directly concerned about the *phenotypic* traits of their offspring, and are only interested in their offspring's genes because they believe that genes determine, predispose towards, or at least affect potential for developing particular phenotypic characteristics. If so, they view genetic selection not as an end in itself, but merely as a means towards the selection of phenotypic characteristics.

With this understood, the first objection to genetic selection that we need to consider is not to genetic selection itself, but to the selection of phenotypic characteristics. More specifically, the objection we have in mind is that it is contrary to human dignity to justify genetic selection on the basis of a desire for the offspring to have[6] particular phenotypic characteristics.

Such an objection might be 'broad': to justify genetic selection on the basis of a desire that the offspring should have particular phenotypic characteristics is contrary to human dignity *whatever* the phenotypic characteristics might be. Alternatively, the objection might be 'narrow': to justify genetic selection on the basis of a desire that the offspring should have particular phenotypic characteristics is contrary to human dignity *only if* the phenotypic characteristics are of *a specific kind.* Thus, for example, it might be claimed that to justify genetic selection on the basis of the desire to avoid a 'serious disorder or disease' is not contrary to human dignity, whereas it is contrary to human dignity to justify genetic selection on the basis of a desire to produce particular 'normal' phenotypic characteristics (especially if these are 'enhancements' that confer special advantages).

These objections might be linked to objections against 'eugenics'. Historically, 'eugenics' refers to activities that are directed at 'improving' the *genetic* stock of the human species (see e.g. Galton 1907). So understood, unless genetic selection has the goal of improving the genetic stock of the human species *as a whole*, it is not strictly 'eugenic'. However, it is natural enough to extend the term to cover activities directed at the genetic characteristics of particular individuals or groups when they are based upon judgements of what are desirable or undesirable genes for human beings *as such* to have.

The genetic stock of an individual or group might be 'improved' by selecting *against* genes judged to be 'undesirable' ('negative eugenics') or by selecting *for* genes judged to be 'desirable' ('positive eugenics').

---

[5] Some manipulations that affect genes of the already born will be considered in Ch. 10.

[6] We will, unless the context otherwise dictates, use 'have' to include 'not have'.

Objections that eugenics (so understood) is contrary to human dignity are related to the objections we have in mind. However, while the broad objection we have in mind is parallel to an objection that eugenics in general is contrary to human dignity, and the example of a narrow objection we gave is parallel to an objection that positive (but not negative) eugenics is contrary to human dignity, the two sets of objections need to be distinguished. This is because the objections we first mentioned are directed at using phenotypic characteristics as the basis for genetic selection (hence at 'improving' *phenotypic* characteristics) rather than at 'improving' *genes as such.*[7]

In this section we will address

1. the broad objection;
2. the narrow objection;
3. objections to eugenics (as we have defined this); and
4. the converse claim that it is not phenotypic or genetic selection that is contrary to human dignity, but failure to engage in such selection (in at least some cases) or to prohibit it that is contrary to human dignity.

The Broad Objection

If the broad objection is accepted, then it must be granted that it is contrary to human dignity to aim to bring it about (by *any* means) that the offspring displays any specific phenotypic characteristics. Put this way, the objection seems absurd. The behaviour that the offspring will subsequently display is part of its phenotype. Some of this behaviour might constitute actions that are contrary to the dignity of other agents. Thus, to accept the objection is, most pointedly, to accept that it is contrary to human dignity to take *any* measures aimed at reducing the likelihood that the offspring will engage in activities that deny human dignity to other persons and agents. Indeed, such an objection can only be taken seriously, we suggest, by a position that does not accept that there is any sound basis for judging that some phenotypic characteristics (including behavioural ones) are unacceptable for a human being to have. However, such a position rests on a form or relativism that does not permit human dignity (or anything else) to be portrayed as a moral value that *must* be supported.

The Narrow Objection

Moral theories differ according to the attributes they identify as necessary and sufficient for a being to possess dignity as the basis for having intrinsic moral status.[8] However, in Gewirthian theory, beings have dignity if and only if they are agents. All agents are, therefore, equal in their dignity and possess equal generic

---

[7] 'Eugenics' has come to be used as a rhetorical device. We comment on this later in this chapter.
[8] Some parts of this section derive from material used in Beyleveld (1999*c*, 2000*b*).

rights on this basis. Genetic selection (by whatever means) justified on the basis of a desire that offspring O should not have particular phenotypic characteristics pPC involves the judgement that it is acceptable to select against O having pPC. That is to say, it involves the judgement that the fact that O will or might have pPC is an acceptable reason for would-be parents to take steps to ensure that O will not have pPC.

However, if selection on the basis of such a judgement is to be contrary to dignity as the basis of human rights then it must, at least implicitly, deny dignity to those who possess it, namely, agents.

An obvious candidate for selection that would deny dignity to agents is surely selection based on the possession of capacities that are fully compatible with being an agent. The thought is that to select against O having pPC when O's having (or not having) pPC *is irrelevant to O's status as an agent*, in some way, implies that those (O or others) who possess pPC do not have the generic rights. The thought, therefore, is that it is not a violation of human dignity to select against characteristics (e.g. anencephaly, where the child is born without a forebrain) if they are incompatible with the offspring ever being able to display agency, but a violation of human dignity to select against any other characteristics (including those that might lead to a shorter life or a very painful or restricted one) that are, nonetheless, compatible with being an agent.

However, is such a thought sound? Consider the following argument, which attempts to show that to suppose that selection against 'agency-irrelevant characteristics' (characteristics that a being can have or lack and still be an agent) is permissible is to suppose that agents can, by their mere existence, deny the rights of other agents, which contradicts the equal moral status of all agents (and, thus, that all agents are equal in dignity).

A potential parent P who wishes to select against having a child with agency-irrelevant characteristics AiC, may be held to claim

(*a*) 'I do no wrong by selecting against my child having AiC'.

Therefore, P claims

(*b*) 'My morally protected autonomy is violated if I am compelled to become a parent of an agent with AiC (when this can be prevented)'.

Thus, P claims

(*c*) 'The mere existence of agents with AiC *against the choice of their parents* (irrespective of how they behave)—whose existence could have been prevented—violates the (generic) rights of their parents'.

Consequently, P claims

(*d*) 'The mere existence of an agent can violate the rights of another agent'.

However, we must assume

(*e*) 'All agents have equal moral status, reciprocal to which all agents have equal duties'.

But this implies that any rights violation can be prevented by observing a duty, which (in turn) implies that the mere existence of an agent cannot be a violation of rights of another agent. Thus

(*f*) (*d*) contradicts (*e*).

Therefore, we must conclude

(*g*) 'Selection against AiC denies that all agents have equal rights, hence the equal dignity of all agents'.

This argument is, however, invalid. The reason is that the valid interpretation of '*the mere existence of an agent cannot* be a violation of the rights of another agent' in (*e*) is '*an agent cannot by its mere existence* violate the rights of another agent'. On the other hand, the valid interpretation of '*the mere existence of an agent can* be a violation of the rights of another agent' in (*d*) is '*Agents who do not permit agents* to select against AiC violate the rights of those agents'. So interpreted, there is no contradiction between (*d*) and (*e*). For there to be a genuine contradiction, it must be read into (*d*) that it is *those agents who have AiC* who are, merely by having AiC, violating the rights of their parents. But (*d*), so interpreted, is not valid.[9]

However, even if it is not possible to show that selection against agency-irrelevant characteristics is *as such* contrary to human dignity, it does not, of course, follow that such selection is morally permissible under the PGC. Consider, for example, the following two cases.

1. Imagine a child with AiC who knows that its parents would have selected against these characteristics if they had been able to do so. Imagine, further, that it is now possible *and accepted as legitimate* for the parents to select against these characteristics. And suppose, as well, that the parents have now had another child whom they have ensured will not have AiC. Might this not be deeply damaging to the self-esteem of the child with X characteristics, in a way that will violate its rights? In addition, will not acceptance of the legitimacy of selection against AiC tend to produce a sense of grievance in parents who, for whatever reason, are

---

[9] It could be argued, conversely, that *any* argument that attempts to show that agency-irrelevant selection logically entails denial of the dignity of agents *must* fail. For example, the following case might be presented: Are not would-be parents, in effect, trying to select for (or against) agency-irrelevant characteristics simply by choosing particular partners to mate with? If so, unless we suppose that mating should be at random, it cannot be contrary to human dignity to select for or against agency-irrelevant characteristics. This, however, is also fallacious. The *effect* of mating partner selection is, indeed, selection for or against various agency-irrelevant traits. But, while mating choices cannot be illegitimate just because they have such an effect (it is, after all, impossible for there not to be such an effect), it is question-begging to maintain that to mate with someone *specifically in order* to produce children with specific agency-irrelevant characteristics is legitimate.

unable to avail themselves of new selection technologies against AiC—perhaps even tending to cause resentment against those of their children with the offending AiC, with the consequence that these children are treated with less than the respect they are entitled to?

2. AiC are, in themselves, morally neutral, which is to say that no intrinsic rights benefit is to be gained by selecting for or against them. However, fashions can develop for such characteristics. Many such fashions are harmless in themselves. However, if they come to be regarded as conditions meriting medical intervention, they cease to be so. Witness the example of the desire for perfectly shaped teeth that has swept the United States, resulting in children whose parents are unable to afford the treatment that can correct 'imperfections' that are now perceived of as deformities suffering deep traumas as a result. By extension, it may be argued that permitting selection against AiC, even if this is (*ex hypothesi*) not contrary to human dignity, is likely to produce a culture in which the possession of AiC becomes morally harmful to those who possess them.

Many at least prima facie plausible arguments of this kind can be produced. We caution that they point to a need for empirical research. However, there is a gap between these arguments, even if they are valid, and showing that selection against agency-irrelevant characteristics *as such* is contrary to human dignity. Furthermore, although it is not difficult to see how (particularly, in the first case) the argument bears on the dignity of the children, whether or not their dignity is violated is a contingent matter and not intrinsic to selection of agency-irrelevant characteristics.

Eugenics and Human Dignity

Is the case different if it is genes *as such* that are the targets of selection? If it is, then there must be a relevant difference between genetic selection *as such* and genetic selection *as a means* to phenotypic selection. The obvious difference between one's genotype and one's phenotype is that one's genotype is not acquired but inherited. But is this relevant? Certainly, to discriminate against an agent (deny an agent generic rights) because of characteristics that the agent cannot in any way be held responsible for would deny equal generic rights to that agent and, thus, violate human dignity. The problem with applying this, however, is that it must apply to genetic selection regardless of the means used to effect it. Thus, if genetic selection *as such* is contrary to human dignity, then it must be contrary to human dignity merely to decide not to try for a child on the ground that it will (or might) have undesired genes (or will or might not have desired genes). The problem with this, in turn, is that such a decision is wholly abstract. If no child (not even an embryo or foetus) will come into being because of such a decision then there is no being that will have *its* genes affected by the choice made. Thus, if there is any affront to human dignity as the ground of human rights here, it must be vicarious.

It is important in any discussion of eugenics not to forget the actual history of programmes that have had genetic selection as their aim. After all, the Holocaust carried out by the Nazis during the Second World War was motivated by eugenic ideals. At one level, this association has a tendency to cloud the issues involved in eugenics.

For example, it invites reasoning of the following form.

(1) The Nazis were engaged in eugenics (as we have defined this).
(2) What they did in pursuit of their eugenic aims was contrary to human dignity.
(3) Therefore, eugenics (as we have defined this) is contrary to human dignity

This reasoning is obviously invalid. The eugenic activities of the Nazis were not motivated merely by the goal of improving the genetic stock of the human species but by *specific* judgements about what constitutes having a desirable or undesirable genetic make-up (e.g. being a member of a particular race, having a particular skin colour, eye colour, degree of intelligence—all of which they attributed to undesirable genes). *Without more*, it cannot be inferred from the premiss that genetic selection based on *these* judgements is contrary to human dignity (and that still needs to be established) that genetic selection is contrary to human dignity *regardless of the judgements* about what constitutes having a desirable or undesirable genetic make-up *upon which it might be based.*[10] Also, the Nazis employed specific means (including enforced sterilization, enforced selected mating, and genocide) for eliminating 'undesirable' genes or disseminating 'desirable' ones. Again, without more, it cannot be inferred from the premiss that the means the Nazis employed to achieve their eugenic aims are contrary to human dignity (which they clearly are) that any means to achieve eugenic aims would be contrary to human dignity.

Unless the fallacious nature of these inferences is exposed, labelling something 'eugenic' can (and frequently does) function primarily as a rhetorical device by which to condemn by mere association any selection activities of which the labeller disapproves.

However, there is a different danger, which is that recognizing the fallacious nature of these inferences will lead to this history being dismissed as irrelevant. This is a mistake. That genetic selection for its own sake has been associated with this history gives agents with characteristics that might be the targets of avoidance or removal by genetic selection (or those who care deeply for them) reason to attribute motives of a sinister nature to persons wishing to select against their own children having such characteristics. The fact that someone might not wish

---

[10] Of course, if the judgement is not merely that having or not having particular genes is desirable or undesirable for a human being as such to have, but is that an agent has lower *or greater* moral status than other agents if it has or does not have particular genes (and the Nazis based their programmes on just such judgements) then *these judgements* obviously violate human dignity as the basis of human rights.

to have a child with X genes without either judging that persons with X genes are morally inferior or implying such a judgement misses the point. The point is that the historical association gives those fearful of the motives of those who wish to select against genes reason to fear that illegitimate motives might be active. In other words, that a wish to select genetically does not entail 'Nazi motives' does not entail that no 'Nazi motives' are involved, and the historical association, by showing that such motives have been involved, makes it, at the very least, not irrational to fear that such motives might be involved.

This, of course, does not show that genetic selection *as such* is contrary to human dignity. However, it does render not irrational fears that it might be associated with beliefs that dispose towards or require violations of human dignity or are a direct negation of it.

Failure to Select or Prohibition of Selection and Human Dignity

According to some writers, not only are arguments that genetic selection is contrary to human dignity at best tenuous, but if it is possible to ensure by genetic selection that persons will lead better lives (and their lives *will* be better if they do not suffer diseases like cystic fibrosis or live in fear of a late-onset genetic condition like Huntington's chorea),[11] then there is a positive duty not to have children with such conditions (see e.g. Harris 1985: 150). Indeed, on utilitarian premises, if the general good is best served by doing something then it ought to be done, and this will extend to enhancement programmes as well as to those that merely target diseases and conditions with poor quality of life.

Given that we are also fairly sceptical about selection policies being shown to be against human dignity as the ground of human rights (at least *intrinsically*, unless they are based on judgements that *deny* human dignity directly—e.g, by denying that all human agents have equal generic rights), how does Gewirthian theory stand on the issue of a positive duty to select against particular characteristics. In particular, would *a failure* to select against some characteristics be a violation of human dignity?

Clearly, under the PGC, just as it cannot be a violation of dignity to select against a being *that is not or cannot be an agent*, there cannot be a duty *to* beings

---

[11] A foetus is homozygous if it has inherited genes for a condition from both parents. Cystic fibrosis is a recessive condition, meaning that if the gene for the condition is inherited from only one parent (in which case the foetus will be 'heterozygous') the foetus will not have cystic fibrosis. If both parents are heterozygous carriers, then their children have a 1 in 4 chance of inheriting it from both parents and thus of having cystic fibrosis, a 2 in 4 chance of being heterozygous 'carriers' who are symptom-free, and a 1 in 4 chance of not inheriting the gene at all. The symptoms of the disease include severe respiratory problems, caused by the lungs accumulating mucus. The condition is treatable but is associated with a restricted lifespan. Huntington's chorea is due to a dominant mutation (there is a 50% chance that a child will develop it if one parent carries the gene—and anyone carrying it will develop the disease sooner or later). It is a late-onset disorder (symptoms tend to appear between the ages of 15 and 70, with average onset at about 45 years of age), which involves untreatable dementia that is invariably fatal within about fifteen years.

that are not or cannot be agents, and hence there cannot be a violation of *their* dignity in not preventing their birth (because they do not possess this quality). The issue, therefore, is confined to whether or not it is a violation of dignity not to select against (or for) particular characteristics *of agents*. These characteristics may be divided into two categories.

(*a*) Characteristics that, while compatible with being an agent, are (to one or other degree) debilitating or restrictive in relation to agency or successful agency in general. Such characteristics, under the PGC are those with symptoms that it would be a violation of the PGC to inflict upon an agent who did not possess them (supposing this were possible). Thus, conditions like cystic fibrosis, Huntington's chorea, and Down's syndrome would all be included within this category.

(*b*) Characteristics that would give agents enhanced capacities with respect to action and successful action.

In relation to (*a*), the issue is somewhat different in two scenarios:

(i) the only means available are such (say abortion of a foetus homozygous[12] for cystic fibrosis) that the agent (AF) the foetus might become either will exist with cystic fibrosis if the means to select against cystic fibrosis are not used, or will not exist at all if the means are used; versus

(ii) if the means of selection available are such (e.g., germ-line gene manipulation, or somatic gene manipulation—which, for the present context, we will assume can only be employed before birth) that AF can exist with or without cystic fibrosis.

In (i), AF could not say that AF's rights have been violated by permitting AF to be born with cystic fibrosis, because AF would not have existed if the available means to prevent AF existing with cystic fibrosis were used. In (ii), on the other hand, the claim that AF has a right not to be born with cystic fibrosis is perfectly intelligible.

Under the PGC, agents owe duties to future agents *as agents* equal to those that they owe to present agents. Thus, if agent B has a choice between doing something that would damage future agent AF as an agent and doing something that would not, then B has a prima facie duty (i.e. subject to the duty not being overridden by countervailing duties) to do what B can to avoid that damage. Not to do what is necessary to avoid this damage to AF is qualitatively on a par with not taking steps to avoid equivalent avoidable damage to C, who is another presently existing agent. The fact that the damage will result from an omission rather than a positive commission is of no significance, since all generic rights under the PGC are positive as well as negative.[13]

---

[12] Meaning that the child has inherited a cystic fibrosis gene from each parent.

[13] This is not to say that there are no *quantitative* differences between harm to present generations and harm to future generations. However, that the person being harmed is 'present' rather than 'future' is not a *qualitative* difference, because all action takes time to have effect and so all actions have their

Suppose, then, that somatic gene manipulation is available for cystic fibrosis at the embryonic or foetal stage (but not beyond), and that there are no countervailing and overriding rights of others that would be violated by employing it. In such a case, it would be a violation of AF's generic rights not to have employed it. However, would it be a violation of AF's dignity not to have done so? In that AF could argue that not to do so would mean treating AF not on a par with other agents, then the answer is Yes![14]

What, then, of (*b*)? It might be thought that the key here is whether or not agents have positive generic rights to have such characteristics, and that if they do, then parallel reasoning with case (*a*) will require us to argue that there is a duty to bring it about that agents are born with these characteristics when both doing and not doing so are compatible with their existing.

Suppose, then, that C wants to be a great violinist. Does C have a generic right that others do what they can to bring this about? No! For C does not need to be a great violinist in order to be able to act at all or with general chances of success. Thus, the argument that would have us believe that there is a duty to ensure that offspring have 'enhanced' characteristics falls down at its first stage. However, it might be objected that this is only so because of the particular example, and that the first stage could succeed for other 'enhanced characteristics'. We do not think so, and believe that to argue this is to misunderstand the generic nature of the rights the PGC grants. But even if, *ex hypothesi*, we are wrong about this, it doesn't matter, for the argument would fail at its second stage. This is because, while there can be a general presumption that agents would not want cystic fibrosis if they could avoid it (because of its agency-debilitating effects), there can be no general presumption that someone would value having the ability to be a great violinist rather than something else. This is for agents to decide for themselves.

To draw the threads together, our discussion indicates that it is not necessarily contrary to human dignity as the basis of human rights to aim to select for 'enhanced' characteristics or against 'debilitating' ones, or to fail to select for 'enhanced' ones; but that it is prima facie contrary to human dignity to fail to select against 'debilitating' ones—*provided that* the means for doing so are compatible with the same child existing whether or not these means are employed.

That, however, and it needs repeating, is not to say that there are not valid moral concerns with selection that targets agency-irrelevant characteristics.

---

effects in the future. However, where the delay is long before the effects occur things can be done to prevent or ameliorate them.

[14] On the assumptions we are making, the same arguments would apply to germ-line gene modification.

**Does Selection that Involves or Exploits Abortion or Embryo Destruction
Violate Human Dignity?**

The impact of different views about the substantive basis of human dignity is
nowhere more clearly seen than in relation to the question as to whether abortion
or embryo destruction, which are involved in many genetic selection strategies,
violate human dignity.

For example, if the dignity possessed by human beings is held to be *constituted* biologically (i.e. by being a member of the species *Homo sapiens*) then
human beings acquire dignity from the moment of conception, when the sperm
and ovum fuse to form a zygote. Furthermore, the possession of dignity is not,
then, something that permits of degrees. From the moment of conception the
zygote possesses human dignity to the full extent possible, and no discrimination
may be made between the dignity of the zygote, the implanted embryo, the foetus,
or any human being at any stage of development up to adulthood, at least until
death.[15] The 'rights' of the zygote must be equal to the rights of any living human
being. Furthermore, such rights must derive entirely from duties owed to human
beings by agents. Thus, while all human beings will be held to have equal rights,
they will not have equal duties, since only those with the power to exhibit agency
can carry out duties. Hence, it will not be possible to operate with a will conception of rights.

Clearly, *on such premisses*, not to implant a viable zygote or embryo and to
destroy a human being at any stage of its development must be a violation of its
dignity and a violation of its right to life, which is equal to that of any other
human being.[16]

Things look rather different if dignity is held to be possessed by virtue of an
ability to experience pain or pleasure. For, *on this basis*, only sentient creatures
have any moral status, and sentience (or at least the capacity to display it) is
something that seems to develop and to be associated with the development of a
nervous system. *On such premisses*, there can be no basis for saying that only
human beings have dignity (which view will, as Peter Singer has expressed it,
amount to 'speciesism' (see e.g. Singer 1993: 293–5), which will be an offence

[15] On Gewirthian premisses, the dead clearly cannot have the generic rights. However, whether the
living have duties to the dead (and, indeed, whether the dead can be treated in ways that violate human
dignity) is another matter and something that a comprehensive analysis of human dignity needs to
deal with. However, we do not take it to be within the scope of bioethics or biolaw as commonly
understood.

[16] For this reason, a strict 'pro-life' position will have considerable difficulties if it attempts to say
that the life of the foetus may be sacrificed for the sake of the life of the mother, for there can be no
basis for discriminating between the life of the mother and the life of the foetus. Equally it cannot
justify saving the foetus at the expense of the mother on the grounds that this is the free choice of the
mother, for that supposes that the mother may choose not to exercise her right to life and that seems
to imply that her right to life is a right under the will conception of rights. However, that implies that
her right to life (and the duties of others in relation to this) does not derive from her being human as
such, but from her being an agent.

as grave as racism, for the evidence we have that other non-human animals can experience pain is as good as the evidence we have for saying that human beings can experience pain).

Those who adopt this view will be inclined to say that the unborn human being has no dignity until a fairly well-advanced stage of gestation. However, there are a number of complexities here. First, it is possible to view sentience as the ground of dignity as something that admits of degrees or of different qualities, in which case dignity (and rights) will admit of degrees. Thus, for example, one might hold that there is a qualitative difference between the pain that beings who can reflect upon their own existence can experience and the pain that beings without this can experience, and that only the capacity for the former qualifies the being for moral status.[17] If so, then this view will be very close to making agency at least a necessary condition for dignity. Alternatively, no threshold may be envisaged and what will matter is the extent to which the being is capable of experiencing pain. Second, sentience (at least if viewed as a subjective state, and not merely as a set of behavioural capacities) will, as the basis for dignity, generate similar problems to agency as the ground of dignity, because displaying sentient behaviour (of whatever kind) does not conclusively establish sentience. But, then, neither does the absence of sentient behaviour (and associated anatomical structures) conclusively establish non-sentience. Thus, precautionary reasoning of the kind we argued for in the previous chapter will be applicable if sentience as the basis of dignity is combined with the view that morality is categorically binding. The effect is to extend duties of agents to the embryo and foetus into periods before those at which the embryo or foetus begins to display the behaviour that will be taken to be sufficient evidence of intrinsic moral status.

Because we are committed to the view that agency is the ground of human dignity, we will not dwell on these complications. However, it is worth pointing out that, provided that this view is articulated alongside a commitment to morality being categorically binding, the practical implications are unlikely to be very different from a view based on agency, except that the sentience view could be linked to an interest rather than a will conception of rights.[18]

With agency as the basis of dignity, human beings ostensibly only acquire rights (which will be under the will conception) at some point after birth. However, as we argued in Chapter 6, those who do not display the capacities of agency could be agents, and (on the assumption that morality is categorically binding) precautionary reasoning requires agents to recognize duties to the

---

[17] R. M. Hare (1969) distinguishes between pain, which is a sensation, and suffering, which involves evaluative attitudes. Although Hare does not do so, it is arguable that only the latter capacity is relevant to moral status and that non-human animals lack this capacity. (Inasmuch as we would support this we would, however, subject such judgements to precaution.)

[18] Although utilitarianism is often connected with the interest conception of rights, this is not necessarily so. Preference utilitarianism is compatible with the will conception if it views preferences as choices rather than as mere pro-attitudes (se, e.g. Hare 1981).

unborn in proportion to the degree to which the unborn display characteristics associated with the ability to display agency. As we also indicated, however, it is extremely difficult to quantify the proportionality involved. The most that can be asserted unequivocally is that, without a sound rights-based reason to destroy the embryo, considerations of the possibility that the embryo is an agent (and, thus, has dignity equal to that of those displaying fully the capacities of agency) require the embryo not only not to be destroyed but to be nurtured. However, it is important to appreciate that it is not the supposed or presumed dignity of the embryo (from conception) that is the basis of the duties owed to the zygote from conception. Instead, it is the consideration of the possibility that the zygote *might* be an agent (and have dignity) even though there is little evidence for this. Thus, this view does not imply that dignity admits of degrees. To destroy an embryo or foetus cannot, therefore, be said to violate its dignity unequivocally. However, it is on account of considerations of dignity that duties to the embryo arise, and we must agree that not to take account of these considerations is to act in violation of human dignity.

It is also important to emphasize (as we did in the previous chapter) that it is not possible under agency/human dignity under precaution alone to determine the duties that agents have *in relation to* the embryo. Thus, such considerations, by themselves, are inadequate to assess the adequacy of various legislative regimes and proposals in relation to embryo research, abortion, etc. For such purposes, various vicarious considerations relating to the rights of the mother (in particular, but not exclusively) must also be taken into account.[19]

Do Techniques of Selection Violate Human Dignity because they Instrumentalize the Offspring or Predetermine its Phenotype?

According to Article 11 of UNESCO's Universal Declaration on the Human Genome and Human Rights, 'Practices which are contrary to human dignity, such as reproductive cloning[20] of human beings, shall not be permitted.' In line with this, Article 1.1 of the Protocol to the Convention on Human Rights and Biomedicine on the Prohibition of Cloning Human Beings[21] states, 'Any intervention seeking to

---

[19] For a discussion of vicarious situations and how they interact with precautionary reasoning, see Beyleveld (2000*a*: 62–4, 75–7).

[20] 'Reproductive cloning' is aimed at producing a child. 'Non-reproductive cloning' (sometimes called 'therapeutic' cloning, because it is generally contemplated for therapeutic purposes involving tissue or organ transplantation) involves the reproduction of cells or organs—sometimes, though not necessarily, from embryos—which has led those who attribute full moral status to the embryo to object to the term 'non-reproductive' (see e.g. Linacre Centre (1998)). When we refer to cloning (without qualification) in this chapter, unless otherwise stated, it is to be assumed that we have reproductive cloning in mind.

[21] As of 27 Mar. 2001 Croatia, Cyprus, the Czech Republic, Denmark, Estonia, Finland, France, Georgia, Greece, Hungary, Iceland, Italy, Latvia, Lithuania, Luxembourg, Moldova, the Netherlands

create a human being genetically identical to another human being, whether living or dead, is prohibited'[22] with the Preamble making it clear that this is because 'The instrumentalisation of human beings through the deliberate creation of genetically identical human beings is contrary to human dignity and thus constitutes a misuse of biology and medicine.'

Paragraph 3 of the Explanatory Report to the Protocol is more expansive.

Deliberately cloning humans is a threat to human identity, as it would give up the indispensable protection against the predetermination of the human genetic constitution by a third party. Further ethical reasoning for a prohibition to clone human beings is based first and foremost on human dignity which is endangered by instrumentalisation through artificial cloning. Even if in the future, in theory, a situation could be conceived, which might seem to exclude the instrumentalisation of artificially cloned human offspring, this is not considered a sufficient ethical justification for the cloning of human beings. As naturally occurring genetic recombination is likely to create more freedom for the human being than a predetermined genetic make up, it is in the interest of all persons to keep the essentially random nature of the composition of their own genes.

While this passage suggests, in its grammatical structure, that there are three distinct ethical objections being offered to cloning—that it violates 'human identity', that it violates 'human dignity' (through instrumentalization), and that it violates autonomy—we think that this might be misleading. The idea that instrumentalization endangers human dignity strongly suggests reliance on Kant's Categorical Imperative in the terms of the Formula of the End in Itself, 'Act in such a way that you always treat humanity, whether in your own person or in the person of any other, never simply as a means, but always at the same time as an end' (Kant 1948: 91).[23] However, as we saw in Chapter 5, the Kantian notion of persons as ends is the notion of persons acting according to maxims of their own choosing, which is to say 'autonomous persons'.

Thus, it is possible to interpret the third reason, which claims (in part) that cloning is wrong because it produces a predetermined genetic make-up and that this reduces the freedom ('autonomy') of the person produced, as an objection in relation to human dignity. The objection is that to clone a human being is to produce another human being who will not be able to act according

(with the reservation that 'it interprets the term "human being" as referring exclusively to a human individual, i.e. a human being who has been born'), Norway, Poland, Portugal, Romania, San Marino, Slovakia, Slovenia, Spain ('ad referendum'), Sweden, Switzerland, the former Yugoslav Republic of Macedonia, and Turkey had signed the Protocol, but only Georgia, Greece, Slovakia, Slovenia, and Spain had ratified it.

[22] Bearing in mind our comments at n. 2 above, Article 1.2 explains that ' "genetically identical" to another human being means a human being sharing with another the same nuclear gene set'.

[23] Note that the Human Genetics Advisory Commission and Human Fertilisation and Embryology Authority report on cloning (1998*b*, paragraph 4.4) gets this wrong by referring to the principle as being that 'human beings may never be treated merely as a means to an end, but *only* as an end' (our emphasis added). If human beings must only be treated as ends then they may not ever be treated as means (even if they are at the same time treated as ends), which is an injunction that it is impossible to comply with.

to his or her own freely chosen maxims, because these will be predetermined for him or her.

This, in turn, can be linked back to the first objection. Ostensibly, the first objection is that deliberate cloning threatens human identity (which, implicitly, is not to be threatened). However, it is stated that *human identity* is threatened by deliberate cloning *because* permitting deliberate cloning permits one person to determine another's *genetic identity* ('constitution').[24] This is confusing. It suggests two rather different arguments. On one interpretation, the argument is simply:

(1) It is impermissible for one person to predetermine another's genetic constitution.
(2) To deliberately clone a person is for one person to predetermine another's genetic constitution.
(3) Therefore, deliberate cloning is impermissible.

But, in this case, reference to 'human identity' is redundant. On another interpretation, the argument is:

(a) It is impermissible for one person to predetermine another's human identity.
(b) To predetermine a person's genetic constitution is to predetermine that person's human identity.
(c) To deliberately clone a person is for one person to predetermine another's genetic constitution.
(d) Thus, to deliberately clone a person is for one person to determine another's human identity.
(e) Therefore, deliberate cloning is impermissible.

What, however, is the difference between one's human identity and one's genetic constitution? The Explanatory Report is not at all helpful about this. All that we can safely say is that human identity is not violated by *not having* a unique genetic identity, because paragraph 7 of the Explanatory Report makes it clear that it 'does not intend to discriminate in any fashion against natural monozygotic twins' and, if one's human identity and genetic constitution were simply identical, then it would be otiose to try to explain why the one is violated in terms of impermissible action in relation to the other.

Perhaps 'human identity' refers to 'personal identity'. But then, in the context of paragraph 3 of the Explanatory Report, the most natural interpretation of one's personal identity would include one's being as an end in oneself (one's capacity for autonomous agency). If so, then the first objection is, like the third objection, in effect, that cloning violates human dignity by interfering with the clone's existence as an end in itself (an autonomous person).

---

[24] It is actually stated that deliberate cloning permits predetermination, but that *permitting* deliberate cloning permits predetermination must be what is meant.

Thinking along these lines, we can discern two linked claims: the first is that cloning involves treating the clone not as an end in itself (thus not as a possessor of human dignity, and therefore a rights-bearer), but merely as a means to the ends of others. The second is that cloning involves removal of (or at least reduction of) the autonomy of the clone, thus affecting its very existence as an end in itself (thus its having of dignity, and therefore its being a rights-bearer). In short, it is a violation of human dignity in removing or reducing the dignity of the clone.

Neither of these claims is sound.

Were cloning to treat the cloned individual merely as a means and not at the same time as an end, then this would be a paradigmatic violation of the dignity of the clone within Gewirthian theory.[25] But there is a serious problem with this. To violate human dignity by treating X not as an end (a generic rights-bearer) X must be capable of being a generic rights-bearer and, within Gewirthian theory, X is a generic rights-bearer only if X is an agent. However, in relation to the clone, cloning is not something done to an agent but the bringing into existence of a being that might be an agent or might develop into one. In other words, cloning does not treat the clone as not being an agent because the clone does not exist (and, therefore, no agent *can* exist) until cloning is complete.[26] Thus, if cloning is to violate the dignity of the clone by treating it as a means only there must be something about cloning *as such* that makes it impossible for the clone to be treated as an end when it becomes capable of being treated as an end (i.e. when it comes to display the capacities of agency), or which, at the very least, necessarily runs counter to the clone, as a future ostensible agent, being treated as an end.

The first and third objections in the Explanatory Report (relating to human identity and predetermination) may be viewed as attempts to claim that cloning violates human dignity in just this way. Essentially, the claim is that cloning eliminates or reduces the capacity for free action of the clone (in which capacity its dignity resides).

To assess this, it is necessary to have a view about the nature of the capacity for freedom that constitutes possession of dignity, and also a view about how cloning (which is essentially a gene manipulation) impacts upon this freedom.

In Gewirthian theory, (vulnerable) agency is the ground of dignity. So, whatever freedom must be attributed to agents in the premiss of the argument to the PGC is what must be attributed as the property by virtue of which beings have dignity. Essentially, agents are held to value their purposes in a proactive way,

---

[25] It is worth noting that the idea that instrumentalization is the essence of violating dignity does not sit easily with any ground of dignity other than agency. This is because the concept of an end in a context in which it is juxtaposed to means viewed as means to ends implies that ends refer to actively valued purposes.

[26] Even if having dignity does not consist in being an agent, but, for example, in being a member of the human biological species, then cloning itself cannot violate the dignity of the clone, because that which has dignity does not exist until cloning has been carried out.

and Gewirthian analysis has it that for agents to do this they must have a sense that they choose their purposes and are able to translate their evaluational pro-attitude towards their purposes into action. The psychological sense of freedom involved here is the idea that the purposes they have, and the principles they associate with them, are theirs and not caused by something outside what they are.

Now, it is quite possible that agents might have psychological freedom, yet it be the case that their purposes are determined entirely by factors over which they have no control or even sense of control. So X might believe that what or 'who' X is is determined by, say, X's genetic make-up in interaction with environmental factors, and these may be recognized to be, ultimately, beyond X's control. Nonetheless, X might feel that the purposes X has are X's purposes, in that X connects them inherently with X's view of X's identity. As such, X may be said to act voluntarily for these purposes when X is not prevented by others from pursuing these purposes and feels that the purposes are X's purposes, even though what X is and what X's sense of identity is was determined by genetic and environmental factors (or for that matter, 'essentially random' influences) beyond X's control. Thus, as we have already indicated in Chapter 5, our view is that Gewirthian theory does not suppose free will and is entirely compatible with determinism (though it does not suppose this either).

However, if this is so, then how the clone comes to get its sense of identity hardly matters. Certainly the clone will get it, in the first instance, from somewhere other than itself (its genes, environment, 'random' factors?), whether or not it subsequently has or develops a capacity for free will in the strong sense that places its actions outside the laws of cause and effect as they apply to material objects. It follows that whether or not a person's genetic make-up is chosen for him or her by others or is determined 'randomly' (whatever this is supposed to mean) is entirely irrelevant to the freedom he or she has and requires *as an agent*, and thus to his or her possession of dignity.

It is also worth noting the emphasis that the Explanatory Report places on genetic factors. Modern genetic theory, however, provides no warrant for assuming that *any* phenotypic *characters or traits* are determined entirely (or even mainly) by genetic factors. All of an individual's phenotypic characteristics (not merely behavioural ones) are products of an interaction between the individual's genes and its environment (which will include all factors, including inherited biological ones, external to the genes themselves), whether or not they are monogenic or polygenic.[27] Although 'heritability' studies have produced high figures for the genetic component in relation to many phenotypic characteristics (see e.g. Jensen 1969; Hernstein and Murray 1994), 'heritability' is a concept that applies exclusively to populations and not to individuals. What heritability measures is

---

[27] A monogenic trait is one where the genetic contribution is thought to be a single gene. Where a trait is polygenic, in relation to the contribution of any one gene, it is arguable that the contribution of the other genes should be viewed as environmental rather than genetic.

the *variation* in a phenotypic trait within a particular population attributable to *variation* in the genes within the population as against *variation* in the environment to which that population is subjected. It says nothing whatsoever about the contribution of a person's genes to that person's phenotypic traits, and nothing can be inferred *from heritability figures* as to the extent to which an individual's phenotypic traits can be affected by changes in the environment or genes. Furthermore, whatever figure is obtained for heritability will itself depend on the variation in the population studied in both the environment and the genes (and is in no way fixed) (see Beyleveld 2001: 715–18). Thus, in a population of genetically identical individuals, genetic variation contributes nothing to any phenotypic differences between individuals in the population, and so the heritability of any phenotypic characteristics in such a population will be 0 per cent. Nevertheless, this does not mean that the genes of the individuals do not contribute to the phenotypic characteristics of individuals in this population.

However, once this is appreciated, then it is clear that if there are any problems with pre-selection of genes in regard to human dignity, then there must be equal problems with pre-selection of environmental influences.

In fact, there can be no problem with either genetic pre-selection or environmental pre-selection as such. This is not only because of the above analysis, but simply because it is impossible for there not to be *any* genetic/environmental pre-selection (unless we are to advocate that all mating should be at random—and while this would mean that the *parents* had not selected the determining or influencing factors, this would not mean that the offspring had done so; so from the offspring's perspective, such a policy would be equally predetermining). Thus, any problems there are must be with the specific selection involved and the specific intentions behind it.

Ideally, parents should aim to do what they can to enable their children to have the capacities that will empower them to develop their own life plans and should not attempt to choose for them. Thus, *if* a person wishes to clone himself or herself or another person *in order to predetermine* what they will become, value, do, etc., then that intention can be said to be contrary to the autonomy of agents and a violation of human dignity.[28] And, perhaps, it is this thought that is behind the idea in the Explanatory Report that human identity is threatened by cloning. The problem is that cloning need not have any such intentions, and it certainly cannot reasonably be expected to have any such *results* unless an untenable genetic reductionist position is presumed. In short, while such considerations

---

[28] However, see Beyleveld *et al.* (1998), where it is argued that a mother who subjects her unborn child to exclusionary testing for Huntington's chorea, in principle violates human dignity if she is not willing to grant a child born after a negative test the right to test her later on (the point of exclusionary testing being to prevent the mother from finding out that she has Huntington's chorea should the test be positive—which, because the disease is a dominant mutation, would happen if a direct genetic test for Huntington's chorea performed on the unborn child were to prove positive). The violation of dignity resides in intending not to grant equal rights to the child in the future.

might enable some cases of cloning to be held to be contrary to human dignity, they do not provide warrant for holding that cloning *as such* is contrary to human dignity as the ground of human rights.

Are Certain Techniques of Selection Contrary to Human Dignity because they do not Respect Species Integrity?

According to Recital 38 of Directive 98/44/EC on the Legal Protection of Biotechnological Inventions, 'processes, the use of which offend against human dignity, such as processes to produce chimeras from germ cells or totipotent cells of humans and animals, are obviously also excluded from patentability'. As we understand this, it is asserted that to produce a hybrid between humans and non-human animals is a violation of human dignity. It is possible that behind this lies the idea that it is an affront to human dignity to interfere with the integrity or identity of human beings *as a species*. Certainly, such thinking appears to inform the Council of Europe's Convention on Human Rights and Biomedicine, since the Preamble emphasizes 'the need to respect the human being both as an individual and as a member of the human species . . . [as a means] of ensuring the dignity of the human being'. Also, the notes to UNESCO's Universal Declaration on the Human Genome and Human Rights that outline the main principles behind the Declaration state that the Declaration exists to protect the 'genetic heritage of the human species taken as a value *per se*',[29] and the overriding value in the Declaration is that of human dignity.

If human beings have dignity by virtue of being members of the human species then it might seem that the creation of chimeras that are only part human would be a violation of human dignity. However, even on such a view of dignity, the matter is not straightforward. If the chimera is produced from totipotent cells of humans (the zygote or totipotent cells of early embryonic stages) then we will have violation of dignity by destruction of a human being that possesses dignity. However, if the chimera is produced from germ cells alone then it will not be produced *from* a human being (even in the biological sense), and the product will also not be a human being. Nothing will be manipulated and nothing will be produced that has human dignity to violate. In order to conclude that human dignity is violated, dignity must be attributed to human sperm and ova as such. If such a premiss is to be defended then it seems to us that we must accept that human sperm and ova are created for a purpose (the production of human beings), and that anything that interferes with this is a violation of the 'natural' moral order of things.

---

[29] See http://www.unesco.org/opi/29gencon/eprince.htm, which carries a document, 'The Main Principles behind the Declaration'.

Now, as we remarked in Chapter 1, while such thinking is not alien to, for example, Roman Catholic 'natural law' theology, it is certainly odd if it informs international human rights instruments, since these purport to have multicultural application and so cannot require acceptance of a particular sectarian theology.

If, on the other hand, human beings have dignity by virtue of being sentient, or, as we maintain, on condition that they are agents, then the manipulations that produce the chimera can only be seen to be violations of human dignity if they are performed on a being that is (as the case might be) sentient or an agent. Where the chimera is formed from totipotent cells of human and non-human animals, precautionary reasoning requires us to consider (no more and no less) that these might possibly be sentient/agents and thus possibly have dignity.

What, then, of the chimera produced? If being sentient is what determines having moral status (dignity), then whether or not the chimera produced will have dignity will depend on whether or not it is sentient. Equally, if (as we maintain) being an agent is the qualifying condition, then any chimera produced will have dignity (equal to that of any human agent) if it is an agent (and it must, under the assumptions that drive our precautionary reasoning, be assumed to be an agent if it behaves like one). There is nothing in Gewirthian theory (or Kantian theory for that matter) that permits discrimination between the dignity and moral status of two agents on the grounds that one is human and the other is not. Such discrimination would, following Singer (1993), appropriately be called 'speciesism'. The main difference between Singer's view and ours on this matter, however, is that being sentient is a lower threshold to pass than agency.[30] Consequently, while there is sufficient evidence to attribute full moral status to many non-human animals on a qualifying condition of 'being sentient',[31] the evidence for non-human animals of which we know being agents is certainly insufficient to require attribution of full moral status in almost all cases under Gewirthian theory.[32]

Yet again, however, we must caution that our scepticism that the creation of human/non-human animal chimeras would, *as such*, be violations of dignity in any illuminating sense does not mean that there are no moral problems with such activities, and some of these might relate to violations of human dignity. Certainly, given the capacity (indeed, the propensity) of human beings to discriminate against human beings who merely differ in the colour of their skin, and other wholly irrelevant considerations, the prospects of a human–chimpanzee chimera (let alone of a human–bird or human–dolphin chimera) being treated with equal concern and respect are slim indeed, and this should be

---

[30] But compare the more complex position elaborated in Singer (1995).

[31] This statement would require qualification if moral status is held to be affected by the degree that a being is capable of suffering.

[32] However, higher primates, whales, and some birds might be considered to be borderline cases in that it is unclear whether or not they display sufficient evidence to be considered ostensible agents. See Ch. 6 n. 13.

enough, at present at least,[33] to make the production of such hybrids morally irresponsible.[34]

Do Techniques of Selection Violate Human Dignity when they Set Up a Slippery Slope to Activities that Violate Human Dignity?

It is sometimes argued that activities that are not undesirable or illegitimate in themselves ought to be prohibited, because if they are permitted this will make it difficult or impossible to draw the line between legitimate and illegitimate activities, difficult to prevent illegitimate activities, positively facilitate illegitimate activities, cause illegitimate activities, or make illegitimate activities inevitable. Such arguments, which can be categorized in a number of different ways (see Pattinson 2000), are commonly called 'slippery slope' arguments. They can also be used to argue that activities that do not, in themselves, violate human dignity do so in consequence of the slippery slope that they set up towards activities that do violate human dignity. Thus, for example, those who believe that reproductive cloning of humans or germ-line gene manipulation violate human dignity might argue that the cloning of animals (such as that of Dolly the sheep) and somatic gene modification are contrary to human dignity because they set up a slippery slope to reproductive cloning of humans or germ-line gene modification.

For reasons we have already given, we are not inclined to accept that reproductive cloning or germ-line gene modification are in any specific sense intrinsically contrary to human dignity. However, for the sake of assessing the strategy of slippery slope arguments, we will accept that they are. That being so, we could accept that somatic gene manipulation and cloning of animals are contrary to human dignity if they make it logically impossible to distinguish why germ-line gene modification and human reproductive cloning should not be permitted if somatic gene modification and the cloning of animals are, or if permitting the latter would make it impossible to outlaw the former effectively.

However, whether there is a logical inconsistency in holding that somatic gene manipulation is not a violation of human dignity though germ-line gene manipulation is, or that cloning Dolly was not a violation of human dignity but reproductive cloning of a human being is, depends on the reason why germ-line gene manipulation or human reproductive cloning are held to be violations of human dignity. In principle, if it is held that human reproductive cloning is a violation of

---

[33] Were the world, after global warming, to be covered entirely by water, would the objection to a human–dolphin chimera remain on such grounds if this was the only way in which creatures with a human-agent heritage could survive?

[34] This particular line of objection would not apply to production of human/non-human animal chimeras that were to be destroyed before birth. Considerations of proportionality under precaution would, however, apply and there would be various vicarious considerations that would have to be taken into account.

human dignity because of some essential characteristic of being human that does not necessarily also apply to sheep then the possible absence of that characteristic in sheep will preclude the desired logical inconsistency. Those who argue that human reproductive cloning is contrary to human dignity because of something about being essentially human that does not apply to non-human animals, at least, therefore cannot avail themselves of this strategy.

On the other hand, those who argue that intrinsically acceptable activities are unacceptable because they make it impossible effectively to prohibit activities that are contrary to human dignity need to establish their case. This is no easy matter, once it is appreciated that the end point 'failure effectively to prohibit activities contrary to human dignity' cannot be broadly defined—e.g. so that it is satisfied by the mere possibility of or even the actual doing of things contrary to human dignity by a limited number of individuals. If such an end point is acceptable, then if we accept the argument against cloning of sheep then, in consistency, we must argue that any technological development (or research into it) that provides the means to carry out activities that violate human dignity that ought to be prohibited ought itself to be prohibited. Thus, for example, we should argue that the construction of the printing press (and research and technology that made this possible) should have been prevented, because, for example, the printing press would provide the means for the dissemination of racist propaganda that could (and would, one day, somewhere) be used to aid and abet policies of genocide that are contrary to human dignity. But this logically requires us to argue that all technology, even Stone Age technology and fire-making, should have been prohibited, because such technology could, and would, be used for evil purposes. And it cannot be stopped here; for human beings have, without employing any technology, through using what exists in nature, and by the use of their bare hands, the means to steal, rape, and murder, etc. Hence, accepting this argument requires us to accept that *human beings* ought to be prohibited. In effect, the view that human beings ought not to exist because they have the ability to eat from the tree of knowledge is implicit in the use of a broad end point in slippery slope arguments based on empirical claims.

This carries a message that is relevant to application of the concept of human dignity. But it runs counter to the thrust of 'slippery slope' arguments against activities like somatic gene manipulation and the cloning of animals. The message is that we need to guard against an unrealistically romantic vision of human beings living entirely in harmony with nature, with neither motivation to do evil nor the means to do so. Part of such a vision is the view that knowledge (as measured by the effects it is capable of having) can be divided into two classes—knowledge that is good and knowledge that is evil—and that our duty is to pursue only good knowledge, not evil knowledge. But this view is false. Knowledge is essentially neutral in itself. What is not and cannot be neutral is the manner in which we obtain knowledge and the uses to which we put it, and there is very little (if any) knowledge that can only be used for evil purposes.

This, however, implies that we should confine our prohibitions to methods of pursuing knowledge and using it that are evil. Thus, if reproductive cloning of human beings is so contrary to human dignity that it should be prohibited then we should prohibit it. But, if cloning of sheep is not such an evil in itself and can lead to many benefits for humankind, then it should be permitted—even though prohibiting the use of the results to clone humans will not infallibly prevent the misguided or those of evil intent from one day or on occasion cloning humans. That is simply the price of knowledge and human freedom. But to deny to human beings that freedom is also to attempt to evade moral responsibility, when the capacity for autonomy with its correlative capacity for moral responsibility is fundamental to human dignity.[35]

Conclusion

Our analysis has indicated that there are ways in which genetic selection can violate human dignity. However, we were unable to find convincing reasons for thinking that selection of genes *as such* is contrary to human dignity. While it is arguable that selection for or against agency-irrelevant characteristics can lead to consequences that are contrary to human dignity, these are contingent, not intrinsic to such selection.

This applies both where genetic selection is viewed as a means to phenotypic selection (which is usually the case) or as an end in itself (where the association with 'eugenics') is unavoidable. Thus, we argued that 'eugenics', as the aim of selecting genetic characteristics for their own sake, is not necessarily contrary to human dignity, though it is *when* associated with judgements that having or not having agency-irrelevant characteristics deprives a person of moral status. However, historical association with just such intentions makes it not irrational to fear that 'eugenic programmes' might be associated with evaluations that are untenable in relation to human dignity.

In relation to arguments that it is against human dignity to fail to select for 'enhanced' genes or against 'debilitating' genes, we argued that it is not contrary to human dignity to fail to select for 'enhanced' characteristics (despite the fact that the PGC grants positive as well as negative generic rights), but that it is prima facie contrary to human dignity (in the sense of denying the child *as a future agent* equal rights and thus equal moral status) to fail to select against 'debilitating' ones—*provided that* the means for doing so are compatible with the same child existing whether or not these means are employed.

As far as the idea that any selection procedure that involves destruction of an embryo or termination of a foetus is concerned, our analysis follows more or less directly from the discussion of proportionality under precaution that we presented

---

[35] Some of this analysis was previously published in Beyleveld (1997).

in Chapter 6. With proportionality under precaution in play, rights-relevant reasons of others are necessary to justify such procedures, and to fail to take this into account is to act in violation of human dignity.

Arguments that various techniques are violations of human dignity because they instrumentalize agents are sound in principle. There are problems, however, with their application to reproductive cloning or germ-line gene manipulation because to instrumentalize a being is not merely to treat it as a means to the ends of others but at the same time not to treat it as an end in itself (which, in the Kantian–Gewirthian tradition within which we are operating, requires it to be a setter of ends, and thus an agent). However, reproductive cloning (with the possible exception of embryo-splitting) and germ-line gene manipulation are not performed on beings that, even using proportionality under precaution, are to be considered as possible agents. Hence, the violation of dignity by instrumentalization is, strictly, a matter of how the clone or offspring will, in the future, be treated when it becomes an agent.

However, arguments that appeal to instrumentalization are sometimes conflated with arguments that claim that it is predetermination of the offspring that constitutes violation of its dignity. This has initial plausibility because human dignity, as we conceive it, resides in at least essential part in the capacity of agents to set ends for themselves. However, we maintained that the fact that an agent's character might be determined by factors outside its control does not render it non-autonomous in the sense of lacking dignity. In any event, in so far as predetermination does cause problems, we argued that genetic reductionism is to be rejected and that predetermination is as much of a problem for environmental strategies as for genetic ones. This, however, is not to say that predetermination is not a problem. However, the problem resides in the intention to try to control the character of one's offspring and not restricting one's interventions to doing what one can to enable the offspring to be 'predetermined' to be able to act autonomously, in the sense of being able to make rational (as against irrational) choices.

It has also been suggested that the creation of chimeras is contrary to human dignity. This rests on the idea that a chimera is an admixture that produces a creature lacking dignity from one that possesses dignity and one that does not. Apart from having to overcome the difficulties we pointed out in relation to reproductive cloning and germ-line gene manipulation, this claim is also confronted with the problem that dignity does not reside in being human in the biological sense, but in agency, which is not necessarily restricted to human beings. Thus if the chimera were an agent it would have dignity equal to that of any human agent. However, given the propensities that the human race displays for discriminating against human agents on irrelevant grounds (which is contrary to dignity) the creation of chimeras could be said to recklessly disregard the violations of dignity that would result.

Finally, we considered arguments that allege that if actions that are not in themselves contrary to human dignity set up a slippery slope to results that are, then it is contrary to human dignity to perform (or permit) these actions. We argued that, unless there is no effective way of restricting this, such arguments, by logical implication, imply a denial of the very capacity for moral responsibility that is central to possessing human dignity.

8

Living with Dignity I: Ownership and Commodification of Human Body Parts

Introduction

The suggestion that our bodies, or parts of them, are our property is one of the most contested in bioethics. Even more contentious is the idea that we may sell our bodies. Many who are prepared to concede that we own our bodies *in some sense* will not countenance that the entailed rights are *commercial* property rights.

This controversy is not confined to bioethical debate; it is reflected in divergent legal instruments and legislative proposals. For example, while Article 21 of the Council of Europe's Convention on Human Rights and Biomedicine maintains, 'The human body and its parts shall not, as such, give rise to financial gain,' and Article 4 of UNESCO's Declaration on the Human Genome and Human Rights declares, 'The human genome in its natural state shall not give rise to financial gains,' the erstwhile US Genetic Privacy Act 1997 (S. 422), in its section 301 (6)(B), stated that when samples of DNA are collected or stored for genetic analysis, provision must be made to permit the individual to consent to 'commercial use of the DNA sample, with waiver of, or a provision for, economic benefit to the individual'.[1]

Reflecting the fact that human dignity may be conceived of as empowerment as well as constraint, the need to protect human dignity is frequently central to the positions of *both* sides of the debate. While opponents of the view that we have property rights (or at least commercial property rights) in our bodies claim that *to grant us such rights is incompatible with human dignity,*[2] robust proponents of property rights might assert, on the contrary, that *to deny us these rights is to violate human dignity.*

Coinciding with this, the Kantian dictum that persons must always be treated not merely as means but always at the same time as ends in themselves can be

---

[1] This Act, however, failed to become law, and was withdrawn in late 1999, while being considered by the Senate Employment Committee. Various parts of the Act have been resurrected in new legislative proposals, and given the strong libertarian ethos of the United States it is not unlikely that commodification proposals will reappear.

2 This is clear from the context of Article 4 of UNESCO's Declaration on the Human Genome and Human Rights. Article 1 of the Convention on Human Rights and Biomedicine specifies that the purpose of the Convention is to protect 'the dignity and identity of all human beings'. It follows that the prohibitions contained in the Convention should be viewed as violations of these values.

appealed to by both sides.[3] In such an eventuality, the anti-property position is basically that for us to exercise control over our own bodies in the way that characterizes our having property (or at least commercial property) in our bodies is for us to treat ourselves as means only and not as ends in ourselves (and, thus, to violate our human dignity); while the pro-property position is that to deny us the right to exercise property control over our bodies is not to treat us as ends in ourselves (and, thus, to violate our human dignity).

It is obvious that these protagonists must be operating

(a) with different conceptions of what is involved in treating persons as ends in themselves (i.e. in respecting their human dignity); or

(b) with different conceptions of property (or commercial property); or

(c) both.

In the next chapter we will see the impact of such differing conceptions in relation to transactions (ostensibly contracts) involving the purported sale of human body parts and the commodification of the body (such as surrogacy) as well as the patenting of inventions developed from human biological material. However, in this chapter, in order to be able to bring a critical Gewirthian focus to bear on these practices, we develop our own analysis of the general proposition that we have property in our bodies, and of the more specific proposition that we may have commercial property in them.

First, we will elucidate the general conception of property with which we will be operating. We are interested in the proposition that persons own their bodies according to what we will call the 'rule-preclusionary' conception of property. Under this conception the claim that A owns P is the claim that A has a right to use P in *any legitimate way* and to exclude others (B) from using P, *for the reason that* A stands in a relation R to P that precludes A from having to account on a case-by-case basis for A's right to use P and to exclude B from using P. Property rights, so understood, are not absolute but prima facie only. Thus, although A owns P, in particular circumstances—where there are reasons why B should be permitted to use P against A's will that outweigh the considerations that determine that persons in the position of A should be granted property control over P—A will not be permitted to control the use of P. This will not, however, mean that P is not A's property (that A's property right is negated). It will mean that A's property right is overridden.[4]

Second, we will present three arguments for the general proposition that persons own their bodies in the rule-preclusionary sense. We will argue

---

[3] See Ch. 9.

[4] Confiscation of property (which removes the property right) must, therefore, be distinguished from legitimate removal of control of property from the property owner (which need not remove the property right). Confiscation involves the transfer of property from one person to another. Legitimate removal of control without confiscation may occur, where there is merely prohibition of the right to exercise the property right (to be justified because, in the circumstances, such exercise would conflict with more important rights of others).

(1) that Article 22 of the Convention on Human Rights and Biomedicine presupposes that we own our bodies in the rule-preclusionary sense;[5]

(2) that, *unless* we can own our bodies under the rule-preclusionary conception, we can own nothing in these terms; and

(3) (by adapting Gewirth's own justification for property rights) (see Gewirth 1996: 166–213) that it is dialectically necessary for us to suppose that we own our bodies under the rule-preclusionary conception.[6]

By themselves, however, these arguments do not demonstrate that we may transfer our bodies or body parts to others, let alone that we may transfer our *rule-preclusionary rights over them* to others, still less that we may transfer them for profit (i.e. commodify them). For it to be permissible for us to do these things, such actions must be *legitimate* uses of our bodies (which will not be the case if these uses violate human dignity). However, we will argue that, in Gewirthian theory (at least), none of these transfers is *intrinsically* wrong, from which it follows that if we have rule-preclusionary property in our bodies, then we may, *in principle*, have commercial property in our bodies. This does not mean that, *all things considered*, persons should always be permitted to commodify their bodies. There might be good reasons, *in particular circumstances*, not to permit us to commodify our bodies that *override*, rather than *negate*, our prima facie right to commodify our bodies.

The Concept of Property

Apart from the idea that property rights are rights of control over objects, there is little consensus about what constitutes having an object as one's property. At one extreme, Narveson (1988: 66) holds that to be free to do something *means* to be free to use what one owns, and because he further contends that all rights are freedom rights, he considers it plausible to maintain that all rights are property rights. At another extreme, Honoré (1961) suggests that ownership in the fullest sense has eleven elements,[7] which severely restricts the scope for having property rights.

---

[5] From which it would follow that if the Convention is opposed to the idea of property in the body rather than merely to the idea of commercial property, then there is a contradiction between Articles 21 and 22.

[6] The first two arguments are, of course, dialectically contingent, whereas the third is intended to be dialectically necessary.

[7] According to Honoré, ownership comprises the following conditions: rights (1) to have exclusive physical control over an object; (2) to personally enjoy and use it; (3) to decide how and by whom it shall be used; (4) to derive income from it; (5) to alienate it and consume, waste, or destroy it; (6) to immunity from expropriation; (7) to transfer rights over it to others; (8) to no fixed term being set on the duration of the rights while the holder lives (all of which are (9) subject to the limitation that use harmful to others should not be made of the object, and (10) to liability to removal to pay debts or as compensation or penalty). Finally, it is characteristic of property (11) that, on abandonment, characteristics (1) to (10) will be invested in another.

While some theorists insist on trying to identify an essence of property, which can be stated as a set of necessary and sufficient conditions for something to be property, others, like Judith Jarvis Thomson, maintain that 'ownership is really no more than a cluster of claims, privileges, and powers' (Thomson 1990: 225), and that if the rights that someone has over something are sufficiently like rights that people have over things that are generally recognized as their property (such as 'their houses, typewriters and shoes') (p. 225) then there is no harm in considering those rights to be property rights. This latter view swiftly leads to the widely accepted idea that property consists of a shifting bundle of rights, because not everything that someone will consider to be *sufficiently like* core instances of property will have the same characteristics, and also because there are different ideas of core instances.

In our opinion, the purpose of a definition is crucial in determining both the definition itself and the approach to concept formation in producing it. Thus, if one regards the purpose of a definition as being to summarize or characterize what some group of persons is willing to call 'property', then one is likely to end up with the view that 'property' is a 'cluster concept',[8] or that things called 'property' share no more than a 'family resemblance' (see Wittgenstein 1968: 32–3)[9] to each other, along the lines advocated by Judith Jarvis Thomson. On the other hand, if one uses a definition of property primarily to specify what proposition one is trying to justify when claiming that persons can have X as their property, then a statement of necessary and sufficient conditions for being property will be appropriate, even essential. That some persons might not wish to call 'property' what is property under one's definition, or might wish to call something 'property' that does not qualify under one's definition, is beside the point in this context. Of course, such a justificatory exercise could be entirely trivial. In relation to this, it is worth noting that the broader the definition the easier it will be to justify that something is property. Thus, for example, it is easier, but less interesting, to justify that one has property in one's body under Narveson's definition than under Honoré's. The definition will also be more interesting the more novel the claim it makes about the objects to which it is to be applied.

Gerald F. Gaus suggests the following 'core' definition of property in liberal theory:

for Alf to have unimpaired liberal ownership rights over some thing P, he must have at least the following rights:

---

[8] This term derives from Putnam (1962). In a cluster concept, things sharing a designation will share some necessary characteristics that are sufficient for the designation, there being a fairly indeterminate variety of other conditions that, when added to the necessary conditions, are sufficient.

[9] This idea differs from the idea of a cluster concept in that there may be no common core or set of necessary conditions for a designation. On this model, A, B, C, and D may share a designation. However, while A and B will have characteristics that overlap, as will A and C, and B and D, C and D may share no common characteristics.

(1) *Right of Use*: Alf has a right to use P, i.e.
    (a) It is not wrong for Alf to use P, and
    (b) It is wrong for others to interfere with Alf's using P.
(2) *Right of Exclusion:* Others may use P if and only if Alf consents, i.e.
    (a) If Alf consents, it is prima facie not wrong for others to use P; and
    (b) If Alf doesn't consent, it is prima facie wrong to use P.
(3) *Right of Transfer*: Alf may permanently transfer the rights in rules (1) and (2) to specific persons by consent.
(4) *Right to Compensation*: If Betty damages or uses P without Alf's consent, then Alf typically has a right to compensation from Betty. (Gaus 1994: 213–14)

According to Gaus, when liberal theorists claim that persons own their bodies, their claim is 'attenuated' unless conditions (1) to (4) are held to apply to their relations to their bodies. This is because the four conditions apply to those things liberals most characteristically claim to be property. Gaus then goes on to say that it is condition (3) that distinguishes property rights from rights to bodily integrity, and it is because it is not generally accepted that persons may permanently transfer rights over their bodies to others that the claim that persons own their bodies is controversial.

Stephen Munzer (1990, esp. 37–58), like Gaus, rejects the 'imperial' view that all body rights are property rights, and he also makes transferability the key to property rights. However, he divides bodily rights into 'personal rights' (which include rights to bodily integrity) and 'property rights'. Furthermore, unlike Gaus, he divides property rights into weak and strong property rights (see 1990: 48–9). For Munzer, transfer for value (rather than gratuitous transfer) is the key to strong property rights. In effect, his strong property rights are commercial property rights.

Now, it is not clear whether Gaus's condition (4) is imposed in order to cater for the idea that, at least in his view, liberal property rights are commercial property rights. If it is, then we would drop this condition, siding with Munzer that it is useful (if only at the level of definition) to distinguish property rights in general from commercial property rights more specifically.

If we were to follow the approaches of Gaus and Munzer, then we would begin by noting that

    (*a*) compensation *as such* is not generally thought to attach *only* to what is thought of as property, otherwise the award of damages or compensation for bodily injury must be held to imply property in one's body; and
    (*b*) if transferability is the key to property rights in general, then a right to donate an organ would seem to imply that the organ is the owner's property. For, surely, the kind of *physical transfer* that takes place in organ transplantation transfers *the right* of exclusive use (as captured by something along the lines of Gaus's conditions (1) and (2)) to the recipient of the organ.

However, contemplation of such matters need not detain us, because we will seek the key to the concept of property elsewhere.

There are two basic issues that arise in relation to developing a conception of property. The first issue is *methodological* (and we have already made some brief comments on this). The second issue is *semantic*, 'What does A mean when A claims P as A's property?' The pre-theoretical answer is that A claims that P belongs to A, that P is A's. 'It's mine!', says A. In these terms, philosophical answers are directed at specifying what the relation is between A and P that constitutes P belonging to A. As we have noted, it is generally agreed that this relation is a relation of control. Furthermore, it is agreed that it is not a relation of actual control, but one of normative control, which is best specified in terms of *rights* of control. However, as such, it can be specified further along two dimensions. The first dimension is *substantive*, specification along which involves identifying characteristic rights of control. The second dimension is *functional*. Specification along this dimension directs our attention to the fact that claims to property are not merely claims to some bundle of rights of control, but function to justify rights of control. 'Why should I be able to exert control over P?', or even more pointedly, 'Why do I have a right to exclusive use of P?', can be answered by saying, 'Because P is my property!'

We agree with Gaus and Munzer that having P as one's property involves having rights of control over P in the form of a right to exclusive use (a compound of a right to use and a right to exclude use by others). We also agree that a right of exclusive use is not sufficient to establish that P is one's property. However, the approach taken by Gaus and Munzer, in their related but different ways, is to try to identify further necessary rights of control, which, together with a right to exclusive use, will sufficiently determine that P is one's property or commercial property. As such, their approach is purely substantive. We, on the other hand, believe that it is at least as important to grasp the way in which claims to property function to justify control over their objects, because we believe that what is most interesting about claims to property is that the way in which a claim to a property right over P purports to justify control of P is distinct from the way in which claims to other rights purport to justify control of P.

Some remarks by Andrew Grubb provide us with a useful starting point. According to Grubb,

English law has developed in the last decade to provide significant protection to individuals' self-determination—by recognising a 'right of bodily integrity'—such that the taking of any tissue from a competent adult person would be unlawful without the consent of the source. The law is, however, solely concerned with the 'taking' rather than the 'use' of extra-corporeal organs or tissue. By contrast, property law would have something to say about subsequent 'use' and 'control'. (1998: 299)

A right to bodily integrity is essentially a right not to be harmed physically against one's will. A right not to have one's body parts removed without one's consent derives from a right to bodily integrity *in so far as* the reason for requiring consent is that such removal constitutes physical harm. As such, any control given to the source person over subsequent uses cannot be accounted for by a right to bodily integrity.

Grubb is, furthermore, surely right that recognition of property in one's body parts would involve recognition of control over subsequent use. However, it is too swift a move to infer that recognition of control over subsequent use requires the presumption of property in the removed parts. This is because rights to bodily integrity are not the only rights that can be appealed to apart from property rights in order to give the source person control over the use of his or her body parts after their removal. Thus, for example, a right to prevent certain uses might be claimed as an exercise of a right to *personal* integrity. For instance, Roman Catholic women may claim a right to prevent the use of ovarian tissue that has been removed from them for their treatment to develop chemical contraceptives, on the ground that such a purpose is something that they cannot in good conscience be involved in furthering. Furthermore, in this particular case, their objection might be linked to a right to freedom of religion.[10]

Now, in order to focus on the functional aspect of claims to property, we should not ask, 'What rights of control are necessary in addition to rights of control over subsequent use to characterize claims to property?' Instead, we should ask, 'What distinguishes a claim to the effect that body parts removed for treatment should not be used for other purposes without the source's consent *because* those body parts are the source's property from a claim that those parts should not be used for other purposes *because*, otherwise, such purposes would violate a right to personal integrity, a right to bodily integrity, or whatever?'

We suggest that a right to exclusive use of an object is necessary and sufficient to characterize property rights *substantively*, and that the essential *function* of a justification on the basis of a property right is to justify a right to exclusive use in a characteristic way. If a right to exclusive use of X is justified by a specific right, such as a right to bodily integrity, a right to personal integrity, or a right to freedom of religion, then the success of the justification depends on such a right being threatened by others using X without one's consent. In contrast, justification of a right to exclusive use of X on the basis that X is one's accepted property renders it irrelevant whether or not the claimant needs that control, or will be able to serve some good purpose through that control, or (on the other side) (at least within the scope of the claim to a property right) whether or not someone else needs it or can serve some good purpose through being able to use it. The function of claims to property rights might, thus, be said to be 'preclusionary' (in

---

[10] Which is granted by Article 9 of the European Convention on Human Rights. Alternatively, it might be linked to the right to privacy under Article 8.1 of the same Convention because the European Court of Human Rights interprets the right to privacy so broadly as to use it to protect a person from attacks against 'mental integrity or his moral or intellectual freedom' (Velu 1973: 92). We see no reason why, in principle, the right to personal integrity cannot be claimed both to prevent removal of tissue (where removal may permit a use that violates this right) and to prevent such a use after the tissue has been removed.

being to preclude the need for specific justification). 'Because it's mine!' functionally means 'It is so related to me that I do not have to say why I should be able to use it or why I may exclude others from using it!'

Of course, this does not mean that one does not have to justify the claim that P is one's property. What we are talking about is the functional meaning of a claim to justify a right to exclusive use by claiming that P is one's property. However, the functional meaning of such a claim indicates the form that a justification of something as one's property must take in moral theory. Essentially, to justify P as one's property requires it to be shown that P stands in such a relation to one that the protection of one's rights to bodily integrity, personal integrity, or whatever, *as a rule or matter of first presumption*, requires one to be accorded preclusionary control over its use. Therefore, if it is asked, 'Why should it be recognized that persons (generally or individually) have property in P?', under what we may call the 'rule-preclusionary' conception of property, the appropriate answer needs to take the form 'Because not granting persons generally (or that specific person) preclusionary control over P, as *a general rule*, does not provide adequate protection for their specific rights'.

The functional meaning of a claim to property can be incorporated into a specification of the right to exclusive use that is the substantive focus of a claim to property by reformulating Gaus's conditions (1) and (2) as

(A) Alf has a prima facie right to use P *in any legitimate manner*, even if such use is not of any benefit to Alf or anyone else in the particular circumstances that pertain;

(B) Alf has a prima facie right to prevent others from using P in a legitimate manner even if Alf does not need P and the others do in the particular circumstances that pertain.

Property rights, therefore, are *secondary* rights, which are required by other *primary* rights as a matter of general presumption. As such, they may, however, come into conflict with the rights of others *in particular circumstances*. They are, thus, only prima facie, and may be overridden by conflicting (primary) rights of others in particular circumstances. In such cases, however, it is not that P ceases to be Alf's property. It is just that Alf's property right is overridden. On the other hand, if the use to which Alf proposes to put P is illegitimate (intrinsically wrong) then Alf's property right would not extend to cover that use. Property rights themselves, even as only prima facie, are only rights to legitimate uses.

Of course, others may define property rights differently if they wish. With reference to the remarks we made at the beginning of this section, we will say only that our conception is driven by our aim of justifying the claim that persons have property rights in their bodies under the rule-preclusionary conception. This, in itself, is a far from trivial claim. It becomes even more interesting when it is used (as we shall) as a springboard to justify the claim that persons may commodify their bodies and permit others to make commercial use of them.

Three Arguments for Rule-Preclusionary Rights in Body Parts

The Argument from the Consent Regime of the Convention on Human Rights and Biomedicine

Article 22 of the Council of Europe's Convention on Human Rights and Biomedicine maintains, 'When in the course of an intervention any part of a human body is removed, it may be stored and used for a purpose other than that for which it was removed, only if this is done in conformity with appropriate information and consent procedures.'

The Explanatory Report accompanying the Convention makes it clear that the phrase 'body parts' covers 'organs and tissues proper, including blood' (paragraph 132) but not products such as 'hair and nails, which are discarded tissues, and the sale of which is not an affront to human dignity' (paragraph 133).

However, it is less clear whether 'intervention' covers removal in the context of both treatment and non-treatment, for the Explanatory Report simply says that body parts 'are often removed in the course of interventions, for example surgery' (paragraph 135).

There can be no doubt, though, that the spirit and purpose of Article 22 is to keep faith with the general principle of informed consent (as set out in Article 5 of the Convention), because the Explanatory Report continues that 'parts of the body which have been removed during an intervention for a specified purpose must not be stored or used for a different purpose unless the relevant conditions governing information and consent have been observed' (paragraph 136). That said, the Explanatory Report indicates that the 'information and consent arrangements may vary according to the circumstances, thus allowing for flexibility' (paragraph 137).

Our first argument is that it is difficult to account for Article 22 without presupposing that we have rule-preclusionary property in our own bodies and body parts. As far as we can see, acceptance of Article 22 presupposes acceptance of property (so conceived) in our own bodies and body parts.

Under the rule-preclusionary conception of property, consent is required not only for removal but for subsequent use, *regardless* of whether or not such use would specifically promote or threaten the source person's interests. In requiring that parts removed for a specified purpose must not be used for a different purpose unless there has been *relevant* information and consent, Article 22 does not explicitly require that consent for *any* further use must be obtained, as it is *just* possible that it might be an acceptable interpretation of Article 22 to hold that, in some circumstances, relevant information and consent is no information or consent.

It is pertinent, therefore, that while the Health Council of the Netherlands (1994) has recommended that specific consent should be obtained for all further uses with no differentiation between cases where tissue is removed for treatment or some other purpose, the Nuffield Council on Bioethics (1995) in the United Kingdom recommends that a distinction should be made between tissue removed during the course of treatment and tissue removed in different circumstances. In the latter case, the Nuffield Council recommends that specific consent should be obtained for all uses (1995: 127, paragraph 13.16). In the former case, on the other hand, it advises that the tissue could be used for research and other legitimate purposes without obtaining specific consent (p. 126, paragraphs 13.12 and 13.13). The reasons given for this, however, do not support the idea that consent is not required. The Nuffield Council suggests that, where tissue is removed during treatment, the tissue is to be regarded as 'abandoned' (p. 73, paragraph 9.14.1). If this does not, in itself, imply (in the view of the Council) that the tissue is the patient's property, it certainly implies that patients are relinquishing all further claims with respect to it, and thus *implicitly consenting* to any further uses.[11] Indeed, the Council's considered view is that 'When a patient consents to medical treatment involving the removal of tissue, the consent should be taken to include consent also to subsequent disposal or storage of the tissue and to any further acceptable use' (p. 126, paragraph 13.12). In line with this, the Council recommends that, because any consent must be informed, patients should be informed that their consent to treatment 'covers acceptable further uses of human tissue removed during treatment' (p. 126, paragraph 13.13).[12] Thus, the Nuffield Council, which might possibly be cited to support the contention that some countries ratifying the Convention[13] might find acceptable the view that consent is not required in all cases, does not clearly support such a view.

This does not, of course, wholly preclude the possibility of 'no consent' for certain cases being compatible with Article 22. However, we suggest that the difficulty of overcoming the problem of specifying why tissue given for one purpose precludes the need for consent for other purposes, while tissue given for another purpose does not preclude the need for consent for other purposes, makes it very unlikely that such a position can reasonably be considered compatible with Article 22.

However, if consent (explicit, implied, or merely imputed)[14] is required for

---

[11] The Council thinks that issues of control of the patient can be handled purely on a consent regime basis and need not implicate the recognition of property (see 1995: 73, paragraph 9.15). If the argument in this chapter is sound, however, then this will not be so, as the requirement for consent will imply property.

[12] The obvious weakness of this approach is that it implies that the only way in which a person can object to further uses of tissue removed during treatment is to refuse the treatment. This introduces a considerable element of coercion into any choice the patient might have, and, without the patient having choice, there is little point in obtaining the patient's consent.

[13] At the time of writing, the United Kingdom has not signed, let alone ratified, the Convention. However, we understand that it intends to do so, entering a reservation only against Article 18(2), which prohibits the creation of embryos specifically for research.

[14] There are a number of ways in which consent may be held to be implied. A's consent is implicit when A responds to a request by action that acquiesces to the request. A's consent may be inferred for actions that are obviously necessary for carrying out requests of A. A's consent to an action may be

any different purposes by Article 22, then it would seem to follow directly that Article 22 presupposes that body parts are the source's property, simply because indifference to purposes entails indifference to the interests that might be involved in the uses.

However, before we can conclude this, two cases must be distinguished:

(*a*) requiring consent in all cases of different use, because these different uses *might* bear upon a specific interest, *in which case* the source could prohibit the use; and

(*b*) requiring consent in all cases of different use, enabling the source to prohibit a different use without any reason having to be given.

It is conceivable that the source might object to certain uses of body parts made after treatment for moral or religious reasons. Subsequent use of body parts without the consent of the source runs the risk of running counter to the conscience or personal integrity of the source. Supposing a right to have one's personal integrity respected, a requirement to obtain consent for further use in all cases could be grounded in the need to protect such a right. This grounding might, however, take two forms. The first form is interest- or primary-right-specific (in this case the interest in personal integrity or a right to it). If the consent requirement is grounded in this way, then it will exist so that it might be established whether or not any subsequent use would offend the source's personal integrity. If so, for the source to prohibit a use, the source would have to cite (and perhaps establish) some sort of conscientious objection in order to prohibit the use. On the other hand, respect for the personal integrity of the source could be considered so important, yet so personal a matter, that it justifies giving the source the right to prohibit further use without having to cite offence to the source's personal integrity (or any other specific interest). That it is the source's body part or tissue is all that is, in effect, relevant. This form of grounding would characterize rule-preclusionary (i.e. property) control being given to the source.

Now, in the case of Article 22, if the grounding of the consent requirement were interest-specific, one would expect the Convention to specify the interests that the source could cite to prohibit subsequent use. No such schedule of grounds for objection exists. Thus, even if the need to protect specific interests (such as that in personal integrity) motivated Article 22, this need must be regarded as explaining why the Convention (through Article 22) grants rule-preclusionary control to the source.[15]

---

presumed on the knowledge that A knows that the action is intended, understands it, and does not object. Mere imputation of consent (which is an extremely dubious procedure) occurs when none of these conditions are met but legitimate action requires consent to be construed.

[15] This argument is presented in more detail in Beyleveld and Brownsword (2000c).

*The Argument from the Premiss that Persons can Have Rule-Preclusionary
Control over Something*

The very concept of rule-preclusionary control suggests that to provide an *unconditional* justification of the proposition that 'P is X's property' requires it to be shown that P stands in such a relation R to X that it is necessary for the protection of X's primary rights that X be granted rule-preclusionary control over P.

Our second argument does not try to establish that each person's body stands in such a relation R to him or her that each person must be granted property control over his or her body. That is the task for our third argument.

Instead, our second argument is that if anything at all can stand in such a relation R to me then my body can. Conversely, if my body does not stand in such a relation to me, then nothing can. This is plausible, given that (whatever the metaphysical relationship between me and my body) it is through my body that I, as a physically embodied being, act.

However, it might be objected, this is only cogent in relation to my body as a whole when I am still alive and my body parts while they are still attached to me. It has no application to my dead body or any of my body parts that have been removed.

This objection is overstated, for we have already seen that unconsented uses of removed body parts are, in principle, capable of violating the source's rights.

However, it is surely right to question that my control of my removed body parts is more important for my agency (hence rights generally) than my control over all other things that I might claim as my property. Thus, if our second argument is to be valid, we must claim only that if my *living* body and *attached* body parts cannot be my property, then nothing else can be.

If this claim is correct, then it does not follow automatically that my removed body parts can be my property; simply because it does not *follow* that *anything else* can be my property. In order to make the move to justifying that anything else can be my property, it needs to be established that other things stand in the same relation to me as my living body and attached body parts do, at least qualitatively (that is to say, that under certain circumstances at least, rule-preclusionary control over objects other than my living body and attached body parts ought to be granted).

Once it is recognized that the importance of rule-preclusionary control can be a matter of degree, that this might be made out should not seem far-fetched. For the same reasons that my having my arm is generically more important for my agency than my having my little finger on my left hand (which, in turn, is more important than my having my hair), so various removed parts or things that have never been part of my body can be more or less important for my agency, without these differences affecting that I should be granted a degree of rule-preclusionary control over use of them.[16]

---

[16] The degree of preclusionary control is proportional to the degree of seriousness of the claims of others required to override my control.

This relatively weak claim, nonetheless, has interesting implications. For it suggests that to recognize something (that is not my body) as my property (my computer keyboard, for instance) is to give it a normative status as though it were related to me as my body is. From this it further follows that to claim something as one's property is to claim that it is to be treated normatively as part of one's body, thus 'metaphorically' that it is part of one's body—my computer keyboard must be treated, so to speak, as an extension of my body. At this level, the claim that X is my property, explicated as 'X belongs to me', is to be understood as 'X is part of my (normative) body'.

This might remind some readers of Locke's thesis of self-ownership: namely, that I own my self (*suum*) and that external things come to be my property through being produced by my labour, which makes those things, *normatively*, part of me (see Locke 1960, paragraph 2.27).

Our present argument, of course, is conditional (whereas Locke's is unconditional) and it makes no claims about how external things might come to be related to me as my property (precisely because it is conditional). So we must recast Locke's position in conditional form. As such, the main difference between Locke's thesis and our own is that we do not claim that unless I can own my *suum* I cannot own anything. We claim only that if (I) my *suum* cannot own (my) its body, then (I) it cannot own anything. Of course, the difference between these two positions will be obliterated if there is strict identity between me and my body.[17]

Here, it will suffice to say that we are agnostic about the metaphysical relationship between me and my body, and that we certainly do not positively subscribe to the view that the self, *as such*, is a physical thing (which would require it to be describable entirely in terms of spatio-temporal predicates).[18]

Unconditional Justification of Private Property Rights

Gewirth's Justification of Private Property Rights
Gewirth views private property rights as rights of individuals (both positive and negative) to 'exclusive powers to possess, use, transmit, exchange, or alienate objects' (Gewirth 1996: 166).

This is more inclusive than our conception in relation to the substantive rights of control required, and there is no indication that Gewirth considers important the functional aspect of claims to property that we have made central to the

---

[17] Stephen Buckle (1991: 169–70) suggests (with no specific reference) that Locke considered my body to be part of me (which implies that his thesis of self-ownership encompasses a thesis of ownership of my body and its parts). Whether or not this is so is not relevant to our present concerns.

[18] Although we will not argue this here, we are inclined to the view that for my body to be my property there must be a distinction between me and my body, if only an aspectual one in terms of the quality of the predicates involved in 'body' and 'self' descriptions, which enables my body to stand as 'object' to the 'subject' that is my self. On this basis, because I *am* my self, I *cannot own* my self.

concept of property. We are not, therefore, able to present Gewirth's justification of private property as a justification of rule-preclusionary property without adaptation. His arguments are, however, instructive.

Gewirth provides two arguments for property rights. The first argument he calls 'consequentialist', because the criteria it draws attention to are consequences for the generic rights of agents of distributing control over objects in a particular way.[19] The consequentialist argument for property rights is that 'Having such rights serves to protect both the well-being and the freedom that are needed for purposive action and generally successful action' (1996: 171). On this basis, the things that one can justifiably claim as one's private property are those things that it is *necessary* for one to have the characteristic property rights of control over if one's generic rights are to be adequately protected.

According to Gewirth, however, a consequentialist justification by itself is not adequate.

For a vital question left open by the consequentialist justification is the issue of justified differential rights, including their sources. If property rights are justified by their consequences for freedom and well-being, then, since all persons as actual or prospective agents have needs for these necessary goods of action, this does not, as such, distinguish between the amounts of property that different persons ought to have; nor does it tell us whether work in producing objects of property should give any privileged position to the producers as against other persons. (p. 181)

Furthermore, although the criterion of degrees of needfulness can be appealed to when more than one person lays claim to P (which is in short supply), a consequentialist justification is powerless to deal with the problem as to who should have P when the claimants have equal need for P (see pp. 182–3).

These issues are addressed by an 'antecedentalist' argument, antecedentalist criteria answering questions about just distribution by reference to circumstances *prior to* the distribution (such as, effort, contribution, and prior agreements) (see Gewirth 1985: 13). According to Gewirth, the primary antecedentalist argument for property rights is that 'Property rights belong to persons who have produced the goods— things or services—that are the objects of the rights' (1996: 182). Why? Gewirth gives two answers. The first answer is that, if a person produces objects that others need, then those others should reward the person by providing income (or objects that the first person needs in exchange) as a matter of right. Not to grant the person property control would exploit the effort made (see p. 183). The second answer is that productive labour (which produces things instrumental to the satisfaction of the generic needs of agency) is itself an exercise of the producer's generic rights.

---

[19] As Gewirth explains (1996: 170), the use of this terminology in no way implies a commitment to utilitarian thinking. See also Gewirth (1978a: 216), where he distinguishes 'utilitarian consequentialism' from 'deontological consequentialism', the former determining rights by reference to consequences for non-moral goods, the latter determining what it is right to do on the basis of consequences for rights and duties determined in a deontological way.

[If] it is by A's own efforts that X is produced or made available in ways that do not harm any other persons, and [if] A's direct purpose in so producing is to have X as her own thing either as a use value or as an exchange value, to say that A does not have a property right in X would be to say that A's purpose in so acting may rightly be frustrated. But this, when generalized, would be an attack on the whole purposiveness of human action itself. For all human action is performed with a view to achieving the respective agents' purposes; and such action is morally permissible insofar as it does not violate the generic rights of other persons. It follows that persons have property rights in things they have produced for the purpose of having such rights. This may be called *the purposive-labor thesis* of property. (1996: 183–4)

As Gewirth points out, the consequentialist and antecedentalist arguments pull in different directions.

The consequentialist argument aims to secure property rights for all persons as fulfilling their respective needs of agency; it is not contingent on any special actions or transactions on anyone's part. . . . The antecedentalist argument, on the other hand, justifies property rights for each person only insofar as she has contributed to the production of goods or services through her own labor. Since persons' productive abilities are unequal . . . this argument may eventuate in a markedly unequal distribution of property. (p. 199)

This, however, does not render the two arguments incompatible. Gewirth's discussion of this is coloured by its context, which is to show how the two sets of considerations contribute to establishing the distribution of goods and services required by a just society (see pp. 200–13). However, it is possible to generalize. In essence, consequentialist and antecedentalist considerations do not offer independent and parallel justifications for property. So viewed, they would generate inconsistency. Instead, the consequentialist argument should be treated as primary in that, *in the absence of conflicting claims on goods and services by others*, persons must be granted property control over objects that satisfy the needs of a consequentialist justification, and consequentialist considerations would be sufficient. However, this is a complete abstraction, as conflicting claims are always present. It is at this point that antecedentalist considerations come into play, for their specific effect is to justify why two persons A and B with otherwise *equal claims* on X as property *on consequentialist considerations* are to be treated unequally by granting B property control over X and depriving A of such control (with the specific consequence that A, thereby, acquires duties towards B that A would not otherwise have had).[20] The application of antecedentalist considerations is, however, always under the control of consequentialist considerations as they can never operate validly so as to deprive A of the generic needs of agency when there is sufficient of X to satisfy A's basic needs without depriving B of B's basic needs. As Gewirth says, under the PGC, A has a positive right to be relieved from 'starvation or destitution through B's taxes' when B can provide such relief.

---

[20] This is a consequence of property rights, because it is a consequence of all rights derived from strong claim rights (like the generic rights) being correlative to duties imposed on others.

So, even if antecedentalist considerations justify X as B's property rather than A's, taxation or removal of part of B's property (on consequentialist considerations overriding B's property right) may be justified (see 1996: 200–1).

Adaptation of Gewirth's Justification to Rule-Preclusionary Ownership of Body Parts

It is important to emphasize that the fact that the concept of rule-preclusionary property requires a Gewirthian justification of some particular X as A's property to take the form of showing that rule-preclusionary control of X is required to provide adequate protection for X's generic rights does not imply that the justification must attend to 'consequentialist' rather than 'antecedentalist' considerations. Antecedentalist arguments, *as much as consequentialist arguments*, purport to show that not to grant property control would have the consequence of violating the PGC, thus generic rights. The difference, at least in Gewirth's primary explanation, which accounts for his labelling, is temporal ('consequential' referring to 'after').

While considerations of time are involved, however, we are not convinced that this contrast really captures the difference between Gewirth's two kinds of considerations. The *essential* difference seems to us to be that the 'consequentialist' considerations apply *universally*, whereas the 'antecedentalist' ones apply *particularistically* to relations between particular objects and agents that are not universal (e.g. to the fact that A has produced X by A's labour, but B has not) as a result of which A's generic rights are worse affected by A being denied property control over X than would be the case with B.[21]

Were Gewirth to have presented his analysis under the rule-preclusionary conception of property, we might have argued simply that Gewirth has shown that we can have our earned income as our property, that our second argument has shown that if we can own something, then we can own our bodies; therefore, we own our bodies. However, this would be invalid, because Gewirth has not argued that adequate protection of our generic rights requires us to be granted rule-preclusionary control over our bodies, and our second argument is not directed at showing that we may transfer our bodies for commercial profit. Thus, we need to address the issue in an independent manner.[22]

We will first of all address the issue of ownership of my body *parts as attached to me*.

However my body and body parts are metaphysically related to me, I act through my body. To deprive me of my body parts generically affects my capacity to act or act successfully, so to do this against my will is to violate my generic rights.

---

[21] This is captured in Gewirth's statement (see 1996: 199) that the two sets of considerations pull in opposite directions, which we have quoted above.

[22] It is for such reasons that we have not elucidated the actual details of Gewirth's justification of private property, and have concentrated on presenting the formal structure of his argument.

Use of my body must, therefore, be placed entirely within my decision (subject to my use of my body not being immoral under the PGC, which is to say subject to my use not violating the rights of others or human dignity as conceived under the PGC).

This, however, is not enough to establish that I must be granted rule-preclusionary control over my body, and it also does not explain why, since others (one-armed persons, those suffering kidney failure, etc.) might need one or more of my body parts, they do not have an equal right to these of my body parts as I do.

Following Gewirth's general approach, we could argue that my body parts are products of my labour in some sense, although we then raise various issues about the extent to which what I am and what I do is or is not determined, in the final analysis, by factors outside my control and not by me.[23]

However, in the present context, an attempt to adapt the 'product of my labour' consideration is not the only antecedentalist consideration that is available. I am related to an arm that is already attached to me differently from the way in which another needing an arm is related to the arm that is attached to me. Most obviously, I stand to lose from the arm being removed, whereas the other stands to gain. Related to this, I have a standing reliance on the arm, whereas the other does not.[24]

But, of course, to show that (legitimate) uses of the arm attached to me must be governed entirely by my consent does not show that I must be granted rule-preclusionary control over it. To show that I must be granted such control over it, it must be shown that I must be granted control (at least as an initial standing presumption) in a form that precludes my having to give any reasons in terms of specific rights for that control. That the arm is attached to me must be regarded as sufficient to grant me control over use of my arm, meaning that the fact that some use of my arm without my consent would not cause me any specific or significant harm would not be relevant to whether or not it was to be presumed that such use was illegitimate without my consent.

Now, it is clear that granting me rule-preclusionary control (which places the onus of having to justify use by others firmly on others on a case-by-case basis, with a standing presumption against their use, unless I have consented to it)[25] would *best* protect me. But is it *necessary* to give me such control?

It seems to us that it is. The effect of not giving me such control is that, in the absence of my having objected to a use, there would no necessary presumption against use by others where the use did not appear to be specifically harmful to me. In such cases, the onus would, effectively, be placed on me to justify why

---

[23] See Gewirth (1996: 188–194), for some discussion of this.

[24] This is related to considerations of first use or 'original acquisition' that often figure in justifications of ownership of land.

[25] Mere absence of my objection, or even absence of any specific grounds for me to object, is not sufficient to imply consent. However, consent could be implied if I had information, knew I could object, but did not object.

others may not make use of my arm without my consent. However, there are at least two conditions under which placing the onus to justify control on me rather than on others will not protect me adequately.

The first is where my reliance on the object is so strong that permitting inquiry as to why I should be permitted to use the object would itself place my agency under threat.

The second is where it is not apparent from the nature of the use itself whether or not unconsented use would cause me specific generic harm, but it might. This will characteristically be the case where legitimate beliefs of agents lead them to have strong objections against uses that impinge on their right to personal integrity. Related to this, their beliefs could be so personal that to insist on them being divulged would constitute violation of a right to privacy.

We suggest that my relation to my body is such that both of these conditions are brought into play. The first condition is satisfied simply because I act through my body. The second condition is satisfied because this close relation makes persons particularly prone to attach religious and other deep (sometimes idiosyncratic) emotional significance to their bodies and body parts.

The second of these conditions is especially important with regard to the question whether persons should be granted rule-preclusionary control over *removed body parts and their bodies and body parts after death*. Indeed, it is also important in relation to rule-preclusionary control over those attached parts that are not only renewable but can be removed without significant lasting harm on bodily integrity (such as hair or fingernail clippings).[26]

Although use of the corpse of a deceased person cannot be to the detriment of the bodily integrity of the deceased (and the same can be said of removed body parts, short of their being used to assault the living person from whom they have been removed), various uses can seriously offend the personal integrity of living persons. Unless rule-preclusionary control is granted to persons to dictate legitimate uses of their bodies after death or removal, persons will be deprived of their legitimate expectation that their most sacred and private beliefs will not be trampled on after they die or have lost immediate control of the objects eliciting their concern. Thus preclusionary control must be granted.[27]

---

[26] In the case of renewable body parts that nevertheless cannot be removed without physical harm being caused, the first consideration applies according to the criterion of degrees of needfulness (see Ch. 4, p.70 above).

[27] Latham J, in *R* v. *Department of Heath, ex p Source Informatics Ltd.* [1999] 4 All ER 185, held that pharmacists who release anonymized information (obtained from patient prescriptions) on GPs' prescribing habits to a database company for marketing purposes would be in breach of confidence. The *ratio decidendi* for this judgment was that, although there are a number of grounds for regarding information as confidential, the duty of confidence imposed on a confidant is that the confidant may not use the information for *any* purpose without the consent (explicit or implied) of the confider. As such, although the duty may be overridden by conflicting duties arising from statute or in the public interest, the scope of the duty itself is determined entirely by the consent of the confider. Since breach of confidence is constituted by unconsented use, anonymization before use does not obviate a breach

Alienation of Body Parts

We will use the term 'alienation of body parts' to cover all cases of the giving up of rule-preclusionary control over one's body or its parts. It is important to distinguish mere alienation (surrender) of rule-preclusionary control of one's body parts from transfer to others of rule-preclusionary control over these parts. When one surrenders one's property right, it need not necessarily become the property of anyone else.

Surrender of Body Parts

Clearly, one may surrender one's body parts. One surrenders one's body when one dies, and parts of one's body when, for example, they are removed in contexts where they cannot be reconnected, when they are removed for treatment, or when they are donated to others for their treatment or for research (before or after one's death). There is nothing that one can do about dying as such, or about loss of one's body parts as the result of accident or the assaults of others, but all the other cases involve some degree of voluntariness.

of confidence (see Beyleveld and Histed 1999), and Latham J did not consider the database company's proposed scheme was in the public interest. In effect, Latham J's view was that the person to whom confidential information belongs has rule-preclusionary control over it. Furthermore, his reasoning why such control should be granted fits our general analysis well. He held (as did Rose J in *X* v. *Y and Others* [1988] 2 All ER 648, 660–1 and Bingham LJ in *W* v. *Egdell* [1990] 1 Ch 359, 419 and 422) that the basis of the duty of confidence in relation to information that patients give to doctors for their treatment is a public interest requirement. More specifically, his reasoning was that such information is very personal (*in the sense of* concerning who and what they are and what they consider to be of the greatest significance to them). If unconsented use is made of this information it *could* offend patients in such a way that they become reluctant to seek treatment or to release information candidly to doctors when they seek treatment. This would not be in the public interest (at 165–6). Though Latham J did not go on to say this, it is clear that, on this reasoning, it is irrelevant to recognition of the duty of confidence whether or not the beliefs of patients that would cause certain uses of their information to offend them are reasonable from someone else's point of view (provided that they are not positively illegitimate). Hence, rule-preclusionary control must be granted if the public interest is to be served.

It should be noted that Latham J's decision was overturned by the Court of Appeal (see *R* v. *Department of Health, ex p Source Informatics Ltd.* [2000] 1 All ER 786). Contrary to Latham J, the Court of Appeal maintained that, at least where the duty of confidence arises in equity, the scope of the duty is determined, on a case-by-case basis, by whether the confidant can make fair use of the information (with it being clearly understood that unconsented use is not necessarily unfair). If unconsented disclosure or use would not be contrary to the legitimate interests of the confider (to be determined by the Court) then there is no breach of confidence. The Court considered that the only legitimate interest of patients in the case before them was in concealment of their personal identities and that, therefore, anonymization would preclude a breach of confidence.

Following refusal by the Court of Appeal of leave to appeal, the Department of Health originally petitioned the House of Lords for leave to appeal, but subsequently withdrew its petition. This is unfortunate, as we consider that the original High Court ruling must be considered to be correct if the basis of the duty is as articulated by, *inter alia*, the Court of Appeal in *W* v. *Egdell* (which contention the Court of Appeal in *Source Informatics* did not take account of), and for a number of other reasons. (See Beyleveld and Histed 2000 for a critique of the Court of Appeal's judgment.)

Now, since justified property rights in one's body serve one's generic rights, and agents may, by the very nature of a generic right, waive the benefits that exercise of a generic right confers, it follows directly that they may waive their rule-preclusionary control (their property rights) over their bodies and body parts. Thus, subject as always to their actions not violating the generic rights of others, they may commit suicide or perform any other voluntary surrender of their body parts, with *one exception*.

The exception derives from the fact that they may not act in such a way as to give up their generic rights as such. These are inalienable and, indeed, it is not merely that waiving the benefit conferred by a generic right is not the same thing as waiving the generic right; the waiving of the benefit of a generic right is itself an exercise of a generic right.[28]

It follows from this that one cannot wholly surrender the right to exclusive use of one's body *while one lives*. It is through one's body that one acts. Thus, giving up the right to exclusive use of one's body *altogether and permanently* involves surrendering one's freedom in such a manner that one has given up one's right to object to anything that is against one's will. This is to surrender one's generic rights per se, because they are, at least, rights to non-interference with one's generic needs *against one's will*.[29]

Transferability of Rule-Preclusionary Rights in Body Parts

Gaus (1994: 216–20) insists that it does not follow from the fact that agents may give up their rights of exclusive use over their body parts that they may transfer these rights to others. The fact that one's property rights are waivable entails only that agents may give up their rights to exclusive use, not that they may transfer them permanently to others.

Now, it is certainly the case that the mere fact that one has waived the benefit

---

[28] It is important to appreciate that any particular property right, *as a power to control*, is a benefit of generic rights, not a generic right itself. Thus, viewed as a benefit, one's property right can be waived. However, one cannot surrender one's general right to property (right to have objects as property), because this is necessary for the protection of generic rights, and therefore itself a generic right.

[29] Slavery is wrong for just the reason that it denies the slave the status of a generic rights-holder. Thus, it seems, no one may consent to being a slave (as a permanent state at least) without denying their own dignity. To do so would involve waiving their generic rights as such, not merely the benefits of their exercise, and these are inalienable. It is important, however, not to misunderstand this. Bearing in mind our discussion of duties to oneself at the end of Ch. 5, this 'duty' not to sell myself into slavery is not a duty *under* the PGC, but a function of rationally necessary commitment to the PGC, the requirement not to deny my dignity not being in order not to violate the PGC, but in order for me not to deny that I am an agent by not accepting the PGC, thus being required logically rather than morally. It follows that, under the PGC, it is not so much that I *may not* sell myself into slavery as that I *cannot* do so. If I purport to sell myself into slavery, then I deny that I have the generic rights, which I can do. But I cannot give up the generic rights, and to sell myself into slavery is to give up the generic rights. Having the generic rights I *may*, even if I have agreed to submit my will to that of another, reassert my right to freedom and free myself, which true enslavement does not permit. Hence any agreement to submit one's will to that of another cannot be unlimited.

of one's generic rights by waiving a right to rule-preclusionary control does not entail that whenever a person gives up rule-preclusionary control that rule-preclusionary control has been transferred to someone else. But this is hardly to the point. What Gaus (were he addressing our argument) would have to show is that the fact that a person *may waive* rule-preclusionary control over P is not sufficient to *permit* the person to transfer rule-preclusionary control of P to someone else.

At this point it is worth reminding ourselves of Gewirth's purposive labour thesis of property, which is to the effect that if someone has produced something with the view to having property in it then that person must be granted a property right to it, on pain of denying that person the generic rights.

This can be adapted to imply that if A already has rule-preclusionary control over P (which will be because having this control serves the generic rights) and surrenders such control over P with the intention of transferring this control to B, then it would be a violation of A's generic rights not to permit A to so transfer A's control of P.

Thus, if A hands over one of A's body parts to B with the intention that B should have rule-preclusionary control over it, then (unless, of course, doing this would violate the more important generic rights of others) B will acquire rule-preclusionary control.[30]

It should be borne in mind that there are circumstances in which A's surrender of P to B will automatically transfer rule-preclusionary control of P to B, so that P becomes B's property. For example, if A *voluntarily*[31] surrenders a kidney to be transplanted to B who lacks one, then B acquires rule-preclusionary control over the kidney. This is simply because the antecedentalist consideration of reliance that granted A rule-preclusionary control over the kidney has now been transferred to B. No one, surely, would suggest that A may demand the kidney back or that the consent required of A in relation to the kidney is not now required of B. And, given that informed consent must be obtained for removal of the kidney from A, circumstances will not be altered if A now loses his other kidney.

There are two ways of viewing this. One way of viewing it is to say that A's voluntary surrender, coupled with B's generic reliance, gives B rule-preclusionary control, even if A has merely intended to surrender the kidney and not positively intended to transfer rule-preclusionary control to B. Reliance by B with A's non-objection to B's having A's kidney is enough.

The other way is to say that A's donation would not have been voluntary without knowing that B would acquire reliance, and that A by surrendering the kidney

---

[30] Thomas Hobbes (1946: 86) held that transferring a right is a benefit-directed waiving of it. Gaus (1994: 217) considers this view as a basis for holding that through waiving one's property right with the intention of benefiting someone else the other person can acquire the right, and rejects it. However, the proposition Gaus attacks is much less specific than our proposition, which presents the view that a transfer of property occurs when the property-holder waives his or her property right with the intention not merely to benefit another but for it to become the property of the other.

[31] Unnecessary complications arise if we do not assume voluntariness.

has implicitly consented to (thus intended) B's acquiring rule-preclusionary control.

However, in either case B will acquire rule-preclusionary control until B voluntarily surrenders it.

Commodification of Body Parts

If the arguments we have presented are sound, then surrendering one's body parts and transferring one's rule-preclusionary control from oneself to another permanently cannot, *as such*, violate dignity as the ground of generic rights, since not to grant this power to agents is to violate their generic rights. Furthermore, we fail to see how such actions could per se violate dignity as a virtue—after all, if this were possible then it must be contrary to dignity as a virtue (or the ground of generic rights) to donate a kidney to save the life of another.

It also follows, simply from my having rule-preclusionary control over the use of my body parts, that, without my consent, others *may not* make commercial use of my body parts.[32]

However, the power to prevent others from commodifying my body parts does not, *by itself*, entail the power to transfer one's body parts and rule-preclusionary control over them for profit or to authorize others to commodify them.

Given that it is permissible, in principle, for one to transfer one's body parts gratuitously (whether the parts are now attached or have already been detached for an independent reason), the only problematic aspect here must be that payment is involved. One aspect of payment is that it might provide an inducement to get one to act against one's best interests, exploiting one's poverty, and rendering one's transfer not fully voluntary. Another aspect of payment is that it might be made a condition of the transfer, thus rendering the transfer not entirely altruistic.

As we will see in the next chapter, the possibility that commodification of organs will exploit the vulnerable is a serious consideration arguing against it as a policy. However, it is difficult to see how this can apply to already detached organs. But, more importantly, it is basically directed at the actions of those who would purchase the organs, rather than at the donor. We have argued that the donor may commodify his or her organs voluntarily. Here the actions of others, or a policy of permitting commodification, is being queried because it might interfere with the autonomy of the donor. As such, it is really about considerations that might override the donor's presumed commodification right rather than considerations that preclude the donor from having such a right. We agree that it would violate the donor's dignity to treat the donor purely as a means and not at

---

[32] Removed body parts can be abandoned. However, to abandon something is to give up all claim on it. To reasonably presume that I have abandoned my body parts, there must be good grounds for believing that I have no objection to someone else appropriating them or using them for their purposes, so that my consent may be implied.

the same time as an end in himself or herself. However, if the donor's action is informed and voluntary then the donor is being treated as an end, and not merely as a means. To demand that the donor never be treated as a means to one's ends would render virtually all social interaction in violation of human dignity.

Undoubtedly, allowing persons to demand payment for organs or other tissue as a condition of use may mean that their actions in donating their tissue are not motivated purely by altruism. However, if doing something (which may very well benefit others and even save their lives) for non-altruistic motives means that these actions are violations of dignity as the ground of generic rights (when they would otherwise not be) then altruistic actions must be perfect duties. On the one hand, this means that, whenever the donor has less need for the organ than the donee, the donor must submit to removal of the organ.[33] On the other hand, it means that if the donor is donating the organ for any reason other than the need of the donee, then the donor is somehow violating his or her own dignity. This is to be rejected because it requires that persons be treated only as ends and never as means, which is impossible without totally surrendering one's own freedom. Even if one may choose to do this, one cannot (as here implied) have a duty to do this, as then one has a duty to treat oneself as a means only, which is contrary to one's dignity.

Conclusion: Rule-Preclusionary Property and Dignity

In this chapter we have suggested that the key to the concept of property, given agreement that property rights involve rights of exclusive use over objects, lies in the function of claims to property being to justify the having of these rights in a particular and characteristic rule-preclusionary way, rather than in a further bundle of rights of control. On this basis we may, *in principle*, distinguish transferable from non-transferable property rights, and transferable property rights may be divided into commercial and non-commercial property rights. We presented three arguments for holding that persons have rule-preclusionary rights to exclusive use of their body parts, our strongest argument being that to deny them such rights is to violate the PGC, which requires agents to act in accordance with the generic rights of all agents. To deny agents rule-preclusionary rights of exclusive use of their body parts is not to provide adequate protection for their generic rights (and, indeed, implies that they do not have the generic rights, which is the clearest possible violation of dignity as the basis of generic rights). While the claim that persons have rule-preclusionary rights of exclusive use does not, without more, entail that they may transfer these rights, let alone that they may

---

[33] Gaus (1994: 213 n. 16) cites with approval the view, which he attributes to Jeremy Waldron, that if body parts are (presumably commodifiable) property then they must be forfeitable to pay one's debts. This is not so. That one may commodify one's body parts does not entail that their retention is not protected by a right to bodily integrity.

commodify their body parts or permit others to commodify them, we argued that these consequences are entailed under the PGC. This is basically because, under the PGC, persons must be permitted to do anything they like, provided only that this does not directly or indirectly threaten the generic rights of others. The benefits of the generic rights are waivable by the agent, subject only to this waiving not threatening the generic rights of others, as there are no direct duties to oneself under the PGC. Thus, if A does X with the intention of transferring preclusionary control over X to B, or with the intention of making commercial profit, then effect must be given to A's intention (subject only to this not being a violation of the generic rights of others). Not to do so is to deny the permissibility of A's action, which is to deny A the generic rights, and is contrary to dignity as the ground of generic rights.

It follows that commodification cannot be a violation of the dignity of the source of the body parts in Gewirthian theory. This does not mean, however, that commodification must always be permitted. It should not be permitted if, given the particular context of commodification, considerations of the generic rights of others (or *their* dignity) conflict with and override the commercial property rights of the source.

9

Living with Dignity II: Patents and Contracts

Introduction

In 1977 John Moore attended the medical centre of the University of California, where he was diagnosed as having a cancer of the spleen. His spleen was duly removed. Following surgery, Moore returned to the medical centre over a period of years, during which samples of his blood and tissue were taken, ostensibly for the sole purpose of post-operative check-up. However, what he did not realize was that his doctors were using his spleen and samples to develop a cell-line that the regents of the university duly patented. When he discovered that his body had been the source of a commercially valuable product, he began legal proceedings.[1] Because one of Moore's claims raised the novel question of whether he had proprietary rights in his own body parts, this case has become a famous chapter in the texts on property law.[2] However, it might have been a very different story. Let us suppose that Moore's physicians had been entirely open, fully informing him of their intentions. Further, let us suppose that Moore had then contracted with the regents for the use and exploitation of his tissue. All being well, in due course, Moore would have taken whatever benefits flowed from this contractual arrangement. However, let us suppose that the regents had second thoughts (perhaps because the commercial value of the cell-line far exceeded their expectations) and decided to renege on the agreement with Moore. Would the courts (and should the courts) have recognized this as an enforceable contract? Or might they have declined to do so on the ground that commerce in body parts (in organs, tissue, and the like) violates human dignity? The story might also have been different if the issue had been raised as a question of intellectual property, an objection being taken to the patentability of the (or any) cell-line derived from Moore (or any other human being). In particular, it might have been objected, as happened in the *Relaxin* case[3] in Europe, that the regents should not be permitted to patent an invention derived from human tissue because such commercial exploitation of the human body violates human dignity.

In this chapter we will consider the bearing of human dignity on two aspects of the commercial exploitation of the human body. First, we will discuss the patentability of human gene sequences. Then we will discuss a number of

---

[1] *Moore* v. *Regents of the University of California* (1990) 793 P 2d 479. For a discussion and critique, see e.g. James Boyle (1996, esp. 21–4, 99–107).

[2] The majority of the Supreme Court of California rejected the claim that Moore had proprietary rights in his own cells.

[3] HOWARD FLOREY/Relaxin [1995] EPOR 541.

contractual questions—for example, whether respect for human dignity requires (*a*) that freedom of contract should be limited where the body is exploited some way, such as where there is an agreement to sell organs or to act as a surrogate or the like, and (*b*) that freedom to contract (or not to contract) should be limited where genetic information is used (for example, by insurers or employers) to guide the choice of contractual partners. In both cases, we will explore the question through the lens of recent legislation that invites an appeal to human dignity. In the case of patenting, the relevant legal lens is Directive 98/44/EC on the Legal Protection of Biotechnological Inventions and, in the case of contract, it is the (English) Human Rights Act 1998.

Patenting

The Relaxin *Opposition*

From the early 1990s, when the US National Institutes of Health (together with Dr Craig Venter) filed patent applications for sequences of DNA taken from brain cells (see Gerald Dworkin 1993: 176–7), the patenting of human gene sequences has developed rapidly to the point where it was estimated that, by the mid-1990s, over 1,000 such patents (worldwide) had been granted (see Thomas *et al.* 1996)—and, indeed, that by the turn of the century over 100,000 applications had been made. The leading case in Europe with regard to the patentability of inventions involving human genetic material is the *Relaxin* Opposition.[4] *Relaxin* is also the clearest example of an objection to a patent being argued on the ground that the exploitation of the invention would be contrary to human dignity.

In *Relaxin* the challenge to the patent, which covered claims *inter alia* to 'a DNA fragment encoding a polypeptide having human H2-relaxin activity' (Claim 3 of 21), was made under the European Patent Convention (EPC). According to the EPC, patentability is determined initially by Article 52(1). At the time this provided that 'European patents shall be granted for any inventions which are susceptible of industrial application, which are new and which involve an inventive step.'[5] However, the technical criteria in Article 52(1) must be read in conjunction with the exclusionary provisions of Article 53. First, Article 53(a)

---

[4] There are now two patent regimes in Europe, one a scheme of regulation under the European Patent Convention, the other a new scheme under the Directive on the Legal Protection of Biotechnological Inventions.

[5] Comprehensive revisions have subsequently been made to the Convention. See Proceedings of the Diplomatic Conference (Munich, 20–9 November 2000), reported in Special Edition No. 1 of the Official Journal of the EPO, 2001. The revisions will enter into force either (1) two years after fifteen Contracting States have ratified it; or (2) on the first day of the third month following ratification by the last of all the Contracting States (if all the Contracting Sstates ratify it), whichever is the earlier. Article 52(1) now states: 'European patents shall be granted for any inventions, in all fields of technology, provided that they are new, involve an inventive step and are susceptible of industrial application.'

provided that patents shall not be granted for 'inventions the publication or exploitation of which would be contrary to "ordre public" or morality, provided that the exploitation shall not be deemed to be so contrary merely because it is prohibited by law or regulation in some or all of the Contracting States'.[6] Secondly, Article 53(b) provided that patents shall not be granted for 'plant or animal varieties or essentially biological processes for the production of plants and animals; this provision does not apply to micro-biological processes or the products thereof'.[7]

Both limbs of Article 53 have given rise to interpretative difficulties in the face of patent applications involving genetic engineering—notably, in the *Oncomouse*[8] application (which concerned a transgenic animal for cancer research), and subsequently in the *Plant Genetic Systems* case[9] (which concerned a genetically modified herbicide-resistant plant). However, with regard to patents on human gene sequences, Article 53(a) is the key exclusionary provision—and in *Relaxin* it was on the basis of this provision that the opponents argued for revocation of the patent.[10]

The opponents' objections were articulated in three specific arguments: (1) that the 'isolation of the DNA relaxin gene from tissue taken from a pregnant woman is immoral, as it constitutes an offence against human dignity to make use of a particular female condition (pregnancy) for a technical process oriented towards profit';[11] (2) that patenting genes of this kind 'amounts to a form of modern slavery since it involves the dismemberment of women and their piecemeal sale to commercial enterprises throughout the world'—thereby infringing 'the human right to self-determination';[12] and (3) that the 'patenting of human genes means that human life is being patented', which is 'intrinsically immoral'.[13] Having conceded that the patenting of human DNA would be immoral 'if it were true that the invention involved the patenting of human life, an abuse of pregnant women, a return to slavery and the piecemeal sale of women to industry',[14] the Opposition Division proceeded to reject each of the specific objections.

As regards the first argument, the Opposition Division pointed out that the

---

[6] As revised, this now states: 'inventions the commercial exploitation of which would be contrary to "ordre public" or morality, provided that such exploitation shall not be deemed to be so contrary merely because it is prohibited by law or regulation in some or all of the Contracting States'.

[7] As revised, this states: 'plant or animal varieties or essentially biological processes for the production of plants or animals; this provision shall not apply to micro-biological processes or the products thereof'.

[8] OJ EPO 11/1989, 451 (first decision by examiners); OJ EPO 12/1990, 476 (Board of Appeal); OJ EPO 10/1992, 590 (reconsidered decision by examiners).

[9] Opposition Proceedings EP 0 242 236 B1 (Opposition Division); T 0356/93 (Board of Appeal).

[10] Generally, see Beyleveld and Brownsword (1993b) and Sterckx (1997).

[11] [1995] EPOR 541, 549 (paragraph 6.1(a)).

[12] Ibid. (paragraph 6.1(b)).

[13] Ibid. (paragraph 6.1(c)).

[14] [1995] EPOR 541, 550 (paragraph 6.3).

tissue was obtained from the women with their consent; and, moreover, there was no reason to doubt the morality of procedures of this kind (because many life-saving substances, such as blood-clotting factors, had been developed in this way). The second argument was held to betray a fundamental misunderstanding. A patent covering DNA encoding human H2-relaxin does not confer on the proprietor a right to any part of any particular human being. No woman was enslaved by the patent; the right to self-determination simply was not affected. As for the idea that the patent entailed the dismemberment and piecemeal sale of women, quite the contrary was the case: the whole point of the invention was to enable human H2-relaxin to be produced in a technical manner outside the human body. Finally, the Opposition Division dismissed the argument that patents on genes (even on the whole human genome) amounted to the patenting of human life. There is, the Opposition Division said, more to a human being than the sum of its genes. Furthermore, if the opponents had no objection to the patenting of human proteins, they could not consistently object to the patenting of human genes encoding such proteins.

Given that the Opposition Division interpreted its exclusionary jurisdiction under Article 53(a) as coming into play only in the most exceptional of cases, essentially where the grant of a patent would be so abhorrent as to be inconceivable, it is not surprising that the opponents failed. Moreover, while the Opposition Division addressed the specific objections raised by the opponents, the more general objection invoking respect for human dignity was not squarely addressed. In the light of the new bioethics (as we called it in Chapter 2) and the deliberations of the European Union, the reasoning in *Relaxin* invites the question whether the opponents' dignity-based arguments would (and should) fare any better if they were to be presented under the legal framework brought in by the Directive on the Legal Protection of Biotechnological Inventions.

Relaxin *and the Directive on the Legal Protection of Biotechnological Inventions*

Revisiting the opposition presented in *Relaxin*, we can look first at the general objection that a patent on a product or process so intimately associated with human life must be inconsistent with human dignity (and, thus, excluded as immoral) and then we can consider the particular objection that the tissue donors (the pregnant women) were 'used'—in the sense that they were treated in a way that failed to recognize their status as bearers of human rights, thus compromising their human dignity. In the light of our analysis in the first part of the book, it will be apparent that, whereas the thrust of the general objection fits with dignity as constraint, the particular objection is in line with dignity as empowerment.

The General Objection

The patentability of human gene sequences was the most contested issue of principle during the ten-year debate that accompanied the passage of the Directive. In that debate the need to respect human dignity was a recurrent theme. Eventually a compromise was struck, which is reflected in Articles 5 and 6 of the Directive, as well as in a number of key Recitals.

Article 5(1) concedes to the objectors that the mere discovery of a gene fails the test of inventiveness: 'The human body, at the various stages of its formation and development, and the simple discovery of one of its elements, including the sequence or partial sequence of a gene, cannot constitute patentable inventions.' On the other hand, the limits of this concession are signalled by Article 5(2), which states: 'An element isolated from the human body or otherwise produced by means of a technical process, including the sequence or partial sequence of a gene, may constitute a patentable invention, even if the structure of that element is identical to that of a natural element.' To this, Article 5(3) adds that it is a condition of patentability that the 'industrial application of a sequence or a partial sequence of a gene [is] disclosed in the patent application'. If we assume a distinction between unisolated human gene sequences (in a person's body) and isolated copies of human gene sequences (in a laboratory), the effect of these provisions is to treat the former as categorically unpatentable (under Article 5(1)), but the latter as patentable *provided that* the copy is produced by means of a technical process (Article 5(2)) and the industrial application of the sequence is disclosed (Article 5(3)). On the face of it, therefore, Article 5 would not exclude the patent granted to the claimants in *Relaxin*.

However, the Directive, like the EPC, incorporates a morality exclusion. First, Article 6(1) of the Directive (in language that very closely resembles that of Article 53(a) of the EPC as revised)[15] provides:

Inventions shall be considered unpatentable where their commercial exploitation would be contrary to *ordre public* or morality; however, exploitation shall not be deemed to be so contrary merely because it is prohibited by law or regulation.

Second, Article 6(2) provides:

On the basis of paragraph 1 [i.e. Article 6(1)], the following, in particular, shall be considered unpatentable:

(a) processes for cloning human beings;
(b) processes for modifying the germ line genetic identity of human beings;
(c) uses of human embryos for industrial or commercial purposes;
(d) processes for modifying the genetic identity of animals which are likely to cause them suffering without any substantial medical benefit to man or animal, and also animals resulting from such processes.

---

[15] See n. 6 above. In our opinion, this revision to the EPC is wholly unnecessary and unhelpful. It is unhelpful because the focus of morality should be on that of granting monopoly control to the patent- holder. It is unnecessary because the morality of publication (and, indeed, that of development) is surely relevant to the morality of commercial exploitation, as is the morality of publication, development, and commercial exploitation to the morality of granting a patent. (See, further, Beyleveld *et al.* 2000: 164–7.)

Article 6 builds on a number of Recitals. Most obviously, Article 6(1) draws on Recital 37 (in conjunction with Recital 39);[16] and Article 6(2) draws on Recital 38 (in conjunction with Recitals 40, 41, 42, and 45).[17] However, other Recitals are also clearly relevant to the interpretation of Article 6, particularly Recitals 16, 26, and 43.[18]

Given that human gene sequences, or copies thereof, are not excluded by the express provisions of Article 6(2),[19] an opposition of the kind advanced in *Relaxin* would need to find a footing in Article 6(1). To some extent, the jurisprudence of European patent law resists such an argument, for it is established at the European Patent Office that exclusions from patentability are to be construed narrowly.[20] It might also be argued that the absence of an *explicit* exclusion for copies of human gene sequences points to the lack of any serious moral concern on the part of the drafters with regard to the patentability of inventive work on the human genome. Granted, concern about human dignity is frequently expressed, but nowhere (and especially in Article 6(2) and Recital 38) is this explicitly connected up to the patenting of copies of human genes.[21]

Against this reading of the Directive, opponents of patents on copies of human gene sequences might respond, first, that the EPC jurisprudence favouring a narrow construction of exclusions simply begs the question. Why should we think of a patent regime as an instrument for granting patents (subject to grudgingly accepted moral constraints)? Why not think of patentability as an exercise involving both technical and moral judgements, with no presumption in favour of a grant simply because the technical criteria are satisfied? Second,

[16] The first part of Article 6(1) copies in Recital 37. Recital 39 is drafted in obscure terms but, whatever else it might mean, it certainly signals that it is important to attend to moral considerations in the field of biotechnological inventions.

[17] For the text of Recital 38, see n. 19 below. Recitals 40, 41, 42, and 45 relate to each of the four specific exclusions listed in Article 6(2).

[18] For discussion of Recitals 16 and 26, see n. 21 below and pp. 202–4. Recital 43 rehearses the EU's commitment 'to respect fundamental rights, as guaranteed by the European Convention for the Protection of Human Rights and Fundamental Freedoms . . . and as they result from the constitutional traditions common to the Member States, as general principles of Community law'.

[19] Nor is there any mention of human gene sequences in Recital 38, which relates very closely to Article 6(2). According to Recital 38, 'Whereas the operative part of this Directive should also include an illustrative list of inventions excluded from patentability so as to provide national courts and patent offices with a general guide to interpreting the reference to *ordre public* and morality; whereas this list obviously cannot presume to be exhaustive; whereas processes, the uses of which offend against human dignity, such as processes to produce chimeras from germ cells or totipotent cells of humans and animals, are obviously also excluded from patentability'.

[20] See e.g. the *Plant Genetic Systems* case (T356/93) [1995] EPOR 357, 367: 'the exceptions to patentability have been narrowly construed, in particular in respect of plant and animal varieties. . . In the Board's view, this approach applies equally in respect of the provisions of Article 53(a) EPC.'

[21] Recital 16, to take a further illustration, is inconclusive as to whether *copies* of human gene sequences might be argued to be unpatentable on *moral* grounds. Although the Recital opens by saying that 'patent law must be applied so as to respect the fundamental principles safeguarding the dignity and integrity of the person', from which it follows that human gene sequences are not to be patented, it ends by reciting that such principles are 'in line with the criteria of patentability proper to patent law, whereby a mere discovery cannot be patented'.

while the argument that the drafters of the Directive would have *expressly* provided for the exclusion of copies of human gene sequences had they so intended is a respectable legal stock-in-trade, it is hardly conclusive—only so much should be read into a failure to make express legislative provision (see Fuller 1949). Moreover, in the context of Article 6, a failure to make express provision in Article 6(2) proves nothing about whether a particular kind of objection is arguable under the general test of Article 6(1).[22] Third, Recital 43 rehearses the commitment of the EU to respect for the rights protected under the European Convention on Human Rights (ECHR). It follows that, if the objection to the patenting of copies of human genes is that human rights under the ECHR are violated, or that human rights logically extended from the ECHR are violated,[23] or that human dignity as presupposed by the ECHR is compromised, then the point must be arguable under Article 6(1).

In principle, these arguments and counter-arguments might lead to one of three interpretations of the Directive: namely, patents on copies of human gene sequences are

(*a*) never open to challenge on moral grounds;

(*b*) open to challenge on moral grounds on a case-by-case basis; or

(*c*) always excluded on moral grounds.

The first of these interpretations is unconvincing because it treats Article 5 as settling not only the technical conditions for the patentability of copies of human gene sequences but also the moral questions addressed by Article 6. The third interpretation, deriving no assistance from Article 6(2), is equally unconvincing. The second interpretation not only looks plausible within the terms of the Directive, it fits better with the jurisprudence associated with the EPC (which, quite clearly, is important if patent law is to be harmonized in Europe).

Assuming that the Directive allows for case-by-case challenges under Article 6, the way would then be clear for a dignity-based opposition of the kind advanced in the *Relaxin* case. Whether or not such a challenge would, or should, succeed is another matter. It is eminently arguable that respect for human dignity is one of the cornerstone principles of the Directive (this can be derived from Recital 38 in conjunction with the first three examples given in Article 6(2) as well as from Recital 16 and the provisions of Recital 43, integrating the Directive with the fundamental rights guaranteed by the ECHR).[24] However, from a

---

[22] Although the UK implementation of Article 6(2) (in the Patents Regulations 2000, SI 2000/2037) drops the qualification that the four exclusions are 'in particular' excluded and nowhere else indicates that these exclusions are, as Recital 38 has it, only an 'illustrative list', it would be hard to argue that this exhausts the scope of the general exclusion as in Article 6(1).

[23] See our discussion in Ch. 4.

[24] It should be noted that, in the Patents Regulations 2000, the UK has not implemented any of the Recitals, which creates a problem as cases will be brought under domestic law and there is, as yet, no EC patent. It is arguable, because the domestic courts are required to give effect to the purpose of Directives (and Recitals are directly relevant to this), that patents could be disqualified where Recital 26 has not been complied with (see Beyleveld 2000c).

Gewirthian perspective, it will not do to echo the new European bioethics by simply insisting that patents on human genes compromise human dignity. Unless it is argued that patents on human genes impinge upon the status of agents as rights-bearers, there is no case to answer. It might be contended, in a particular case, that there is indeed such a violation, whether direct or indirect. For example, alleging a direct violation, it might be claimed that the particular exploitation of the human genome has failed to respect either the capacity that agents have to give informed consent or the conditions that they need to exercise an informed choice (possibly along the lines discussed in the next section, where the objection is that the tissue donors were used). Or the particular violation alleged might be indirect—for example, the argument might be that patents on human genes inhibit research that would otherwise have a positive impact on the basic (dignity-related) interests of agents. At all events, while we take the view that a dignity-based challenge should certainly be heard under Article 6, we also think that it should fail unless patenting of this kind, or in this particular case, fails to respect the distinctive capacities of agency or impacts adversely on the conditions that agents need to have if they are to flourish.

The Objection that the Tissue Donors Were 'Used'

A relevant way of developing the objection to the patent in the *Relaxin* case would be to focus upon the processes under which the tissue was taken by the researchers. Were the tissue donors 'used'? Did the researchers respect the fact that they were dealing with agents? Were the donors taken seriously as consent-competent persons or were they simply 'instrumentalized'? In this sense, was there a violation of the human dignity of the donors? While it is arguable that Article 6(1) is drafted in a way that restricts objections based on anything other than the morality of the future commercial exploitation of the invention, we can assume that it permits a broader range of objections, including objections looking back at the research and development of the invention.[25] On this assumption, Recital 26 of the Directive seems to be a highly relevant provision in relation to objections of this kind.

Recital 26, which appears at the end of a cluster of Recitals dealing with the matters provided for in Article 5, states: 'Whereas if an invention is based on biological material of human origin or if it uses such material, where a patent application is filed, the person from whose body the material is taken must have had an opportunity of expressing free and informed consent thereto, in accordance with national law.' On the face of it, this not only underlines the European view that insists upon there being informed consent as a precondition for taking human material (at least from the living), it also links directly to Article 6(1), inviting opposition to patents where informed consent requirements have not

---

[25] See n. 15 above.

been properly satisfied.[26] Yet, would this combination of provisions have assisted the opponents in the *Relaxin* case where the Opposition Division accepted that 'the women who donated tissue consented to do so within the framework of necessary gynaecological operations'?[27] This, after all, seems a long way removed from the circumstances in which tissue was taken from John Moore.[28]

Given that the general rule is that it is unlawful to take a person's bodily material without their consent, the most robust, literal, and indeed unambiguous interpretation of Recital 26 is that free and informed consent must be given not only to the taking of the tissue *but also to the use of the tissue in research work that might lead to an application for a patent.* In other words, the donor's consent must reach right through to the possibility of patenting (and, by implication, to subsequent patent-protected commercial exploitation). It is not clear whether the consent of the donor women in *Relaxin* would have satisfied such a stringent requirement. If not, on this interpretation of Recital 26 and Article 6(1), the patent should be excluded as immoral. Against this, however, we must reckon with a foreseeable pressure to weaken the requirements set by Recital 26 so that some allowance is made for the inconvenience (or impossibility) of obtaining informed consent.[29]

[26] See, too, Article 22 of the Council of Europe Convention on Human Rights and Biomedicine and the UNESCO Universal Declaration on the Human Genome and Human Rights.

[27] [1995] EPOR 541, 550 (paragraph 6.3.1).

[28] *Moore* v. *Regents of the University of California* (1990) 793 P 2d 479.

[29] In this vein, paragraph 8.15 of the Human Genetics Commission's discussion paper *Whose Hands on your Genes?* (2000) is an interesting case in point. There we read, first, that the wording of Recital 26 'does not make clear whether the consent refers to the original removal of the tissue or the patent application itself'. However, (*a*) we do not think that there is any reasonable grammatical construction of Recital 26 that enables the operative word 'thereto' to refer to the taking of human biological material rather than to the filing of the patent; (*b*) if we are wrong about this and there is grammatical ambiguity, then the fact that the Directive is about patenting, not the removal of human biological material, dictates that 'thereto' should refer to the filing of the patent; and (*c*) even if 'thereto' referred *directly* to removal, we would maintain that it would still refer *indirectly* to the filing of the patent *as well*, because consent to removal would not be free and informed without knowledge of the intention to patent *and the ability to withhold consent from this.* Second, we read that 'recitals do not need to be specifically incorporated into national law'—which, although correct, does not mean (as it might very well be taken to) that national law may be applied in a way that is inconsistent with Recital 26 (see Beyleveld 2000c). This paragraph concludes by saying that 'as a moral principle and for consistency (and commercial prudence) donors should perhaps understand that commercial gain includes the filing of patents in which they will retain no rights'. So the message (astonishingly) is that there is no good reason to obtain the donor's consent to the filing of the patent, but there are good reasons for informing donors that they retain no rights in the patents obtained. In effect, no ground is given to those who argue that dignity is compromised by allowing for financial gain from human body parts but, equally, no concession is made to the view that the dignity of donors is violated where their tissue is exploited without their consent. For further evidence of the pressure to weaken the consent requirement in Recital 26, see the recent Opinion of Advocate General Jacobs in *Kingdom of the Netherlands* v. *European Parliament and Council of the European Union* Case C-377/98. In paragraph 209 of this Opinion the Advocate General asserts that it is unclear whether the consent requirement in Recital 26 relates to the filing of the patent or to the taking of the tissue; and, in paragraph 211, although obtaining consent for all potential uses of human material is recognized to be fundamental, patent law is said to be an inappropriate framework for the imposition and monitoring of such a requirement. The decision of the ECJ is awaited with interest.

In so far as such allowance simply recognizes the validity of some kind of surrogate test (best interests or substituted judgement or the like) where a person is not able to give free and informed consent (whether dispositionally or merely particularly occurrently), there is no great problem. The critical question is how we read the requirement where persons are able (but perhaps unwilling) to give free and informed consent.

Prima facie, the purpose of the closing clause of Recital 26, which speaks of informed consent 'in accordance with national law', is to make the requirement contingent in some sense upon the position taken by national legal systems. If this signals scope for some national variation in relation to the particular procedures used for obtaining consent, or the standards thereof, then there is some cause for concern; for this would mean that a challenge under Article 6(1) would be limited to ensuring that patent-holders respect the consent requirements as understood in their own national legal regimes. On this view, provided that the donors in *Relaxin* were treated in accordance with national consent requirements, they could not be said to have been used. Having said this, however, no such weakening must be permitted to rewrite the fundamental requirement of Recital 26— namely, that the Recital will not be satisfied unless the consent to be obtained runs beyond the taking of the tissue to the filing of a patent (or the attempt to develop the material for the purpose of producing a patentable invention).[30]

In treatment settings, the very idea of free and informed consent is, of course, deeply problematic.[31] From a Gewirthian dignity-based perspective, however, the principal guidelines are clear. If agents have property in their own bodies and body parts (as considered in the previous chapter), the fact that an agent consents to the removal of tissue certainly does not imply consent to any future use of that tissue (and, where tissue might be of commercial value, consent to removal does not imply abandonment of any property interest). Even if agents do not have property in their own bodies and body parts, there is no reason to think that consent to the removal of the tissue implies consent to future commercial exploitation. If those who take and exploit the commercial value in human tissue are to respect the dignity of their sources, Gewirthian morality dictates that this should be on the basis of a free and fully informed consent—which is to say that sources must be put fully in the picture so that they understand precisely what it is that they are being asked to agree to.

Taking Stock

Revisiting the *Relaxin* case, it seems to us that, while the new bioethics might prompt a fresh line of dignity-based challenge, and while the Directive might

---

[30] See n. 22 above for the UK's implementation of the Directive.

[31] Generally, see Schuck (1994). See Ch. 8 for discussion of the approach to consent in the Nuffield Council on Bioethics Report, *Human Tissue: Ethical and Legal Issues* (1995).

permit such a challenge to be argued, such an opposition would not be well founded. Rather than arguing that the patenting of human genes is inconsistent with human dignity (as conceived by a particular community) or that the donor women might have compromised their own dignity, we should continue to question whether the dignity-based autonomy of the donors was respected—whether, in other words, the donors (as agents) were treated as capable of giving informed consent (or refusal) and whether steps were taken to ensure that their consent actually was free and fully informed.

Contracting

In various ways, transactions that might be objected to as 'commodifying' the human body are already regulated. For example, in England section 1 of the Human Organ Transplants Act 1989 prohibits commerce in human organs, section 1A of the Surrogacy Arrangements Act 1985 provides that surrogacy agreements are unenforceable, and the common law treats as illegal any contract tainted by sexual immorality (including the *indirect* promotion of prostitution). In the light of the new bioethics, one might be tempted to read such regulatory measures as an attempt to defend the value of human dignity; and, if John Moore had contracted with the regents in the way hypothesized at the beginning of this chapter, human dignity might again seem to be at risk if such commerce is permitted or enforced as a matter of private law obligation.

With the implementation of the Human Rights Act 1998 (which, broadly speaking, incorporates the ECHR into domestic English law (see, generally, Ewing 1999)), public authorities are clearly bound to act in a way that is compatible with the Convention rights (this being the so-called 'vertical' application of the Act). However, there is an important question about whether the Act will also have a 'horizontal' application, extending beyond the public sphere to impinge on private proceedings, including proceedings involving points of contract law (see e.g. Hunt 1998; Phillipson 1999; and Lester and Pannick 2000).[32] In advance of the jurisprudence of the Act settling down, the general assumption is that the Act will not have a *direct* horizontal effect. This means that the Convention rights may not be treated as, in themselves, the basis of a claim made in private law. In private law disputes, the Convention rights only apply when there is an independent recognized cause

---

[32] Lester and Pannick (2000: 383) suggest that the application of the Act should be thought of as 'more diagonal than directly horizontal. In terms of chess, the judge moves the unwritten law more in the manner of the Knight, that is forward and diagonally, but not directly sideways and horizontally, unlike the Queen or the castle.' Such a flurry of academic debate, it might be thought, is rather peculiar. For according to the spirit (and letter) of at least some pre-1998 case law (notably, perhaps, the Court of Appeal in *Derbyshire County Council* v. *Times Newspapers* [1992] QB 770; [1993] AC 534), the position anyway was that the Convention rights must be taken into account by the courts precisely in order to develop the common law (see e.g. Hunt 1997).

of action on which the claim is based.[33] Rather, the Act will have some degree of *indirect* horizontal application. For present purposes, we can assume that this means that, once a recognized private law claim is up and running, it must be handled in a way that is compatible with the Convention rights.

In this light, we should consider whether the value of respect for human rights and, more particularly, human dignity could have a bearing on the way in which we now understand and apply the principle of freedom of contract.[34] If the very idea that human dignity might have some bearing on contract sounds somewhat implausible, at any rate to English lawyers, the decision of the Supreme Court of Israel in *'Jerusalem Community' Funeral Society* v. *Lionel Aryeh Kesternbaum*[35] should give pause for thought. There the respondent contracted with the funeral society for his wife's funeral arrangements. According to the respondent, it was his deceased wife's wish that her tombstone should show her name, Gregorian date of birth, and Gregorian date of death in Latin characters. However, the funeral society refused to so engrave the tombstone, relying on a term in its standard form of contract to the effect that no letters other than those of the Hebrew alphabet should be engraved on its tombstones. The majority of the Supreme Court held that this term was void on the ground (*inter alia*) that it violated the respondent's right to freedom of expression, conscience, *and human dignity*. Predictably, though, respect for dignity was relied on in support of both majority and minority positions. While the majority saw the preservation of human dignity as a reason for restricting the funeral society's freedom of contract, the minority opinion treated the preservation of the dignity of the cemetery (in the sense of maintaining its traditional character) as an argument in favour of upholding the funeral society's freedom of contract.

---

[33] But famously contra, see a number of papers by Sir William Wade. For Sir William's fourth, and most recent, assertion of strong horizontality, see Wade (2000), this being in response to a very restrictive reading of the Act contended for by the Rt. Hon. Sir Richard Buxton (2000). Although there are numerous complexities and fine distinctions that need to be made if the position is to be stated precisely and accurately, comments made by the judges in the Court of Appeal in *Michael Douglas, Catherine Zeta-Jones, Northern & Shell plc* v. *Hello! Limited* (21 December 2000, available from the Court Service web site) suggest that the Courts may be willing to accept a position in practical effect (if not in procedure) will amount to full horizontality. The judgment by Sedley LJ, in particular, goes in this direction. An uncontroversial way in which horizontality can be achieved indirectly is if, in relation to, say, confidentiality, a value protected by the ECHR (e.g. privacy) is already recognized by domestic law as a relevant interest of the confider. In such a case, horizontal effect is to be achieved simply by requiring that this interest be interpreted in line with the Convention right. More controversially, it might be held that the only thing necessary to achieve indirect horizontality is that the claim be pinned on *some* existing action, *whether or not* the courts already recognize the right being claimed as a value to be protected in such an action. Yet Sedley LJ seems to contemplate just such a controversial mechanism for indirect horizontality, saying that 'if the step from confidentiality to privacy is not simply a modern restatement of a known protection but a legal innovation—then I would accept . . . that this is precisely the kind of incremental change for which the [Human Rights] Act is designed' (paragraph 129).

[34] See Clapham (1993) for the suggestion that the complementary values of democracy and dignity 'are the tools with which to analyse human rights in the private sphere' (p. 145).

[35] (1992) 46(ii) P. D. 464.

Before turning to human dignity in relation to the Human Rights Act and English contract law, we need a thumbnail sketch of the idea of freedom of contract. For, if there are to be dignity-based objections to the enforcement of contracts (such as that between John Moore and the university regents of the kind hypothesized at the start of this chapter), we can be sure that they will be countered by appeals to the pivotal idea of contractual freedom.

Freedom of Contract

From a Gewirthian perspective (although not only from such a perspective), there is a background sense in which agents have 'freedom of contract', meaning that it is permissible for agents freely to enter into agreements with one another or to make exchanges and that, concomitantly, agents have a right that others do not interfere with such permissible activity.[36] Moreover, in so far as dignity is closely related to an agent's capacity for making choices, and in so far as contract is seen as an arena for transactional and cooperative choices, then there is a close relationship between respecting 'freedom of contract' in this background sense and respecting dignity. In principle, such contracting activities can take place in the absence of (or prior to) the development of an institution of contract law; but, in practice, modern societies develop just such a legal institution, with a whole array of rules relating to what constitutes a contract as well as to who can contract, and with a set of sanctions (remedies) available in the event of non-performance. Once such an institution of contract law is in place, it is arguable that the background right of 'freedom of contract' is extended in such a way that agents are not to be improperly excluded from participation in the now legally backed activity of contracting. So understood, the background right of freedom of contract protects agents from interference with permissible (but not legally sanctioned) contracting as well as against exclusion from the contractual arena that is legally sanctioned.

Once an institutional version of contract is in place, 'freedom of contract' comes to be associated with three key principles, each of which seeks to influence the specific design of contract law. These three principles are: (1) that the law should respect the freedom of contracting parties to pursue their own purposes and to set their own terms (that is, to make their own bargains) (we can call this 'term freedom'); (2) that the law should respect the freedom of eligible contractors to choose their own partners (that is, the freedom not to contract) (we can call this 'partner freedom'); and (3) that where agreements have been freely made, the parties should be held to their bargains (usually expressed as 'sanctity of contract'). Unless we indicate otherwise, 'freedom of contract' should now be understood in the institutional sense with 'term freedom', 'partner freedom', and 'sanctity of contract' reflecting its three fundamental threads.

---

[36] The analysis in this section draws to some extent on Brownsword (2000*a,b*).

In the common law world it is trite that freedom of contract was central to the so-called classical law (see Atiyah 1979). As Sir George Jessel MR famously put it in *Printing and Numerical Registering Co* v. *Sampson*,[37] 'men of full age and competent understanding [should] have the utmost liberty of contracting, and . . . their contracts when entered into freely and voluntarily [should] be held sacred and [should] be enforced by Courts of justice'. This articulation of the idea of freedom of contract is best understood as calling for a three-pronged form of legislative and judicial restraint. First, if parties are to have 'the utmost liberty of contracting', it follows that legislatures and courts should be slow to limit the kinds of transactions, or the kinds of terms, that the parties can freely agree upon within the domain of contract (i.e. that there should be restraint as to term freedom). Concomitantly, and second, it might be said that 'the utmost liberty of contracting' implies a freedom *not* to contract, and a freedom to choose one's contracting partners (i.e. that there should be restraint, on the part of the state, in relation to placing restrictions on partner freedom). Third, where agreements have been made freely, the temptation to release parties from hard bargains should be resisted; excusing conditions should be given only limited recognition and applied sparingly—for even well-meaning paternalism betrays a lack of respect for the ideal of sanctity of contract (or *pacta sunt servanda*).

Of course, the idea that parties should be protected against legislative and judicial intervention in setting their contractual terms should not be read as a prescription for licence. The activities of contractors must be subject to whatever restrictions are necessary for the protection of the legitimate interests of third parties or the public interest. More plausibly, then, freedom of contract (*qua* term freedom) holds that parties should be permitted to make their own bargains, to set their own terms, *unless* there is 'a good reason' for non-enforcement or even prohibition. Clearly, the background philosophy of the particular legal order in which freedom of contract is so recognized matters a great deal to the way in which the category of good reasons is understood and applied. Historically, freedom of contract (at any rate, in the common law world) tends to be associated with an ideology of robust individualism coupled with Benthamite utilitarianism.[38] Given such a background philosophy, the *raison d'être* for allowing the parties freedom to set their own terms will be that such an approach (favouring private ordering over public allocation) is expected to maximize utility (or wealth); and, where freedom is restricted, the good reasons supporting the restriction will involve calculations of disutilities (or wealth losses) occasioned by freedom of contract. Where, however, a legal system takes human rights seriously then freedom of contract will need to be operated in a way that is compatible with respect for the rights of both the contractors and third parties. On the one side, if the contractors' freedom is itself seen as an aspect of a protected right to individual autonomy, then

---

[37] (1879) LR 19 Eq 462, 465.
[38] Although, for a more complex history, see Scheiber (1998).

it should not be abridged for simple utilitarian considerations (which will entail a restricted reading of public interest limiting reasons); on the other side, if the contractors' actions threaten the human rights of third parties, this will be a good reason for restricting freedom of contract.

Allowing that it will rarely be the case that we can neatly package a community's background morality within an established school of thinking (whether of a utilitarian or rights kind), we can at least say that, *where freedom of contract is taken seriously*, it will not count as a *sufficient* reason for intervention that the transaction is judged to be harmful to the interests of either or both of the contracting parties and, at strongest (where the contractors' autonomy rights trump other considerations), harm to such interests will not count as a good reason at all. Thus, where commitment to freedom of contract is at its strongest, it is not a good reason for (negative) interference that others would prefer the contractors not so to transact or perceive the contractors to be acting in a way that is self-harming: as it has been said on countless occasions, the price of liberty (and liberty of contract is like any other lifestyle liberty in this respect) is that the mere preferences of the majority (or of the 'community') must give way to the preferences of the contracting parties (see e.g. Ronald Dworkin 1978 and Trebilcock 1993).

With the enactment of the Human Rights Act, we can certainly say that the background morality against which the English law of contract operates has taken an explicit tilt towards acceptance of human rights. At minimum, then, the Courts must ensure that the common law is compatible with the Convention rights and this must mean that any infringement of these rights (when held by third parties)[39] counts as a good reason for restricting freedom of contract.

Human Dignity: Reinforcing or Restricting Freedom of Contract?

Let us assume that contractual terms should be interpreted in a way that renders them compatible with the Convention rights and that contracts that cannot be so interpreted will be unenforceable as contrary to public policy. Even if this proves to have a significant impact on contract law (which one might doubt), it is the need to respect human rights rather than to avoid compromising human dignity, as such, that is acting as the constraint on freedom of contract. For that matter, human dignity is not yet explicitly in the picture. Yet, when neither the ECHR nor the Human Rights Act explicitly mentions human dignity, can we draw on human dignity and, if we can, then to what effect?

The first of these questions is readily answered. For, it is trite that the ECHR copies across for Europe the principles agreed in the Universal Declaration of Human Rights, in which human dignity is explicitly declared as one of the

---

[39] The relationship between freedom of contract and Convention rights held by the contracting parties themselves is dealt with in the next section.

foundational ideas. Indeed, as we said in Chapter 1, human dignity is the infra-structure on which the modern superstructure of human rights is constructed. Moreover, while the Council of Europe might have drafted the ECHR without explicitly relying on the notion of human dignity, it has conspicuously changed its practice in the recent Convention on Human Rights and Biomedicine 1996. As we saw in Chapter 2, this is an instrument drafted on the basis that human dignity is the essential value to be upheld. Accordingly, unless one stands on an extreme literalism, it is difficult to resist the proposition that respect for human dignity is the implicit foundation of the Human Rights Act.[40] If so, what does this imply?

One way of unpacking the principle of respect for human dignity might be to reinforce (rather than to limit) the scope and importance of freedom of contract (at any rate, as between the contracting parties themselves). As we have indicated already, the idea of a dignity-based background right to freedom of contract has more than a little plausibility. There is a widely accepted chain of thinking that links respect for dignity with respect for individual autonomy, the latter of which is expressed (although not exclusively so) through the exercise of contractual choice (see e.g. McCurdy 1998: 168). On this view, respect for human dignity and freedom of contract form a virtuous circle: without at least the right to make our own contracts (whether within or outwith an institutional framework of contract law), our dignity is violated; with such a right, to this extent at least, our dignity is respected. Now, if we assume that background rights (such as the suggested right to freedom of contract but also human rights of the kind enumerated by the ECHR) are to be given the standard Gewirthian reading, then they are to be interpreted under a will conception of rights; in principle, and by virtue of the dignity of agents, the benefit of these rights may be waived (by consent or contract);[41] and, unless a particular legal institution such as the law of contract signals otherwise, these rights must continue to be read under the will conception post-incorporation. It follows that, in the absence of contrary institutional signals, the benefits of the rights recognized by the law must be open to waiver. This is no surprise in relation to freedom of contract (within the institution). For example, a party might agree to waive the benefit of partner freedom for a period by entering into a lock-out or exclusive dealing agreement. However, the possibility of waiving the benefits of newly incorporated human rights, and of doing so by virtue of contractual agreement, points to the potential power of (dignity-based) contractual freedom. For example, if respect for dignity entails that agents must be permitted freely to contract out of (or waive) the benefit of their ordinary

---

[40] See Clapham (1993: 143) for examples of the recurrent use of human dignity in international human rights Declarations, Covenants, Conventions, and Resolutions.

[41] There is a puzzle about how far it is possible (logically) to waive the benefit of the right of freedom of contract if we treat the act of waiver as itself an exercise of this right. There is no difficulty in conceiving of a waiver of the ordinary benefits of contractual freedom within the institution of contract, nor of limited waivers outside the institution. However, to purport to waive all benefits of freedom of contract implies a contradiction unless there is a proviso saving the right and its benefit for the purpose of making this otherwise all-encompassing waiver.

Human Rights Act entitlements, then (for instance) one might purport to contract away the benefit of what would otherwise be a protected right to family life or freedom of expression.[42] If this is correct, then the focal question would be whether or not there had been a free waiver, not whether freedom of contract took priority over freedom of expression (or whatever) in a balance of competing interests.[43]

We might, however, read the import of human dignity rather differently. It will be recalled that Article 21 the Convention on Human Rights and Biomedicine 1996 provides: 'The human body and its parts shall not, as such, give rise to financial gain.' In so prohibiting such commerce, according to the Explanatory Report to the Convention, the intention is that 'body parts' should apply to 'organs and tissues proper, including blood' (paragraph 132) but not to products such as 'hair and nails, which are discarded tissues, and the sale of which is not an affront to human dignity' (paragraph 133).[44] If the idea of respect for human dignity can be read into the Human Rights Act, it is at least arguable that it constitutes a 'good reason' for restraining certain forms of biocommerce—and the Convention on Human Rights and Biomedicine clearly signals a European view that freedom of contract should be so limited. Furthermore, we might also draw on the new bioethics to argue for a restraint on freedom to contract (i.e. freedom of choice in relation to one's contractual partners), particularly where genetic information is implicated in a refusal to contract. A familiar question (foreshadowed by the *'Jerusalem Community' Funeral Society* case) thus takes shape: if, following the enactment of the Human Rights Act, the principle of respect for human dignity is relevant to English contract law then does it serve to underpin freedom of contract (the autonomy of contractors) or to constrain it?

---

[42] *Attorney General* v. *Barker* [1990] 3 All ER 257 is an interesting case in point. There the Attorney General, representing the Queen's private interests, sought to restrain the publication of a book the contents of which (if published) would clearly breach a contractual undertaking given by Barker when he entered into the service of the royal family. The question for the Court of Appeal concerned the territorial scope of the restraint. It was argued that Article 10 of the ECHR militated against the UK courts setting a restraint extending outside the United Kingdom. However, a worldwide restraint was put in place, with Lord Donaldson MR emphasizing the importance of sanctity of contract. 'For my part, I would have thought that much more relevant was the question of whether a man's word is his bond and whether contractual obligations freely entered into shall be maintained. It is not a question of what foreigners are entitled to read, but what somebody subject to the jurisdiction of this court is entitled to publish and it is an incidental result that, if he cannot publish, foreigners cannot read. . . . I cannot believe that there is a foreign country which would regard the sanctity of contract as not being of enormous importance and central to the necessities of a democratic society' (p. 261).

[43] For an excellent general discussion of the nature of rights under the ECHR, see McHarg (1999); and for an indication of the European Court of Human Rights' willingness to accept agreement as a legitimate waiver of the benefit of a right, see e.g. *Stedman* v. *UK* (1997) 23 EHRR CD 128.

[44] Similarly, although most proximately under the rubric of respect for *integrity*, Article 3 of the Charter of Fundamental Rights of the European Union prohibits 'making the human body and its parts a source of financial gain'. The prohibition of trafficking in human beings in Article 5 of the Charter, however, is said to stem directly from the cornerstone principle of respect for human *dignity*.

Human Dignity, Term Freedom, and Partner Freedom

The spirit of the institutional version of freedom of contract, we have suggested, is that there should be 'good reasons' for restricting (or failing to support) the choices made by contractors. If we practise what we preach, contractors will enjoy freedom in two spheres—in relation to their choice of contractual projects, purposes, and particular terms (term freedom) and in relation to their choice of co-contractors (partner freedom). Given a Gewirthian approach to the freedom of contracting agents, to what extent is respect for human dignity a good reason for restricting contractual choice?

Term Freedom

The Gewirthian approach to term freedom centres on a clear guiding principle— namely, provided that agents enter into contracts on the basis of free and informed consent, and provided that the contract does not violate the generic rights of third parties, then the transaction is at least morally permissible and, other things being equal, the State should respect the common will of the contractors. The dignity of agents includes the capacity for making contractual choices, and we respect that dignity precisely by allowing agents to make their choices. Having said this, it is worth reiterating that the prerequisite of informed consent is an important proviso: human dignity as conceived by Gewirthians is the basis for the exercise of autonomy, not a licence for the exploitation of other agents. It follows that term freedom is not a licence for one contractor to abuse its bargaining power by compromising the dignity of a fellow contractor, nor for the contractors to act in concert with a view to abusing the dignity of third parties.[45]

Against this approach, human dignity is appealed to as a reason for restricting various manifestations of term freedom. Even if we can overcome the property objection (on the basis of the arguments presented in Chapter 8), the sale of human organs, tissues, and the like is an obvious case in point. As we have just said, in Europe Article 21 of the Convention on Human Rights and Biomedicine relies on respect for human dignity in order to prohibit financial gain from commerce in the human body or body parts; and, writing from a North American vantage point, Michael Trebilcock remarks that the legal prohibitions on the sale of organs reflect 'the commonly held notion that body parts are among those things which ought not to be bought and sold, because they are intrinsic to our personhood' (Trebilcock 1993: 38).[46] Surrogacy agreements, too, may fall foul of

---

[45] Arguably, the actions of the Funeral Society in the *Kesternbaum* case (in text above) involved a violation of the dignity of a fellow contractor (or so the majority ruled). In the context of a surrogacy contract, the majority judgment of Panelli J in *Johnson* v. *Calvert* (1993) 851 P 2d 776 (Cal SC) nicely illustrates the concern that the parties should enter such an agreement on an informed and free basis.

[46] For a stimulating discussion of various contractual or quasi-contractual arrangements that might be seen as falling within the range of Article 21, see Brazier (1999); and, famously, see Landes and Posner (1978).

the objection put to the Warnock Committee in England that 'it is inconsistent with human dignity that a woman should use her uterus for financial profit and treat it as an incubator for someone else's child' (Warnock Committee 1984, paragraph 8.10).[47] However, whether such objections are traced back to the Kantian duty of self-esteem, or to the idea that human dignity has no price, or to the vision of human dignity that is taken to define one's community as the particular community that it is, they cannot stand (given a Gewirthian view) unless such transactions violate the principle of free and informed consent between the parties or respect for the PGC-protected rights of third parties.

Nevertheless, where contractors are manifestly vulnerable, there are dignity-based considerations that must be taken seriously by Gewirthians. The dwarf-throwing case that we discussed in the first part of the book nicely illustrates two such dignity-based arguments. First, there is the argument that the dwarfs could not have freely entered into their contracts with the clubs. Even allowing that respect for dignity involves respect for free choice, it simply is not plausible to regard the choice made by the dwarfs as free. Second, there is the argument that the dwarfs were simply used as a means (by the clubs who employed them, and by the customers who threw them). Again, the dignity of the dwarfs (even for Gewirthians) was surely violated. What do we make of these two arguments, each of which could be applied equally plausibly to organ-selling, surrogacy, prostitution, and the like?

With regard to the first of these points, let us concede that there is no bright line to be drawn between those situations where a party 'freely' contracts and those where a contractor's choice is no longer 'free'. To be sure, we can agree that there is no free choice where a party is subject to physical coercion, but it is much more difficult to characterize a choice as free or unfree relative to the economic context in which a particular contract is made. Other things being equal, however, we can say that the more options the market offers, the less pressure there is to enter into any particular contract and the more plausible it is to characterize the choice as free. What makes the choice of the dwarfs problematic (similarly, the choice of organ-sellers where the transaction involves an *inter vivos* transfer) is that we suspect that these choices would not have been made had there been (*a*) other options and (*b*) less pressure to raise money or find employment. This is not the place to attempt to theorize the conditions of free choice and informed consent. Nevertheless, if we deny the dwarfs, organ-sellers, and others these problematic options, we run into the trap of the double bind. For, where an agent has just the one viable option, to close off that option (whether on the ground of lack of free choice or as compromising dignity) is to reduce what little room for manoeuvre that agent has anyway. As Michael Trebilcock says,

---

[47] In the United Kingdom no surrogacy arrangement is enforceable as a contract by or against any of the parties (see section 1A of the Surrogacy Arrangements Act 1985, inserted by section 36 of the Human Fertilisation and Embryology Act 1990). Generally, for discussion of the legal position, see e.g. Mason and McCall Smith (1999: 77–85).

The problem of the double bind arises because in many contexts prohibiting commodification or exchange may make the plight of the individual whose welfare [dignity] is central to the commodification objection actually worse. For example, banning prostitution or commercial surrogacy contracts, as morally offensive as these may be to many people, may eliminate one of the few income-earning options available to poor women and thus exacerbate their plight and that of their families. (1993: 25)

Indeed, in the case of the dwarfs, the bind was even more severe because it was the opportunity of gainful employment that the dwarfs saw as the key to retaining their self-esteem and sense of dignity.

The second argument (that the dwarfs were simply used as a means) certainly strikes a Gewirthian chord. However, we fail to respect the dignity of others not by treating them as a means (otherwise any kind of cooperative or contractual activity would be an affront to dignity), but by treating them *merely* as a means. In the clearest case, we fail to respect the dignity of others when we treat them as though they lack the capacities of agency, particularly the ability to express their will by giving or refusing their consent. Once this objection is focused in this way, it becomes much more difficult to cash the objection that the dwarfs, organ-sellers, and so on were simply used. If the dwarfs had been treated as being incapable of giving their consent, or in a way that paid no attention to whether or not they had consented to participate in dwarf-throwing, then their dignity would have been violated, and they would have been treated as a mere means or object. However, they were not treated in this way; they had consented; and, at least in the case of the dwarfs, they sought to uphold rather than to escape from their contracts.[48] These considerations surely take the sting out of the objection (similarly, in relation to organ-sellers, surrogates, and prostitutes provided that the consent condition is satisfied).

Is this not a bit too quick with the objection, though? After all, might there not be some *indirect* effects of licensing commerce in body parts and the like? Even if commerce of this kind cannot be legitimately objected to as compromising human dignity per se, might not the consequences of allowing markets of this kind to operate be corrosive of respect for the dignity of others (in the Gewirthian sense)? Might we not come to view one another as mere repositories of body parts? Or might some buyers use the market as a vehicle to demean sellers (in the sense of making sellers feel that they have demeaned themselves)? To establish whether some such risks might materialize in practice, there would have to be empirical research over a period of time, including testing out the effect of different market settings. However, even if some such risks materialized, we should not think that dignity would be powerless to protect those who were so demeaned or used. For, it must not be forgotten that respect for human dignity has an important protective dimension, including the insistence that agents' choices are only

---

[48] This is not like the case of, say, an extortionate credit agreement where the debtor pleads a violation of dignity with a view to rescinding or avoiding the contract.

to be enforced where they are made on a free and informed basis. Moreover, even if we concede that there might be some such risks, to insist that commerce of this kind should be prohibited on the basis of simple speculation would imply either a high level of risk aversion or a fear of extraordinarily grave consequences (should preventive steps not be taken). Given that, on a *non-speculative* basis, we do not insist that 'sexual intercourse should be prohibited because it permits the possibility of rape' (Harris 1998: 32),[49] this might seem to be something of an overreaction.

Genetic Discrimination and Partner Freedom

Article 11 of the Convention on Human Rights and Biomedicine, reflecting widespread concern about the potentially exclusionary effects of genetic discrimination, prohibits 'any form of discrimination against a person on grounds of his or her genetic heritage'. As is well known, particular concern has been expressed about the possibility of one's genetic profile being a required part of one's curriculum vitae, which will then lead to bad genetic risks being excluded from contracts, notably by insurers and employers (see e.g. Nuffield Council on Bioethics 1993, Chs. 6 and 7; Gannon and Villiers 1999; Human Genetics Commission 2000, section 9). In the United States, for instance, President Clinton barred American Federal government agencies from discriminating against employees on the basis of genetic tests,[50] as well as giving his backing to a Senate Bill designed to extend similar protection to the private sector and insurance purchasers. If such a scenario of adverse selection were to materialize, the practice of declining bad risks might be defended under the rubric of freedom of contract (specifically the freedom not to contract). Would the Human Rights Act, with the aid of human dignity, have any purchase on such exercises in partner freedom?

A natural starting point is the provision in Article 14 of the Convention that the Convention rights and freedoms are to be secured without discrimination on any ground, including the standard grounds of sex, race, colour, language, religion, political opinion, or the like. Although the Convention does not specifically identify genetic discrimination as a prohibited ground, it is eminently arguable that such a ground could be read as within the ambit of Article 14. For instance, one might cite in support of this view, not only Article 11 of the Convention on Human Rights and Biomedicine but also Article 2 of the Universal Declaration of Human Rights (UDHR). The latter, which articulates a broad principle of non-discrimination, might then be tied to Article 2 of the UNESCO Universal Declaration on the Human Genome and Human Rights, according to which

---

[49] Generally, for a sceptical commentary on appeals to dignity in the context of commerce in body parts, see Duxbury (1996).

[50] See *The Guardian*, 9 Feb. 2000, 14.

(a) Everyone has a right to respect for their dignity and for their rights regardless of their genetic characteristics.
(b) That dignity makes it imperative not to reduce individuals to their genetic characteristics and to respect their uniqueness and diversity.

As we pointed out in Chapter 2, this Article is seen as being derived from Article 2 of the UDHR and as adding the genetic criterion to it. Moreover, according to the chair of the Legal Commission of UNESCO's International Bioethics Committee, 'Many other instruments adopted by UNESCO also refer to this principle of non-discrimination . . . In taking the dignity of the human person as its reference, the Declaration seeks above all to condemn any attempt to draw political or social inferences from a purported distinction between 'good' genes and 'bad' genes' (Espiell 1999: 3). At the very least, then, it is arguable that a principle of non-discrimination (including genetic discrimination) protects the implementation of the Convention rights; and, if the ECHR provided *explicitly* that there was a right to insist upon a contract of employment, or a contract of insurance, or whatever, there would clearly be a 'good reason' in the Human Rights Act to limit the freedom *not* to contract. However, there is no such right and, thus, no such direct route to a legitimate restriction on freedom of contract. Is there, then, an indirect route?

The most promising indirect argument is to view the specific principle of non-discrimination in the Human Rights Act as a particular application of a general principle of non-discrimination. In England, where there is a considerable jurisprudence relating to racial and sexual discrimination (and, more recently, recognition and regulation of disability discrimination), it seems plausible to argue from a general principle of non-discrimination (including genetic discrimination) as well as to argue that such a principle applies to the field of contract (as is already the case in respect of racial and sexual discrimination). Plausible though this all might seem, we need to be clearer about why (and to what extent) choices based on genetic information should be thought to be questionable.

From a number of starting points in the liberal tradition, we might have reason to question the legitimacy of genetic discrimination. For example, for those who think the Rawlsian thought (see Rawls 1972) that racial or sexual discrimination is unjust, genetic discrimination will seem to be a similar case. Behind a Rawlsian veil of ignorance, contractors will have no more knowledge of their actual genetic profile than of their race or sex. In consequence, their risk-averse approach will dictate that, in the absence of good reasons, the basic principles of fair dealing in society should not allow for one's genetic characteristics to be used against one. Alternatively, one might arrive at a similar conclusion by reflecting on the damage that might be occasioned to a person's self-esteem (to an agent's additive interests in Gewirthian theory) as a result of discriminatory practices that relate to a non-relevant feature of agency.

It is true, of course, that the tide of Gewirthian thinking runs strongly in favour of individual choice—the right to say yes but equally the right to say no—but only so long as this is compatible with the rights of fellow agents, including the right to be protected against actions that represent an affront to one's dignity.[51] If discrimination on genetic grounds involves regarding bad-risk agents as incapable of exercising choice, or as inferior, or something of that kind, then this is certainly something to be targeted. Similarly, if genetic discrimination has the effect of excluding agents from the enjoyment of conditions in which one can maintain a sense of one's own value, or if it consigns persons to circumstances that are demeaning or degrading, then respect for human dignity is also violated. However, where selection (and non-selection) is illegitimate only if specific discriminatory reasons or attitudes or effects are in play, this means that genetic discrimination *tout court* is not ruled out. In principle, it is plainly right to identify the particular form of discrimination that is to be checked; in practice, though, this might weaken the regulatory control—which, in turn, might invite a precautionary strategy under which genetic discrimination is self-consciously *over*-regulated in order to ensure that most, if not all, cases of illegitimate discrimination are caught.[52]

Clearly, there is a good deal more to be said about genetic discrimination in general and its relation to human dignity and human rights in particular (see e.g. O'Neill 1998). So far as the Human Rights Act is concerned, however, there is a real difficulty about continuing this debate so long as the horizontal application of the legislation is restricted to existing actions that already recognize the right claimed as a value to be respected.[53] If this proves to be the case, the technical challenge in English law will be how to plead unlawful (genetic) discrimination, particularly in the sphere of contractual negotiation. Perhaps the long-standing recognition of good faith in insurance contracts and its more recent reception in consumer contracts might coalesce to support a duty to negotiate in good faith which would then act as a conduit leading from contract negotiation to a general principle of non-discrimination (see, generally, Brownsword *et al.* 1999).[54]

---

[51] See further Gannon and Villiers (1999) for comments on the significance of autonomy where genetic tests are proposed for employees who are already in employment.

[52] If, instead, we consider genetic discrimination from the standpoint of human dignity as constraint, we might also judge that genetic discrimination should be prohibited. To allow for discrimination on genetic grounds is to make a certain sort of statement about the kind of community that this is. If this is not the community vision that we share, if this is not our idea of a civilized society, then a limit must be placed on partner freedom. Again, this particular vision might be refined so that genetic discrimination is regulated only in certain contexts or only where specific discriminatory reasons or attitudes are employed. On the other hand, a more robust view might be taken, prohibiting all forms of genetic discrimination: in other words, there would be a prohibition on the use of genetic information for the purposes of selection or non-selection, irrespective of the particular reason for which that information would be employed. Such a precautionary approach might make very good sense where the protection of the culture is judged to be more important than the preservation of the maximum amount of freedom and choice. It would be ironic, indeed, if human dignity as constraint proved the more effective basis for regulating genetic discrimination in an otherwise freedom-loving society.

[53] But see n. 33 above.

[54] For some signs that the tide of opinion might be turning in favour of a general principle of good faith in contracts, see several of the papers in Forte (1999).

Failing this, where the boundary between the public and the private is hazy, there might be opportunities to plead abuse of contractual right by way of judicial review (see Brownsword 1999). Generally, though, without some common law engineering, the Human Rights Act (even backed by the principle of respect for human dignity) might not be the answer to this particular problem.

Conclusion

The key to respecting dignity (other than in the special sense of living in accordance with the virtue of dignity) is to respect the fact that agents have a range of distinctive capacities: the capacity for free and purposive action, including the capacity to make informed choices, to give or refuse consent, and so on. It follows that, where the generic rights of agents are at issue, we need to attend very carefully to whether or not there is a covering consent for our actions. Consent is the green light; an absence of consent is at best an amber light; and a refusal of consent is clearly a red light. Hence, contrary to a number of the currents in the new bioethics, we believe that, in principle, property and commerce in body parts, as patents on inventions derived from human tissue, are compatible with human dignity. If the story in John Moore's case had been different, the question should have been whether the physicians acted with Moore's consent, not whether the enforcement of a contract between Moore and the physicians, or the patenting of the cell-line, involved the parties in compromising their own dignity or acting against the community's conception of human dignity. This is not to say that there is not a good deal more to consider in licensing patents and contracts of this kind—not least, precisely how we conceive of free and informed consent and whether we can secure it. However, respect for human dignity is, if anything, an argument in favour of, rather than against, biocommerce.

10

Living with Dignity III: Prolonging Life, Denying Death, and Cosmetic Augmentation

Introduction

Medical science enables life to be prolonged and its quality to be improved. While this is independent of advances in genetics and molecular biotechnology, the latter open up the possibility of treatments and manipulations so radical that the possibility of bodily immortality is sometimes mooted.

This is loose talk, designed to create headlines for a sensation-seeking media. Certainly, spare part surgery,[1] the possibility of being able to slow down the process of cell ageing, or the possibility of giving cells the capacity to divide in a controlled way indefinitely suggest that doubling, trebling, or even further extending current lifespans is not a mere pipe-dream. However, immortality is not merely a long time, not even a *very* long time. It is not measured in hundreds of years, thousands of years, trillions of years, or in any order of number of years one chooses to mention, but—like infinity—has no measure. For bodily immortality to be taken seriously, almost everything current scientific thinking claims to understand about the nature of physical matter and the universe would need to be rejected. Nevertheless, a world in which people routinely live to 200 or more years would be a very different world from the one we live in, and the possibility that aspiring to live that long, or to create such a world, is contrary to human dignity is something that must be considered.

Alongside prolongation of life, scientific advances enable conditions that were previously incurable or irreversible to be no longer so, and the list of possible treatments is being extended continually. Since new treatments rest increasingly on fundamental knowledge about molecular and genetic processes, however, they not only offer the possibility of alleviating or curing conditions that are life-threatening, physically or mentally debilitating, or painful, but also (at least in theory) enable alterations that can radically enhance physical or mental performance, or confer purely social or aesthetic advantages.

Of course, interventions that are designed to prolong life may also improve its quality and vice versa. However, if only for convenience, we will divide this chapter into two sections—the first dealing with interventions *as designed* to

---

[1] For which organs may be obtained, not merely from living donors or from those who have died, but from genetically modified animals, more radically from the use of non-reproductive cloning to grow new organs, and most radically in the form of mechanical devices (leading, ultimately, to human–machine hybrids).

prolong life, the second dealing with interventions *as designed* to improve the quality of life.

Prolongation of Life

Interventions designed to prolong life might be carried out with the consent of the treated person, without this consent, or against the treated person's will. In this chapter we will deal mainly with interventions designed to prolong life that the treated person has consented to. Interventions designed to prolong life without the treated person's consent, or even in the face of the treated person's objection, will be dealt with mainly in the next and final chapter.

We have already said that the proposition that science might achieve literal bodily immortality for us should not be taken seriously. Some persons, nevertheless, desire such immortality, and the possibility that pursuing this aim is not merely silly but contrary to human dignity is the first thing to be considered.

Following that, we will focus on the realistic aim of great extension of bodily life and the (perhaps) not impossible one of indefinite (but not infinite) extension of bodily life, during which we will distinguish the aim of prolongation of one's own bodily existence and 'prolongation' through the continued existence of succeeding generations and future persons (the aim of 'vicarious' prolongation).

Finally, in this section we will consider some specific issues raised by suggested means for achieving prolongation.

Trying to Live For Ever

For literal bodily immortality to be possible, it must be possible for embodied beings to be indestructible by any means whatsoever. Embodied immortal beings would have to be free of any requirements for food or outside sources of energy, and impervious to nuclear explosion or even to contact with anti-matter. The thought is ludicrous. That, on our most advanced theories and knowledge of matter, cannot be achieved by any physical entity. To aspire to such immortality is wholly without warrant. Indeed, it is silly.

It is not merely silly, however. If our analysis in Chapter 6 is correct, then it is contrary to human dignity. The mere aspiration is a refusal to accept conditions that are necessary to give point to morality. As such, it is an attempt to transcend moral responsibility. It is an attempt to transcend dignity by pretending that it does not exist. We argued that this is the essence of undignified conduct, as well as being dispositionally dangerous.

Trying to Extend One's Life Indefinitely

Trying to live for ever as an embodied being must be distinguished from the aim of indefinite extension of one's bodily existence. By indefinite extension of bodily existence rather than bodily immortality we mean a conditional bodily immortality, an immortality conditional on getting food (or fuel, if we think about extension via human–machine hybrids) and not getting in the path of nuclear explosions etc. We do not see how the possibility of this can be ruled out a priori.

Because such extension recognizes the vulnerability of bodily existence, it is not open to the critique that can be directed at the aim of literal immortality. It is not, however, free of problems in relation to respect for human dignity.

Most obviously, there are problems of distributive justice. All agents are equal in dignity under the PGC. Thus, equality of dignity requires all agents to be treated equally with respect to their generic rights. Suppose, then, that it is technically feasible to grant indefinite bodily existence to anyone. Could this be granted to everyone? If so, then recognition of the equal dignity of all would require it to be granted to all who desire it. Suppose, however, which is highly likely, that costs make this impossible; or suppose that costs do not preclude all receiving the necessary treatment, but that the consequences of treating everyone would put such a strain on the earth's resources that some would have to die despite their potential for indefinite existence if others are to enjoy such an existence. How would the decision be made as to who is to receive the treatment or who is to receive the available resources to enable their potential indefinite existence to be actualized? It does not take much imagination to foresee that it is the powerful, the rich, and the influential who would, in practice, receive the 'gift' of indefinite existence and that the weak, the poor, and the 'unimportant' would be deprived; and there is no doubt that this would be a denial of their equal dignity.

There is a solution to this, in principle, however. This is that those who are to receive it are to do so on a purely random basis, as decided by lottery. This would not result in all receiving the necessary interventions, but would give all an equal chance of doing so, and this would be consistent with the equal dignity of all. However, anyone who believes that the powerful and rich would permit this to their possible detriment knows nothing about human psychology.

These reflections do not apply only to the availability of treatments that promise to extend life indefinitely. They apply to the distribution of health care and all treatments that prolong life. Prima facie, any treatments and interventions are consistent with the equal dignity of all agents only to the extent that all have an equal chance to benefit from them if they so wish.[2]

Vicarious Extension

The media has carried stories about persons who would like to be cloned in order

---

[2] The application of this principle, however, raises numerous issues and involves a host of complexities that we are unable to go into here, but must leave for another occasion. Readers may, however, consult Gewirth (1996: 74–5, 158–9), for relevant discussion about the requirement for equality of opportunity rather than equal (i.e. the same) treatment.

to survive their bodily deaths. If there are people who believe that a genetically identical person created from one of their cells would be themselves, then they are sadly deluded. Cloning technology can only reproduce a person's genes, and persons are (or so genetic theory has it) products of their genes in interaction with their environments. But even if the clone could be given an environment that would produce a qualitatively identical personality (which is unimaginable), the clone would still be a distinct individual (quantitatively not identical). The clone might grow up to be indistinguishable in appearance and personality from the parent, but it would not be the parent. The parent would not literally continue to live in the clone. How could this be so if the parent were still alive? And what possible reason could there be for believing that the parent's psyche would transfer to the clone when the parent 'died'? If it did, what would happen to the clone's psyche?

However, there are those, who include the distinguished moral philosopher Derek Parfit, who might regard having such a clone exist after one's death as being 'about as good as' one's continued existence (Parfit 1984: 201). Is such an attitude silly? While we do not share this view, we suspend judgement, as we see no reason not to regard this as a purely individual matter. It is to be noted, too, that such an attitude is not very different from the feeling that very many people have that they can continue to 'live through' their children and succeeding generations. Of course, they literally cannot; but the idea that 'they' continue to exist, at least in part, as long as they have descendants is comforting to them. Furthermore, this attitude is not all that different from the desire that many have to 'live on in the minds of others', to 'continue to live' as long as there are those who remember them or what they have done.

Such attitudes might not be harmful in themselves. However, they are not altogether neutral in relation to human dignity. The 'feeling' that one can live through others (before or after one's bodily death) need not be a mere feeling, as it can (and sometimes does) lead to steps being taken to try to make the subject of one's 'vicarious existence' be like oneself (or do what one would have liked to have done, but failed to do). *If so*, the attitude contradicts and actively threatens the autonomy and dignity of the person through whom one hopes to 'exist vicariously'.[3]

Issues in Relation to Specific Means of Extension

Telomere Manipulation

Normal cell division results in cells with telomeres[4] that are shorter than the telomere of the parent cell. When this shortening has progressed to a particular

---

[3] It is because, as we observed in Ch. 7, cloning (to cite just one example) does not necessarily involve such controlling desires and actions that it cannot, independently of the contingent motives that attend it, be said to be contrary to human dignity on grounds of this kind.

[4] Telomeres are DNA-protein complexes at the end of linear chromosomes.

extent, the cells produced are unable to divide further. The enzyme telomerase can regenerate telomeres *in vitro*. This raises the possibility that understanding the processes involved will enable treatments to be developed that would give differentiated cells the capacity to reproduce themselves indefinitely, which (at present) only cancerous cells (which divide uncontrollably) can do in humans. Such treatments might constitute a very large step in the direction of indefinite extension of life (see e.g. Fossel 1996; Nash 1997).

However, it does not seem to us that this raises any special problems in relation to human dignity that are not raised by the pursuit of indefinite extension of embodied life as such.

Standard Transplantation from Other Humans

By standard transplantation from other human beings, we mean transplantation from living donors and from dead human beings, *excluding* (i) the use of non-reproductive cloning of organs or tissue for transplantation from embryos or from the cells of persons other than the recipient of the transplant (which we will comment on in the next subsection); or (ii) reproductive cloning by which anencephalic[5] humans are produced as spare part factories for the persons from whom they are cloned (which we will comment on in the next subsection but one).

Issues concerning human dignity arise in relation to commercialization of standard transplantation, and we considered these in the last chapter. Issues are also raised, however, by the use of standard transplantation for the prolongation of life, and we will comment on two of them.

First, parents who have a child requiring a transplant might have another child in order to produce a transplantable organ for their first child. Indeed, this might well have happened. In the United Kingdom, at least, it is not forbidden by law for children who are too young to give free and informed consent to be donors of regenerable tissue (like bone marrow) or even of a kidney for their siblings. This cannot be justified solely on the grounds that the recipient needs the donation to live, whereas the donor can survive donation. That would justify enforced donation from any suitable donor. So it is more tenable to argue that the interests of the donor sibling (in having a happy family), which favour donation, outweigh the interests of the donor sibling in not being subjected to the risks of donation, provided that he or she does not positively object. However, the issue is not altogether straightforward. For one thing, the family context itself increases rather than decreases the possibility of coercion, and this means that judgements that the sibling does not object must be arrived at only after very careful scrutiny. In addition, if the donor sibling has been conceived *in order to* provide an organ, then the situation is not described adequately simply as one in which the interests of the donor sibling in having a sibling live rather than die (and in being a member

---

[5] Anencephaly is a congenital condition in which the child is born without all or part of the brain. What we have in mind here is human beings produced without a brain at all or without a forebrain.

of a happy family) are to be weighed against the donor sibling's interests in not undergoing a risky operation to provide an organ or tissue. The situation in which that conflict exists has not just happened, but has come about as the result of the deliberate choice and intention of the parents.

This might suggest that the dignity of the donor has been violated because the donor child has been conceived merely as a means to prolong the life of the sibling recipient. However, it must be appreciated that the donor child would not have existed at all without this decision. So, as we have already seen,[6] the donor child's dignity cannot be violated *by the decision* to have the donor child. If there is violation of the donor child's dignity, then this is because the donor child *is actually used* to save the sibling without being able to consent.

Matters are made more complicated here if the donor child is too young to be an agent; for then the donor child's dignity is not violated by such use, because it does not have dignity in our theory. However, we must employ precautionary reasoning, and this, in practice, would prevent a child who does not yet appear to be an agent from being used in this way if there are any feasible alternatives. Furthermore, it is necessary to differentiate cases where the use will harm the donor child when he or she becomes an agent (e.g. donation of a kidney) from where the donor child can reasonably be expected not to suffer lasting harm (e.g. marrow donation). In the former case, the issue of dignity can and must be referred not only to precautionary reason, but also to 'futurality' considerations, which require a child who does not yet appear to be an agent to be treated from the perspective of the ostensible agent it might become in the future.

With all these complications in play, we suggest that there are circumstances in which the use of children unable to consent is, at least prima facie, a violation of their dignity, but that there are circumstances, provided no other alternatives are available, that would render it, *all things being considered*, not so.

Second, it should be apparent that if standard donation is not of regenerable tissue then it is a method that sets up two groups: a group that benefits (recipients) and a group that does not (and might even be harmed) (donors). Because this is so, the possibility of using it as a means to indefinite extension of life without distributive inequality contrary to equal dignity is severely limited. In order for organs to be produced to enable recipients to live indefinitely without such inequality, organs must have been obtained either from those who have died but cannot be assisted by transplantation themselves (which will provide inadequate supplies), or from the living, who, unless they are willing to assist others to live indefinitely while damaging their own chances of doing so, will be exploited.

Non-Reproductive Cloning

Non-reproductive cloning of organs or tissue can be effected either by directing embryonic development or by directing de-differentiation and redifferentiation of

---

[6] See the discussion in Ch. 7, pp. 158–64.

cells that never go through an embryonic stage in this process. In the latter case, at least, it is possible to 'grow' new organs for recipients of a donation entirely from their own cells.[7]

In our opinion, the latter raises no special issues in relation to human dignity. The former raises the kinds of issues we considered in Chapter 7. However, we anticipate that the development of technologies that allow self-cloning will largely obviate the usefulness of embryo-involved methods of non-reproductive cloning.

Reproductive Cloning

Non-reproductive cloning of organs grown from cells of the would-be recipient also obviates the usefulness of another possibility. This is the reproductive cloning of a person (either the would-be recipient or another person) to produce an anencephalic human to serve as a spare part factory for the recipient.

Since an anencephalic clone lacks a forebrain, it is not even a potential ostensible agent. So, even under precaution, agents are not required to regard it as having a degree of dignity equal to that of the 'normal' foetus at an early stage. However, the fact that unless (or until) artificial or mechanical wombs become available[8] a woman would have to become pregnant for such donors to be created, and the instinctive (albeit not necessarily rational) repugnance that many persons feel for such a proposal, render this development unlikely.

Xenotransplantation

Much effort has been expended on the genetic manipulation of non-human animals, especially pigs, in order to produce an adequate supply of organs for donation.

Again, we suspect that, since this method (without much improvement in the science) would remain very much a second best because of continuing rejection problems, and because of doubts about the safety of this approach that will be difficult to dispel,[9] the development of cloning from cells of the recipient that does not involve embryos will render it obsolete.

For the record, however, xenotransplantation is not free from issues in relation to dignity. Since the PGC grants dignity to agents, not to human beings biologically defined, non-human animals are to be respected in proportion to the possibility, under precaution, that they might be agents. Nevertheless, if the choice is between the lives of non-human animals that are not ostensibly agents and the lives of human ostensible agents, then this would not be decisive in protecting the

---

[7] In the former case, this is also possible if the embryo is produced by use of an enucleated egg from the donor and nucleation from a somatic cell of the donor. However, creation of an embryo, in itself, may be considered to be creation of a distinct individual.

[8] This is a distinct possibility. See Hannaford (1998).

[9] A major concern is that xenotransplantation might lead to xenoses—diseases caused by viruses that normally only affect one species crossing the species barrier, possibly with epidemic effect.

non-human animals. However, once again, note must be taken that it is a general principle of precautionary reasoning that risks of violating the PGC must not be incurred if they are avoidable. Thus, if the development of cloning from cells of the recipient (without involving embryos) will render xenotransplantation unnecessary, the latter must be considered contrary to the possible dignity (rights-bearing status) of non-human animals under precaution in this context.

It is also worth noting that the possibility that xenotransplantation is contrary to human dignity by rendering human beings, in effect, partly not human, is to be discounted under the PGC. This is, again, because the dignity of human beings resides in their agency, and xenotransplantation short of a brain transplant (which would, presumptively, end the life of the human recipient as an agent) would not, in itself, affect the status of the human recipient as an agent.[10]

Cyborgs and Such

Perhaps the most radical proposal for achieving indefinite extension of life is the creation of human–machine hybrids, which might even involve the transfer of a human personality to a machine. At the extreme end, this raises metaphysical issues that should give anyone who contemplates such a move pause for thought. Perhaps it will become possible to effect what appears to be transfer of a person's memory and personality to a computer or android, while 'wiping' the mind of the person. However, would that mean that the person continued to live in the computer? Or would the person have died? If the person had died, would the computer be a person or would it only appear to be so?

Under precaution, if a computer or android appears to behave as though it is an agent, then agents must grant it agency status. So any problems with this are not in relation to dignity as such, and probably not moral at all if the person whose mind has ostensibly been transferred to the machine gave free and informed consent. But this would not mean that, if the machine had been created by an apparent transfer of a human personality to an android, the human person was now living in the machine. Derek Parfit (1984: 199–201) offers us relevant scenarios in relation to teleportation (or 'teletransportation', as Parfit calls it) to reflect upon. Teleportation of a human body involves the conversion of a human body into energy, which is then 'beamed' at the speed of light to a distant point, where the energy is reassembled into the structures of the original human body.[11] The being assembled at the place to which the beam is directed looks like the being who entered and behaves exactly like the being who entered. In short, it is a perfect clone. But would you enter the teleporter knowing that your body is to be atomized and dematerialized in the process? Do you believe that the being that appears at the other end will be you, just because it will look and act exactly as

---

[10] This parallels our comments on the creation of chimeras in Ch. 7.

[11] When Captain James T. Kirk and his crew, in the television series *Star Trek*, beam themselves down to a planet they are teleporting.

you would, and 'think' that it is you? We do not think that there is any way of answering this.[12]

Thus, to be on less speculative ground, we should perhaps look to something less radical, which would merely involve a being along the lines of Robocop, the Hollywood film character with a human brain enhanced by connection to a machine body and brain (but without the brain damage of Robocop). In principle, such a being could live much longer than ordinary human beings could.

We do not consider that there are any special problems with this in relation to human dignity.

Improving the Quality of Life

The general issue here is whether (and, if so, where) a line is to be drawn between interventions designed to improve quality of life that violate human dignity and those that do not. This issue is similar to the issue we addressed in Chapter 7 as to whether (and, if so, which) selection of genetic characteristics of offspring is contrary to human dignity. There are, however, differences between these two sets of issues. In particular, prenatal selection necessarily occurs without the consent of the offspring, whereas post-natal interventions (except when affecting very young children and babies) offer the possibility of consent, or at least non-objection, of the person undergoing the intervention.

For simplicity, we will confine our attention to interventions for which the person is able to consent. We will consider improvement of the quality of life from the viewpoint of the agent who wishes to undergo an intervention. In other words, if agent X freely wants to undergo an intervention because X considers that the intervention will improve X's quality of life then we will not question that the result to be achieved would be an improvement in X's quality of life. However, so viewed, it is possible for an improvement in X's quality of life to involve a specific violation of human dignity or to be immoral in other ways.

To focus the issue a bit, it might be helpful to have an example in mind, such as the case of assisted reproduction. Assisted reproduction might, in theory, be

---

[12] Derek Parfit (1984, ch. 12) does not consider that the clone produced by the teleporter is me. However, he argues that personal identity is not what matters. What matters is 'Relation R: psychological connectedness and/or psychological continuity, with the right kind of cause' (p. 279) with the clone produced by the teleporter. Parfit's arguments are complex and not to be dismissed out of hand. However, while we agree that 'Relation R' is what matters, we are not satisfied that Parfit takes adequate account of the distinction between what we might call 'forward-looking connectedness', in which my psychological awareness continues through me to the clone, and 'backward-looking connectedness', in which this awareness exists only in the clone and my awareness has ceased. Related to this, Parfit considers that a person's life can be subdivided into successive selves, on which model great imprudence is to be regarded as immoral. To put my future self at risk is analogous to putting another person at risk (see pp. 319–20). However, as we noted in relation to use of a similar model by Gewirth (see Ch. 5, p. 107), the analogy is flawed, because, while I become my future selves, I do not become other persons.

offered to persons in a number of different circumstances or for a number of different reasons. For example, it might be offered to

(*a*) women of normal child-bearing age who are unable to have children because of factors associated with their own or their partner's biology;

(*b*) women of normal child-bearing age who are to undergo treatment that will leave them sterile, or which is likely to cause chromosomal or other genetic damage to their germ cells;

(*c*) women who experience the menopause prematurely;

(*d*) lesbian women who do not wish to engage in sexual intercourse with a man in order to become pregnant;

(*e*) women who chose not to have a child before the onset of their menopause; or

(*f*) men who would like to be able to become pregnant and give birth.

With this in mind, we might repose our question, as follows: 'Which, if any, of these interventions is contrary to human dignity, and for what reason or reasons?' However, it is not our intention to try to give definitive answers to these questions. We will not, therefore, consider each case individually, and the different examples will merely be a backdrop against which we will consider some grounds that might be (and have been) appealed to in order to draw lines between them. In particular, we will consider whether anything can be made of the claim that what matters is whether the intervention is (i) for treatment of an illness or is merely for 'cosmetic' purposes; or (ii) 'natural' or 'against nature'. We will also consider whether, and in what sense, there can be said to be a right to have a child, as this has a bearing on the issue.

Treatment of Illness versus Cosmetic Improvement

It might be suggested that assisted reproduction is contrary to dignity if it is cosmetic but not if it is used to treat a harmful condition.

If anything is to be made of this, however, then we must be able to distinguish what is harmful or an illness from what is merely cosmetic *in a morally relevant way*. Under the PGC, this is readily done. Harmful conditions generally are those that diminish or threaten the generic capacities for action and successful action. On this basis, treatment interventions may be distinguished from cosmetic ones on the basis that 'treatment' is designed to minimize or remove a threat or interference with generic needs, whereas cosmetic interventions aim to bring about desired results that are not generic needs.

However, it is ridiculous to suggest that cosmetic interventions, so defined, are necessarily immoral, let alone that they are necessarily contrary to dignity in any specific sense. Under the PGC, agents are permitted to do anything to others or themselves that they freely choose to do, provided only that this does not threaten the generic rights of others or run counter to the basis of the PGC itself. It follows from this that, prima facie, agents not only may seek cosmetic interventions to alter their own characteristics, but may also seek interventions that are generically *harmful* to themselves (or even to others if this is with the others' free and informed consent). Thus, in the abstract, none of our examples of assisted reproduction would seem to violate dignity *on the grounds that* the would-be recipients of assisted reproduction were receiving cosmetic treatments.

Natural versus Against Nature

Many persons feel that a number of scientific interventions are 'unnatural', and cite this as the reason why it is wrong to employ them. This reaction may be linked to the idea that such interventions are contrary to dignity by the following reasoning. Dignity is the property by virtue of which human beings have moral rights or moral standing. All human beings have dignity simply by virtue of being human. Dignity is thus an essential part of human nature. Therefore, to act contrary to human nature is to act contrary to human dignity, and it might, then, be alleged that, for example, assisted reproduction itself is against nature; or 70-year-old women bearing children is against nature; or lesbianism is against nature; or men bearing children is against nature.

Since, under the PGC, dignity does not belong to human beings by virtue of their being human, but solely by virtue of their being agents, any reasoning about what is natural as against contrary to nature has to be modified to refer to the nature of agents rather than to human nature.

Now, if the dialectically necessary argument for the PGC is sound, then agents deny that they are agents if they do not accept the PGC. Thus, there is a sense in which agents act against their nature if they violate the PGC. However, that they contradict that they are agents by acting against the PGC does not mean that they cease to be agents or that it is impossible for them to act against the PGC. It only means that they act contrary to the way in which agents must act if they are to be rational on the criterion of not denying that they are agents. Thus, we must still keep separate what agents can do from what they may do. This means that while we may, if we wish, say that it is unnatural for agents to violate the PGC, what is natural is now being defined normatively in a way that makes what is natural depend on what the PGC permits, whereas the line of thinking that would have dignity explicated in terms of what is natural characteristically tries to justify what may be done on the basis of what can be done. On the other hand, if we define the nature of agents in terms of what they can do (as against what they may do), then it can only be observed that all the examples in our list of assisted reproduction scenarios will be natural if they can be done.

An attempt to explicate respect for human dignity in terms of human nature is not without its problems even if couched within a framework that links having dignity to being human (in a biological sense).

Suppose that it is held that it is unnatural for a lesbian woman to bear a child, or for a man to bear a child. What is meant by saying that it is unnatural? Clearly, it cannot be meant that it goes against the laws of nature. If something is contrary to the laws of nature then it cannot (physically) happen. And, if it is not possible for it to happen then there is no need to prescribe that it ought not to happen or to take steps to prevent it from happening.

Perhaps, then, what is meant is that it cannot happen without human intervention. However, there are so many things that cannot happen without human intervention that this threatens to imply that human action itself is contrary to human nature. Certainly, anyone who adopts such a view must, it seems, hold that all medical intervention without which a person would die is contrary to human nature. Furthermore, such a stance requires human interventions to be divided into those that are against nature and those that are not. However, if being against nature is a *non-normative* matter then surely anything that human beings can do is natural. Human beings are part of nature and what they do is natural.

Of course, as we saw might happen within Gewirthian theory, it might be responded that 'natural' is not a non-normative concept. However, while it is clear that 'X is unnatural' is often used in a normative way (more or less equivalent to 'X is highly immoral'), this misses the point entirely. The point is that 'being unnatural' is, within the context in which we are considering it, supposed to explain why something is immoral or contrary to dignity. The rejoinder, however, abandons such an intention, and, indeed, attempts to explain what is 'natural' as against 'unnatural' on the basis of judgements about morality or immorality or respect for dignity.

We must conclude in general, then, that the discourse of what is 'natural/unnatural' will not enable us to determine which examples of assisted reproduction (or other interventions) are contrary or not contrary to dignity, unless it conceals a moral standard, in which case that standard should be made explicit.

Is there a Right to Have a Child?

In relation to the case of assisted reproduction, the question whether there is a right to have (to bear) a child is relevant to the question whether or not assisted reproduction might be contrary to human dignity. If there is a positive *generic* right for anyone to have a child who can (i.e. a duty on those who can assist someone to have a child to do so, when this is possible but cannot be secured by their own unaided efforts), then it *cannot* be contrary to human dignity to enable anyone to have a child who wants one.

It is sometimes argued that there is no positive right to have a child, only a negative right (i.e. others have a duty not to prevent those who can have a child from having one) (see e.g. McLean 2000). However, under the PGC, all generic rights are both positive and negative, so that if there is a negative generic right to have a child, then there is a positive generic right to have a child as well.[13]

Of course, there can be no right to *have* a child as against a right to take steps that might lead to the having of a child (both because success in trying to have a child cannot be guaranteed and because some steps might interfere unacceptably with the rights of others). Hence, when we refer to the generic right to have a child we refer merely to the right to take steps to have a child that do not interfere with the generic rights of others.

However, even so qualified, it should be clear that there is no generic right per se to have a child, and this is simply because having a child (or providing the opportunities to try to have a child) is not necessary for action or successful action in general.[14]

Therefore, consideration of the question of a right to have a child leaves it open whether or not particular instances of assisted reproduction might or might not violate human dignity.

General Principles

Since an agent may, under the PGC, choose to do anything, provided only that this does not violate the rights of others or deny the grounds of morality itself, nothing that an agent chooses to do freely can be contrary to human dignity if no violation of the rights of others or denial of the grounds of morality itself is involved.

Following our analysis in Chapter 6, there are three particularly relevant ways in which freely chosen intervention designed to improve one's quality of life can be contrary to human dignity. These are that the intervention

(*a*) produces, or is premissed on, an inequality of rights of agents;

(*b*) generates a disposition to violate or deny the rights of others by one's pursuit of agency-irrelevant improvements;

(*c*) makes a fetish of irrelevant considerations (i.e. treats qualities that are irrelevant to moral status as relevant to moral status).

The first of these violations is possible in relation to the allocation of 'treatments'. If 'cosmetic' interventions (i.e. those designed to produce agency-irrelevant improvements) (e.g. to increase breast size, or reverse baldness, or remove

---

[13] This is because the argument for positive rights is parallel to the argument for negative rights. See Gewirth (1984: 228–9). See also Beyleveld (1991: 334–6).

[14] That said, many women (in particular) are, or would be, considerably distressed by being unable to have a child. So much so that to prevent them from having a child when they can, or to withhold assistance to them to have a child when this is possible, would constitute interference with their generic rights. To the extent that the consequences of not having a child derive from factors beyond their control, whether of a biological nature or socialization, there are good reasons under the PGC to grant them a right (both positive and negative) to have a child. However, any such right is not a generic right to have a child, but a right deriving from various other generic rights (to mental equilibrium, physical health, etc.).

wrinkles) are provided at the expense of agency-relevant ones, then this is contrary to human dignity.

The second of these violations occurs when the importance attached to 'cosmetic' qualities predisposes an agent to seek an allocation of 'treatments' or to make judgements premissed on the idea that those who lack the desired quality have a lower moral status than those who possess it.

The third of these violations occurs when an agent attaches an importance to agency-irrelevant characteristics such that its functioning as an agent is affected by an inability to secure the improvement.

In the latter case, it is true, the fetish may more appropriately prompt pity rather than retribution. Indeed, there may even be a duty to provide the treatment required to satisfy the fetish, if other methods (such as counselling) do not relieve the trauma. However, that does not show that fetishes are not contrary to human dignity, and there is at the same time a duty not to encourage fetishes and to institute educational and other programmes that aim to modify the social attitudes that are very often responsible for them.

If we attempt to apply these general principles to the case of assisted reproduction then it seems to us that, while there may be good reasons supported by the PGC to offer assisted reproduction in at least some of the cases we listed,[15] we do not consider that issues of human dignity, as such, enable us to discriminate these cases independently of the specific circumstances that attend them. Having a child is not a generic need. But neither is the desire to have a child a fetish, though it can become one. Provision of assisted reproduction can disturb the equality of rights, but need not do so. And, as with all the examples we have considered, we cannot reduce the issue of whether or not it is permissible or impermissible to do something to whether or not it is a violation of human dignity.

---

[15] Subject to conditions such as adequate resources to do so, proper attention being given to the interests of the future child, etc.

11

Dying with Dignity

Introduction

We started this book by remarking that it is a little surprising to find the notion of human dignity being so heavily relied upon in debates relating to the regulation of the most modern forms of bioscience and medicine. There is one context, however, where we have been accustomed for some time to encounter arguments incorporating the rhetoric of respect for human dignity. This is the context of 'euthanasia' (which covers a range of actions and omissions designed to terminate life) and physician-assisted suicide. True to form, human dignity is pressed into service by both those who advocate more permissive legal frameworks as well as those who oppose any relaxation in the law. As Mohammed Bedjaoui, president of the International Court of Justice, has commented:

[A] legal framework for potential new practices or those already engaged in which concern the human body is absolutely essential in that it protects man in his freedom and dignity. But it is by no means an easy task. . . . Take, for example, the concept of . . . 'human dignity'. It is an expression which seems simple: one immediately apprehends its prospective import, if not its exact meaning. But, paradoxically, it is also an expression full of fragility, for in the name of the same argument of 'human dignity' some refute the legitimacy of euthanasia, whilst others claim it as the ultimate right of those who wish to 'die in dignity'! (1995: 144)

It scarcely needs emphasizing, however, that the term 'euthanasia' is itself employed rather loosely, covering a range of possible end of life scenarios. To take just three well-known English cases from the last decade: the term might be applied to the case of Dr Nigel Cox, who at the request of his arthritic patient Mrs Lillian Boyes administered a lethal injection of potassium chloride; or it might be applied to the case of Annie Lindsell, who, suffering from motor neurone disease, campaigned for the right to a lawfully assisted death; or the term might be applied to the withdrawal of feeding and hydration and/or general medical care and support from a person such as Tony Bland, one of the victims of the Hillsborough football stadium tragedy, who was diagnosed as being in a permanent (or persistent) vegetative state.

Observing a tendency for 'the "death with dignity" movement [to link] arms with the "patient autonomy" and "control over one's life" movements' (Frey 1998: 17), one might question whether it is right to assimilate these several cases of euthanasia to one another. It is arguable that there are material differences between cases involving persons who are seemingly competent to consent or refuse (such as Lillian Boyes and Annie Lindsell) and those involving persons who no longer seem to have such a capacity (as was the case with Tony Bland), between cases involving 'active' steps to end life (such as the steps taken by Dr Cox) and those involving the 'passive' withdrawing or withholding of life-sustaining support (as in the Bland case), or between a party giving advice and assistance with the preparatory steps for the ending of life (as in Annie Lindsell's case) as against actually executing the life-ending action itself (as with Dr Cox's giving of a lethal injection), and so on. Can we do justice to debates about 'death with dignity' without going beyond the broad label 'euthanasia' and without taking seriously distinctions of this kind?

Of course, how seriously we should take distinctions of the kind intuitively invited by this trio of cases just referred to (Cox, Lindsell, and Bland), or that we find criss-crossing the field in the very extensive literature on the ethics of euthanasia, depends on the particular moral theory that we employ. If we start, as we do, with a Gewirthian agency perspective, then it follows that, in general, the distinctions that will matter for us will be those that are material relative to this perspective, specifically this perspective as it operates under the principle of precaution (in the sense detailed in Chapter 6).

In this final chapter we will discuss three contexts in which 'death with dignity' is an issue. First, there are cases where we are dealing with ostensible agents, cases such as that of Dr Cox and Lillian Boyes. While there are times when ostensible agents are in no position to express or to make their own choices (for example, when they are asleep or incapacitated by drink or drugs), they are treated as ostensible agents precisely because they seem to have a developed capacity for making their own decisions (that is, acting in a free and purposive way, including giving or withholding their consent). On the face of it, we violate the dignity of ostensible agents if we fail to recognize that they have this capacity (for example, by failing to respect their life-terminating choices). Second, there are cases, such as that of Tony Bland, where a once ostensible agent not only no longer seems to have the relevant decision-making capacity but seems to have lost it irretrievably. This is not a case of a temporary or occasional lack of consent competence; where a permanent vegetative state is diagnosed, while precaution dictates that we hold open the possibility of agency, the implication of the diagnosis is that this person is no longer an ostensible agent. Moreover, the implication of characterizing another as no longer an ostensible agent is that they do not have dignity to be violated—or, at any rate, their dignity exists only in the realm of possibility. Yet we know that this is just the kind of case where appeals to 'death with dignity' are commonly made in a way that implies that the nature and basis of the claim is perfectly obvious. Third, we look at a particular case of 'death with dignity', but a case arising at the beginning rather than the end of life. This is the much debated case of the Siamese twins Jodie and Mary, which was litigated under the name *Re A (children) (conjoined twins: surgical separation)*.[1]

---

[1] [2000] 4 All ER 961.

From a Gewirthian precautionary perspective, neither of the twins is to be regarded as an ostensible agent: the stronger of the twins, Jodie, is to be regarded as at best a potential ostensible agent and the weaker, Mary, as merely a possible agent. The question is whether separating the twins so that Jodie can survive (but knowing that Mary will then die) is compatible with dignity. In other words, would the taking of the life of Mary (in order to give the chance of life to Jodie) respect the possible dignity of Mary? Moreover, would this action respect the dignity of the twins' parents, the latter being ostensible agents who have refused to give their consent to the separation? From this extraordinarily complex case, we can extract a point of fundamental practical (and moral) importance encapsulated in the idea of dignity as a virtue. Dignity as a virtue enjoins agents as individuals to confront adversity (most acutely in the form of our existential anxiety) in a way that succumbs neither to blind (optimistic) faith nor to a nihilism that denies all point or purpose to life. However, dignity as a virtue also has a collective application, guiding societies that aspire to a moral ordering when confronted with moral conflict, complexity, and uncertainty. Uniting these various contexts, we will close by suggesting that dignity as a virtue speaks to both our personal and our civic responsibilities, to what it means to die with dignity but also to what it means to live with dignity.

Euthanasia and End of Life Settings: Terminology

The broad term 'euthanasia', as we have said, covers a number of end of life scenarios. Before broaching any questions concerning 'death with dignity', we need some terminological clarification.

The Walton Report (Walton Committee 1994) defines 'euthanasia' as 'a deliberate intervention undertaken with the express intention of ending a life to relieve intractable suffering' (paragraph 20). The standard, but controversial, distinction between 'active' and 'passive' euthanasia is not drawn as such and, in fact, the Committee prefers not to use the term 'passive euthanasia', speaking instead of 'withdrawing or not initiating treatment or of a treatment-limiting decision' (paragraph 21).[2] Having said that 'The state of mind of the person whose death might be brought about by an act of euthanasia . . . is . . . significant' (paragraph 23), the Committee goes on to differentiate between 'voluntary', 'non-voluntary', and 'involuntary' euthanasia in the following terms:

Voluntary euthanasia occurs when the patient's death is brought about at his or her own request. Non-voluntary euthanasia may be used to describe the killing of a patient who does not have the capacity to understand what euthanasia means and cannot therefore form

---

[2] The Committee also says: 'Some people use the term passive euthanasia to describe the act of a doctor or other person who prescribes or administers pain-killers or other (e.g. sedative) drugs necessary for the relief of a patient's pain or severe distress, but in the knowledge that a probable consequence of the prescription is a shortening of the patient's life. Again we think that this usage is incorrect. We speak instead of the double effect' (Walton Committee 1994, paragraph 22).

a request or withhold consent. Involuntary euthanasia has been used to describe the killing of a patient who is competent to request or consent to the act, but does not do so. (paragraph 23)

For the Committee, patients are 'competent' if they are

able to understand the available information about their conditions, to consider with medical advice the risks, benefits and burdens of different treatments or courses of action, and thus to make informed decisions. (paragraph 24)

Patients are 'incompetent' if they are

unable, whether permanently or temporarily, to make decisions about their medical care. (paragraph 24)

Of the other terminological uses given by the Committee, at this stage we need only note that 'assisted suicide' refers to a case where

a competent patient has formed a desire to end his or her life but requires help to perform the act, perhaps because of physical disability. (paragraph 26)

For the sake of argument, let us follow the Committee by supposing that 'euthanasia' means 'a deliberate intervention [by A] undertaken with the express intention of ending a life [B's life] to relieve intractable suffering [by B]'. Now, from a Gewirthian perspective, the obvious first move towards organizing our thinking about euthanasia is to distinguish between cases where B (whose life is to be ended by A) is to be regarded as an ostensible agent and cases where B is not to be so regarded. Ostensible agents have the (apparent) capacity to make free and informed choices; (other things being equal) they have competence as understood by the Select Committee; and they have the capacity to make requests, and to give or refuse their consent in just the way contemplated by the Committee. In precautionary terms, it follows that, whereas what the Committee refers to as cases of voluntary and involuntary euthanasia (together with assisted suicide) fall on one side of the line (because B is an ostensible agent, with a developed capacity to choose as well as, in the ordinary way, the competence to consent or refuse), cases of non-voluntary euthanasia (where we can treat B as a non-ostensible agent, lacking a developed capacity to choose, or to consent or refuse) fall on the other side.

Next, if we think about the cases of voluntary and involuntary euthanasia, there seem to be two matters that invite some tidying up. First, as a matter of principle, whether or not B 'requests' A to terminate B's life hardly seems relevant. The important question is whether or not A is terminating B's life against B's will—or, to put this slightly differently, the important question is whether or not B is consenting to the termination. In practice, a procedure requiring there to be a request by B to A might well assist in confirming that B is consenting to the termination. However, to carry this instrumental feature back into the organization of the field seems to be a mistake. Second, in principle, there are three answers to the question of whether B has consented to the termination by A. B might have consented; B might have refused (or denied consent); or B might have neither consented nor refused. To avoid any misunderstanding, this third possibility (that B has neither consented nor refused) should not be mistaken for the case of non-voluntary euthanasia: it is one thing to deal with ostensible agents who are competent to signal consent or refusal but who have not yet done so, quite another to deal with those who lack this capacity.

Even though our particular interest is in human dignity rather than informed consent as such, the distinction between ostensible agents (who are, apparently capacity-wise if not always opportunity-wise, consent-competent) and those who are not to be regarded as agents of this kind is central to Gewirthian thinking. Accordingly, this is the distinction that we will use to structure our discussion.

Death, Dignity, and Ostensible Agents

Justice Brennan, dissenting (together with Justices Marshall and Blackmun) in the famous US Supreme Court decision of *Nancy Beth Cruzan* v. *Director, Missouri Department of Health*,[3] held that Cruzan had 'a fundamental right to be free of unwanted artificial nutrition and hydration . . . [and she was] entitled to choose to die with dignity'.[4]

Given that Cruzan (like Tony Bland in the parallel English case) was in a persistent vegetative state (PVS), there were difficulties in making an accurate determination of Cruzan's choice—and, indeed, it was in relation to these difficulties that the majority and the minority divided. Contrary to the facts, had Cruzan been an ostensible agent who was, in the ordinary way and at the material time, consent-competent (in the sense given by the Walton Committee 1994), she could have advised the medical team (and, if necessary, the Court) of her choice and Justice Brennan's ringing declaration of her fundamental right could have been given an easy application. As it was, the application of the right of self-determination was tricky and we shall return to this point later when we deal with those who are not to be regarded as ostensible agents. Nevertheless, so far as ostensible agents are concerned, many would believe that Justice Brennan has the right idea.

In the well-known exchange between John Harris and John Finnis (see Harris 1995*a,b,c*; Finnis 1995*a,b,c*) the former argues for a position that is similar to that taken by Brennan. According to Harris, a life form (whether human or otherwise) becomes a 'person' when it is 'capable of valuing its own existence' (Harris 1995*a*: 9). Hence,

---

[3] 497 US 261, 110 S Ct 2841 (1990); 111 L Ed 2d 224. Of the many commentaries on *Cruzan*, see e.g. Cantor (1993, ch. 1).
[4] 111 L Ed 2d 224, 257.

Persons who want to live are wronged by being killed because they are thereby deprived of something they value. Persons who do not want to live are not on this account wronged by having their wish to die granted, through voluntary euthanasia for example. Non-persons or potential persons cannot be wronged in this way because death does not deprive them of anything they can value. If they cannot wish to live, they cannot have that wish frustrated by being killed. (p. 9)

From this perspective, it is respect for persons and, concomitantly, for the life of persons (so long as they wish to live) rather than respect for life itself that is fundamental. From this perspective, too, it is 'persons' who have the capacity not only to value their existence (i.e. to value being alive) but also to give particular value to their lives through the exercise of their autonomy (i.e. to value their particular identities). Thus,

The point of autonomy, the point of choosing and having the freedom to choose between competing conceptions of how, and indeed why, to live, is simply that it is only thus that our lives become in any real sense our own. The value of our lives is the value we give to our lives. And we do this, so far as this is possible at all, by shaping our lives for ourselves. Our own choices, decisions and preferences help to make us what we are, for each helps us to confirm and modify our own character and enables us to develop and to understand ourselves. So autonomy, as the ability and the freedom to make the choices that shape our lives, is quite crucial in giving to each life its own special and peculiar value. (Harris 1995*a*: 11)

It follows that respect for persons goes beyond respecting a person's choice in favour of life over death: it extends to respecting the particular life choices that a person makes (because this is what makes the person that particular person). Turning this coin over, respect for persons also involves respecting a person's choice in favour of death over life. So, for Harris, euthanasia should be permitted because 'to deny a person control of what, on any analysis, must be one of the most important decisions of life, is a form of tyranny, which like all acts of tyranny is an ultimate denial of respect for persons' (pp. 19–20).

If we were to cast Harris's approach in terms of respect for human dignity, it would clearly fall under the conception of dignity as empowerment. Humans, *qua persons*, have the capacity to attribute value to their lives (in both the general and the particular sense) and, thus, to accord themselves dignity. In this way, 'the dignity of the person' becomes a shorthand for a cluster of capacities which, in turn, act as the basis on which the right of autonomy is asserted.

Responding to Harris, John Finnis contends that euthanasia cannot be permitted without violating the common bond between humans, namely their humanity. As Finnis presents it, 'human bodily life is the life of a person and has the dignity of the person. Every human being is equal precisely in having that human life which is also humanity and personhood, and thus that dignity and intrinsic value' (Finnis 1995*a*: 32). Far from denying the value of free choice, such a view celebrates autonomous participation in *intelligible* goods; and, indeed '[human] dignity is most fully manifested in the dispositions and activities of people and communities who think wisely, and choose and act with the integrity and justice of full reasonableness' (p. 31). Nevertheless, Finnis contends,

If one is really exercising autonomy in choosing to kill oneself, or in inviting or demanding that others assist one to do so or themselves take steps to terminate one's life, one will be proceeding on one or both of two philosophically and morally erroneous judgments: (i) that human life in certain conditions or circumstances retains no intrinsic value and dignity; and/or (ii) that the world would be a better place if one's life were intentionally terminated. (pp. 33–4)[5]

The practical consequences of such erroneous thinking, Finnis concludes, are particularly dangerous for the vulnerable. What we must hold on to is the true judgement that it is always 'irrational, hubristic, and . . . deeply sinister' (1995*c*: 66) to make a judgement of the form 'this person is a *person who should die*' (p. 66). For, without this controlling standard, we are liable to fail to acknowledge both the dignity and the right to life of those who are damaged or whose existence is burdensome for others (see Finnis 1995*a*: 34).[6]

Perhaps the neatest way of capturing the contrast between Harris and Finnis is to imagine a human, B, in circumstances that are judged to be undignified (i) by B and (ii) by persons other than B. What most troubles Harris is the thought that, in the first of these cases, B (assuming, crucially, that B remains a 'person' as conceived by Harris) should be denied the right to put an end to that undignified condition (if necessary by taking steps for the termination of B's life). What most troubles Finnis is the thought that, in the second of these cases, others should think themselves justified in putting an end to what they see as B's undignified condition (if necessary by the termination of B's life). Moreover, for Finnis, this troubling thought applies regardless of whether B is a 'person' as conceived by Harris; for Finnis, it is enough that B is a member of the human species. In this light, it will be understood that, although Harris and Finnis appear to have some common ground in insisting that the intrinsic dignity of persons (for Harris) and

---

[5] Compare Harris (1995*b*: 43–4) and Finnis (1995*c*: 70).

[6] Harris emphasizes that his position gives no warrant for euthanasia other than where persons 'autonomously choose to die' (Harris 1995*b*: 42): 'non-voluntary and involuntary euthanasia of *persons* is always wrong' (Harris 1995*c*: 60; our emphasis). However, throughout his exchange with Harris, Finnis is suspicious of Harris's intentions vis-à-vis those whom Harris treats as non-persons. For example, Finnis says, 'Harris more than once suggests that "the persons whose deaths are permitted must autonomously choose to die". This purported restriction of permissible euthanasia to voluntary euthanasia must be taken cautiously and with a large pinch of salt. Cautiously, because as he says in the essay's chilling final words, "non-persons, even if human, are . . . a different matter". And with a large pinch of salt, because in his book *The Value of Life* . . . Harris unambiguously affirms that the persons who may rightly (indeed should) be killed include not only those who autonomously choose to die but also "those who are living in circumstances to which death is preferable or who face a future in which this will be true, but who are unable to express a preference for death", and also those other innocents whose death, although not desired by them, is expected to "promote . . . other values" of sufficient weight. Are Harris's present essays really recanting his book's promotion of both non-voluntary euthanasia and the deliberate and intentional killing of innocent and unwilling persons? It would be rash to think so' (1995*c*: 67–8).

humans (for Finnis) holds good even where persons/humans find themselves in undignified circumstances, they have fundamentally different ideas about what it means to respect the dignity of persons/humans. Whereas, for Harris, to respect the dignity of persons is to respect their right to choose and control their immediate circumstances, whether dignified or undignified, for Finnis it is respect for humanity and life itself that is axiomatic.[7]

If we approach such matters from a Gewirthian perspective, respect for dignity attaches to agents (in precautionary terms, to ostensible agents) rather than to humans or persons. Against Finnis, while the idea of an agent is itself the intellectual construct of humans and while, in our present state of knowledge and understanding, the paradigm of ostensible agency is the developed member of the human species, Gewirthians do not equate agency with humanity and nor do they operate with Finnis's baseline view that human life is an intrinsic good. With regard to Harris, while Gewirthians would certainly reject any overarching scheme of utilitarian reasoning (and, concomitantly, the implicit preference utilitarianism which takes us from the fact that a person values his or her existence to the moral judgement that such a person is prima facie wronged by being killed), the Harrisian conception of personhood bears a considerable resemblance to Gewirthian agency. How, then, should we analyse and respond to the demand made by ostensible agents that they should be permitted to die with dignity?

The main Gewirthian argument, it will be recalled, runs through three stages. In that argument it is perfectly possible to move from agency to the PGC without relying at any point on the notion of respect for dignity (of humans, persons, or agents). However, in so far as dignity is thought of as relating to the capacities of agents that ground their having rights, then it is the first stage of the Gewirthian argument that, so to speak, does the dignity groundwork, laying the foundations for the subsequent claiming of rights (at the second stage) and acceptance of correlative duties (at the third stage). In the first stage, to which we have added a context of vulnerability and existential anxiety, it is argued that (conatively normal)[8] agents will consider that their particular purposes have value; and that agents must then reflexively consider that the conditions (the generic conditions) that make it possible to pursue particular purposes, whatever those particular purposes might be, must also have value—that is, the generic conditions must be

---

[7] For an approach that is very close to that argued for by Finnis, see Gormally (1995). First, contends Gormally, because there will always be some arbitrariness in specifying certain abilities as the criterion for human dignity (and, thus, eligibility as a bearer of human rights), the only alternative is to treat 'dignity and value as an *ineliminable* attribute of human beings' (p. 115). Second, he says that any justification for killing must be compatible with respect for the dignity and value of humans. Then, third, it is asserted that, with regard to both voluntary and non-voluntary euthanasia, the 'real work of justifying the killing' is the judgement that '*the patient lacks a worthwhile life*' (p. 115). Hence, on Gormally's analysis, there is no material difference between voluntary and non-voluntary euthanasia, and in neither case is the justification adequate.

[8] According to Gewirth, an agent as a 'conatively normal person', is a being who 'has the self-interested motivations common to most persons and is willing to expend the effort needed to fulfil them' (1978a: 90).

viewed as the valued means towards each and every valued particular end. If it is accepted that those generic conditions are constituted by an agent's freedom and basic well-being (as Gewirth contends), then an agent must value its freedom and basic well-being (not as ends in themselves, but as the essential means to its particular purpose fulfilment).[9] Accordingly, in just the way that a Harrisian person has the capacity to think 'I value my own existence', but equally 'I no longer value my own existence', so too a Gewirthian agent has the capacity to think (in relation to particular purpose selection) 'I value my own existence, because it is a necessary means for my achieving my particular valued purposes (which do not include putting an end to my life)', but equally 'My particular purpose is to put an end to my life. For the fulfilment of this particular purpose, I need and must value my own existence. Beyond this, however, I no longer value my own existence'. And, crucially, for a Gewirthian, an agent thinking such thoughts does not contradict its status as an agent. Life is a generic instrumental, not an instrinsic, value.

Applying a Gewirthian analysis, the first line of defence for an agent is that others should not engage in (unwilled) interferences with its generic conditions. To take the life of an agent, *against the will of that agent*, is the most serious violation of the PGC. However, there is no violation of the PGC if the agent has waived the benefit of the right which otherwise would have been compromised—and this holds good in relation to the rights to the basic goods and their benefits as much as to lesser rights. Thus, if it is the will of agent B that agent A should take agent B's life, no wrong is committed (as between A and B) if A then takes B's life.[10] Of course, just because it is permissible for A to take B's life, it does not follow that it is permissible for C or D to do so; nor does it follow that it is permissible for A to take the life of C or D. Permissibility is determined by both the scope and the specific addressee of the waiver in question. Nor, of course, does it follow that B does no wrong: B's life-terminating actions are permissible only so long as they are consistent with B's responsibility to respect the rights of fellow agents.

If the thrust of this is correct, it means that an agent is subject to no final constraint with respect to the preservation of its own life. Granted, so long as B is an agent, B must proactively value and preserve B's generic conditions of agency; for without these conditions, B cannot flourish as an agent. However, an agent does not contradict its own agency by selecting a purpose which involves the termination of its life and, with that, the termination of its agency. Agents, in other words, have no duty to maintain their own lives if their freely chosen particular purposes involve the loss of their lives. In the final analysis, then, respect for the dignity of agency has no self-regarding dimension placing an agent under a categorical duty to preserve its own life; and, in the other-regarding dimension, respect

---

[9] See our discussion in Ch. 4. But, for a non-instrumental view, see e.g. Joseph Boyle (1995: 192).

[10] The question of whether A has a duty to assist B is to be resolved in accordance with the usual Gewirthian principles concerning positive rights and duties. The answer will vary from case to case; and it will hinge on whether B actually needs A's assistance as well as on the level of the cost to A.

for the dignity of agency translates into respect for the generic conditions (which are conditions facilitating free choice and autonomy) of each agent, *save where the particular agent has willed and authorized interference with some good associated with those conditions.*

It follows that, in relation to ostensible agents, Gewirthians must side with the line advanced by Justice Brennan, John Harris, and others in the liberal tradition. The right to choose is a basic expression of one's dignity;[11] and there is no more fundamental expression of one's dignity than the right to make life-saving or life-terminating choices. Dignity, in other words, is embedded in the right to choose itself, irrespective of the particular choice that one makes. Now, when we say (with Justice Brennan) that an agent is entitled to choose to die with dignity, dignity remains implicitly embedded in that entitlement, but what we are explicitly highlighting is the particular choice made, namely to die with dignity. Another way of putting this is to say that agents have a fundamental right to choose and to control the circumstances of their death; in this sense, they express their dignity in the chosen manner of their death. Some ways of dying may appeal more than others; in particular, an agent may wish to avoid those situations in which the lead-up to death seems undignified, or demeaning or degrading. Where this is the case, where an agent chooses to avoid an undignified death, then the agent's will is to die with dignity.

From a Gewirthian standpoint, therefore, there is little mystery about the moral position of (ostensible) agents: first, there is at least a prima facie right to choose the manner of one's death and such agents are to be protected against the loss of their dignity in the sense of being denied this right to choose and control when and how they die;[12] second, if the right to choose is exercised in a way that is designed to avoid what are judged to be undignified circumstances, then there is a right to have this particular choice respected (similarly, if, to the contrary, the particular choice were to be to die in what are judged to be undignified circumstances). The so-called right to die with dignity is, thus, elliptical: it runs together the dignity-based right to choose when and how one dies (i.e. the primary right to make the choice) with the right that a particular choice be respected, namely the choice that the circumstances surrounding one's death should be dignified (i.e. the secondary right).

---

[11] Commenting on the *Cruzan* case and its background jurisprudence, Norman Cantor picks up this connection between choice and dignity: 'Identification of the integral tie between choice and human dignity in the context of death-and-dying decisions follows the path of prior state court decisions in the field. Some of those decisions had stressed the blow to dignity when a patient's autonomous preferences regarding medical interventions are not respected. Other decisions had acknowledged the relation between human dignity and the avoidance of both suffering and a dying process deemed undignified or degrading according to the affected individual. All these voices emphasized the importance of an individual's choice to reject medical interventions deemed distasteful or to decide when a prospective existence is so painful or dismal that life-preserving intervention is unwanted' (1993: 6).

[12] However, there are further issues to be resolved concerning the rights of agents to decline to assist with a killing in a certain manner.

Does it follow, then, that active euthanasia (of the kind practised by Dr Nigel Cox on Mrs Lillian Boyes) was at least morally permissible? Does it follow that those many legal systems that take it as axiomatic that cases of this kind should be treated as (serious) criminal offences are in error? Similarly, does it follow that assisted suicide (of the kind requested by Annie Lindsell and publicized internationally by the activities of Dr Jack Kevorkian) is morally permissible and that those many legal systems that criminalize such assistance are in error? To each of these questions the answer in principle must be in the affirmative—or, at any rate, the argument from dignity supports recognizing (rather than contesting) the permissibility of active euthanasia and assisted suicide.

To avoid any misunderstanding, however, it must emphasized that this is not the final word. From a Gewirthian perspective, active euthanasia is permissible only *provided that the consent conditions are properly satisfied* (and this is a major caveat); only if this proviso can be satisfied should it be declared that active euthanasia is not unlawful. So, for instance, in a case such as that presented to the Canadian Supreme Court by Sue Rodriguez,[13] we would need to examine the consent proviso very carefully. There Rodriguez, who was suffering from Lou Gehrig's disease, applied for a declaration that section 241(b) of the Criminal Code (according to which it is a criminal offence to aid or abet a person to commit suicide) violated the Canadian Charter of Rights and Freedoms. In a split 5/4 decision, the Court ruled against Rodriguez. What divided the Court, however, was not a rival approach to respect for human dignity. On both sides of the Court there was acceptance of the importance of respecting autonomy. The question was how best to put in place a legal framework that both facilitates free choice by agents (if necessary, by giving effect to an agent's freedom to confer immunity on 'interfering' others) but also protects vulnerable agents against coerced choice masquerading as autonomous consent (thus protecting an agent's freedom to be immune from unwilled interferences). What the majority, in ruling against Rodriguez, wished to preserve was not the dignity of life, but the dignity-based free choices of all Canadians, the vulnerable as much as the non-vulnerable; and they were not satisfied that this could be safeguarded if the criminal code was relaxed. From a Gewirthian standpoint, this outcome is moot; but the argument is a legitimate one concerning the consent condition, rather than a misguided one relating to human dignity.

We can turn now from the case of ostensible agents (who, in the ordinary way, are consent-competent) to a special case of incompetence. Here, we will focus on those who are no longer ostensible agents but rather who are (for want of a better term) ex-ostensible agents, such as Tony Bland and Nancy Cruzan, who are diagnosed as being in PVS at the material time.

---

[13] *Re Rodriguez and Attorney-General of British Columbia* (1993) 107 DLR 4th 342.

Death, Dignity, and the Incompetence of Ex-Ostensible Agents

At more than one level Lord Justice Hoffmann's opinion in the *Bland* case,[14] when it was before the Court of Appeal, is striking. Remarkably, Lord Hoffmann (as he now is) opened by saying that the question for the court (which, as in *Cruzan*, was whether the feeding and hydration of a person in PVS could be lawfully withdrawn) was one where no difference could be allowed to exist 'between what is legal and what is morally right'.[15] For our purposes, it is the way in which respect for human dignity is worked into the ensuing analysis that is of particular interest.

First, respect for the sanctity of life is presented as a cornerstone moral principle. However, Lord Hoffmann sees this as just one of several ethical principles that are relevant.

Another [principle] is respect for the individual human being and in particular for his right to choose how he should live his own life. We call this individual autonomy or the right of self-determination. And another principle, closely connected, is respect for the dignity of the individual human being: our belief that quite irrespective of what the person concerned may think about it, it is wrong for someone to be humiliated or treated without respect for his value as a person.[16]

This passage resonates with the Gewirthian conception of dignity: respect for human dignity is closely connected to the right of self-determination or autonomy and it is to be distinguished from respect for the sanctity of life (with which, indeed, it may sometimes move into tension).[17] However, immediately following this passage, we read: 'The fact that the dignity of an individual is an intrinsic value is shown by the fact that we feel embarrassed and think it wrong when someone behaves in a way which we think demeaning to himself, which does not show sufficient respect for himself as a person.'[18] This seems badly off the mark. In the liberal human rights account, human dignity is an intrinsic value because all humans (strictly, for Gewirthians, all ostensible agents) have dignity and, importantly, they retain it even when they behave in a way that we think is demeaning; the presence or absence of dignity has nothing whatsoever to do with our embarrassment when we encounter demeaning behaviour in others. More seriously, by suggesting that the intrinsic value of human dignity is evidenced by a critical reaction when a person fails to show sufficient respect for himself as a

---

[14] *Airedale NHS Trust* v. *Bland* [1993] 1 All ER 821.

[15] Ibid. 850.

[16] Ibid. 851.

[17] This tension is underlined: 'There is no formula for reconciling this conflict of principles and no easy answer. It does no good to seize hold of one of them, such as the sanctity of life, and say that because it is valid and right, as it undoubtedly is, it must always prevail over other principles which are also valid and right. . . . For many people, the sanctity of life is not at all the same thing as the dignity of the individual. We cannot smooth away the differences by interpretation' (Ibid. 854).

[18] Ibid. 851.

person, Lord Hoffmann seems to be toying with the idea that one might compromise one's own dignity.

By and large, in what follows, Lord Hoffmann gets back on track. If, as his Lordship says, 'Anthony Bland were to be momentarily restored to consciousness with full knowledge that he would shortly revert to his persistent vegetative state, and if he were to instruct those caring for him that he no longer wanted artificially to be kept alive, the doctors and nurses would be obliged to respect his wishes'.[19] Short of such a miraculous restoration, however, the spirit of respect for human dignity must be maintained by making a substituted judgement: 'Anthony Bland is an individual human being and the principle of self-determination says he should be allowed to choose for himself and that, if he is unable to express his choice, we should try our honest best to do what we think he would have chosen.'[20]

Yet, what would Bland have chosen? Bland left no advance directive and, as his Lordship observed, 'There is nothing to show that in the course of [Bland's] short life he gave the matter any thought.'[21] Faced with this difficulty, Lord Hoffmann relied, to some extent, on the evidence of the family that, given Bland's general attitude to life, 'he would not have wanted to survive in his present state'.[22] Additionally, though, he relied on the assertion that 'Most people would like an honourable and dignified death';[23] and Bland, presumably, was no exception to this normal preference.

Although Bland was unconscious and had no awareness of his situation, Lord Hoffmann strongly resisted the idea that a person's interests endure only so long as there is consciousness. 'It is demeaning to the human spirit to say that, being unconscious, [Bland] can have no interest in his personal privacy and dignity, in how he lives or dies.'[24]

Following Lord Hoffmann in taking a leaf from Ronald Dworkin's book (Dworkin 1993),[25] we can conceive of a person as having a set of critical interests in the sense of a number of autonomously chosen character-defining interests. With such interests as our reference point, we can evaluate particular choices as being 'in character' (in line with a person's critical interests) or 'out of character' (out of line with a person's critical interests). But we can also draw on our understanding of a person's critical interests to construct an account of what a person would have chosen in a particular situation; and we can do this even where that person is unconscious or dead. So, doing his 'honest best' to divine what Bland would have chosen, Lord Hoffmann was guided by the family's evidence as to Bland's general attitude to life (his critical interests) coupled with the assumption that, as a general rule, humans prefer to have a dignified death (and

---

[19] Ibid. 852.   [20] Ibid, 854.   [21] Ibid. 853.
[22] Ibid.   [23] Ibid.   [24] Ibid. 854.
[25] For Dworkin's distinction between 'experiential' and 'critical' interests, see Dworkin (1993, esp. 201–2).

that the regime of support for Bland was what most would judge to be undignified).

As we have seen, where the right to die with dignity is proclaimed, one might
be arguing for the dignity-based right to choose, or for protection of the particular choice made, or for both. In his opinion, Lord Hoffmann largely focuses on
the extended recognition, despite Bland's lack of consciousness, of his fundamental right to choose. However, approaching Bland's right to die with dignity
from the other end, the avoidance of undignified circumstances is the imperative.
So long as the analysis is anchored to Bland's right to choose, there should be no
misunderstanding of what is being said. Nevertheless, in a famous critique of the
Bland judgments, John Finnis (1993) detects a serious equivocation in Lord
Hoffmann's opinion.

There is an important distinction, argues Finnis, between respect for human
dignity in the sense first given by Lord Hoffmann, namely that 'it is wrong for
someone to be humiliated or treated without respect for his value as a person'[26]
and the other thread in Lord Hoffmann's judgment according to which we respect
human dignity by taking steps to put an end to the undignified circumstances in
which a person such as Bland was placed. Memorably, Finnis remarks: 'Failure
to distinguish being subjected to indignities from being (or being put) in an
undignified condition (or position) is a deeply unsettling aspect of *Bland*. Many
are those who might be rescued from undignified conditions by benevolent termination of their life' (1993: 336).[27]

Finnis's concern is that *Bland* articulates the wrong idea of respect for human
dignity, which it then prioritizes over the right idea. Lord Hoffmann starts with
the right idea: that it is wrong to treat others without respect for their value as a
person, that it is wrong to humiliate others or subject them to indignities; and, as
Finnis sees it, to continue with the hospital support for Bland would not in any
way violate his dignity in this sense (the sense that really matters). What must be
guarded against is the tendency to drift into thinking that we respect the dignity
of others by putting an end to the undignified circumstances in which they are
placed, if necessary by terminating their lives. This, Finnis contends, is very definitely the wrong idea; and, recalling Finnis's exchange with John Harris, it will
be appreciated that Finnis fears that *Bland* gives the green light for lawfully
ending the lives of the vulnerable whose continuing existence is inconvenient or
burdensome to others.

Is this fear well founded? As we have said already, it is important to read Lord
Hoffmann's analysis as anchored to Bland's right to choose the manner of his
death. If the dignity-based right to choose is detached from the commentary on
the avoidance of an undignifed death, there is some scope for misinterpretation.
In Finnis's reading, the two threads are detached; but, even more significantly,

---

[26] *Airedale NHS Trust* v. *Bland* [1993] 1 All ER 821, 851.
[27] To similar effect, see Joseph Boyle (1995, esp. 195).

what he takes to be the right idea of respect for human dignity (not subjecting Bland to indignities by failing to respect his value as a person) does not correspond to the liberal dignity-based right to choose that surely is the root of Lord Hoffmann's reasoning (again recall the exchange between Finnis and Harris, where there is a similar root difference). Provided, then, that we read Lord Hoffmann's judgment as a steadfast attempt to respect Bland's right to choose, even where we can make only our best guess as to what he would choose, it is coherent and it does not suffer from the equivocation alleged by Finnis. Nevertheless, is there not something in Finnis's background fear for the welfare of the vulnerable? Consider the following three cases where we must try to apply the principle that Bland's choice should be respected:

(1) Magically, Bland recovers consciousness for long enough to tell the medical team whether or not he wishes the feeding and hydration to continue when he loses consciousness again.

(2) Before the Hillsborough disaster, Bland had made an advance directive saying that if he was ever diagnosed as being in PVS, he would not wish the feeding and hydration to continue after three years.

(3) As in the actual case, there was no miraculous short-term recovery of consciousness, no advance directive, and no direct evidence of what Bland would have wished should he ever be in PVS.

In (1), where consent incompetence is briefly interrupted by a spell of consent competence, we might be reasonably confident about acting in accordance with Bland's choice. In (2), where we act on an ex-ostensible agent by relying on a specific indication given during an earlier period of ostensible agency, we might be confident about acting in accordance with the earlier directive but we might be uncertain whether the earlier expression of choice holds good when the contingency actually eventuates and we have no means of confirming *present* choice.[28] In (3), we can make only a substituted judgement. We might get it right; we might get it wrong. In good faith, we can try to put ourselves in the position of Bland; but, there is no getting away from the fact that the dignity-based right to choose is now being applied in a relatively speculative fashion. Decision-makers can be assisted to some extent by the evidence of Bland's family and friends; and the law can operate with a default position that fits with what one takes to be the choice that would normally be made. This, we suggest, is where Finnis's fears are well founded. If Bland's continuing existence is burdensome, how reliable is the evidence of family and (so-called) friends? Even more significantly, where the culture regards long-term feeding and hydration of those who are in PVS as undignified, and where it also militates against the choice of prolonged support of this kind, then the default position will certainly ease the passing.

We must return to the *Bland* case shortly, to comment on the major fear that

---

[28] For a valuable discussion of such uncertainty, see Morgan (1994).

the courts had, which is that, by declaring that the withholding of feeding and hydration was not unlawful, they were, as Lord Goff put it, in danger of 'cross[ing] the Rubicon which runs between on the one hand the care of the living patient and on the other hand euthanasia—actively causing his death to avoid or to end his suffering'.[29] However, before we move on to this question, we should look briefly at the reasoning of the US Supreme Court in the *Cruzan* case,[30] because this sheds light on the matter of the default position.

The point at issue in *Cruzan* concerned the requirement in Missouri that, before feeding and hydration of a patient in PVS could be withheld lawfully, there must be clear and compelling evidence that the individual patient would have so wished. The majority of the Supreme Court upheld this requirement; the minority rejected it as inconsistent with the individual's right to refuse treatment and to elect to die with dignity. One way of reading the difference between the majority and minority opinions is to focus on the default position that the law takes in dealing with end of life decisions in relation to the incompetence of non-ostensible agents. On this account, both the majority and the minority in *Cruzan* (on both sides, just like Lord Hoffmann in *Bland*) are doing their honest best to make an accurate determination of the choice that the incompetent non-ostensible agent would have made. Would, or would not, Nancy Cruzan have wished that the medical support regime should continue? In principle, three general default positions might be operated by the law.

(*a*) The default presumption is that an individual in PVS would ordinarily choose the regime of feeding and hydration to continue; the onus, therefore, is on those who wish to discontinue the support to adduce evidence showing that this particular individual would not have so chosen.

(*b*) The default position makes no presumption either way as to whether an individual in PVS would ordinarily choose the regime of feeding and hydration to continue. Accordingly, the onus of adducing evidence as to the individual's wishes lies equally on both sides.

(*c*) The default presumption is that an individual in PVS would ordinarily choose the regime of feeding and hydration to be discontinued. The onus, therefore, is on those who wish to continue with the support, to adduce evidence showing that this particular individual would not have so chosen.

These positions can be refined by specifying a particular standard of proof. For example, in *Cruzan*, the majority's approach fits with the first default position, but it is operated in an extremely precautionary way by upholding the Missouri standard that the (rebutting) evidence must be clear and compelling.

While we say that the majority approach in *Cruzan* fits with the first default position, this is not the only reading of the case. In the minority opinions, there is

---

[29] *Airedale NHS Trust* v. *Bland* [1993] 1 All ER 821, 867.
[30] 497 US 261, 110 S Ct 2841 (1990); 111 L Ed 2d 224.

an unconcealed suspicion that the majority were prioritizing the sanctity of life rather than the individual's right to self-determination. As Justice Brennan emphasizes in his dissent, if the governing principle is keeping faith with Cruzan's choice, then to give weight to the irrevocability of withholding support is to misdirect ourselves.

An erroneous decision to terminate artificial nutrition and hydration, to be sure, will lead to failure of that last remnant of physiological life, the brain stem, and result in complete brain death. An erroneous decision not to terminate life support, however, robs a patient of the very qualities protected by the right to avoid unwanted medical treatment. His own degraded existence is perpetuated; his family's suffering is protracted; the memory he leaves behind becomes more and more distorted.[31]

On this view, the majority would need to justify adopting the first default position by reference to general attitudes to life and death in Missouri, rather than by assuming that erroneously withdrawing support would involve a greater harm (because death would irretrievably ensue) than the harm involved in erroneously continuing with the support regime. Similarly, the minority would need also to justify adopting one of the other default positions by reference to the pattern of general attitudes to life and death in Missouri (or wherever the immediate context was located).

Returning to *Bland*, a plausible reading of Lord Hoffmann's speech (and quite probably of the general approach of the courts hearing the case) is that the third default position should apply and that it should apply in the following modified terms:

(*c′*) The default presumption is that an individual in PVS would ordinarily choose the regime of feeding and hydration to be discontinued, *on the ground that it is generally thought to be undignified to be maintained in such a condition and people (in South Yorkshire, the North of England, or wherever the immediate context) generally do not desire to be kept in undignified circumstances.* The onus, therefore, is on those who wish to continue with the support, to adduce evidence showing that this particular individual would not have so chosen.

In so far as we are anxious about the accuracy of the judgement made as to the individual's choice, we need to be reassured that the law's reading of local culture (particularly typical local attitudes to life and death) is reliable. If it is, at least the default position seems to have the right trajectory.

In *Bland* itself, the courts, as we have said, seem less troubled about the accuracy of the default position that they are implicitly presupposing than that they might be opening the door to the legalization of (active) euthanasia. Throughout the judgments, there is a mixture of denial and concern. Lord Hoffmann, having

---

[31] 111 L Ed 2d 224, 268.

hypothesized that it might be more humane to end Bland's life by administering a lethal injection, immediately rejects any such suggestion. According to his Lordship, we would be appalled by such a suggestion because it is incompatible with our commitment to the sanctity of life (which entails its inviolability by an outsider). 'Subject to exceptions like self-defence, human life is inviolate even if the person in question has consented to its violation. That is why although suicide is not a crime, assisting someone to commit suicide is. It follows that, even if we think Anthony Bland would have consented, we would not be entitled to end his life by a lethal injection.'[32] On the face of it, this is a pretty remarkable line. How can we square the proposition (*a*) that it is permissible to withhold feeding and hydration from Bland (knowing that death will ensue), when we are relying on no more than an honest guess as to whether he would have consented to this, with (*b*) that it is not permissible to administer a lethal injection to Bland, even where we have incontrovertible evidence that he consents to the termination of his life in this way?

Similarly, in the House of Lords Lord Browne-Wilkinson concluded by posing much the same moral conundrum:

the conclusion I have reached will appear to some to be almost irrational. How can it be lawful to allow a patient to die slowly, though painlessly, over a period of weeks from lack of food but unlawful to produce his immediate death by a lethal injection, thereby saving his family from yet another ordeal to add to the tragedy that has already struck them? I find it difficult to find a moral answer to that question.[33]

In both cases, the critical consideration is to understand (for a Gewirthian) which waters are flowing in the Rubicon: namely, the waters of consent. What is absolutely prohibited is acting against an agent's generic conditions without having the appropriate consent for such interference. From this perspective, it is wholly irrational to treat the administration of a lethal injection to a consenting agent as impermissible; starving a non-consenting ostensible agent to death is no better or worse than administering a lethal injection to such an agent; and, if we are dealing with patients who are irretrievably consent-incompetent, it remains to be seen whether starvation is any better or worse morally speaking than the administration of a lethal injection.

What, then, is the Gewirthian approach to questions of dignity when we are dealing with ex-ostensible agents who are no longer (or, so it seems) consent-competent? To repeat, following our discussion in Chapter 6, while we can say that, in principle, particular human beings either are or are not agents, we cannot with confidence make our classificatory judgements in particular cases. Even in what we take to be the clearest case of agency, precaution dictates that we treat a human being as an *ostensible* agent (and, thus, for practical purposes, as an agent). Conversely, even where we believe that a particular living thing falls

---

[32] *Airedale NHS Trust* v. *Bland* [1993] 1 All ER 821, 855.
[33] Ibid. 884.

clearly on the non-agent side of the line, precaution dictates that we recognize the *possibility* of agency. In between these supposedly clear cases, we have cases of partial and intermittent agency where precaution again dictates that we operate in practice in a way that recognizes the possibility of agency. What do we say, though, about tragic cases such as *Bland* and *Cruzan*, where those who were once ostensible agents no longer seem to be agents, where consent competence is seemingly gone for good? Where there is still the capacity to choose, Gewirthians will be guided by consent principles and the dignity-based right to choose will govern. However, in the PVS cases, how are we to act in a way that respects human dignity? Or, do we even need to trouble to attempt so to act?

One approach might be to echo Lord Mustill's blunt observation in *Bland* to the effect that it was stretching a point to ask whether the withdrawal of support was in the young man's best interests, because the 'distressing truth which must not be shirked is that . . . [Bland] has no best interests of any kind'.[34] Or, to cast this in Gewirthian terms: it makes little sense to ask whether the withdrawal of support might be in accordance with Bland's will because Bland seemingly no longer has the capacity to will anything. And, if this painful truth is not to be shirked, we must accept that Bland no longer has the wherewithal to be treated as an ostensible agent—indeed that he should be treated at best as a possible (but remotely possible) agent. Yet, if Bland is not to be treated as an ostensible agent, he has no straightforward rights, and less than a full (ostensible agent) entitlement to respect or resource. Again, Lord Mustill's forthright speech makes an important point:

Threaded through the technical arguments addressed to the House were the strands of a much wider position, that it is in the best interests of the community at large that Anthony Bland's life should now end. The doctors have done all they can. Nothing will be gained by going on and much will be lost. The distress of the family will get steadily worse. The strain on the devotion of a medical staff charged with the care of a patient whose condition will never improve, who may live for years and who does not even recognise that he is being cared for, will continue to mount. The large resources of skill, labour and money now being devoted to Anthony Bland might in the opinion of many be more fruitfully employed in improving the condition of other patients, who if treated may have useful, healthy and enjoyable lives for years to come.[35]

Such a cost–benefit calculation is, of course, alien to Gewirthian thinking where we are dealing with ostensible agents; but, where we are dealing with one who is not an ostensible agent, maybe we should be even more hard-nosed. Why expend any resource on such a being? Why spend time formulating the content of a hypothetical will when the capacity to formulate an actual will seemingly has been lost? Why not channel the resource to ostensible agents in need rather than to those who no longer are capable of recognizing their own needs?

Let us suppose that we were to try to resist this chain of thinking by appealing

---

[34] Ibid. 894.   [35] Ibid. 893.

to the importance of human dignity. We might object, first, that respect for human dignity demands that we preserve the life of humans even when the human capacity for practical reason ostensibly has been lost. From a Gewirthian perspective, we cannot get very far with an objection based, as this is, on the intrinsic good of human life. Even so, there are two features of PVS cases that must give Gewirthians pause.

First, there is the matter of the precautionary principle which perhaps we lose sight of as we pursue Lord Mustill's blunt line of thinking. It will be appreciated that such precautionary reasoning is not to be confused with the precautionary conclusions that we might derive from the debate about whether PVS is reversible (so that, if there is a chance of recovery, however remote, we should not act in a way that eliminates that possibility). Rather, assuming that PVS is irreversible, Gewirthian precautionary reasoning asks whether there is a possibility that a living being in PVS whom we once took to be an agent (i.e. treated as an ostensible agent) is still an agent. If the answer is that the evidence does not support treating this person as an ostensible agent but we still cannot rule out the possibility (albeit a remote possibility) that this is an agent, then we must respect that possibility in our actions. It follows that (other things being equal) we should maintain the life of such possible agents, not in the expectation or hope that they might once again present themselves as ostensible agents, but simply because of our minimal obligations to those who are *possible* agents.

The second feature of PVS cases is that we are dealing with beings who, prior to entering into PVS, were ostensible agents. Such ex-ostensible agents invite special consideration. At strongest, they (when they were ostensible agents) might have secured undertakings from others concerning their treatment if they entered into PVS; at weakest they (when they were ostensible agents) might have been encouraged to believe that they might be treated in a certain way if they entered into PVS, and they might then have acted in the expectation that they would be so treated. In such circumstances, it is at least arguable that an obligation is owed to such ex-ostensible agents to treat them in accordance with the undertakings given or the expectations so engendered. In the absence of prior obligation of this kind, it is unclear why there should be an inquiry as to what the ex-ostensible agent would have preferred once PVS was diagnosed. On the other hand, even if an inquiry of this kind is not a matter of moral requirement under the PGC, it is not obviously impermissible. To pursue this any further, however, takes us beyond our brief (which is about the import of respect for human dignity rather than about the broad application of the PGC).[36]

---

[36] Arguably, though, there is still more mileage in respect for human dignity bridging from agency to ex-agency. For example, Norman Cantor suggests: 'In significant part, a person's control over a post-competence dying process is an effort to mold other people's posthumous recollections of the person's character and values. The desire to shape recollections is grounded on common recognition of a tie between human dignity and a personal image projected to others. And because of a perceived tie between dignity and lifetime image, individual self-fulfillment and self-respect are seen as dependent

What, then, can we say about the right to die with dignity in cases such as those of Bland and Cruzan where we are dealing with at best possible agents? Gewirthian precautionary reasoning allows for the view that beings in PVS are possible agents and, thus, that their well-being (life) should be sustained. If, notwithstanding such precautionary protection, feeding, hydration, and the like are to be withdrawn (leading to death) this might be justified on one of three grounds as follows:

1. as the fulfilment of an obligation undertaken to the previously ostensible agent; or
2. as a permissible fulfilment of a preference that one assumes the previously ostensible agent would have had; or
3. as a reallocation of scarce resources in order to protect the generic interests of ostensible agents.

Whereas, in the first of these cases, the thrust of the justification is that the previously ostensible agent did, indeed, have a (dignity-based) right to die with dignity, in the second case, the justification rests on respect for the previously ostensible agent's assumed preference for a death that is not undignified. In the third case, the reasoning respects the possible dignity of the person in PVS but, where possible dignity is in competition with ostensible agency (and dignity) the latter must prevail.

Before we turn to our third 'death with dignity' context, it is worth noting how dignity as a virtue might be related to the attitude of an ostensible agent at the end of life. This virtue keys in to the dignity-relevant capacities of agency; in particular, without the capacity to choose, we cannot display the virtue of dignity. Specifically, we have suggested that this virtue can be understood in terms of an ability to display fortitude in the face of adversity, striking a balance between premature submission and futile resistance, and making one's choices accordingly. For all agents, it is the existential anxiety that, above all, represents the running adversity of the human social condition. To respond to this adversity with dignity is to live a life that presupposes neither certain extinction nor certain immortality; and to die with dignity is to leave this life in a way that submits (consistent with one's rational hope in immortality) but that also displays resistance (consistent with one's fear of extinction). If we take this idea seriously, we can understand the right to die with dignity in a rather different light. The agent who lives in accordance with the virtue of dignity will wish to die in a way that reflects a radical agnosticism about the afterlife. For such agents, it is not the prospect of a culturally defined undignified condition (particularly associated with invasive hospital treatment) that is the real concern. Rather, the concern is

not just on dominion over important decisions while the person is still competent and acutely aware but on dominion over a lifetime image' (1993: 105). In terms of what we have said in the text, such considerations might translate into an argument that we respect the dignity-based expectations of agents by treating ex-ostensible agents in a way that is consistent with the importance generally attached to lifetime image and posthumous recollection.

that life-sustaining measures should not be continued once it is clear that the onset of death is inevitable—and, arguably, from an agency perspective, the concern (and the requirements of the virtue) kick in once it is clear that agency cannot be retrieved. For the virtuous agent, to die with dignity is the final act of a life lived with dignity; it is to meet one's fate with resistance and submission balanced in just the right measure.

Death with Dignity at the Beginning of Life

If tragic cases such as those of *Bland* and *Cruzan* raise complex questions about death with dignity, so too does a case such as that of *Re A (children)(conjoined twins: surgical separation)*,[37] where the English courts were asked to rule on the lawfulness of separating the Siamese twins Jodie and Mary. The essential facts (and, concomitantly, the dilemma to which the facts give rise) are set out in Ward LJ's judgment as follows:

Jodie and Mary are conjoined twins. They each have their own brain, heart and lungs and other vital organs and they each have arms and legs. They are joined at the lower abdomen. Whilst not underplaying the surgical complexities, they can be successfully separated. But the operation will kill the weaker twin, Mary. That is because her lungs and heart are too deficient to oxygenate and pump blood through her body. Had she been born a singleton, she would not have been viable and resuscitation would have been abandoned. She would have died shortly after her birth. She is alive only because a common artery enables her sister, who is stronger, to circulate life sustaining oxygenated blood for both of them. Separation would require the clamping and then the severing of that common artery. Within minutes of doing so Mary will die. Yet if the operation does not take place, both will die within three to six months, or perhaps a little longer, because Jodie's heart will eventually fail. The parents cannot bring themselves to consent to the operation. The twins are equal in their eyes and they cannot agree to kill one even to save the other. As devout Roman Catholics they sincerely believe that it is God's will that their children are afflicted as they are and must be left in God's hands. The doctors are convinced they can carry out the operation so as to give Jodie a life which will be worthwhile.[38]

At first instance, Johnson J ruled that separation would be lawful. Unanimously, although without always agreeing with Johnson J's reasoning, the Court of Appeal agreed that the separation could proceed lawfully. The parents elected not to pursue the appeal any further. The operation took place, resulting, as anticipated, in Mary's death and Jodie's survival.

Of the many questions invited by *Re A (children)*, the principal question for us is whether the separation was compatible with respect for human dignity. In particular, did separation respect the dignity of each of the two girls and their parents (the latter of whom refused to consent to the operation)? Beyond this,

---

[37] [2000] 4 All ER 961.   [38] Ibid. 969.

there is an important point to be made about dignity in relation to the parents' accepting the ruling of the Court of Appeal, even though they disagreed with it. Before looking at the Court's approach, though, we must sketch a Gewirthian (precautionary) analysis of this case.

Gewirthian Analysis

The primary meaning that we have attached to human dignity is as the basis of the rights of agents. If we assume that nothing other than this is relevant to the decision in *Re A (children)* (which is equivalent to assuming that nothing other than the intrinsic status of the twins in relation to their being agents is relevant), then the decision is straightforward.

Following the precautionary framework of reasoning developed in Chapter 6, neither Jodie nor Mary is ostensibly an agent at the time of the proposed separation. It is *possible* that both Jodie and Mary are agents. However, the evidence is that Jodie is a potential ostensible agent (or an ostensible potential agent), whereas Mary is not. From this, it follows that the probability that Jodie is an agent is greater than the probability that Mary is an agent. Hence, while both Jodie and Mary are to be accorded some direct moral status as possible agents under precaution, Jodie must be granted higher status.

It follows that, essentially, the conflict between Jodie's life and Mary's life is on a par with that between the life of a mother and that of her unborn child where both cannot live but the mother can be saved at the expense of the unborn child (when the unborn child cannot be saved at the expense of the mother). There is a difference between the two cases in that the mother could choose to die with her unborn child, whereas Jodie has no capacity to choose to die with Mary, but this difference is not relevant to the issue at hand. The two cases can be made equivalent, for practical purposes, by assuming that the mother has expressed no wish about this situation in the past and is unconscious at the point at which a decision must be made. Where probability of harm and severity of harm are both measured on scales of 0 to 1, these two (analogous) situations can be represented as follows:

	Mother	*Foetus*
Moral status	1	<1
Severity of harm	1	1
Probability of harm	1	1

	Jodie	*Mary*
Moral status	$<1 \ (= z)$	$<z$
Severity of harm	1	1
Probability of harm	1	1

So expressed, the conflict between Jodie and Mary must be resolved in favour of the former (as the lesser of two moral evils). However, the human dignity of the twins in these terms is not the only consideration; for example, the human dignity of the parents and others can also be affected and this dimension of the puzzle must also be considered.

On the facts of *Re A (children)*, to separate the twins is to act contrary to the wishes of the parents. It might be contended that this is to violate the generic rights of the parents (and implicitly their dignity as the basis of their generic rights). Furthermore, it might be argued that since the parents are ostensible agents, whereas Jodie (on whose behalf we might argue for the chance to survive) is not, it follows that the twins should not be separated. This, however, is fallacious reasoning. The parents do not have a generic right to do whatever they want. Their generic right to freedom of action gives them rights to do whatever they want provided that they do not violate their duties under the PGC. Precautionary reasoning imposes duties on them to protect Jodie as a possible agent (indeed, an ostensible potential agent), which means that only if saving Jodie impacts on their generic rights as such is there any case for giving their wishes preference.[39] Again, putting this in the form of a balance, we have the following:

	Jodie	*Parents*
Moral status	<1 (human dignity value under precaution)	1
Severity of harm	1	<1 (of adverse consequences to parents of Jodie living)[40]
Probability of harm	1	<1

Having set up the question in these terms, however, it is not at all obvious how we should weigh these competing considerations. For, there are at least two major problems. First, there is an inexactitude about the value that we give to any of the variables where it is less than 1. To some extent, we can make ordinal judgements (1 takes precedence over <1) but we cannot translate <1 so readily into a cardinal value. Second, even if we could give all variables precise values, and assuming that there is commensurability between the same variable on either side of the balance, is there nevertheless commensurability between *different* variables? For example, in the balance between Jodie and her parents, is there commensurability between, say, moral status and severity or probability of harm? Does the 1 value for the parents' moral status equate to the 1 value for Jodie with regard to the severity or probability of harm? In short, where different variables are in play is there a common tariff allowing for commensurability? Or, if not, is there some other way of conducting the balance?

The difficulty of identifying a common tariff is obvious. Even if one might be able to weigh, say, a low probability of a severe harm against a high probability

---

[39] It seems to us that there is no case for saying that moral status as an ostensible agent (with full human dignity) is the only thing that matters. To argue that would be to contradict that any duties are generated by precaution towards those that are not ostensibly agents. Our duties to Jodie are generated by the possibility that she may be an agent, not by her being presumed to be an agent.

[40] Compare Ward LJ's assessment of the impact on the parents in [2000] 4 All ER 961, 1009.

of a minor harm (and it is not at all clear that one might be able so to translate these options into a common currency), how can one proceed once the probability of agency is factored in? For example, which is the lesser of two evils, a low probability of medium-level harm to a very high probability (ostensible) agent, or a very high probability of medium-level harm to a low probability (non-ostensible) agent? Is it plausible to think that there might be a common tariff allowing this calculation to be made? If not, one might think it more plausible perhaps that the moral status variable should be privileged in the calculation. After all, the precautionary principle is designed to prevent ostensible agents from harming those who, while not ostensible agents, actually are agents—that is to say, the imperative is to prevent the violation of generic rights, whether of those who appear to be or who actually are (appearances notwithstanding) agents. It follows that, if one has to weigh the interests of an ostensible agent against those of a merely possible agent, one must judge that the probability of violating generic rights is higher in relation to the former than the latter. Of course, it is not controversial to say that, other things being equal (or the balance otherwise being in equipoise), one should favour the interests of an ostensible agent. However, one might go beyond this, contending either (i) that, even where one simply does not know whether other things are equal, one should favour the interests of an ostensible agent, or (ii) that, even where other things seem to be marginally inclined towards the merely possible agent, one should still favour the interests of an ostensible agent. On these matters, at least for now, we express no opinion.

Our difficulties, moreover, are not yet all in view. Once we have resolved the balance between Jodie and her parents, we must take into consideration the interests of any other ostensible agents. To (over)simplify, let us assume that no other (third party) ostensible agents will be *directly* affected by the decision. Nevertheless, any *indirect* effects (on ostensible agents) of sanctioning the separation of the twins must be taken into account. For example, despite the Court's heroic attempt (see below) to disavow making any judgment as to the quality of life of the girls, the decision might have the effect of inviting just such slippery slope thoughts (and encouraging practices that evince a lack of respect for the intrinsic dignity of agents). Such considerations add to the complexity of the case, for 'tendency' arguments of this kind are speculative. Moreover, at the end of the chain of indirect effect, we return to the central question of how we compare one kind of (indirect) impact on an ostensible agent with another kind of (direct) impact on a merely possible agent.

If Gewirthian theory does allow for a calculation of this kind to be conducted by way of a *direct* application of the PGC, we confess that we do not yet know how this should be done. Specifically, with regard to the balance between Jodie and her parents in *Re A (children)*, we are unable to offer an answer. This is not because we think that the arguments are evenly balanced (that there is equipoise with the arguments equally weighted on either side); rather, it is simply that we do not know how the balance stands: if this is a case of equipoise, it is equipoise due to complexity and uncertainty. Such an admission takes us to the possibility of an indirect application of the PGC. As we argued in *Law as a Moral Judgment*, any politico-legal system that aspires to a legal–moral order must have a strategy for dealing with differences of moral opinion (see Beyleveld and Brownsword 1986, chs. 5 and 7). This is that an authorized body, such as a court, must be charged with making a good faith attempt at applying the PGC. Such indirect applications, we argued, must be treated as having practical authority. With the Gewirthian analysis taking us in this direction, we can turn to consider the way in which the Court approached the issue in *Re A (children)*.

The Court of Appeal's Approach

The Court of Appeal in *Re A (children)* did not regard the case as an easy one. Far from it, it was headline news that the judges were agonizing over their decision and, indeed, the Court made no secret of its difficulties. According to Ward LJ:

In this case the right answer is not at all . . . easy to find. I freely confess to having found it exceptionally difficult to decide—difficult because of the scale of the tragedy for the parents and the twins, difficult for the seemingly irreconcilable conflicts of moral and ethical values and difficult because the search for settled legal principle has been especially arduous and conducted under real pressure of time.[41]

The Court declared its intention to relegate the moral considerations to the background, saying that the Court was one of law not morals. Manifestly, though, this was easier said than done. While the Court could decline to arbitrate between the many competing moral views of the case and could focus instead on the recognized principles of positive law in order to frame the issues, the moral problematic of taking Mary's life in order to save that of Jodie could not be silenced or suppressed. How, then, did the Court of Appeal approach the case?

Broadly speaking, the Court's approach (guided by recognized legal principles) falls into two parts: (i) a consideration of whether, as a matter of family law, separation would be compatible with respecting the best interests of the children; and (ii) if so, whether separation (given that this would involve the foreseen killing of Mary) would be compatible with the criminal law. Ward LJ leads the Court on the family law issues and, for our purposes, this is the focal part of the judgment because it is here that we find the Court weighing the interests of the children, taking into account the wishes of the parents, and touching on questions of dignity.

At first instance, it was taken as read that both children, crucially Mary, were live and separate persons. Responding to some doubt about this assumption, however, Ward LJ reiterated this view:

Here Mary has been born in the sense that she has an existence quite independent from her

---

[41] [2000] 4 All ER 961, 968–9.

mother. The fact that Mary is dependent upon Jodie, or the fact that the twins may be inter-dependent if they share heart and lungs, should not lead the law to fly in the face of the clinical judgment that each child is alive and that each child is separate both for the purposes of the civil law and the criminal law.[42]

If anything, Brooke LJ put the point even more forcibly:

I am satisfied that Mary's life is a human life that falls to be protected by the law of murder. Although she has for all practical purposes a useless brain, a useless heart and useless lungs, she is alive, and it would in my judgment be an act of murder if someone deliber-ately acted so as to extinguish that life unless a justification or excuse could be shown which English law is willing to recognise.[43]

The baseline for the Court, therefore, was that Mary and Jodie, each as a life in being, enjoyed the same protected status under English law. Accordingly, when endeavouring to apply the (governing) welfare principle, the Court should not open with the interest of one child already prioritized over that of another; the Court starts 'with an evenly balanced pair of scales'.[44] Having determined that separation would be in Jodie's best interests (giving her the chance of an inde-pendent life) but that it would be contrary to Mary's best interests (resulting in the loss of her life), Ward LJ recognized that 'the conflict between the children could not be more acute'.[45] To decline to decide the case, Ward LJ thought, would be an abdication of duty. Yet how could the balance be struck?

First, the parents' wishes must be taken into account. However, the task of the Court is not simply to endorse the parents' wishes without more, nor even to endorse their wishes provided that they are not wholly unreasonable. Whether the parents' wishes are patently irreconcilable with the welfare of the children or a perfectly reasonable view, the case law requires the judge to make an independent decision as to the child's welfare. Here, although the position taken by the parents of Mary and Jodie was 'pre-eminently reasonable',[46] Ward LJ detected an incon-sistency in the way in which they rightly emphasized that Mary's right to life should be respected and yet seemingly minimized the same right on Jodie's part in the light of perceived burdens that would be borne by Jodie and her carers. Thus:

In their natural repugnance at the idea of killing Mary they fail to recognise their conflict-ing duty to save Jodie and they seem to exculpate themselves from, or at least fail fully to face up to the consequence of the failure to separate the twins, namely death for Jodie. In my judgment, parents who are placed on the horns of such a terrible dilemma simply have to choose the lesser of their inevitable loss. If a family at the gates of a concentration camp were told they might free one of their children but if no choice were made both would die,

---

[42] Ibid. 996. [43] Ibid. 1025.
[44] *Per* Balcombe LJ in *Birmingham City Council* v. *H (a minor)* [1994] 1 All ER 12, [1994] 2 AC 212, cited by Ward LJ at [2000] 4 All ER 961, 1005.
[45] Ibid. 1006.
[46] Transcript (www.courtservice.gov.uk), 148. This does not appear in the All England Reports.

compassionate parents with equal love for their twins would elect to save the stronger and see the weak one destined for death pass through the gates.[47]

Returning to the balance as between the twins, Ward LJ repeats the pattern of reasoning that he believes the parents should have followed. Whereas Mary is doomed for death, Jodie's actual bodily condition is such that, with separation, she has the chance of life. So viewed, 'the scales come down heavily in Jodie's favour'.[48] It is again strongly emphasized, however, that what moves the scales in this way is not that Jodie's life is regarded as more valuable than Mary's— 'Mary's life, desperate as it is, still has its own ineliminable value and dignity';[49] nor does the balance turn on the worthwhileness of the lives of these children. Rather, it is the worthwhileness of the separation (the 'treatment' as Ward LJ calls it) that is relevant.[50] So far as Mary is concerned the separation is worse than futile; but, for Jodie, separation is the key to life itself and to 'the dignity of her own free, separate body'.[51]

What do we make of this approach relative to the Gewirthian analysis that we have outlined? Superficially, the approach adopted by the Court is not dissimilar to our Gewirthian sketch. The conflicting interests of the twins are considered and, in fact, as in the Gewirthian analysis, the interests of Jodie prevail. The interests of the parents, too, are brought into the Court's assessment of the best interests of the children. However, there are two striking differences between the Court's approach and what we find in the Gewirthian analysis.

First, the Court treats the legal (and, implicitly, the moral) status of the children as not only equal but, so far as their dignity is concerned, full. In the Court's eyes, Jodie and Mary are each entitled to the full protection of the law. Despite the fact that Jodie cannot choose whether or not she wishes to proceed with the separation, and despite the fact that Mary has been born with 'a useless brain, a useless heart and useless lungs', these children are to be treated (in Gewirthian terms) as though they are agents.[52] From a Gewirthian perspective, this approach

[47] [2000] 4 All ER 961, 1009–10.
[48] Ibid. 1011.
[49] Transcript (www.courtservice.gov.uk), 147. Again, this does not appear in the All England Reports.
[50] This distinction between the worthwhileness of treatment as against the worthwhileness of a person's life draws on Keown (1997). In general, Keown presents a sanctity of life principle as a middle way between vitalism (preserving life at all costs) and a Quality of Life approach (involving (arbitrary) judgements as to the worthwhileness of persons and their lives). The sanctity of life principle, unlike vitalism, does not require treatment to be given, or continued, where it is futile. As Keown is at pains to emphasize, though, 'the question is always whether the treatment would be worthwhile, not whether the patient's life would be worthwhile' (ibid. 485).
[51] Transcript (www.courtservice.gov.uk), 147. Once again, this does not appear in the All England Reports.
[52] On this basis, it might be argued that the law is wrong to treat the newly born as having full moral status (that is, a human dignity value of 1). Alternatively, it might be argued that, as a rule of thumb, and taking into account various policy reasons under the PGC driven by precaution (e.g. brutalization and similar negative indirect effects), this is permissible. However, such a rule of thumb would have to be suspended when there is a direct conflict at the level of the most basic value of life.

displays an over high degree of precaution. However, at this point in the Court's argument, the obvious physical differences between Mary and Jodie are not relied on. It is only when the Court moves on to consider the worthwhileness of the treatment (separation) to each of the girls that these differences become critical. By contrast, in our Gewirthian analysis, the fact that Mary, unlike Jodie, has been born with 'a useless brain, a useless heart and useless lungs' makes a difference to how we regard these two girls. Of course, it is not a matter of abandoning precaution in relation to Mary. We must apply a precautionary approach to both girls but, under such an application, we must judge that the possibility of Jodie being an agent is higher than that of Mary. To put this another way, on the evidence, we have insufficient grounds to believe that either girl is an agent and, thus, has dignity; but we could be wrong and, on the evidence, the chances are that we are more likely to be wrong in relation to Jodie than to Mary.

Second, the way in which the Court pays attention to the preferences of the parents in its assessment of the best interests of the children is quite different from the way that this operates in our Gewirthian analysis. Whereas, in our Gewirthian analysis, the parents (as ostensible agents) must be treated as having a higher moral status than Jodie (who is no more than a potential ostensible agent), the Court draws no distinction between the status of parent and child in this respect. Indeed, in the Court's view, because its task is to act in whatever way is in the child's best interest, the relevance of the parents' preference for non-separation of the twins is simply that the setting for Jodie's survival and future well-being will necessarily be coloured by the parents' declared opposition to the separation. For the Court, it is true, the parents' refusal counts against the separation but this operates indirectly and within the framework of the *child's* best interests. By contrast, in our Gewirthian analysis, the parents have a direct and independent claim that their generic rights should not be harmed against their will. So far as Jodie is concerned, the parents' duty is to act in a way that is compatible with respecting the welfare of possible agents. To express this in terms of the parties' interests: in our Gewirthian analysis, there is a conflict between the interests of ostensible agents and those of a potential ostensible agent.

So much for the Court's general approach to the question, but what is its view of human dignity? In the judgments, we find a number of explicit, but essentially passing, remarks concerning the relevance and importance of dignity. For example, the Court pauses to admire the 'fortitude and dignity'[53] displayed by the parents (a point to which we will return); it asserts that Mary 'has a full claim to the dignity of independence which is her human entitlement';[54] and, in a similar vein, there are references to bodily integrity and human dignity as well as personal privacy and human dignity.[55] Possibly the Court confuses at times the idea of intrinsic dignity with its understanding of a dignified existence (a conjoined existence being treated as less dignified than a separated existence).

[53] [2000] 4 All ER 961, 987.   [54] Ibid. 1010.   [55] Ibid. 1069 (Robert Walker LJ).

However, the most significant facet of the Court's thinking is its reliance (particularly in Ward LJ's judgment) on the work of John Keown, which ties it to one particular conception of human dignity. According to Keown:

The dignity of human beings inheres because of their radical capacities, such as for understanding and rational choice, inherent in their nature. Some human beings, such as infants, may not yet possess the ability to exercise these radical capacities. But radical capacities must not be confused with abilities: one may have, for example, the radical capacity but not the ability to speak Swahili. All human being [*sic*] possess the capacities inherent in their nature even though, because of infancy, disability or senility, they may not yet, not now, or no longer have the ability to exercise them. (1997: 483)

And, in the words of Ward LJ:

The sanctity of life doctrine holds that human life is created in the image of God and is therefore possessed of an intrinsic dignity which entitled [*sic*] it to protection from unjust attack.[56]

At first sight, this conception of dignity seems to share ground with a Gewirthian or Kantian view, because it aligns dignity with the capacity for understanding and rational choice. However, it is very different.

The example Keown uses to illustrate the concept of a radical capacity is not clear. Is the difference between having the ability to speak Swahili and having the radical capacity to speak Swahili the difference between actually being able to speak Swahili and having the actual ability *to learn to* speak Swahili? If so, then to have the radical capacity to speak Swahili one must be an agent (and not merely have potential to develop into an agent). So this understanding cannot be applied assertorically to infants or those who no longer appear to be agents. Is the distinction, then, between actually having the ability to speak Swahili and having the potential to develop the abilities needed to learn to speak Swahili? But, if so, then while Jodie (who, ostensibly, has the potential to develop into an agent) would seem to have the radical capacity to speak Swahili, Mary does not (for she appears not to have the potential to develop into an agent) and neither does someone like Tony Bland (who appears, irreversibly, to be no longer an agent). In fact, to be able to attribute the radical capacity to speak Swahili to *all* human beings, 'radical potential' must be understood as something like 'species potential', in the sense that an individual A may be said to have the radical potential to be able to do X if the ability to do X is something that characterizes the species to which A belongs (either on the basis that some members of A's species are able to do X, or on the basis that most 'normal' adult members of A's species have the ability to do X), *whether or not* A actually has the potential to develop the ability to do X or actually has the ability to do X. In short, the function of 'radical' is to deem all humans (by virtue of species membership) to be on a par with regard to their dignity, even when individually they are not equal with respect to having the abil-

56 [2000] 4 All ER 961, 999.

ities on the basis of which dignity is attributed to the species. If this is not simply specious, then it must be coupled with theological or teleological premisses that are at the very least highly contentious. Thus, in so far as the Court accepts Keown's submission, we believe that it takes up what is *at best* a dubious speciesism that cuts through some significant distinctions, and that is difficult to defend.

This leads us to a final general point concerning the adequacy of the Court's reasoning. The Court's attribution of full status to Mary and Jodie, together with its espousal of the sanctity of life approach, has some considerable support in positive law. It might be said, therefore, that any Gewirthian critique of these premisses is *external* to the Court's legal deliberations (and, as such, of less practical relevance and weight)—indeed, is this not precisely one of the implications of Ward LJ's remark to the effect that the Court is one of law not morals? However, for a Court committed, as this Court is, to the protection of human rights, the Gewirthian critique cannot be put at a distance so readily. As we argued in Chapter 4, a (contingent) commitment to human rights (dialectically contingently, or immanently) commits one to the PGC; so, where that human rights commitment is within a legal system or a particular legal institution such as a court, the commitment to the PGC is *internal* to that system or institution and its discourse. It follows that, in *Re A (children)*, the Court was one of law not (external) morals, but the relevant law was legal–moral in its nature, with the PGC as the governing internal standard.[57]

Conclusion: Dignity and Uncertainty—Towards a Civilized Society

At the same time that the new bioethics seeks to attribute dignity to human life, it emphasizes the importance of being mindful of the vulnerability of human life. From such a standpoint, dignity and vulnerability would surely combine to oppose the taking of Mary's life. Although we have argued against much of the new bioethics, we suggested in Chapter 6 that the vulnerability of agents (in the context of the existential anxiety of humans) invites an understanding of dignity as a virtue; and we can close this book by outlining how dignity as a virtue offers guidance as to the resolution of hard cases such as that of Jodie and Mary.

In Chapter 6, we argued that agents must regard themselves as vulnerable in the sense that they can be harmed (at worst, fatally harmed) against their will. Moreover, without any certainties as to an 'afterlife', the taking of an agent's life against the will of that agent cannot be passed off as no more than an *apparent* harm; such an action must be regarded as at least a possible *real* harm. It is because agents must so regard themselves as vulnerable that the protective prin-

---

[57] Of course, on dialectically necessary considerations, the Court was also internally bound by the PGC.

ciples of morality make sense. In other words, the *raison d'être* for morality is closely related to the rationally perceived vulnerability of agents. One might, however, draw a rather different lesson from the vulnerability of agents. If there is no afterlife, or at any rate no external sanctioning of the moral life, then while one might benefit at times from the protective effect of a moral code, there is no final reason, purpose, or point demanding that morality should be taken seriously. Again, though, because we cannot be certain about the premises that lead us down this potentially nihilistic train of thinking, rational agents should not entertain such thoughts. In Chapter 6, we suggested that agents, confronting their existential anxiety, should eschew two polar responses to their possible vulnerability: they should not (trusting to faith) treat themselves as invulnerable and, thus, come to see morality as unnecessary; but nor should they treat themselves as (definitely) vulnerable and limited by human finitude and mortality and, thus, come to deny the point of morality. We also suggested that a practical attitude eschewing these two responses might be captured in the form of dignity as a virtue.

Dignity as a virtue tells us something about how, as individual agents, we should confront our possible vulnerability and mortality as well as shaping our attitude (as moral agents) to natural and social adversity. However, it also points to how societies, striving to take morality seriously, should address their collective difficulties. In particular, how are societies (morally aspirant orders) to resolve their uncertainties and differences? In practice, there may well be intractable differences generated by what Rawls (1993, *passim*) calls incompatible 'comprehensive' doctrines. However, we are assuming the simpler case of just one comprehensive view, namely collective acceptance of Gewirthian moral theory backed by collective commitment to a PGC polity. Even in this exceptional (simpler) case, though, there are conflicts, uncertainties and differences representing adversities which must be addressed. Dignity as a virtue demands that we confront these problems in a way that is consistent with our commitment to serious and rational moral engagement. In this context, two considerations will lead agents to accept procedures for making *indirect*, but authorized and binding, practical applications of the PGC. First, where agents are in dispute because they are unable to agree about the right interpretation or direct application of the PGC in a particular case, such a dispute must not be allowed to escalate to the point where it threatens more important values than those actually at issue. To guard against this risk, rational agents will agree to defer to some decision-making procedure, the outcome of which will be treated for practical purposes as binding.[58] Second, because on occasion (as in a case such as that of Jodie and Mary) the application of the PGC genuinely is uncertain, we should recognize that we have reached the current limits of competence in relation to the processing of our moral knowledge. This is not something for which we should apologize; rather, we should openly recognize this aspect of human finitude, accept with humility

---

[58] As we argued in chs. 5 and 7 of *Law as a Moral Judgment* (Beyleveld and Brownsword 1986).

that the problem is beyond us and that it would be inappropriate to insist on one's own view, and defer again to an agreed decision-making procedure.

There is quite a lot that might be said about the appropriateness of particular decision-making procedures relative to particular kinds of problems that require an indirect resolution. However, for present purposes, it suffices to say that dignity as a virtue insists that, while we do not give up on morality, we accept that we cannot press our own favoured view no matter what. Let us suppose, then, that in the case of Jodie and Mary, it was appropriate for the dispute to be placed before the court on the understanding that the judicial ruling, whichever way it went, would bind the parties.

Having passed the puzzle to the court, what then? Is there any reason to suppose that a court might do better than the agents directly involved in the dispute? To the extent that judges are professional problem-solvers operating at some distance from the parties (implying both competence and impartiality), we might expect them to cope a little better. Even so, there is a real possibility that the court might find the arguments equally balanced (so that, for example, it is judged that the parents' refusal to agree to the separation of the twins merits precisely as much respect as Jodie's chance of life), in which event the indirect process needs to have a tie-breaking procedure. Or the court might find the puzzle beyond its competence (so that, for example, it admits that it is too uncertain about the weight to give to Jodie's interest as against those of Mary or the parents), in which event it cannot even say (as in the tie-break situation) that either of two possible answers is as good as the other. If the court judges that the question is beyond its competence, dignity as a virtue might again guide it through the adversity but it could do so in more than one way. For instance, it might be read as a pointer to allowing nature to take its course, both girls then dying; or it might suggest that we should resort to some random process. In neither case could we defend the particular outcome on the basis of reason, because we would be operating beyond the limits of reason in relation to the particular decision itself. However, even if leaving the fate of the twins to natural selection or to random intervention takes us a step beyond reason, it is better to be honest in the face of our difficulties than to cloak our decisions in pseudo-reason.

The tragic case of Jodie and Mary is a fitting point at which to conclude our commentary on human dignity. The intrinsic dignity of agents, we have argued, relates to those capacities that constitute beings as agents. Central to those capacities is the power to choose, which leads us to the fundamental importance of respecting the choices made by others (so long as these choices are consistent with respect for the rights of other agents). Even if an agent chooses to act in an 'undignified' way, we should respect the choice that has been made; for if we fail to respect that choice, undignified though it may be, we fail to respect the dignity of the agent who so chooses. In the case of Jodie and Mary, the parents made two critical choices, first to oppose the separation and, second, to accept the decision handed down by the Court of Appeal. The first of those choices undoubtedly merited respect; the parents legitimately asserted their right to refuse to the separation of their children. Whether or not it was right to override the parents on this matter we simply do not know. In some respects, though, the second of the parents' choices was as significant as the first. For to choose to accept the decision of the Court was to act with dignity. If the first of these choices asserts the dignity of right (the right to choose), it is the second that expresses the dignity of responsibility; and the broader lesson that we should draw from our commentary on human dignity is that a community of dignity-based right will flourish only where dignity also inspires our sense of virtue, specifically our sense of personal and civic responsibility.

References

ALEXY, ROBERT (1989), *A Theory of Legal Argumentation* (Oxford: Clarendon Press).

ALLISON, HENRY E. (1990), *Kant's Theory of Freedom* (Cambridge: Cambridge University Press).

ATIYAH, PATRICK S. (1979), *The Rise and Fall of Freedom of Contract* (Oxford: Clarendon Press).

BAIER, KURT (1958), *The Moral Point of View* (Ithaca, NY: Cornell University Press).

BEAUCHAMP, TOM L., and CHILDRESS, JAMES F. (1979), *Principles of Biomedical Ethics* (New York: Oxford University Press).

BECK, LEWIS WHITE (1960), *A Commentary on Kant's* Critique of Practical Reason (Chicago: University of Chicago Press).

—— (1965), 'Kant's Theoretical and Practical Philosophy', in Lewis White Beck (ed.), *Studies in the Philosophy of Kant* (Indianapolis: Bobbs-Merrill), 3–53; repr. (Westport, Conn.: Greenwood Press, 1981).

BECKER, ERNEST (1973), *The Denial of Death* (New York: Free Press).

BEDAU, HUGO ADAM (1992), 'The Eighth Amendment, Dignity, and the Death Penalty', in Michael J. Meyer and William A. Parent (eds.), *The Constitution of Rights: Human Dignity and American Values* (Ithaca, NY: Cornell University Press), 145–77.

BEDJAOUI, MOHAMMED (1995), 'Speech by Mr. Mohammed Bedjaoui', in *Proceedings of the Third Session of the International Bioethics Committee of UNESCO, September 1995,* vol. i (Paris: International Bioethics Committee of UNESCO), 137–45.

BENN, S. I., and PETERS, R. S. (1959), *Social Principles and the Democratic State* (London: George Allen & Unwin).

BEYLEVELD, DERYCK (1991), *The Dialectical Necessity of Morality: An Analysis and Defense of Alan Gewirth's Argument to the Principle of Generic Consistency* (Chicago: University of Chicago Press).

—— (1996), 'Legal Theory and Dialectically Contingent Justifications for the Principle of Generic Consistency', *Ratio Juris,* 9: 15–41.

—— (1997), 'The Trouble with Tendential Slippery Slope Arguments', *Biomedical Ethics: Newsletter of the European Network on Biomedical Ethics,* 2: 42.

—— (1998a), 'Some Observations on Human Dignity and Human Rights', in Elisabeth Hildt and Dietmar Mieth (eds.), *In Vitro Fertilisation in the 1990s: Towards a Medical, Social and Ethical Evaluation* (Aldershot: Ashgate), 335–7.

—— 1998b), 'The Moral and Legal Status of the Human Embryo', in Elisabeth Hildt and Dietmar Mieth (eds.), *In Vitro Fertilisation in the 1990s: Towards a Medical, Social and Ethical Evaluation* (Aldershot: Ashgate), 247–60.

—— (1999a), 'Gewirth and Kant on Justifying the Supreme Principle of Morality', in Michael Boylan (ed.), *Gewirth: Critical Essays on Action, Rationality and Community* (New York: Rowman & Littlefield), 97–117.

—— (1999b) 'Ethics for the Vulnerable by the Vulnerable: Attending to the Concept of Vulnerability in Bioethics', Paper presented at the World Congress on Philosophy of Law and Social Philosophy, PACE University, New York, 29 June.

BEYLEVELD, DERYCK, (1999c),'Does PID Solve the Moral Problems of Prenatal Diagnosis? A Rights Analysis', in Elisabeth Hildt and Sigrid Graumann (eds.), *Genetics in Human Reproduction* (Aldershot: Ashgate), 135–40.

—— (2000a), 'The Moral Status of the Human Embryo and Fetus', in Hille Haker and Deryck Beyleveld (eds.), *The Ethics of Genetics in Human Procreation* (Aldershot: Ashgate), 59–85.

—— (2000b), 'Is Embryo Research and Preimplantation Genetic Diagnosis Ethical?', *Forensic Science International*, 113: 461–75.

—— (2000c), 'Why Recital 26 of the EC Directive on the Legal Protection of Biotechnological Inventions should be Implemented in National Law', *Intellectual Property Quarterly*, 4: 1–26.

—— (2001), 'Ethics of Statistics in Genetics', in David Balding, Chris Cannings, and Martin Bishop (eds.), *Handbook of Statistical Genetics* (Chichester: John Wiley & Sons), 697–720.

—— and BROWNSWORD, ROGER (1985), 'The Practical Difference between Natural-Law Theory and Legal Positivism', *Oxford Journal of Legal Studies*, 5: 1–32.

—— —— (1986), *Law as a Moral Judgment* (London: Sweet & Maxwell; repr. Sheffield: Sheffield Academic Press, 1994).

—— —— (1993a), 'The Dialectically Necessary Foundation of Natural Law', in Alan Norrie (ed.), *Closure or Critique: Current Directions in Legal Theory* (Edinburgh: Edinburgh University Press), 22–44.

—— —— (1993b), *Mice, Morality, and Patents* (London: Common Law Institute of Intellectual Property).

—— —— (1998a), 'Articles 21 and 22 of the Convention on Human Rights and Biomedicine: Property and Consent, Commerce and Dignity', Paper presented at the workshop of EU Project PL 950207, Utrecht, Nov. 1997, in Peter Kemp (ed.), *Research Projects on Basic Ethical Principles in Bioethics and Biolaw* (Copenhagen: Centre for Ethics and Law), 33–67.

—— —— (1998b), 'Human Dignity, Human Rights, and Human Genetics', *Modern Law Review*, 61: 661–80; repr. in Roger Brownsword, W. R. Cornish, and Margaret Llewelyn (eds.), *Law and Human Genetics: Regulating a Revolution* (Oxford: Hart, 1998), 69–88.

—— —— (2000a), 'Human Dignity, Human Rights, and the Human Genome', Paper presented at the workshop of EU Project PL 950207, Sheffield, Apr. 1996, in Jacob Rendtorff and Peter Kemp (eds.), *Basic Ethical Principles in European Bioethics and Biolaw*, vol. ii (Copenhagen: Centre for Ethics and Law), 15–44.

—— —— (2000b), 'Final Statement on the Concerted Action "Basic Principles of Bioethics and Biolaw" ', in Jacob Rendtorff and Peter Kemp (eds.), *Basic Ethical Principles in European Bioethics and Biolaw*, vol. ii (Copenhgen: Centre for Ethics and Law), 45–55.

—— —— (2000c), 'My Body, my Body Parts, my Property?', *Health Care Analysis*, 8: 87–99.

—— —— and LLEWELYN, MARGARET (2000), 'The Morality Clauses of the Directive on the Legal Protection of Biotechnological Inventions: Conflict, Compromise, and the Patent Community', in Richard Goldberg and Julian Lonbay (eds.), *Pharmaceutical Medicine, Biotechnology and European Law* (Cambridge: Cambridge University Press), 157–81.

—— and HISTED, ELISE (1999), 'Case Commentary: Anonymisation is not Exoneration: *R v Department of Health, ex parte Source Informatics Ltd.* [1999] QB. Latham J.', *Medical Law International*, 4: 69–80.

—— —— (2000), 'Betrayal of Confidence in the Court of Appeal', *Medical Law International*, 4: 277–311.

—— and PATTINSON, SHAUN (1998), 'Proportionality under Precaution: Justifying Duties to Apparent Non-Agents', unpublished paper available from the authors.

—— —— (2000), 'Precautionary Reason as the Link to Moral Action', in Michael Boylan (ed.), *Medical Ethics* (Upper Saddle River, NJ: Prentice-Hall), 39–53.

—— and QUARRELL, OLIVER, and TODDINGTON, STUART (1998), 'Generic Consistency in the Reproductive Enterprise: Ethical and Legal Implications of Exclusion Testing for Huntington's Disease', *Medical Law International*, 3: 135–58.

BIRNBACHER, DIETER (1998), 'Do Modern Reproductive Technologies Violate Human Dignity?', in Elisabeth Hildt and Dietmar Mieth (eds.), *In Vitro Fertilisation in the 1990s* (Aldershot: Ashgate), 325–33.

BOXILL, BERNARD R. (1992), 'Dignity, Slavery, and the Thirteenth Amendment', in Michael J. Meyer and William A. Parent (eds.), *The Constitution of Rights* (Ithaca, NY: Cornell University Press), 102–17.

BOYLE, JAMES (1996), *Shamans, Software, and Spleens* (Cambridge, Mass.: Harvard University Press).

BOYLE, JOSEPH (1995), 'A Case for Sometimes Tube-Feeding Patients in Persistent Vegetative State', in John Keown (ed.), *Euthanasia Examined* (Cambridge: Cambridge University Press), 189–99.

BRANDT, RICHARD B. (1981), 'The Future of Ethics', *Nous*, 15: 31–40.

BRAZIER, MARGARET (1999), 'Can you Buy Children?', *Child and Family Law Quarterly*, 11: 345–54.

BRISTOW, PETER E. (1997), *The Moral Dignity of Man*, 2nd edn. (Dublin: Four Courts Press).

BROWNSWORD, ROGER (1999), 'General Considerations', in Michael Furmston (ed.), *The Law of Contract* (London: Butterworths), 137–45.

—— (2000a), 'Freedom of Contract', in American Bar Association, *Common Law, Common Values, Common Rights* (San Francisco: ABA and West Group), 135–41.

—— (2000b), *Contract Law: Themes for the Twenty-First Century* (London: Butterworths).

—— HIRD, NORMA J., and HOWELLS, GERAINT (eds.) (1999), *Good Faith in Contract: Concept and Context* (Aldershot: Ashgate).

BUCKLE, STEPHEN (1991), *Natural Law and the Theory of Property* (Oxford: Clarendon Press).

BURCHELL, JONATHAN (1988), 'Beyond the Glass Bead Game: Human Dignity in the Law of Delict', *South African Journal on Human Rights*, 4: 1–20.

BURKE, EDMUND (1973), *Reflections on the Revolution in France 1790* (New York: Anchor).

BUXTON, RICHARD (2000), 'The Human Rights Act and Private Law', *Law Quarterly Review*, 116: 48–65.

CAMPBELL, ALASTAIR V. (2000), 'Dignity of the Human Person in Relation to Biomedical Problems', in Peter Kemp, Jacob Rendtorff, and Niels Mattson Johansen (eds.), *Bioethics and Biolaw* vol. ii: *Four Ethical Principles* (Copenhagen: Rhodos International Science and Art Publishers and Centre for Ethics and Law), 103–11.

CANTOR, NORMAN L. (1993), *Advance Directives and the Pursuit of Death with Dignity* (Bloomington, Ind.: Indiana University Press).

CHAPMAN, JOHN W., and GALSTON, WILLIAM A. (eds.) (1992), *Virtue: Nomos XXXIV* (New York: New York University Press).

CLAPHAM, ANDREW (1993), *Human Rights in the Private Sphere* (Oxford: Clarendon Press).

CRISP, ROGER, and SLOTE, MICHAEL (eds.) (1997), *Virtue Ethics* (Oxford: Oxford University Press).

DAVIDSON, SCOTT (1993), *Human Rights* (Buckingham: Open University Press).

DEVLIN, PATRICK (1959), 'The Enforcement of Morals', Maccabaean Lecture in Jurisprudence, *Proceedings of the British Academy*, 45: 129–51.

—— (1965), *The Enforcement of Morals* (Oxford: Oxford University Press).

DUXBURY, NEIL (1996), 'Do Markets Degrade?', *Modern Law Review*, 59: 331–48.

DWORKIN, GERALD (1993), 'Ethics of Human Genome Analysis: Intellectual Property and Ownership of Data', in Hille Haker, Richard Hearn, and Klaus Steigleder (eds.), *Ethics of Human Genome Analysis* (Tübingen: Attempto Verlag), 175–95.

DWORKIN, RONALD (1978), *Taking Rights Seriously*, rev. edn. (London: Duckworth).

—— (1993), *Life's Dominion* (London: HarperCollins).

EDELMAN, BERNARD (1997), 'La Dignité de la Personne Humaine, un Concept Nouveau', *Recueil Dalloz*, 23e Cahier, Chronique, 185–8.

ENGELHARDT, H. TRISTRAM, JR. (2000), 'Autonomy: The Cardinal Principle of Contemporary Bioethics', in Peter Kemp, Jacob Rendtorff, and Niels Mattson Johansen (eds.), *Bioethics and Biolaw*, vol. ii: *Four Ethical Principles* (Copenhagen: Rhodos International Science and Art Publishers and Centre for Ethics and Law), 35–46.

ESPIELL, HECTÓR GROS (1999), 'Introduction', in *Birth of the Universal Declaration on the Human Genome and Human Rights* (Paris: Division of the Ethics of Science and Technology of UNESCO), 1–7.

EWING, KEITH (1999), 'The Human Rights Act and Parliamentary Democracy', *Modern Law Review*, 62: 79–99.

FAGAN, ANTON (1998), 'Dignity and Unfair Discrimination: A Value Misplaced and a Right Misunderstood', *South African Journal on Human Rights*, 14: 220–47.

FEINBERG, JOEL (1973), *Social Philosophy* (Englewood Cliffs, NJ: Prentice-Hall).

FELDMAN, DAVID (1999), 'Human Dignity as a Legal Value: Part I', *Public Law*, 682–702.

—— (2000), 'Human Dignity as a Legal Value: Part II', *Public Law*, 61–76.

FINNIS, JOHN (1984), *Natural Law and Natural Rights* (Oxford: Clarendon Press).

—— (1993), 'Bland: Crossing the Rubicon?', *Law Quarterly Review*, 109: 329–37.

—— (1995a), 'A Philosophical Case against Euthanasia', in John Keown (ed.), *Euthanasia Examined* (Cambridge: Cambridge University Press), 23–35.

—— (1995b), 'The Fragile Case for Euthanasia: A Reply to John Harris', in John Keown (ed.), *Euthanasia Examined* (Cambridge: Cambridge University Press), 46–55.

—— (1995c), 'Misunderstanding the Case against Euthanasia: Response to Harris's First Reply', in John Keown (ed.), *Euthanasia Examined* (Cambridge: Cambridge University Press), 62–71.

FORTE, ANGELO D. M. (ed.) (1999), *Good Faith in Contract and Property Law* (Oxford: Hart).

FORTIN, JANE (1999), 'Rights Brought Home for Children', *Modern Law Review*, 62: 350–70.

FOSSEL, MICHAEL (1996), *Reversing Human Aging* (New York: William Morrow).

FRANKL, VICTOR (1984), *Man's Search for Meaning* (New York: Washington Square).

FREY, R. G. (1998), 'Distinctions in Death', in Gerald Dworkin, R. G. Frey, and Sissela Bok (eds.), *Euthanasia and Physician-Assisted Suicide* (Cambridge: Cambridge University Press), 17–42.

FROMM, ERICH (1942), *The Fear of Freedom* (London: Routledge & Kegan Paul).

—— (1974), *The Anatomy of Human Destructiveness* (London: Jonathan Cape).

FULLER, LON L. (1949), 'The Case of the Speluncean Explorers', *Harvard Law Review*, 62: 616–45.

GALSTON, WILLIAM A. (1992), 'Introduction', in John W. Chapman and William A. Galston (eds.), *Virtue: Nomos XXXIV* (New York: New York University Press), 1–22.

GALTON, FRANCIS (1907), *Inquiries into the Human Faculty and its Development* (1883), 2nd edn. (London: J. M. Dent & Sons).

GAMWELL, FRANKLIN I. (1984), *Beyond Preference: Liberal Theories of Independent Associations* (Chicago: University of Chicago Press).

GANNON, PHILIPPA, and VILLIERS, CHARLOTTE (1999), 'Genetic Testing and Employee Protection', *Medical Law International*, 4: 39–57.

GAUS, GERALD F. (1994), 'Property, Rights and Freedom', in Ellen Frankel Paul, Fred D. Miller Jr., and Jeffrey Paul (eds.), *Property Rights* (Cambridge: Cambridge University Press), 209–40.

GAUTHIER, DAVID (1986), *Morals by Agreement* (Oxford: Clarendon Press).

GEWIRTH, ALAN (1960), 'Positive "Ethics" and Normative "Science" ', *Philosophical Review*, 69: 311–30.

—— (1978a), *Reason and Morality* (Chicago: University of Chicago Press).

—— (1978b), 'The Golden Rule Rationalized', *Midwest Studies in Philosophy*, 3: 133–47.

—— (1981), 'Are there Any Absolute Rights?', *Philosophical Quarterly*, 31: 1–16.

—— (1982a), *Human Rights* (Chicago: University of Chicago Press).

—— (1982b), 'There are Absolute Rights', *Philosophical Quarterly*, 32: 348–53.

—— (1984), 'Replies to my Critics', in Edward Regis Jr. (ed.), *Gewirth's Ethical Rationalism: Critical Essays with a Reply by Alan Gewirth* (Chicago: University of Chicago Press), 192–255.

—— (1985), 'Economic Justice: Concepts and Criteria', in K. Kipnis and D. T. Meyers (eds.), *Economic Justice: Private Rights and Public Participation* (Totowa, NJ: Rowman & Allanheld), 7–32.

—— (1991), 'Can Any Final Ends be Rational?', *Ethics*, 102: 66–95.

—— (1996), *The Community of Rights* (Chicago: University of Chicago Press), 166–213.

GOLDING, MARTIN P. (1981), 'From Prudence to Rights: A Critique', in J. R. Pennock and J. W. Chapman (eds.), *Nomos XXIII: Human Rights* (New York: New York University Press), 165–74.

GOODIN, ROBERT E. (1981), 'The Political Theories of Choice and Dignity', *American Philosophical Quarterly*, 18: 91–100.

GORMALLY, LUKE (1995), 'Walton, Davies, Boyd and the Legalization of Euthanasia', in John Keown (ed.), *Euthanasia Examined* (Cambridge: Cambridge University Press), 113–40.

GRUBB, ANDREW (1998), ' "I, Me, Mine": Bodies, Parts and Property', *Medical Law International*, 3: 299–317.

HABERMAS, JÜRGEN (1984), *The Theory of Communicative Action* (Cambridge: Polity Press).

HABERMAS, JÜRGEN (1988), 'Law and Morality', *The Tanner Lectures on Human Values*, vol. viii (Salt Lake City: University of Utah Press), 217–79.

HANNAFORD, RICHARD (1998), 'Brave New World of Medicine around the Corner', BBC News, 3 Dec. Available at http://news.bbc.co.uk/hi/english/health/newsid_226000/226856.stm, downloaded 28 Mar. 2001.

HARE, R. M. (1969), 'Pain and Evil', in Joel Feinberg (ed.), *Moral Concepts* (Oxford: Oxford University Press), 29–42.

—— (1981), *Moral Thinking* (Oxford: Clarendon Press).

HARRIS, JOHN (1985), *The Value of Life* (London: Routledge & Kegan Paul).

—— (1995a), 'Euthanasia and the Value of Life', in John Keown (ed.), *Euthanasia Examined* (Cambridge: Cambridge University Press), 6–22.

—— (1995b), 'The Philosophical Case against the Philosophical Case against Euthanasia', in John Keown (ed.), *Euthanasia Examined* (Cambridge: Cambridge University Press), 36–45.

—— (1995c), 'Final Thoughts on Final Acts', in John Keown (ed.), *Euthanasia Examined* (Cambridge: Cambridge University Press), 56–61.

—— (1998), *Clones, Genes, and Immortality* (Oxford: Oxford University Press).

—— (1999), 'Clones, Genes, and Human Rights', in Justine Burley (ed.), *The Genetic Revolution and Human Rights* (Oxford: Oxford University Press), 61–94.

HART, H. L. A. (1963), *Law, Liberty and Morality* (London: Oxford University Press).

—— (1967), 'Social Solidarity and the Enforcement of Morality', *University of Chicago Law Review*, 35: 1–13.

HEALTH COUNCIL OF THE NETHERLANDS (1994), *Proper Use of Human Tissue*, Publication No. 1996/01E (The Hague: Health Council of the Netherlands).

HENKIN, LOUIS (1992), 'Human Dignity and Constitutional Rights', in Michael J. Meyer and William A. Parent (eds.), *The Constitution of Rights* (Ithaca, NY: Cornell University Press), 210–28.

HERNSTEIN. R. J., and MURRAY, C. (1994), *The Bell Curve: Intelligence and Class Structure in American Life.* (New York: Free Press).

HICK, JOHN (1977), *Evil and the God of Love*, 2nd edn. (London: Macmillan).

HILL, JAMES F. (1984), 'Are Marginal Agents "Our Recipients"?', in Edward Regis Jr. (ed.), *Gewirth's Ethical Rationalism: Critical Essays with a Reply by Alan Gewirth* (Chicago: University of Chicago Press), 180–91.

HOBBES, THOMAS (1946), *Leviathan* (1651), ed. Michael Oakeshott (Oxford: Blackwell).

HONORÉ, A. M. (1961), 'Ownership', in A. G. Guest (ed.), *Oxford Essays in Jurisprudence* (Oxford: Clarendon Press), 107–47.

HOTTOIS, GILBERT (2000), 'Dignity of the Human Body: A Philosophical and Critical Approach', in Peter Kemp, Jacob Rendtorff, and Niels Mattson Johansen (eds.), *Bioethics and Biolaw*, vol. ii: *Four Ethical Principles* (Copenhagen: Rhodos International Science and Art Publishers and Centre for Ethics and Law), 87–102.

HUMAN GENETICS ADVISORY COMMISSION and HUMAN FERTILISATION AND EMBRYOLOGY AUTHORITY (1998a), *Cloning Issues in Reproduction, Science and Medicine* (London: Human Genetics Advisory Commission and Human Fertilisation and Embryology Authority, Jan.).

—— (1998b), *Cloning Issues in Reproduction, Science and Medicine* (Dec.) Available at www.dti.gov.uk/hgac/papers/papers-d.htm (downloaded 10 May 2000).

HUMAN GENETICS COMMISSION (2000), *Whose Hands on your Genes?* (London: Human Genetics Commission, Nov.).

HUNT, MURRAY (1997), *Using Human Rights Law in English Courts* (Oxford: Hart).

—— (1998), 'The Horizontal Effect of the Human Rights Act', *Public Law*, 423–43.

HURSTHOUSE, ROSALIND (1997), 'Virtue Theory and Abortion', in Roger Crisp and Michael Slote (eds.), *Virtue Ethics* (Oxford: Oxford University Press), 217–38.

JENSEN, A. R. (1969), 'How much can we Boost IQ and Scholastic Achievement?', *Harvard Educational Review*, 39: 1–123.

KADIDAL, SHAYANA (1996), 'Obscenity in the Age of Mechanical Reproduction', *American Journal of Comparative Law*, 44: 353–85.

KANT, IMMANUEL (1934), *Critique of Pure Reason* (1787), trans. J. M. D. Meiklejohn, introd. A. D. Lindsay (London: Dent Dutton).

—— (1948), *Groundwork of the Metaphysic of Morals* (1785), Trans. with introd. H. J. Paton as *The Moral Law* (London: Hutchinson).

—— (1956), *Critique of Practical Reason* (1788), trans. Lewis White Beck (New York: Liberal Arts Press).

—— (1991), *The Metaphysics of Morals* (1797), trans. and ed. Mary Gregor (Cambridge: Cambridge University Press).

KEIGHTLEY, RAYLENE (1995), 'Torture and Cruel, Inhuman and Degrading Treatment or Punishment in the UN Convention against Torture and Other Instruments of International Law: Recent Developments in South Africa', *South African Journal on Human Rights*, 11: 379–400.

KEMP, PETER (2000), 'Four Ethical Principles in Biolaw', in Peter Kemp, Jacob Rendtorff, and Niels Mattson Johansen (eds.), *Bioethics and Biolaw*, vol. ii: *Four Ethical Principles* (Copenhagen: Rhodos International Science and Art Publishers and Centre for Ethics and Law), 13–22.

KEOWN, JOHN (ed.) (1995), *Euthanasia Examined* (Cambridge: Cambridge University Press).

—— (1997), 'Restoring Moral and Intellectual Shape to the Law after *Bland*', *Law Quarterly Review*, 113: 481–503.

KIERKEGAARD, SØREN (1954), *Fear and Trembling and The Sickness unto Death*, trans. with introd. and notes by Walter Lowrie (Princeton: Princeton University Press); *Fear and Trembling* first pub. 1843; *The Sickness unto Death* first pub. 1849.

—— (1980), *The Concept of Anxiety* (1844), ed. and trans. with introd. and notes by Reidar Thomte in collaboration with Albert B. Anderson (Princeton: Princeton University Press).

KOLNAI, AUREL (1976), 'Dignity', *Philosophy*, 51: 251–71.

KORSGAARD, CHRISTINE (1985), 'Kant's Formula of Universal Law', *Pacific Philosophical Quarterly*, 66: 24–47.

KRAMER, MATTHEW H., and SIMMONDS, NIGEL E. (1996), 'Reason without Reason: A Critique of Alan Gewirth's Moral Philosophy', *Southern Journal of Philosophy*, 34: 301–15.

KUHSE, HELGA (2000), 'Is there a Tension between Autonomy and Dignity?', in Peter Kemp, Jacob Rendtorff, and Niels Mattson Johansen (eds.), *Bioethics and Biolaw*, vol. ii: *Four Ethical Principles* (Copenhagen: Rhodos International Science and Art Publishers and Centre for Ethics and Law), 61–74.

LANDES, ELIZABETH, and POSNER, RICHARD (1978), 'The Economics of the Baby Shortage', *Journal of Legal Studies*, 7: 323–48.

LEIBNIZ, WILHELM GOTTFRIED (1934), *Philosophical Writings*, trans. Mary Morris with introd. by C. R. Morris (London: Dent Dutton).

LESTER, ANTHONY, and PANNICK, DAVID (2000), 'The Impact of the Human Rights Act on Private Law: The Knight's Move', *Law Quarterly Review*, 116: 380–5.

LEVINSON, JERROLD (1982), 'Gewirth on Absolute Rights', *Philosophical Quarterly*, 32: 73–5.

LINACRE CENTRE (1998), 'A Response to the Consultation Document "Cloning Issues in Reproduction, Science and Medicine" '. Available at www.linacre.org/clone.html (downloaded 10 May 2000).

LOCKE, JOHN (1960), *Two Treatises of Government*, ed. Peter Laslett (New York: Mentor).

MCCURDY, CHARLES W. (1998), 'The "Liberty of Contract" Regime', in Harry N. Scheiber (ed.), *The State and Freedom of Contract* (Stanford, Calif.: Stanford University Press), 161–97.

MCHARG, AILEEN (1999), 'Reconciling Human Rights and the Public Interest: Conceptual Problems and Doctrinal Uncertainty in the Jurisprudence of the European Court of Human Rights', *Modern Law Review*, 62: 671–96.

MCLEAN, SHEILA (2000), 'A Moral Right to Procreation: Assisted Procreation and Persons at Risk of Hereditary Genetic Diseases', in Hille Haker and Deryck Beyleveld (eds.), *The Ethics of Genetics in Human Procreation* (Aldershot: Ashgate), 13–25.

MASON, J. K., and MCCALL SMITH, R. A. (1999), *Law and Medical Ethics*, 5th edn. (London: Butterworths).

MEYER, MICHAEL J. (1992), 'Introduction', in Michael J. Meyer and William A. Parent (eds.), *The Constitution of Rights: Human Dignity and American Values* (Ithaca, NY: Cornell University Press), 1–9.

—— and PARENT, WILLIAM A. (eds.) (1992), *The Constitution of Rights: Human Dignity and American Values* (Ithaca, NY: Cornell University Press).

MILL, JOHN STUART (1962), *On Liberty* (1859), in Mary Warnock (ed.), *Utilitarianism* (Glasgow: William Collins Sons), 126–250.

MORGAN, DEREK (1994), 'Odysseus and the Binding Directive: Only a Cautionary Tale?', *Legal Studies*, 14: 411–42.

—— and LEE, ROBERT G. (1997), 'In the Name of the Father? Ex parte *Blood*: Dealing with Novelty and Anomaly', *Modern Law Review*, 60: 840–56.

MUNZER, STEPHEN R. (1990), *A Theory of Property* (Cambridge: Cambridge University Press).

—— (1994), 'An Uneasy Case against Property Rights in Body Parts', in Ellen Frankel Paul, Fred D. Miller Jr., and Jeffrey Paul (eds.), *Property Rights* (Cambridge: Cambridge University Press), 259–86.

NARVESON, JAN (1988), *The Libertarian Idea* (Philadelphia: Temple University Press).

NASH, J. MADELEINE (1997), 'The Immortality Enzyme', *Time*, 150/9 (http://www.time.com/time/magazine/1997/dom/970901/medicine.the_imortalit.html).

NELSEN, KAI (1984), 'Against Ethical Rationalism', in Edward J. Regis Jr. (ed.), *Gewirth's Ethical Rationalism: Critical Essays with a Reply by Alan Gewirth* (Chicago: University of Chicago Press), 59–83.

NUFFIELD COUNCIL ON BIOETHICS (1993), *Genetic Screening: Ethical Issues* (London: Nuffield Council on Bioethics).

—— (1995), *Human Tissue: Ethical and Legal Issues* (London: Nuffield Council on Bioethics).

OCKLETON, MARK (1988), 'Review of *Law as a Moral Judgment,* by Deryck Beyleveld and Roger Brownsword', *Legal Studies,* 8: 234–8.

OLIVER, DAWN (1997), 'The Underlying Values of Public and Private Law', in Michael Taggart (ed.), *The Province of Administrative Law* (Oxford: Hart), 217–42.

O'NEILL, ONORA (1998), 'Insurance and Genetics: The Current State of Play', *Modern Law Review,* 61: 716–23; repr. in Roger Brownsword, W. R. Cornish, and Margaret Llewelyn (eds.), *Law and Human Genetics: Regulating a Revolution* (Oxford: Hart), 124–31.

PAINE, THOMAS (1973), *The Rights of Man* (New York: Anchor); pt. 1 first pub. 1791, pt. 2 1792.

PARENT, WILLIAM A. (1992), 'Constitutional Values and Human Dignity', in Michael J. Meyer and William A. Parent (eds.), *The Constitution of Rights* (Ithaca, NY: Cornell University Press), 47–72.

PARFIT, DEREK (1984), *Reasons and Persons* (Oxford: Clarendon Press; repr. corr. 1987).

PARIZEAU, MARIE-HÉLÈNE (2000), 'The Tension between Autonomy and Dignity', in Peter Kemp, Jacob Rendtorff, and Niels Mattson Johansen (eds.), *Bioethics and Biolaw,* vol. ii: *Four Ethical Principles* (Copenhagen: Rhodos International Science and Art Publishers and Centre for Ethics and Law), 47–59.

PASCAL, BLAISE (1966), *Pensées,* trans. A. J. Krailsheimer (London: Penguin).

PATTINSON, SHAUN (2000), 'Regulating Germ-Line Gene Therapy to Avoid Sliding down the Slippery Slope', *Medical Law International,* 4: 213–22; Paper delivered at the 13th World Congress on Medical Law, Helsinki, 10 Aug.

PHILLIPSON, GAVIN (1999), 'The Human Rights Act, "Horizontal Effect" and the Common Law: A Bang or a Whimper?', *Modern Law Review,* 62: 824–49.

PRITCHARD, MICHAEL (1972), 'Human Dignity and Justice', *Ethics,* 82: 299–313.

PUTNAM, HILARY (1962), 'The Analytic and the Synthetic', in Herbert Feigl and Grover Maxwell (eds.), *Minnesota Studies in the Philosophy of Science,* vol. iii. (Minneapolis: University of Minnesota Press), 358–97.

—— (1999), 'Cloning People', in Justine Burley (ed.), *The Genetic Revolution and Human Rights* (Oxford: Oxford University Press), 1–13.

RAE, SCOTT B., and COX, PAUL M. (1999), *Bioethics: A Christian Approach in a Pluralistic Age* (Grand Rapids, Mich.: William B. Eerdmans).

RALAIMIHOATRA, CHANTAL (1996), 'Seventh Meeting of the Legal Commission of the IBC—Paris, 3 and 4 October 1996', in *Proceedings of the Fourth Session of the International Bioethics Committee of UNESCO, October 1996,* vol. i (Paris: International Bioethics Committee of UNESCO), 45–53.

RAWLS, JOHN (1972), *A Theory of Justice* (London: Oxford University Press).

—— (1993), *Political Liberalism* (New York: Columbia University Press).

RAZ, JOSEPH (1979), *The Authority of Law* (Oxford: Clarendon Press).

REGIS, Edward J., Jr. (ed.). (1984), *Gewirth's Ethical Rationalism: Critical Essays with a Reply by Alan Gewirth* (Chicago: University of Chicago Press).

RENDTORFF, JACOB, and KEMP, PETER (1999), *Basic Ethical Principles in European Bioethics and Biolaw,* vol. i: *Autonomy, Dignity, Integrity and Vulnerability* (Copenhagen: Centre for Ethics and Law).

ROUAULT, MARIE-CHRISTINE. (1996), 'Note', *Les Petites Affiches* (24 Jan.), no. 11: 30–2.

SCANLON, THOMAS (1992), 'The Aims and Authority of Moral Theory', *Oxford Journal of Legal Studies*, 12: 1–23.

SCHEIBER, HARRY N. (ed.) (1998), *The State and Freedom of Contract* (Stanford, Calif.: Stanford University Press).

SCHEINGOLD, STUART A. (1974), *The Politics of Rights: Lawyers, Public Policy and Political Change* (New Haven: Yale University Press).

SCHUCK, P. (1994), 'Rethinking Informed Consent', *Yale Law Journal*, 103: 899–959.

SÉGUIN, PHILIPPE (1995), 'Speech by Mr. Philippe Séguin', in *Proceedings of the Third Session of the International Bioethics Committee of UNESCO, September 1995*, vol. i (Paris: International Bioethics Committee of UNESCO), 119–23.

SINGER, MARCUS G. (2000), 'Gewirth, Beyleveld, and Dialectical Necessity', *Ratio Juris*, 13: 177–95.

SINGER, PETER (1993), 'Animals and the Value of Life', in Tom Regan (ed.), *Matters of Life and Death*, 3rd edn. (New York: McGraw-Hill), 280–321.

—— (1995), *Rethinking Life and Death* (Oxford: Oxford University Press).

SPIEGELBERG, HERBERT (1970), 'Human Dignity: A Challenge to Contemporary Philosophy', in Rubin Gotesky and Ervin Laszlo (eds.), *Human Dignity: This Century and the Next* (New York: Gordon & Breach), 39–64.

STERCKX, SIGRID (ed.) (1997), *Biotechnology, Patents and Morality* (Aldershot: Ashgate).

THOMAS, S. M., DAVIES, A. R. W., BIRTWISTLE, N. J., CROWTHER, S. M., and BURKE, J. F. (1996), 'Ownership of the Human Genome', *Nature*, 380 (4 Apr.), 387–8.

THOMSON, JUDITH JARVIS (1990), *The Realm of Rights* (Cambridge: Cambridge University Press).

TOULMIN, STEPHEN E. (1950), *An Examination of the Place of Reason in Ethics* (Cambridge: Cambridge University Press).

TREBILCOCK, MICHAEL J. (1993), *The Limits of Freedom of Contract* (Cambridge, Mass.: Harvard University Press).

UNESCO, *Birth of the Universal Declaration on the Human Genome and Human Rights* (Paris: Division of the Ethics of Science and Technology of UNESCO, 1999).

VELU, JACQUES (1973), 'The European Convention on Human Rights and the Right to Respect for Private Life, the Home and Communications', in A. H. Robertson (ed.), *Privacy and Human Rights* (Manchester: Manchester University Press), 12–128.

VOLTAIRE, FRANÇOIS-MARIE AROUET DE (1971), *Candide and Other Tales* (1759), trans. Tobias Smollett, rev. J. C. Thornton (London: Dent Dutton).

WADE, SIR WILLIAM (2000), 'Horizons of Horizontality', *Law Quarterly Review*, 116: 217–24.

WALTON COMMITTEE (1994), *Report of the Select Committee on Medical Ethics* (London: HMSO).

WARNOCK COMMITTEE (1984), *Report of the Committee of Inquiry into Human Fertilisation and Embryology* (London: HMSO).

WILLIAMS, BERNARD (1985), *Ethics and the Limits of Philosophy* (Cambridge, Mass.: Harvard University Press), 62–3.

WITTGENSTEIN, LUDWIG (1968), *Philosophical Investigations* (Oxford: Blackwell).

WOLBERT, WERNER (1998), 'The Kantian Formula of Human Dignity and its Implications for Bioethics', *Human Reproduction and Genetic Ethics*, 4: 18–23.

Index